D1617474

COLLABORATIVE LEARNING, REASONING, AND TECHNOLOGY

The Rutgers Invitational Symposium
on Education Series

O'Donnell/King, Eds. • *Cognitive Perspectives on Peer Learning*

Vitello/Mithaug, Eds. • *Inclusive Schooling: National and International Perspectives*

Golbeck, Ed. • *Psychological Perspectives on Early Childhood Education: Reframing Dilemmas in Research and Practice*

Shimahara/Holowinsky/Tomlinson-Clarke, Eds. • *Ethnicity, Race, and Nationality in Education: A Global Perspective*

O'Donnell/Hmelo-Silver/Erkens, Eds. • *Collaborative Learning, Reasoning, and Technology*

COLLABORATIVE LEARNING, REASONING, AND TECHNOLOGY

Edited by

Angela M. O'Donnell
Cindy E. Hmelo-Silver
Gijsbert Erkens

2006

LAWRENCE ERLBAUM ASSOCIATES, PUBLISHERS
Mahwah, New Jersey   London

Camera ready copy for this book was provided by the editors.

Lawrence Erlbaum Associates, Inc., Publishers
10 Industrial Avenue
Mahwah, New Jersey 07430
www.erlbaum.com

Cover design by Kathryn Houghtaling Lacey

Library of Congress Cataloging-in-Publication Data

Collaborative learning, reasoning, and technology / edited by Angela M. O'Donnell, Cindy E. Hmelo-Silver, Gijsbert Erkens.
　　p. cm.
Includes bibliographical references and index.
ISBN 0-8058-4778-2 (cloth : alk. paper)
1. Team learning approach in education. 2. Reasoning—Study and teaching. 3. Computer-assisted instruction. I. O'Donnell, Angela M. II. Hmelo-Silver, Cindy E. III. Erkens, Gijsbert, 1949– IV. Series.
LB1032.C567　2005
371.33'4—dc22
　　　　　　　　　　　　　　　　　　　　　2004056426
　　　　　　　　　　　　　　　　　　　　　CIP

Books published by Lawrence Erlbaum Associates are printed on acid-free paper, and their bindings are chosen for strength and durability.

Printed in the United States of America
10　9　8　7　6　5　4　3　2　1

*This book is dedicated
to the memory of
Jos van der Linden,
a warm and caring colleague.*

Table of Contents

Series Foreword

Rutgers Invitational Symposia on Education (RISE)
Rutgers Graduate School of Education

Ever since 1988, a distinguished group of local, national, and international educational scholars and practitioners has traveled to the campus of Rutgers University in New Brunswick, New Jersey to participate in a topic-specific symposium that presents original findings and ideas. This volume is based on a recent RISE symposium that considered the use of technology to support collaboration and reasoning. The symposium itself was originally scheduled to occur on October 19, 2001 but was delayed until May 17, 2002, due to the terrorist attacks that occurred in the eastern United States on September 11, 2001. Citizens throughout the world were profoundly affected by the events of September 11, 2001 and life since that tragic day has never felt quite the same for most of us. One aspect of this profound discontinuity in daily existence is the felt need for people throughout the world to attempt to transcend ignorance, prejudice, and outright hatred. Our efforts at transcendence must surely be based, at least in part, on two of the most powerful tools at our disposal, namely, education and modern technology. Although either tool can be used to as an instrument of evil, investigations of how technology can be used within educational settings to support collaboration and reasoning have at least the promise of contributing to the greater good.

In wealthy countries like the United States, students have near-universal access to Internet-connected computers in their schools, classrooms, homes, or local libraries. Given the tremendous investment that has been made in providing students with these resources, it is natural for government officials and policymakers to ask for evidence about the effectiveness of this investment. States are developing technology standards for students, teachers, and administrators. There is widespread agreement about the kinds of academic knowledge, cognitive skills, and social competencies that education needs to foster in students. There is much less agreement about how technology can be used to achieve these goals. A similar progression from issues of access to technology in homes and schools to issues of strategies for utilization to optimize learning is now occurring in countries with less wealth.

The chapters that comprise this volume then, seem especially timely and important. An international group of educational researchers presents original findings of how technology can be used to scaffold the development of critical reasoning skills, collaboration, and argumentation in both student and teachers at the K-12 and college levels. The chapters should be of interest to both researchers and practitioners. The volume is divided into 14 chapters. These chapters together address some of the key issues in using technology to support collaborative learning, reasoning, and argumentation. The importance of human and technological scaffolding in supporting such learning is also addressed. I am pleased to have this volume added to the series, *The Rutgers Invitational Symposium on Education.*

—**Richard De Lisi**
Dean and Professor of Educational Psychology
Graduate School of Education
Rutgers, The State University of
New Jersey

List of Contributors

Jerry Andriessen, Department of Educational Sciences, Utrecht University, Heidelberglaan 2. 3584 CS Utrecht, The Netherlands. E-mail: J.Andriessen@fss.uu.nl

Jeannine Bailey, Department of Psychology, 1007 W. Harrison St. (MC 285), University of Illinois, Chicago, IL 60607.

Katerine Bielaczyc, Harvard Graduate School of Education, Technology in Education, Longfellow 325 Cambridge, MA 02138. E-mail: bielacka@gse.harvard.edu

Carla van Boxtel, Department of Educational Sciences, Utrecht University, Heidelberglaan 1, 3584 CS Utrecht, Netherlands. E-mail: C.vanBoxtel@fss.uu.nl

Qi Chen, Department of Psychology, Beijing Normal University, Beijing, 100875 China. E-mail: chenqi@email.bnu.edu.cn

Clark A. Chinn, Department of Educational Psychology, Rutgers, The State University of New Jersey, 10 Seminary Place, New Brunswick, NJ 08901-1183. E-mail: cchinn@rci.rutgers.edu

Allan Collins, E-mail: collins@bbn.com

Sharon Derry, Educational Sciences Building, 1025 W. Johnson St., University of Wisconsin at Madison, Madison, WI 53706. E-mail: sharond@wcer.wisc.edu

Richard De Lisi, Department of Educational Psychology, Rutgers, The State University of New Jersey, 10 Seminary Place, New Brunswick, NJ 08901-1183. E-mail: delisi@rci.rutgers.edu.

Jannet van Drie, Department of Educational Sciences, Utrecht University, Heidelberglaan 2, 3584 CS Utrecht, The Netherlands. E-mail: j.vandrie@fss.uu.nl

Gijsbert Erkens, Department of Educational Sciences, Utrecht University, Heidelberglaan 2, 3584 CS Utrecht, The Netherlands. E-mail: G.Erkens@fss.uu.nl

Cindy Hmelo-Silver, Department of Educational Psychology, Rutgers, The State University of New Jersey, 10 Seminary Place, New Brunswick, NJ 08901-1183. E-mail: chmelo@rci.rutgers.edu.

Jos Jasper, Department of Educational Sciences, Utrecht University, Heidelberglaan 1, 3584 CS Utrecht, The Netherlands.
E-mail: J.Jaspers@fss.uu.nl

Marcia C. Linn, Graduate School of Education, 4533 Tolman Hall, University of California at Berkeley, Berkeley, CA 94720.
E-mail: mclinn@socrates.berkeley.edu

Jos van der Linden (deceased).

Angela M. O'Donnell, Department of Educational Psychology, Rutgers, The State University of New Jersey, 10 Seminary Place, New Brunswick, NJ 08901-1183. E-mail: angelao@rci.rutgers.edu.

Maaike Prangsma, Department of Educational Sciences, Utrecht University, Heidelberglaan 1, 3584 CS Utrecht, The Netherlands.
E-mail: M.Prangsma@fss.uu.nl

James D. Slotta, Graduate School of Education, 4533 Tolman Hall, University of California at Berkeley, Berkeley, CA 94720.
E-mail: slotta@socrates.berkeley.edu.

Arja Veerman, TNO - Human Factors, Dep. of Training and Instruction, Kampweg 5, P.O. Box 23, 3769 ZG Soesterberg, The Netherlands.
E-mail: arja@xs4all.nl

Else Veldhuis-Diermanse, Wageningen University & Research Centre. Staff Dept. for Education, P.O.Box 9101, 6700 HB Wageningen, The Netherlands.
E-mail: Else.Veldhuis-Diermanse@wur.nl

Jennifer Wiley, Department of Psychology, 1007 W. Harrison St. (MC 285), Office Number 1054D, University of Illinois, Chicago, IL 60607. E-mail: jwiley@uic.edu

Susan Williams, Instructional Technology, Curriculum & Instruction Department
George I. Sanchez Building, Room 406, The University of Texas at Austin Austin, TX 78712-1294. E-mail: susan.williams@mail.utexas.edu

Jianwei Zhang, Educational Technology Institute, Tsinghua University, 100084 China E-mail: zhangjw@tsinghua.edu.cn

Acknowledgments

We are thankful for the support of many who contributed to the completion of this book in addition to the authors of various chapters. We wish to thank the Dean of the School of Education, Dr. Richard De Lisi for continued support of this project that was begun with the support of former Dean Louise Wilkinson. We would also like to express our appreciation to the Department of Educational Psychology for logistical support provide for this project. We thank Nicole DiDonato for her careful assistance with checking references and copyediting, Elvira Katić for her attention to detail as she checked the final camera-ready copy and created the author index, and to Emily Matos, Rebecca Giagnacova, and Peija Zha for assistance with the subject index. We also thank Gary Silver for his help with resolving software problems while preparing the camera-ready copy.

Chapter 1

Introduction: Learning with Technology

Angela M. O'Donnell

Rutgers, The State University of New Jersey

A major initiative in considering the potential contribution of technology to education was the appointment of the Web-Based Education Commission. In December 2000, the commission released its report, *The power of the Internet for learning: Moving from promise to practice.* An important issue addressed by the commission was the need to build a research framework for how people learn in the Internet age. According to the commission, this research framework would need to address learning outcomes and should be developed from an "understanding of how people learn and, of how new tools support and assess learning gains, what kinds of organizational structures support these gains, and what is needed to keep the field of learning moving forward" (Kerrey & Isakson, 2000, p. iv). Clearly much work remains to be done in understanding how and when to use various technologies to promote learning and instruction.

The use of technology in education can, under the right circumstances, have positive effects on teaching and learning in elementary and secondary schools (Honey, 2001; Norris, Smolka, & Soloway, 2000). According to Honey (2001), the benefits of educational technology implementations include increases in standardized test scores, support for the development of early literacy skills, promotion of students' mastery of mathematical concepts, and increases in students' understanding of core science concepts. However, these benefits are likely to accrue only when there is leadership around technology that is focused on clear educational goals, there is sustained and intensive professional development, there are adequate technology resource available, sufficient time is allowed for change to occur, and evaluations are conducted to identify whether educational goals are being met. In reporting on the Snapshot Survey of approximately 1000 k-12 classroom teachers, Norris and colleagues concluded that educational technology has had little impact on teaching and learning because students have little access to computers. (Norris, Sullivan, Poirot, & Soloway, 2003). Sixty-seven percent of respondents to the survey indicated that they had access to a computer lab once or less than one a week. The use of technology for instruction in higher education is less constrained than in k-12 environments as students do a great deal of their learning outside of the classroom. Access to computing facilities is not constrained to a single time period or location.

Many key aspects of learning and instruction may be influenced by the use of technology. For example, the report by the National Center for Post-secondary Education (Gumport & Chun, 2000) described a number of areas of impact of technology on teaching and learning in higher education including the nature of knowledge, the relationships among participants in the learning and teaching process, the content of courses, and the dimension of time as an influence on the processes of learning and teaching. The kind of knowledge students can acquire may be different in that new research becomes more readily available via the Internet than was previously possible. Multiple sources can be easily located and different perspectives on particular topics can also be easily found. Students must be more careful about the trustworthiness of sources and data available on the Internet, as the rigors of peer review are not applied to all the materials that are available on the Internet. The relationships among participants in the teaching and learning process can change from those typically found in most college classrooms. Participants have more equal access to opportunities to participate when using online tools. In face-to-face groups, students may feel intimidated by other students in their groups. In asynchronous online interaction, students can choose to participate when they feel prepared to do so. The content of courses may be changed because of the availability of technological resources such as videos. Learning is not limited to particular times of day or particular days. Students can tailor their learning environment to their own needs. Technology can be used to enhance existing strategies for instruction or to fundamentally alter the roles of teachers and students. The wealth of writing about the role of technology in higher education includes concerns about the role of faculty, the incentives for faculty to improve their own technological competence, the costs of introducing and maintaining the infrastructure needed to support instructional uses of technology, and access and equity.

Attention to what students are learning as a result of the introduction of technology has received less attention, and rigorous evaluations of the impact of technology on student learning are few (Merisotis, 1999; Phipps & Merisotis, 1999). However, despite the promises of the contribution of technology to effective learning and instruction, the assumption that the use of technology for learning and instruction is necessary and effectively promotes learning is so pervasive that it is virtually unexamined as an assumption. Some would argue that to query its use is not even appropriate. It is difficult, nevertheless, to justify an uncritical approach to any educational intervention when one considers the costs involved in both human and financial capital. Frequently, claims are made for the importance of technology to student learning although the empirical basis for such claims is limited. The enormous costs involved in the introduction, maintenance, and expansion of instructional uses of technology in terms of money and faculty and student time warrant a serious examination of the claims made. The report of the Web-Based Education Commission (Kerrey & Isakson, 2000) notes that only 0.1% of the budget allocated to education is dedicated to examining outcomes from education.

Given the enormous costs involved in developing an infrastructure to support the use of technology in education and the human capital involved, it is important to consider the outcomes associated with the introduction and use of technology. Jones and Paolucci (1999) noted that less than 5% of published research on the effectiveness of educational technology could adequately address the question of the role of technology in contributing to learning outcomes. Their criticisms rest largely on their viewpoint that quantitative measures were inadequately used. Merisotis (1999) also criticized the lack of rigor in evaluation of the outcomes from the use of technology. An alternative view, however, was provided by Agnew (2001), who criticized some of the research on the effectiveness of educational technology in instruction because of its dependence on quantitative measures that lacked sensitivity to changes in learning and instruction. The difference in opinions voiced by Agnew and by Jones and Paolucci is indicative of the general disarray in the consideration of learning outcomes that result from the use of technology in learning and teaching. Although these authors were writing about the use of technology for instruction in higher education contexts, it is likely that the same differences of opinion can be found at any educational level.

The goal of this book is to provide a critical analysis of work involving the use of technology in instruction and learning and to present research findings related to that work. The contents of the book center on two themes: the use of technology to promote argumentation and reasoning and the use of technology as a scaffold for learning. Collaboration among peers is a key element of both of these strands.

FOCUS ON COLLABORATION

Many of the justifications for the use of technology in instructional contexts are made on the basis that higher levels of learning goals can be accomplished if supported by various technological applications. Examples of tools that can foster higher levels of thinking include the visualization tools in CoVIS (Pea, Edelson, & Gomez, 1994) or the data collection and manipulation tools such as those students encounter in the Global Lab (Tinker & Berenfeld, 1994). The CoVis project provides students with the kinds of tools that researchers use in their work. Participating students use these tools when engaged in inquiry-based activities related to the study of atmospheric and environmental science. The focus is on the use of scientific visualizations conducted in collaborative groups. The Global Lab curriculum is a year- long interdisciplinary science course in which students learn to investigate scientific topics in collaboration with others.

The current focus on technology to support higher order learning is markedly different than the focus that permeated the 1970s and 1980s when computer-based instruction was largely directed toward the acquisition of basic skills (Kulik, Kulik, & Cohen, 1980). The change in emphasis on the expected role of technology in education paralleled a change during the same time frame in the conceptualization of human learning and how it can be supported or promoted. In the early 1970s and 1980s, learning was still construed within a more behavioral tradition. Issues such as the complex contribution of social context to individual learning had not received broad consideration. Human learning as described in more recent writings (e.g., the American Psychological Association's Learner-centered Principles (1997); the National Research Council's project How people learn (Bransford, Brown, and Cocking, 1999) is viewed as complex; strongly influenced by social context; involving metacognitive, motivational, and cognitive components; and characterized by individual differences in almost every facet. Technology in support of instruction and learning may be deployed to support or enhance one or more of these facets of human learning.

Collaboration among peers or others such as domain experts is generally considered to be an important contributor to students' conceptual development. Such collaborations have the potential to increase the quality of discourse, provide alternative explanations for phenomenon, generate multiple solutions to problems, and allow for the inclusion of many different kinds of skills in solving problems. It is also true, however, that successful collaborations are not easy to create or sustain (O'Donnell, 1999; Salomon & Globerson, 1989).

The use of technology by groups of students to support their learning also requires a model of the nature of the anticipated collaboration. A variety of theoretical approaches to peer learning have been delineated (O'Donnell & O'Kelly, 1994) and include those based on developmental psychological theories of Piaget and Vygotsky or on social psychological theory drawing on Lewin's field theory (Deutsch, 1949). Explanations of why collaboration is important to conceptual growth based on Piagetian theory rely on the concept of cognitive conflict that may be engendered by group discussions and arguments. The opportunity for differing opinions is enhanced in collaborative groups and those differences that may provoke conceptual change. Explanations of the utility of collaboration based on Vygotskian theory focus on both individual learning and group learning. Individuals may benefit in a collaborative group because there is an opportunity for their learning to be scaffolded by a more knowledgeable or experienced peer. The group may also come to shared understandings and involve individuals at different levels of participation. Other approaches to understanding collaboration include those based primarily on information ,essing theory and focusing on cognitive elaboration as a mechanism promotes learning in collaborative groups. From this perspective, col-ɔration provides opportunities for deeper processing of content and the elaboration of existing knowledge structures. The quality of discourse in a collaborative group is critical for learning to occur. A final approach to describing collaboration is a sociocultural approach in which the collaborative is seen as a community of learners.

The chapters in this book describe various forms and uses for technology. Understanding the model of collaboration that underpins the work is important to understanding the contribution that the technology made to the enhancement of learning. Chapters address the following questions:

- What theoretical perspective on collaboration is being adopted in the chapter?
- Within this theoretical framework, how and for whom does collaboration facilitate learning?
- How is technology conceptualized as a contributor to learning within the theoretical framework adopted and in what way does it contribute?

Theme of Argumentation

As collaboration among students is intended to foster higher level learning outcomes, a major theme in this book is argumentation. A number of the chapters in this book focus on the use of technology to support argumentation. Across all domains, students need to learn to make arguments, draw on reasons to support ideas, use evidence in support of their ideas, and draw valid conclusions. Skills in argumentation are very much in demand in school and also out of school. There is no end to the opportunities that people have to engage in argumentation. Public meetings of school boards, public hearings about development in a township, political meetings, and so on, provide many opportunities to use skills in argumentation. All too often, the quality of argumentation skills one observes is often lacking. Students can benefit greatly from developing skills in argumentation and technology can be fruitfully used to support that development.

Collaboration among students provides a context in which argumentation can be promoted. A number of researchers have shown that collaboratively constructed arguments are more beneficial than individually constructed arguments (Chinn, O'Donnell, & Jinks, 2001; Schwartz, Neumann, Gil, & Ilya, 2003).

Theme of Scaffolding

The complexities of collaboration in a computer-based environment are well illustrated in the chapters that specifically address argumentation. Clearly students need support as they learn to develop arguments or engage in higher levels of learning objectives. Much of how such scaffolding is conceptualized in the various chapters depends on the authors' orientation toward collaboration. To provide instructional environments that can support higher level reasoning, instructors need to consider how to design supports in the environment that will make it possible for students to engage in these higher order cognitive processes.

In the next few pages, I provide an overview of the contents of the book and how the various contributions address collaboration, argumentation, and scaffolding. The chapters are not discussed in the order in which they appear. Many chapters contribute to the themes of argumentation and scaffolding to varying degrees. In some chapters, these themes are integrally related. In others they are less tightly woven. Together, the chapters contribute to our understanding of the complexity of using technology effectively for the purposes of instruction and meaningful learning.

COLLABORATION, ARGUMENTATION, AND SCAFFOLDING

De Lisi's chapter (chap. 2) provides a developmental perspective on virtual scaffolding and the use of technology in learning. He identifies two communalities in the work of Piaget and Vygotsky, two theorists who provided influential theoretical perspectives on how collaboration among peers might promote cognitive development or facilitate learning. The two points of common ground are (a) the use of developmental methods, and (b) a constructivist approach to learning and instruction that emphasizes both individual and social processes. The chapter provides a very clear characterization of sociocultural constructivist theory. This overview is very useful, as most of the other chapters in the book draw on such theory in framing their analysis of collaboration and the use of technology. De Lisi describes the main themes in the work of Vygotsky and Piaget and examines how these are manifest in the chapters in this volume.

Three themes were identified that formed the core of Vygotsky's work (Wertsch, 1985): (a) use of a developmental methodology, (b) that individuals' higher mental processes have their origins in social processes, and (c) mental processes can only be understood by understanding mediators of these processes such as tools and signs. De Lisi notes that although the authors draw on Vygotskian theory, the methods used in the studies reported are not developmental in that intraindividual growth is not measured. In addition, the studies do not involve the students working with more competent others as might be expected when work is framed from a Vygotskian perspective. Although most of the studies reported in this volume were concerned with the use of technology as a cultural tool that mediates cognitive processes, De Lisi points out that it is difficult to draw conclusions about the contributions of these tools. Piaget's constructivism, social relationships, and the importance of the sociomoral climate in the chapters in this volume are described. The latter part of this chapter analyzes the concept of scaffolding and how it is utilized in these chapters. This chapter provides a critical framework, which can be used to analyze the contributions of the remaining chapters in this volume.

The chapter by Bielaczyc and Collins (chap. 3) provides an overview of knowledge-building communities, illustrates such communities by reference to historically documented instances of such communities, and describes the characteristics of such communities. The theory of collaboration that underlies this chapter has its origins in the sociocultural theory described by De Lisi. In knowledge-building communities, there is a concentration of expertise, knowledge is shared among participants, and scaffolds for such knowledge sharing either exist or are developed. Such communities of practice include multiple perspectives and strategies and are likely to promote argumentation. The mechanisms that are thought to foster knowledge-building are illustrated in the use of Knowledge Forum (Scardamalia & Bereiter, 1991, 1994) by teachers and students at two separate schools.

Chapters by Erkens, Prangsma, and Jaspers (chap.10), Andriessen (chap.9), Wiley and Bailey (chap.12), and Van Drie, van Boxtel, and van der Linden (chap.11) focus on computer support for the development of argumentation skills. The complexities of collaboration in a computer-based environment are well illustrated in these chapters that specifically address argumentation. Clearly students need support as they learn to develop arguments or engage in higher levels of learning objectives. Erkens et al. (chap.10) describe a computer-supported collaborative written argumentation environment and describe how students coordinated their activities and adjusted their actions in the process of problem solving and knowledge construction. Andriessen et al. (chap. 9) present an analysis of 5 years of work in asynchronous learning environments that were designed to engage students in argumentative computer-mediated communication. Wiley and Bailey (chap.12) broaden the scope of inquiry into the development of argumentation skills as they examine the contribution of collaboration in the context of students writing arguments based on multiple sources. Van Drie et al. (chap.11) also focus on learning history and the presentation of arguments using historical resources.

Erkens et al. (chap.10) focus on the way collaborating students manage to coordinate and adjust their actions to the processes of knowledge construction and problem solving when engaged in computer-supported collaborative argumentative writing. Discussion of planning activities was more frequent than were discussions related to the nature of the arguments being made. The chapter also contributes to our understanding of the kinds of supports that assist students when engaged in demanding activities. The software developed for use in the tasks described has a number of interesting features. The authors of this chapter also address some important methodological issues in relation to the study and analysis of collaborative learning.

Andriessen and his colleagues (chap.9) describe the evolution of efforts to engage students in argumentative computer-mediated communication within the context of college courses. Analyses of data collected in three separate courses examined the kind of discussions that took place among students in an asynchronous chat format. Aspects of these discussions that were of interest included the content-related nature of the discussions, whether they represented construction of knowledge or argumentation, and the degree to which messages posted by different participants were connected to other messages. The authors conclude that students need experience in collaboration before they can be effective in jointly developing arguments. The students' discussions rarely involved argumentation and messages were often disconnected from one another. The chapter describes some of the ways in which efforts were made to ameliorate these difficulties.

Wiley and Bailey (chap.12) also examine the effects of argumentation and collaboration on learning. This work is a bit of a departure from other work in the book. Many of the chapters involve the use of online discussions as part of a learning task. These discussions were subsequently analyzed in terms of many characteristics, including the quality of argumentation present. In some cases (e.g., Erken et al.'s argumentation writing task), students were explicitly directed to generate arguments. Wiley and Bailey directed students to either create a summary from multiple web pages or generate an argument. In both scenarios, students worked in pairs. Argumentation in this study was a manipulation in contrast to other work in which it was an outcome. Asking students to develop arguments when learning from multiple web pages appears to hold some promise as an element of instructional design in such environments. Argumentation seems to prompt more co-construction of ideas by students but did not seem to encourage more extensive evaluation of sources. It may be that such skills must be directly taught.

Students in this study (and the sample was small) did not argue with one another, contradict one another, or voice any disagreement. Better evaluation of sources of evidence might have occurred in the presence of some disagreement. The absence of this kind of dialogue is not atypical. Person (1995) found that politeness rituals between tutors and their tutees often interfered with the tutorial process and the kind of feedback provided to tutees.

Van Drie and colleagues (chap.11) also compare the effects on interaction of two different instructional scenarios. Their chapter is concerned with historical reasoning, defined by the authors as "describing, explaining, or judging phenomena of the past with the use of historical concepts" (p. xx). Van Drie et al. required students to explain the changes in students' behaviors in the 1950s and 1960s in the Netherlands. In a second condition, students were asked to evaluate whether the behavior exhibited by students in the 1950s and 1960s was revolutionary or not. Students worked in pairs

with multiple sources to respond to the assigned task. Being asked to explain or evaluate influenced students' historical reasoning. Students who
were asked to evaluate tended to talk about their points of view and use
evidence to support their arguments. Those who were asked to explain
tended to focus on identifying causes. Overall, students used relatively little
historical reasoning (13% utterances were associated with historical reasoning). This is a rather low level of historical reasoning on a task that deliber-
ately called for students to engage in such reasoning.

It is clear from these various chapters that look at collaborative and
technological support for argumentation that engaging students in high
quality argumentation is not a simply task . Generating good arguments is
complex and requires high levels of cognitive activity. Chinn's chapter
(chap.14) addresses some of the issues with the difficulty in learning to
argue well. He organizes his chapter around a set of research questions related to argumentation. The first set of questions concerns whether argumentation was worth doing; that is, does it offer any instructional benefits?
The second set of questions assumes that a positive answer can be found in
response to the first set and is related to instructional goals. Specifically,
Chinn asks what students are supposed to learn when they engage in argumentation. The final set of questions concerns the kinds of instructional
practices that might help students learn to argue well. Chinn refers to many
of the other chapters in the book as he considers these questions.

It is clear that creating the necessary prompts, supports, or instructional
contexts within which students can use technology to support the development of higher order skills is not simple. A number of chapters deal explicitly with software that is designed to support student learning of complex
content. Examples of these are Hmelo-Silver's chapter (chap.7) on the use
of the Oncology Thinking Cap (Day, Shirey, Ramakrishnan, & Huang,
1998) that provides a modeling tool for cancer researchers as they design
clinical trials, Qi and Zhang's chapter (chap. 7) on a simulation environment for reasoning about buoyancy, and Veerman and Veldhuis-
Diermanse's chapter (chapt.13) on the use of a variety of technology tools.

Hmelo-Silver (chap.7) and Qi and Zhang (chap.6) describe simulation
environments that are intended to reduce the processing burden on the part
of participants, and thus allow students to perform at higher levels with
respect to reasoning because of the reduced load related to issues of compu-
tation. Hmelo-Silver worked with a group of medical students using a modeling tool for the design of cancer researchers. The simulation environment,
the Oncology Thinking Cap, could be used to model clinical trials of particular cancer drug treatments. The simulation clearly indicated the need to
specify the dose, schedule, and conditional rules for designing a trial. Under
such circumstances, the medical students who used the simulation acquired
some knowledge of the structure of the task. The statistical computations
needed for the full completion of the task were hidden from students. Essentially, when elements of the task structure are made explicit, students
learn. It is interesting to consider how training using this kind of simulation

would compare to direct, explicit instruction in the elements of the task and practice in executing the task.

Qi and Zhang (chap.6) found that peer collaboration had positive effects on students' overall discovery outcomes. Students typically experience difficulty in the consideration and manipulation of multiple variables in experimentation and the software described in this chapter is designed to support students' experimentation. Pairs more successfully discovered rules linking the features of an object (shape, mass, and volume) and the size of its buoyant force under circumstances where the object floated or sank. They also demonstrated more intuitive understanding of the task. However, there was no effect of an additional manipulation in the experiment that contrasted the performance of students who were provided with explanatory prompt cards that they could use to guide their activity. These cards included questions they might ask themselves or a partner. Students seemed unable to use these effectively. In this study, the combination of supports provided by the simulation program, the presence of a partner, and the availability of a prompt card may have created an excessive cognitive load for students.

Veerman and Veldhuis-Diermanse (chap.13) analyzed the characteristics of effective computer-mediated communication systems in four separate studies. They show that the effective use of educational technology to support collaborative learning is associated with the roles students adopt and the characteristics of the computer-mediated communication systems used.

Linn and Slotta (chap.4) describe the design of collaborative forums that enable students to learn science. They lay out the many separate decisions necessary to design a collaborative experience. They report on a study involving the iterative design of online discussion. The study involved a group of teachers selected to participate in a program of activities with researchers from the American Physiological Society to help them implement science activities on topics of physiology. The initial experience with the online discussions of this group was characterized by a lack of participation and peer exchange. The chapter describes the changes made to substantially improve the quantity and quality of participation.

Two additional chapters focus on preservice teachers and in-service teachers. Derry (chap.8) describes a project in which a large undergraduate class in a teacher education program is transformed into a learning environment in which students study video cases of actual classroom instruction and formulate ideas about instructional redesign that prompt exploration of content in the learning sciences. The software environment described in this chapter supports problem-based learning of content in educational psychology. A theoretical framework called the activity field hypothesis guides the design of the software and its instructional use.

Williams and Kelly (chap.5) examine how in-service teachers use online interaction to support professional development activities. This chapter describes a model of professional development called Anchored Collaborative Inquiry. It combines an actual in-service workshop to promote the implementation of standards-based reform in the participating teachers' classrooms. Their implementation of this reform effort was supported by ongoing online discussion facilitated by the workshop faculty. Participants had difficulty in effectively communicating about the contexts in which they worked.

SUMMARY

The chapters of this book together contribute to an increased understanding of the complexity of using technology effectively to support higher-level learning. The provision of technological support can facilitate complex learning but still leaves challenges to be addressed. Chinn (chap.14) correctly points to the difficulties in learning to argue and the kinds of instruction that promote the development of effective argumentation. De Lisi (chap.2) also points to the need for more refined conceptualizations of scaffolding, the result of which might be to develop more successful supports for the kind of learning outcomes desired. The chapters provide the reader with a range of strategies that the authors adopted to solve some of the difficulties that arose in implementing the projects described. There is a wealth of experience and knowledge about how to use technology effectively for learning embedded in these chapters.

The chapters also contribute to our understanding of the kinds of research that might be conducted on topics related to technology. Each chapter presents a critical analysis of data collected for the specific projects being described. Different authors have selected varied research strategies in collecting, analyzing, and interpreting data and these decisions can be understood against the backdrop of the theoretical orientation researchers have adopted with respect to the nature of collaboration, the role of technology in supporting learning, and the desired outcomes from the interaction of individuals in a collaborative context supported by the technology.

REFERENCES

Agnew, C. (2001). Evaluating changes in teaching and learning. *Journal of Geography in Higher Education, 25*, 293–298.

American Psychological Association. (1997). *Learner-centered psychological principles: A framework for school redesign and reform.* Retrieved December 19, 2004 from http://www.apa.org/ed/lcp.html

Bransford, J. D., Brown, A. L., & Cocking, R. R. (Eds.). (1999). *How people learn*. Washington, DC: National Academy Press.

Chinn, C. A., O'Donnell, A. M., & Jinks, T. S. (2001). The structure of discourse in collaborative learning. *Journal of Experimental Education, 69*, 77-97.

Day, R., Shirey, W., Ramakrishnan, S., & Huang, Q. (1998, April). *Tumor biology modeling workbench for prospectively evaluating cancer treatments*. Paper presented at the 2nd IMACS International Multi-conference: CESA '98 Computational Engineering in Systems Applications, Tunisia.

Deutsch, M. (1949). A theory of cooperation and competition. *Human Relations, 2*, 129–152.

Gumport, P. J., & Chun, M. (2000). *Technology and higher education: Opportunities and challenges for the new era* (Tech. Rep. No.1-02). Stanford, CA: Stanford University, National Center for Postsecondary Improvement.

Honey, M. (2001). Testimony before the Labor, HHS, and Education Appropriations Subcommittee, United States Senate, July 25, 2001. Retrieved 12/19/2004 from http://main.edc.org/newsroom/features/mhtestimony.asp

Jones, T. H., & Paolucci, R. (1999). Research framework and dimensions for evaluating the effectiveness of educational technology systems on learning outcomes. *Journal of Research on Computing in Education, 32*, 17–28.

Kerrey, R., & Isakson, J. (2000). *The power of the Internet for learning: Moving from promise to practice* (Report of the Web-Based Education Commission). Retrieved December 19, 2004 from http://www.ed.gov/offices/AC/WBEC/FinalReport/WBECReport. pdf.

Kulik, J. A., Kulik, C., & Cohen, P. (1980). Effectiveness of computer-based teaching: A meta-analysis of findings. *Review of Educational Research, 50*, 525–544.

Merisotis, J. P. (1999). The "What's-the-difference?" debate. *Academe, 85*(5), 47–51.

Norris, C., Smolka, J, & Soloway, E. (2000). Extracting value from research: A guide for the perplexed. *Technology & Learning, 20(11)*, 45-48.

Norris, C., Sullivan, T., Poirot, J., & Soloway, E. (2003). No access, no use, no impact: Snapshot surveys of educational technology in K-12. *Journal of Research on Technology in Education, 36*, 15-27.

O'Donnell, A. M. (1999). Structuring dyadic interaction through scripted cooperation. In A. M. O'Donnell & A. King (Eds.), *Cognitive perspectives on peer learning* (pp. 179–196). Mahwah, NJ: Lawrence Erlbaum Associates.

O'Donnell, A. M., & O'Kelly, J. (1994). Learning from peers: Beyond the rhetoric of positive results. *Educational Psychology Review, 6,* 321–349.

Pea, R., Edelson, D., & Gomez, L. (1994, April). *The CoVis Collaboratory: High school science learning supported by a broadband educational network with scientific visualization, videoconferencing, and collaborative computing.* Paper presented at the symposium Issues in Computer Networking in K-12 Classrooms: A Progress Report of Four NSF Testbeds, at the Annual Meeting of the American Educational Research Association, New Orleans, LA.

Person, N. K. (1995). Pragmatics and pedagogy: Conversational rules and politeness strategies may inhibit effective tutoring. *Cognition and Instruction, 13,* 161–188.

Phipps, R., & Merisotis, J. P. (1999). *What's the difference? A review of contemporary research on the effectiveness of distance learning in higher education.* Retrieved from http:/www.ihep.com/difference.pdf

Salomon, G., & Globerson, T. (1989). When teams do not function the way they ought to. *International Journal of Educational Research, 13,* 89–99.

Scardamalia, M., & Bereiter, C. (1991). Higher levels of agency for children in knowledge building: A challenge for the design of new knowledge media. *The Journal of the Learning Sciences, 1,* 37–68.

Scardamalia, M., & Bereiter, C. (1994). Computer support for knowledge building communities. *The Journal of the Learning Sciences, 3,* 265–283.

Schwartz, B. B., Neuman, Y., Gil, J., & Ilya, M. (2003). Construction of collective and individual knowledge in argumentative activity. *The Journal of the Learning Sciences, 12,* 219-256.

Tinker, B., & Berenfeld, B. (1994). Patterns of US Global Lab adaptations. *Hands on!* Retrieved from http://hou.lbl.gov.

Wertsch, J. V. (1985). *Vygotsky and the social formation of mind.* Cambridge, MA: Harvard University Press.

Chapter 2

A Developmental Perspective on Virtual Scaffolding for Learning in Home and School Contexts

Richard De Lisi
Rutgers, The State University of New Jersey

As the 21st century enters its fourth year, nations throughout the world continue to make significant investments in technology for homes, schools, and workplaces. In some cases, technological advances have supplanted older technologies. For example, modern teenagers believe that CD or MP3 players are the only means to listen to music, as they have had little to no exposure to vinyl records and turntables, or to cassette tapes and tape players. In a similar vein, in the United States, DVD players are fast overtaking VCRs as the means to view movies in the home. Although new technologies sometimes replace older technologies, new technologies often coexist with previously developed and older technologies. For example, despite the availability of electronic versions of newspapers, magazines, and journals, "hard" copies continue to be bought, sold, and read in homes, libraries, and places of business.

As a society we are still working out various aspects of our relationship to modern technology. For example, there is a tension between the need to protect children from access to harmful material and from being "accessed" by predators, and the need for freedom of information in our democratic society. For example, the U.S. Supreme Court has been asked to decide whether or not local and state governments can restrict Internet surfing at public libraries. The tension is between the right for free speech and the need to protect children from harmful materials. Specifically, the Court will decide if federal funding can be withdrawn from libraries that do not install filters on their computers (Associated Press, 2002). This issue is of obvious concern to educators who want their students to use the Internet for learning (Schwartz, 2002).

Students also need to learn that what appear to be private e-mail and instant messaging communications between and among friends are really in the public domain. In particular, what students may intend as jokes or as fanciful boasting can be interpreted as more than that when brought to the attention of authority figures. In a recent case, a high school student in Queens, New York, was arrested for making shooting spree threats in a chat room. The apologetic student claimed he was new to chat rooms and never intended to really harm anyone, but instead was trying to scare and impress a female high school student in Arkansas (Kilgannon, 2003).

Given the central role that technology plays in the modern world, few would disagree with the proposition that schoolchildren, especially the educationally disadvantaged whose parents lack resources, need to be exposed to technology in schools as part of preparation for the world after school. In K–16 educational settings, new technology, especially high-speed Internet access, is rapidly becoming ubiquitous in nations that can afford this investment. Even in schools that have made significant investments in technology, however, long-standing educational methods and practices can still be found. Students still work alone with books, dittos, and pencil and paper; and they still work together in face-to-face classroom discussions. In both individual and group settings, modern students still work under the face-to-face guidance and direction of teachers. The use of computers to support collaborative learning or computer-supported collaborative learning (CSCL) is an instance of technology blending into previously worked out methods and approaches, rather than an example of technology leading to the abandonment of the old in favor of the new.

Educators recognized the importance of cooperative and collaborative learning well before the introduction of networked computers in classrooms. Two of the "giants" of developmental psychology, Piaget and Vygotsky, provided theoretical foundations for the practice of using networked computers to support collaborative learning. This chapter examines these theoretical foundations with a particular focus on "virtual scaffolding" to clarify the strengths and weaknesses of current research and practice on CSCL.

In recent years the tendency to contrast or juxtapose the ideas of Piaget and Vygotsky has diminished with an increasing recognition that there is much common ground in their respective theories (Kuhn, 1996; Shayer, 2003; Smith, Dockrell, & Tomlinson, 1997). This is the approach that I take in this chapter, although each theorist is discussed separately in some parts of the chapter. Two of the most important points of common ground between Piaget and Vygotsky that are relevant for research on virtual scaffolding are (a) the use of developmental methods, and (b) a constructivist approach to learning and instruction that emphasizes both individual and social processes. In addition, from Piaget we get important insights about children's relations with peers and with adults. These insights help to clarify the social aspects of constructivism. From Vygotsky we get insights about the importance in children's lives of societal artifacts and tools. These insights help to clarify the cultural aspects of constructivism. I use these ideas about developmental methods, and the individual, social, and cultural aspects of constructivism to frame my discussion of CSCL and virtual scaffolding.

In this chapter I also discuss scaffolding as a psychoeducational process. I argue that it would be helpful if some kind of definitional consensus and clarity could emerge in future work. At present, the term is being used in so many different ways that virtually any effort that results in student learning can be considered to be an example of scaffolding. I propose dimensions of instructional design as a framework to classify or categorize various modes of instruction, including scaffolding.

SOCIO-CULTURAL-CONSTRUCTIVIST THEORY

Overview

If you had to select one theory that was the basis for most modern work on using technology to scaffold learning in schools and colleges, that theory would be sociocultural constructivist theory. Indeed, many of the authors in this book explicitly adopt this theoretical framework and present cogent summaries of their theoretical foundations. Here is a quick summary of the main ideas that most authors explicitly adopted in their work:

- Constructivism: Students are active learners.
- Higher forms of thinking develop from experiences with more competent other persons who serve as scaffolds for learning.
- Higher forms of thinking develop from experiences with peers who coconstruct learning outcomes.
- Cultural tools and artifacts play a formative role in learning processes.
- The quality of discourse is an important factor in the quality of learning.
- Modern technology is an important example of a cultural tool that can be used to support learning in both scaffolding and coconstructing relationships.

Student motivation receives less explicit attention in sociocultural constructivist approaches. In part this is due to the assumption that students are active, intrinsically motivated learners rather than passive learners who need extrinsic motivation. In addition, there is the assumption that peer experiences are intrinsically motivating or at least more motivating than passively listening to teacher talk. Similarly, there is an implicit assumption that working with a more competent other person in scaffolding, rather than a direct instruction environment, can also be viewed as intrinsically motivating. Some of the work reported in this volume contradicts these assumptions about motivation. Motivation cannot necessarily be assumed and may require specific attention in various learning contexts.

Vygotsky's Theoretical Foundations

As a psychoeducational process, scaffolding is most widely associated with the work of Vygotsky (Rieber & Carton, 1987; Van der Veer & Valsiner, 1994; Wertsch, 1985). To my knowledge, Vygotsky did not use the terms *scaffold* or *scaffolding*, but his theory is widely understood to provide a theoretical foundation for this type of instructional approach.

According to Wertsch (1985), three themes formed the core of Vygotsky's theoretical framework: (a) use of a developmental methodology, (b) the assertion that higher mental processes in the individual have their origin in social processes, and (c) the assertion that mental processes can be understood only if we understand the tools and signs that mediate them.

Developmental methodology

Early developmental theorists like Vygotsky and Piaget were profoundly influenced by Darwin's theory of evolution. The idea that to understand a phenomenon, you have to describe and explain how it comes about, is at the heart of an evolutionary approach. Vygotsky, for example, made frequent reference to the work of the early Gestalt researchers who studied tool use in great apes. Vygotsky referred to these data in presenting his own findings concerning children's acquisition of cultural tools, especially speech and language, during the course of child development. In discussing child development, Vygotsky made reference to natural-psychological development and cultural-psychological development. The former is linked to phylogenesis and early childhood the latter to ontogenesis from early childhood through adulthood. Vygotsky also assumed that cultures could be developmentally scaled and together with Luria, he studied differences in certain cognitive abilities, like classification in parts of the Soviet Union thought to be "primitive" versus "modern." In each of these examples of a developmental approach to a problem, there is an explicit scale ranging from less well developed to more well developed that reflects differences in underlying qualitative organization.

On a more technical note, modern-day developmental psychology recognizes three main classes of developmental methodology: simple designs, sequential designs, and microgenetic methods. Simple designs include cross-sectional, longitudinal, and time-lag studies. Of these three types of simple designs, only longitudinal work measures intraindividual change directly as it entails repeated measurements. Sequential designs combine these simple designs in one study, consisting of two or more cross-sectional, longitudinal, and time-lag studies. Microgenetic designs entail direct measures of intraindividual change as individuals are observed repeatedly in a short period of time. Microgenetic methods can be traced to Vygotsky's ideas about dynamic assessment in the zone of proximal development. Longitudinal studies typically span weeks, months, years, or even decades, but microgenetic studies might entail a single problem-solving session or several sessions that are completed in a short period of time. Microgenetic methods are well suited for the study of the development of problem solving strategies. (Granott & Parziale, 2002; Kuhn, 1995, 1997; Siegler & Crowley, 1991; Siegler & Svetina, 2002).

Developmental Methods in This Present Volume

None of the studies of scaffolding reported in this book used either simple or sequential developmental methods. Each study focused on one and only one "grade" level such as middle school students, college students, preservice teachers, medical students, and teachers. It would be possible, of course, to introduce either cross-sectional or longitudinal approaches in any of this work. For example, computer simulations of physics problems could be tried on students in different grade levels. As another example using a developmental framework, teacher experience could be built in as a design variable to look for differences in reactions to and participation in professional development workshops and Web-based assignments. This be could done by tracking changes in teacher performance following longitudinal participation in professional development programs over multiple years.

Researchers in the field of instructional design can use microgenetic analyses if scaffolding is a focus. Modern versions of computer programs used for courseware, for example, are ideal for keeping records of student participation in communicative and collaborative endeavors. The data analytic technique would be to record: (a) amount of participation, (b) type of participation, and, most important, (c) any changes in the type or quality of participation that occur over time. Note that the methodology becomes developmental (microgenetic) if and only if the third component includes measures of intraindividual, not just group change. The studies in this volume that report students' participation in virtual communities do not, for the most part, take this last step. If they did examine changes in amount or type of participation, the analyses stop short of a focus on individual change.

Social Origin of Higher Mental Processes

The idea that higher cognitive functions originate in social processes is perhaps the most widely recognized of Vygotsky's themes. Vygotsky's prototypical example of this theme is the differentiation in early childhood of human speech into two major functions—interpersonal communication, and as a tool for voluntary self-regulation and thought. This differentiation is based on the child's experiences with parents and other adults who use speech to not only communicate with the child, but also to regulate the child's behavior. Based on these experiences, the child comes to recognize and internalize the regulatory function of speech and to use speech as a tool for thinking. Anticipatory planning based on inner speech is Vygotsky's prototypical example of a higher cognitive process that has its origin in social experience. Vygotsky's analysis of speech developing from social speech to egocentric speech to inner speech is an excellent example of a general developmental approach that identified changes in the underlying structural and functional organization of human speech in childhood.

Vygotsky's notion of the *zone of proximal development* reflects his use of microgenetic analysis as well as the idea that higher forms of cognition have a basis in social experiences. For example, Vygotsky (1978) reported finding that two children at the same developmental level as measured by an IQ test performed at different levels of performance on a difficult problem (a problem that exceeded their present IQ level) when given the same assistance by another person whose level of individual functioning exceeded that of the children. In this type of research investigation, a person is assessed on three separate occasions. First, the person is studied when working alone to establish a baseline, then when working in the company of a more competent other person who provides assistance, and finally when working alone again. The third phase of the investigation provides a measure of the degree to which the person has *internalized* key aspects of the joint problem-solving session. In this type of (developmental) microgenetic methodology in a classroom or laboratory setting, the presence of another person in a problem-solving situation introduces a social element that makes dynamic assessment of a learner's competencies possible. Vygotsky stressed the importance of dynamic assessment in psychology and education. Two pupils with the same IQs could have different zones of proximal development, or distances between current level of functioning and potential functioning as indexed by performance with social assistance. This fact is not uncovered by measures in which the child performs alone and without social assistance. Vygotsky argued that these kinds of experiences in the zone of proximal development eventually lead the child to internalize the sociocultural tools and techniques used by the more competent problem solver. At this point, the child is less dependent on the other and can employ higher forms of problem solving on his or her own. With Vygotsky's theory as a basis then, the term *scaffold* suggests a temporary, supportive interpersonal framework in which the more competent other person uses social tools and artifacts (e.g., societal speech) to assist the less competent person in achieving a learning or problem-solving objective. A scaffold is assumed to be temporary in the specific sense that the social support and guidance will not be necessary at some point in the future as the target individual incorporates the tools and strategies into his or her repertoire.

Social Origins of Higher Mental Processes in This Present Volume

Despite almost universal acceptance of Vygotsky's ideas, none of the authors in this volume study learners working with a more competent other person using dynamic, microgenetic methods. Instead, learners are observed working with other coequal learners on either scientific reasoning and inquiry problems, or professional development problems using technology as a mediator. In some of these studies, computer software is the more competent "other." In other studies, software programs are used to support communication, discussion, and argumentation.

It is interesting to note that as Vygotsky's theory predicts, many of the present investigators found it necessary to build in a human interface at the start, and often throughout their study, to get the learners to use and benefit from the software in the ways intended by the researcher. In this volume, whether the participants were middle school students, college students, graduate students, or professionals, the instructional designs included face-to-face, social components in which members of the research team were present to help participants understand the technological demands of the tasks at hand. So, even in instances where the goal was to have participants benefit from virtual rather than human scaffolds, a kind of double scaffolding was needed. First, the researchers needed to scaffold participants such that they could use the technology on their own. Then, the software provided another kind of scaffolding by presenting materials, allowing for information access, keeping track of comments, and so forth. Often, the researchers maintain their involvement by asking questions, making suggestions for revisions or new discussion directions, and so forth. If the investigators had analyzed the learners' reactions to their (the investigators') roles, then these studies would have had a distinctive "Vygotskian" flavor. For example, no doubt all learners were novices at first, but some probably internalized the instructions about how to use available technology more quickly than others. In other words, participants had different zones of proximal development. It would be interesting to track how students with smaller and larger zones of proximal development regarding technology use and facility fared in the research studies and in classrooms over time.

Cognitive Processes Are Mediated by Cultural Tools

Cole and Wertsch (1996) discussed the fact that the second theme in Vygotsky's work, social origin of higher mental processes, is often misinterpreted to mean that Vygotsky ignored or downplayed the role of the individual in the development of higher cognitive processes. Indeed, it has often been asserted that Piaget's theory of cognitive development highlights the role of individual constructivism and ignores sociocultural constructivism, whereas Vygotsky's theory does the reverse. Most modern-day scholars reject this view. Piaget and Vygotsky each discussed both individual and social influences on cognitive constructivism (Kuhn, 1996; Shayer, 2003; Smith, et al., 1997).

Cole and Wertsch (1996) emphasized that the third major theme in Vygotsky's theory, cognitive processes are mediated by cultural tools, is emphasized in Vygotsky's theory but not in Piaget's theory. This theme stresses the fact that our human environment is enriched with the cultural achievements of previous generations. These cultural achievements (artifacts and tools) serve to shape and enrich the cognitive processes of those who develop in that environment. According to Cole and Wertsch (1996),

> In their early writings on this subject, the Russian cultural-historical psychologists coupled a focus on the cultural medium with the assumption that the special mental quality of human beings is their need and ability to mediate their actions through artifacts and to arrange for the rediscovery and appropriation of these forms of mediation by subsequent generations. (p. 252).

The authors went on to indicate that although Vygotsky focused on human language as a critical cultural artifact, Vygotsky also discussed other cultural artifacts including algebraic symbol systems, works of art, diagrams, maps, and other conventional signs. Thus, it seems safe to assume that modern technology including the various kinds of computer software programs used in instructional design studies, would be considered to be important cultural tools and artifacts within a Vygotskian theoretical framework.

In a recent report, Harmon (2003) noted that the use of computers by chess players at the highest level of the sport is fundamentally changing the way humans think about chess, plan for competitive matches, and conduct games of chess. Many of the experts interviewed believe that the ingenuity and strategy of the game is being sacrificed for memorization of machine-derived computational lines of play. As another example, Schiesel (2003) discussed how computer tools have transformed the field of probabilistic risk assessment, helping mathematicians, engineers, and insurance executives to assess risks of disasters such as hurricanes, nuclear power plant failures, or space shuttle catastrophes. These trends are fully consistent with Vygotsky's ideas about the importance of cultural tools in shaping the nature of human thought. We can anticipate new lines of research on the impact of technology on the development of thought from its formative stages to that of high-end experts in many fields, not just in chess grandmasters and scientists.

The Study of Cultural Tool Mediation in This Present Volume

The idea that cultural tools mediate cognitive processes is at the heart of much of the work reported in this book. Indeed, the work presented is attempting to apply this idea with new and modern tools such as computer software that supports communication in asynchronous and synchronous formats and high-speed access to audio, visual, and text-based information on the Internet. As you read some of this work you will discover that learners' reactions can be unpredictable. For example, Chen and Zhang (chap. 6) did not find the expected benefit from a condition designed to enhance physics learning (prompt condition). These authors concluded that Chinese students are not used to social-reciprocal activities in school contexts and therefore did not benefit in the ways intended by the instructional designers. This suggests that the use of cultural—tools here, a software simulation of a physics experiment—needs to be considered in light of larger the larger, sociocultural context. Older, more established classroom norms and expectations influenced the degree of influence of the newer, computer-based tools. In different chapters that summarize work with teachers, both Williams and Kelly (chap. 5) and Linn and Slotta (chap. 4) reported that teachers interpreted and reacted to technology-mediated professional development activities in ways that were not intended by the research design team. For example, teachers were reluctant to post comments that could be seen as critical of fellow teachers, resulting in "flat" rather than hierarchical and integrative discussions. Here again, a long-standing cultural expectation, "thou shall not critically evaluate a fellow teacher," muted the effect intended by the instructional design team. In other chapters, it is clear that the use of technological-based cultural tools can vary within very similar instructional contexts. For example, Veerman and Veldhuis-Diermanse (chap. 13) found that college students' collaborative participations varied across asynchronous versus synchronous virtual formats with the former leading to higher levels of higher quality participation. Hmelo-Silver (chap. 7) found that advanced medical students needed "black-box" scaffolding in addition to "glass-box" scaffolding as they attempted to master the complexities of design and analysis of clinical trials.

From these studies it is difficult to draw any firm conclusions about how modern technology influences the development of higher cognitive processes, as there are too many uncontrolled variables operating. Specifically, the participants were from different birth cohorts were from different cultural contexts, had different degrees of experience with technology, had different technologies available, and were observed in different subject areas with different amounts of support for different durations. A much larger corpus of data is needed in each area studied. It is interesting that several studies found that participants' relationships with other participants and with the research team itself provided an important source of performance variability. This general finding is well captured by Piaget's ideas about the role and importance of social experiences in intellectual development. These ideas are summarized in the next section.

Piaget's Theoretical Foundations

Constructivism

Over the course of a nearly sixty-year career, Piaget articulated a comprehensive theory of intellectual development predicated on an evolutionary
biological notion of self-regulation (Piaget, 1970). Like Vygotsky, Piaget
was interested in the development from "natural" or biological regulation to
deliberate, psychological regulation. Also, like Vygotsky, Piaget recognized
the role and importance of social factors in the development of various
forms of regulation. Although Piaget was certainly aware of the existence
of cultural factors in the development of the intellectual operations he described, Piaget did not investigate cultural factors in the same way or to the
same extent as did Vygotsky. Instead, Piaget focused on types of social
relations as they pertain to child and adolescent development. In particular,
Piaget described structural and functional differences between child–adult
and child–child relationships and discussed their respective roles in moral
development, intellectual development, and education (Piaget, 1965/1995).

Piaget acknowledged the importance of social relations in intellectual
development right from the start of a child's life. It is not correct to assert
that Piaget believed development proceeds from the individual level at first
and then after sufficient intellectual development has occurred, shifts to a
social level. Instead, Piaget acknowledged the importance of biological-
maturational factors, experiences in the physical world, and experiences in
the social world including teaching, as factors in intellectual development.
Piaget maintained, however, that each of these factors is coordinated or
"orchestrated" by the central self-organizing factor called *equilibration*
(Piaget, 1975/1985). The theoretical framework described by Linn and
Slotta (chap. 4), which recognizes both autonomous and social aspects of
learning, is very consistent with Piaget's view. As Linn and Slotta cogently
argue, instructional design efforts need to be mindful of both the social and
individual aspects of student performance and learning.

With this construct of equilibration, Piaget reminded us that individuals
are constantly needing to work out a balance or relationship between their
current, immediate experiences and their underlying cognitive system.
Cognitive systems are open to potential revision and refinement, changing
via differentiation and integration. The nature of the person's underlying
cognitive system is critical according to Piaget, because it plays a major
role in cognitive performance. For example, Inhelder and Piaget's (1958)
classic studies of scientific problem solving and reasoning showed that
young children, who lacked even concrete logical operations, would misin-
terpret their own role in the causal operations of systems like pendulums.
Older children who developed concrete operational schemes could systematically isolate and control variables but only to a limited degree. Only
when students had developed a full-fledged combinatorial system did they

begin to observe, manipulate, and control variables in accordance with scientific methods. Thus, a key idea in Piaget's constructivist theory is that the underlying cognitive system determines the child's meaning making, and level of success and understanding, in a given problem-solving context.

In Piaget's theory, constructivism has a second meaning as well. In the first sense of the term just illustrated, constructivism refers to current, "online" meaning making as a function of the person's cognitive system. In the second sense of the term, constructivism refers to changes in the present cognitive system initiated by meaning making in a given context. This meaning making opens up the possibility for revisions to the cognitive system. Meaning making can be thought of as Step 1 in the process of differentiating and integrating the cognitive system. It is important to note, however, that whereas the first type of constructivism is always in play, maintenance of the cognitive system, not revision, is the default for the second type of constructivism. That is to say, often Step 1 is the only step in the process, and the cognitive system remains unchanged (De Lisi & Golbeck, 1999).

For the cognitive system to be revised, gaps (e.g., factors ignored) in meaning making and perturbations (e.g., feedback that errors have occurred) must be incorporated into the cognitive system. This incorporation leads to revision of the cognitive system or constructivism in the second sense of the term. Students are often only momentarily aware of gaps or perturbations and do not take the next steps of trying to incorporate them into the present cognitive system. In this case, change does not occur. This general model of constructivism was used by Piaget to describe functioning at both lower (sensory motor) and higher levels (operational) of cognitive functioning (Piaget, 1975/1985).

Given this model of constructivism, it is important to understand what factors lead to differentiation and integration of the cognitive system via incorporation of gaps and perturbations. This same question can be posed about Vygotsky's construct of *internalization* of higher cognitive functions and processes within scaffolding experiences. Given that the student is in a social setting in which learning is supposed to be occurring, what factors contribute to the student being able to benefit from this experience such that when faced with the same or similar circumstances, the social support is no longer necessary for successful performance?

Social Relationships

One important factor pertaining to meaning making and to change in cognitive systems studied by Piaget in his early work was the type of social relationship children were experiencing (Piaget, 1965/1995). In particular, Piaget described how the "social factor" in development is not a single factor but instead consists of (at least) two main types of relationships: child–adult and child–child relationships. Although Piaget felt that children and their parents could experience mutual love and affection, the intellectual and social-moral balance of power in a child–adult relationship resides with the adult. The child is not a coequal with an adult, and children do not begin to think of themselves as equals until adolescence. In the prototypic child–adult relationship, the child has a unilateral respect for the adult, authority figure. Given this imbalance, Piaget was particularly skeptical about the intellectual and moral benefits of having adults "tell" the children what to do. Especially in a classroom setting, students might feel constrained to simply "spit back" what the teacher says and memorize what is in source materials, despite only having a superficial level of understanding and even a lack of conviction in what is being repeated. This does not mean that Piaget rejected Vygotsky's notion of scaffolding in which adults provide supports for children. However, Piaget believed that the teaching–learning relationship must be carefully orchestrated for cognitive advancement on the part of the child to occur (Piaget, 1973).

In child–child relationships, in contrast, it is more likely that neither party is the intellectual and moral authority. In a social relationship between equal partners, each one feels freer to express his or her true ideas and convictions. This occurs because children feel a mutual respect for their peer and believe it be reciprocated in kind. Lacking an authority figure to tell them what is right and wrong, children must, of necessity, coconstruct courses of action, demonstrations, and explanations. This process is open-ended and potentially more likely to have children become aware of gaps and perturbations in their efforts. Thus, Piaget's theory provides a firm foundation for peer learning in school contexts. Again, however, it is not the case that peer learning, in and of itself, is beneficial. The relationships must be of a certain kind for both parties to benefit. In particular, participants must feel that their ideas and efforts will be valued and respected by other team members. If instead, there is a perceived intellectual imbalance between members, then unilateral respect might cause the intellectually inferior team member to mindlessly imitate what the intellectually superior team member proposes. This situation would be similar to the prototypical child–adult relationship.

The Importance of the Sociomoral Climate in This Present Volume

As I just suggested, it is important to acknowledge that not all child–adult relationships are fully tinged with constraint, and not all child–child or student peer relationships contain equal partners. The underlying social-moral climate that characterizes the relationship is at least as important as whether an adult or peer is involved. In classrooms, for example, teachers can create contexts in which students feel that their teachers respect them as persons for their ideas and efforts. In such classrooms, students are more likely to have mutual respect for their fellow students. On the other hand, in classrooms in which a supportive, social-moral climate has not been created, peer work might devolve into relationships of constraint and unilateral respect such that one child takes the lead and the other is either passive or merely following along. As I already noted, Chen and Zhang (chap. 6) found that middle school students did not react to a peer prompt condition in the ways they expected due to larger context and previous experiences in the educational system in China. Similarly, both Williams and Kelly (chap. 5) and Linn and Slotta (chap. 4) found that teachers reacted to opportunities for peer collaboration in unexpected ways, due in part, to a cultural norm in which K–12 teachers do not formally evaluate each and are reluctant to criticize one another. In this case, the teacher peer relationship of mutual respect means that one teacher does not criticize the practices of another teacher. In both studies, the university researchers had to work to create a socio-moral context in which teachers used technology to have the intended collaborative discussions about practice.

SCAFFOLDING WITH TECHNOLOGY AND LEARNING ACROSS CONTEXTS

To this point, an overview of theoretical ideas from Vygotsky and from Piaget has been presented as an analytical framework for the studies reported in this book that use modern technology to support student learning. Now I expand on some of these ideas by noting current trends in the larger cultural context and in interpersonal relationships due, in part, to the rapid advances that have occurred in technology. I use scaffolding as a central frame of reference for this analysis and discussion.

Scaffolding Reconsidered

A General Definition

In modern educational psychology, the term *scaffold* connotes a temporary, supportive framework involving at least one student who has been judged to need assistance in an educational context. As I noted earlier in this chapter, from the second major component of Vygotsky's theory, one could argue that this supportive framework needs to be an interpersonal one. However, in modern usage, these supportive frameworks are often said to consist of general cultural tools and processes or specially designed tools and processes that may or may not require the immediate involvement of a second person, either another student or a teacher. As cultural artifacts, these computer applications are based on prior cultural beliefs and knowledge, but they differ in the degree to which users are in direct communication with other learners or teachers. In previewing the studies reported here, we also saw that in the work that attempted to use computer programs as scaffolds for learning, the researchers needed to be either physically or virtually present to help participants benefit from the tools provided in the intended ways. In some cases, the researchers' presence was not temporary or faded, but was required throughout. It would be premature to reach any firm conclusions at this point, but the need for social support to benefit from cultural artifacts intended to facilitate higher forms of cognitive processing is interesting. It suggests that the nature of human learning may always require a social component despite increased, rapid technological advances. As I also suggested earlier, this is, no doubt, an individual difference variable that can be studied with a microgenetic approach.

Scaffolding as a Specific Type of Learning Process

The variety of ways in which scaffolding is discussed in this book and in the field, in general, raises the question of whether scaffolding is a component of other learning processes, or a separate learning process that stands apart from other processes of learning. Consider the following seven terms: collaborative learning, lecturing, mentoring, modeling, problem-based learning, repetitive practice, and tutoring. Each of these is a form of instructional activity that a teacher can build into a lesson as a matter of instructional design. For each of these seven terms, one could argue that a scaffold for learning is being provided. I believe this approach—viewing scaffolding as a component of learning—is not useful. With this approach, almost any activity that leads to learning can be considered to be a scaffold. Instead, I think it is more useful to view scaffolding as a separate process that can and should be differentiated from each of these other seven terms for conceptual and theoretical clarity. In so doing, I propose that scaffolding remain closely tied to its original origins in social-cultural developmental psychology.

Four Sociocultural Dimensions of Instructional Design

To distinguish among these eight forms of instruction, I propose that four dimensions of instructional design be considered: (a) whether or not the process is tailored to individual needs, (b) whether or not the learning relationships (student–student, student–teacher) are impersonal, (c) the expected degree of learner activity versus passivity, and (d) the degree to which the instructional design is intended to be temporary or "fading" in nature. Reported in Table 2.1 is a classification of these eight forms of instructional processes along each of these four dimensions.

The characterization of the instructional processes is intended to capture their prototypical essence, rather than peripheral exemplars. The use of the term maybe for some terms on some dimensions in Table 2.1 reflects a judgment on my part that there is no definite prototypical case in that instance. For example, it is possible to lecture to only one or a handful of homogeneously grouped students, and in this exceptional case, lecturing can be tailored to individual needs. The prototypical case of lecturing, however, has at its core the notion that the material is targeted to some subset of a heterogeneous group of students. Therefore, lecturing is classified in Table 2.1 as not being tailored to individual needs. Similarly, although many teachers who lecture form personal relationships with their students outside of the classroom, when they are lecturing in a classroom, the relationship is impersonal. I think it is clear why lecturing is characterized as a process in which students are passive. Finally, lecturing is not designed to be faded. Indeed, if the lecture stops, no more learning is possible if lecturing is the only means of instruction.

TABLE 2.1

Differentiation of Eight Instructional Processes Along Four Dimensions

| Instructional Processes | Dimensions of Instructional Design | | | |
	Individually Tailored	Impersonal	Active Student	Fading
Collaborative Learning	N	N	Y	N
Lecturing	N	Y	N	N
Mentoring	Y	N	Y	Y
Modeling	M	M	M	N
Problem-based Learning	N	M	Y	N
Repetitive practice	M	Y	N	N
Scaffolding	M	M	Y	Y
Tutoring	Y	M	M	M

Mentoring and scaffolding contrast with lecturing and repetitive practice in that students are meant to be active, and fading is an explicit part of the instructional design. Like mentors, scaffolds are meant to be temporary and removable, as the intention is for students to internalize the requisite knowledge and skills and eventually to no longer need the scaffolding supports. For example, providing a novice with training wheels on a bicycle or with double-bladed ice skates would be examples of scaffolding because these supports are intended to allow the novice to practice the skills necessary to be able to ride a bicycle with only two wheels or ice skates with only a single blade. In contrast, eyeglasses with lenses that correct vision or a wheelchair for a person who has lost the use of his or her legs would not qualify as examples of scaffolds. Although eyeglasses and wheelchairs provide necessary supportive frameworks, they are expected to be permanent rather than temporary, and therefore do not qualify as scaffolds. Mentoring and scaffolding differ in that mentoring is always tailored to individual needs and based on a relationship that is more than impersonal, whereas scaffolding is not necessarily individually tailored and can be impersonal. Thus, in the present state of technological innovation, computer software can be designed to provide scaffolds for learning, but not mentoring experiences.

Modeling and tutoring are each only fixed on one dimension and can vary on the other three. Consider the difference between modeling provided by an instructional video versus a real-life coach. An instructional video provides a general, impersonal model Students viewing a video model may or may not be passive when viewing (e.g., a yoga vs. a skiing video viewed indoors). Coaches typically tailor their modeling demonstrations to the needs of individual students in relationships that can be more or less impersonal. When watching a coach, students may or may not be actively involved. In all forms of modeling, however, there is no expectation of fading during the instructional process. Unlike modeling, tutoring is always designed to an individual's needs, but like modeling, tutoring may or may not be based on an impersonal relationship. Tutoring does not have firm requirements for degree of student activity or for fading. In some forms of tutoring, students are active; in other forms of tutoring, they are passive. Tutors sometimes have the expectation that their involvement should diminish as instruction continues, but at other times, tutors assume their role will not fade during the instructional process.

In sum, I propose that scaffolding be reserved for instructional designs that assume an active student in need of temporary learning supports. That support may be based on a personal relationship in which learning activities are individually tailored, but the support may be impersonal, or virtual, and consist of a general, not individually tailored program for mastery.

Issues in Interpersonal Scaffolding

Here I briefly consider the special case in which scaffolding is not impersonal, but instead entails an interpersonal relationship of some kind. Linn and Slotta (chap. 4) note some of the problems that can occur when learning activities have a social-interpersonal dimension. Here I discuss two additional pitfalls. In each case, as the scaffolding relationship approaches either end of the stated dimension it is unlikely that the target student will benefit from the scaffolding relationship in ways that the teacher intended.

Indifference–Enmeshment

The more competent other person may be ineffective in a scaffolding relationship because he or she falls at either end of this dimension. Erring on the side of *indifference* occurs whenever too little support is provided or the right kind of support is not provided. *Enmeshment* occurs when the person in charge does not see the importance of "fading" his or her involvement with the target student. For example, Lewin (2003) reported that many parents are using modern technology (wireless phones, e-mail, and instant messaging) to stay in touch with their college student children on a weekly or even daily basis to monitor their academic work and even help the student to complete assignments. The parents interviewed justified their continuous involvement due to the high stakes of postsecondary education (cost and importance of earning a degree). To provide a temporary, supportive framework, those with greater competence in the scaffolding relationship need to strike a balance between being overly involved and not involved enough in the target student's learning experiences.

Inappropriate Maturity Demands–Infantalization

Errors on this dimension reflect misjudgments about either the cognitive or emotional capabilities of the target students. Teachers always need to check that instructional designs are appropriate for the students they actually have, rather than the students that they anticipate having. An effective "scaffolder" is able to adjust maturity demands in either direction based on how the "scafoldee" is progressing. Infantalizing errors occur when the other person continues to perform functions that the target student is capable of performing on his or her own. Inappropriate maturity demand errors occur when the target student is asked to perform functions that he or she is not yet capable of performing without assistance. When errors occur at either end of this spectrum, the scaffolding relationship will neither be temporary nor supportive.

Issues in Virtual Scaffolding

Optimizing the Development of Higher Mental Processes

As communication and access to information continue to be expanded by technology, it will be important that a focus on developing higher mental processes, such as reasoning, argumentation, critical analysis of information, and metacognition (Kuhn, 1997) be maintained. Bielaczyc and Collins (chap. 3) provide a nice description of these types of cognitive processes in "knowledge-creation communities." Other authors in this book describe work in which development of higher forms of thinking has been a goal, although you will see when reading about these efforts that this goal was not always realized.

This may turn out to be an important problem that goes beyond the specifics of any one study. Increased use and availability of technology in schools do not guarantee that higher forms of thinking will be developed. For example, it was recently reported that as students expect to be in constant contact with their friends and families, and in constant contact with Web sites, college professors find themselves in competition to keep their students' attention and to keep them productively engaged during class time (Schwartz, 2003). Students who submit to turning off their cell phones insist that their laptops be used for taking notes and that wireless connections to the Internet in classrooms be left on. As wireless connections to the Internet become ubiquitous, it is not too far fetched to envision middle school and high school students bringing laptops to class to use as tools for amusement rather than for learning. Helping students to balance their use of technology for amusement and for personal communication versus as tools for learning will soon become a major challenge in middle school through university classes. Teachers may have to work even harder to have students buy into and adopt academic learning goals. Use of technology may "signal" personal amusement and interpersonal communication rather than disciplined inquiry and the development of academic skills. As mentioned earlier in this chapter, sociocultural approaches to mentorship were developed in societies in which scaffolding was typically based on close personal relationships and contexts in which the less able and more able participants had shared values and motivations. More attention may have to be paid to issues of student motivation as this model now includes technology, virtual relationships, and different motivations on the parts of apprentices and their students.

The Apprentice Model Has Been Transformed

In discussing a traditional apprentice model, Hmelo-Silver (chap. 7) asserts that the most meaningful forms of learning occur when the target individual participates in the authentic activities of a community. Rogoff and Angelillo (2002) made the point that this type of apprentice model is not a typical cultural practice of middle-class European-American communities, but is still typical in nonindustrialized communities. In the former cultural context, children are (for the most part) segregated from adult activities and placed in child-focused activities designed as preparation for a lifetime of extensive schooling. In this cultural pattern, schools are designed to prepare students for the world of work that commences after schooling has been completed (Rogoff & Angelillo, 2002). See Rogoff (2002) for additional discussions of research on the cultural aspects of human development.

This cultural shift in which school experiences occur apart from the real world of adult work and commerce has been ongoing for some time now. A recent development along this same line is an importance placed on school performance, per se, and the need to provide activities that prepare children for school (so that school can prepare them for the real world). The rapid rise in voluntary preschool programs, the increased availability of "educational" toys, games, and media are examples of this newer cultural development.

Another change in the traditional apprentice model envisioned by Vygotsky is the fact that when technology is involved as a critical component of the learning process, children and students are often more competent and conversant with modern technology than their parents or teachers. This was certainly the case some 10 years ago when computer programs and workstations first found their way into schools and classrooms. Teachers can use their students' technological expertise to provide a role model of what it means to be an inquisitive student (even though they are the teacher) and to have students benefit from adopting the teacher role (even though they are the student).

Accountability in Educational Contexts

One upshot of the trend toward increased importance placed on schooling and the increased investment in technology is that the public demands and expects children's learning in school to be optimized by technology. Demonstrations of learning outcomes are typically being measured by high-stakes, large-scale tests. This trend is especially pronounced in the United States following adoption of the No Child Left Behind legislation. Funding for future instructional design innovations might become contingent on inclusion of measurable outcomes such as performance on statewide testing programs or national testing programs such as AP exams, the ACTs and SATs. Here there is a kind of cultural clash, as many modern researchers and commentators view such tests as "inauthentic." However, it appears likely that these tests are firmly a part of modern culture and need to be more explicitly acknowledged as such by the instructional design research community. One of the major challenges in current instructional design efforts is to try to ensure that technology-based communication and information access contribute to student learning and development in ways that are acknowledged and valued by the larger culture. Many of the authors whose work is reported in this volume are working towards this objective but it is clear that the issues are complex and in no danger of immediate resolution.

REFERENCES

Associated Press (2002, November 12). Supreme court to hear internet por-
nography case [Electronic version]. *The New York Times.* Retrieved November 12, 2002, from http://www.nytimes.com
Cole, M., & Wertsch, J. V. (1996). Beyond the individual-social antinomy
in discussions of Piaget and Vygotsky. *Human Development, 39,*
250–256.
De Lisi, R., & Golbeck, S. L. (1999). The implications of Piaget's theory
for peer learning. In A. O'Donnell & A. King (Eds.), *Cognitive
perspectives on peer learning* (pp.3–37). Mahwah, NJ: Lawrence
Erlbaum Associates.
Granott, N., & Parziale, J. (Eds.). (2002). *Microdevelopment: Transition
processes in development and learning.* New York: Cambridge
University Press.
Harmon, A. (2003, February 6). Queen, captured by a mouse; More chess
players use computers for edge. *New York Times.* Retrieved May
10, 2004, from
http://query.nytimes.com/gst/fullpage.html?res=9CODE7DC173B
F9
Inhelder, B., & Piaget, J. (1958). *The growth of logical thinking from child-
hood to adolescence: An essay on the construction of formal op-
erational structures* (A. Parsons & S. Milgram, Trans.). New
York: Basic Books.
Kilgannon, C. (2003, January 26). Student apologizes for "foolish" Internet
threats. *The New York Times,* p. A30.
Kuhn, D. (1995). Microgenetic study of change: What has it told us? *Psy-
chological Science, 6,* 133–139.
Kuhn, D. (Ed.). (1996). Where is mind? Building on Piaget and Vygotsky
[Special issue]. *Human Development, 39*(5).
Kuhn, D. (1997). Postface: The view from giants' shoulders. In L. Smith, J.
Dockrell, & P. Tomlinson (Eds.), *Piaget, Vygotsky and beyond:
Future issues for developmental psychology and education* (pp.
246–259). London: Routledge.
Lewin, T. (2003, January 6). Parents' role is narrowing generation gap on
campus. *The New York Times,* pp. A1, A18.
Piaget, J. (1970). Piaget's theory. In P. Mussen (Ed.), *Carmichael's manual
of child psychology* (3rd ed., Vol. 1, pp. 703–732*).* New York:
Wiley.
Piaget, J. (1973). *To understand is to invent.* New York: Viking.
Piaget, J. (1985). *The equilibration of cognitive structures: The central
problem of development* (T. Brown & K. J. Thampy, Trans.). Chi-
cago: University of Chicago Press. (Original work published 1975)
Piaget, J. (1995). *Sociological studies* (L. Smith, Ed.). London: Routledge.
(Original work published1965)

Rieber, R. W., & Carton, A. S. (Eds.). (1987). *The collected works of L. S. Vygotsky: Vol.1. Problems of general psychology.* New York: Plenum.

Rogoff, B. (Ed.). (2002). How can we study cultural aspects of human development? [Special issue]. *Human Development, 45*(4).

Rogoff, B., & Angelillo, C. (2002). Investigating the coordinated functioning of multifaceted cultural practices in human development. *Human Development, 45,* 211–225.

Schiesel, S. (2003, February 6). What are the chances? Computer tools refine the ability to understand the odds of catastrophe. *The New York Times,* pp.G1, G6.

Schwartz, J. (2002, December 11). Internet filters block many useful sites, study finds [Electronic version}. *The New York Times.* Retrieved December 11, 2002, from http://www.nytimes.com.

Schwartz, J. (2003, January 2). Professors vie with web for class's attention [Electronic version]. *The New York Times.* Retrieved January 2, 2003, from http://www.nytimes.com.

Shayer, M. (2003). Not just Piaget; not just Vygotsky, and certainly not Vygotsky as *alternative* to Piaget. *Learning and Instruction, 13,* 465–485.

Siegler, R., & Crowley, K. (1991). The microgenetic method: A direct means for studying cognitive developments. *American Psychologist, 46,* 606–620.

Siegler, R. S., & Svetina, M. (2002). A microgenetic/cross-sectional study of matrix completion: Comparing short-term and long-term change. *Child Development, 73,* 793–809.

Smith, L., Dockrell, J., & Tomlinson, P. (Eds.). (1997). *Piaget, Vygotsky and beyond. Future issues for developmental psychology and education.* London: Routledge.

Van der Veer, R., & Valsiner, J. (Eds.). (1994). *The Vygotsky reader.* Oxford, UK: Blackwell.

Vygotsky, L. S. (1978). *Mind in society. Development of higher psychological processes.* Cambridge, MA: Harvard University Press.

Wertsch, J. V. (1985). *Vygotsky and the social formation of mind.* Cambridge, MA: Harvard University Press.

Chapter 3

Fostering Knowledge-Creating Communities

Katerine Bielaczyc
Harvard University

Allan Collins
Northwestern University

Throughout history there have been hotbed communities where knowledge creation has taken on a life of its own. Sagan (1980) attributed the development of science to the Greeks living in the region of Ionia off the coast of Turkey 2,500 years ago. Before then, phenomena in the world were attributed to the gods, who controlled nature and often intervened in the lives of people.

> But in the sixth century BC, in Ionia, a new concept developed, one of the great ideas of the human species. The universe is knowable, the ancient Ionians argued, because it exhibits an internal order: there are regularities in Nature that permit its secrets to be uncovered (p. 140).

The first Ionian scientist was Thales of Miletus, who figured out how to measure the height of a large object from the length of its shadow and the angle of the sun above the horizon: "He was the first to prove geometric theorems of the sort codified by Euclid three centuries later" (Sagan, p. 142). Like the Babylonians, he believed the world to once have been made of water, but unlike the Babylonians he did not attribute the formation of land to a god, but rather to a process like the silting that occurred in the Nile delta. Anaximander of Miletus, a friend of Thales, was "one of the first persons we know of to do an experiment" (p. 143). By examining the moving shadow cast by a vertical stick he determined accurately the length of the year, and was the first person in Greece to make a sundial. A string of great Ionian scientists and mathematicians followed, including Pythagoras, Anaxagoras, Empedocles, Hippocrates, and Democritus.

In the small city of Cremona, Italy, during the 16th to 18th centuries, there developed a tradition of violin making that has never been equaled anywhere in the world. Andrea Amati in 1564 is credited with developing the modern shape of the violin and the characteristic amber-colored varnish of the Amati instruments. His two sons followed him as string makers and his grandson Niccolo trained the founders of the other great violin-making families of Cremona, Andrea Guarnieri and Antonio Stradivari. The two sons of Andre Guarnieri developed their own refinements on the Amati design, and one is credited with moving the F-holes—the figures cut into the belly of the violin—further apart to improve the resonance. The most famous of the Guarnieris, known as Giuseppi del Gesu, was the grandson of Andre, but he abandoned the Amati-inspired designs for the bolder style of the Brescian school. Antonio Stradivari, who is the most famous of the violin makers of Cremona, devoted his life to perfecting the design of the violin. His improvements consist chiefly in lowering the height of the arch of the belly, making the four corner blocks more massive, giving greater curvature to the middle ribs, altering the setting of the sound holes, and making the scroll more prominent. The flowering of creativity in Cremona is a story that has many parallels in history.

One such similar story, as told by Krugman (1991), involves the development of the carpet industry in the small city of Dalton, Georgia, after World War II. The story starts in 1895 when a teenaged girl, Catherine Evans made a tufted bedspread as a wedding gift. The craft of tufting, although developed earlier, had fallen into disuse at the time, so that it was an unusual gift. The recipient and her neighbors were so delighted with the tufted bedspread, Catherine Evans began making other tufted items as gifts. Around 1900 she discovered a trick of locking the tufts into the backing, and then began selling the bedspreads. Soon she and her friends started a local handicraft industry that sold items beyond the local vicinity. The industry became semi-mechanized in the 1920s to satisfy the demand for chenille sweaters, but remained mainly an industry that was carried out by different households. After World War II a machine was developed for making tufted carpets, which turned out to be much cheaper to make than woven carpets. As the expertise in tufting at that time was centered in Dalton, many small carpet firms sprang up in and around Dalton, while the existing carpet firms that stuck to weaving went out of business. At the time that Krugman (1991) reported the story, 19 of the top 20 carpet-making firms in the United States were located in and around Dalton. In his book, Krugman detailed how other industries similarly develop in focused geographical areas.

The most famous recent story of such a concentration of industry and creativity took place in Silicon Valley. This story began when Frederick Terman, the vice president of Stanford University, decided to help William Hewlett and David Packard start their own electronics firm, Hewlett-Packard, by providing capital and setting up a research park on Stanford land. Other occupants soon followed. The Research Park became the nucleus for the growth of Silicon Valley. It created a synergistic relationship, where Stanford benefited from the proximity of the new high-technology firms that were started by its staff and students, and the firms benefited from the rich source of knowledge and personnel that Stanford provided.

Many of the new startups in Silicon Valley were spun off from the early firms that were started with Stanford support, so that it is possible to construct a kind of genealogical chart of the growth of firms in the Valley. Clearly ideas and techniques have spread easily from firm to firm, as for example the user-interface approach developed at Xerox PARC spread to Apple and then to Microsoft Windows. The strategies for supporting creativity in Silicon Valley are being widely copied in many other places (e.g., the Research Triangle in North Carolina) with greater or lesser success.

SAGAN'S EXPLANATION FOR KNOWLEDGE CREATION IN IONIA

Sagan (1980) suggested there was a combination of several factors that made Ionia a suitable site for the development of science. First, it was an island realm, which bred diversity and weak political control, which in turn supported free inquiry. "Political power was in the hands of the merchants, who actively promoted the technology on which their prosperity depended" (p. 141). Also, it was at the crossroads of cultures between Greece, Egypt, Phoenicia, and Babylonia, which "met and cross-fertilized in a vigorous and heady confrontation of prejudices, languages, ideas and gods" (p. 141). The Ionians were traders and so came in contact with all these cultures.

> What do you do when you are faced with several different gods each claiming the same territory? The Babylonian Marduk and the Greek Zeus were each considered master of the sky and king of the gods. You might decide that Marduk and Zeus were really the same. You might also decide, since they had quite different attributes, that one of them was merely invented by the priests. But if one, why not both? (p. 141).

In addition, they were the first Greeks to adopt the Phoenician alphabet, which led to widespread literacy. This meant "the thoughts of many were available for consideration and debate" (p. 141). So for Sagan the creativity of the Ionians derived from the freedom to inquire, the conflict of different cultural perspectives, and the importation of writing as a tool for thinking.

MARSHALL'S EXPLANATION FOR THE CONCENTRATION OF INDUSTRIES

Krugman (1991) described how the early 20th-century economist Alfred Marshall explained the concentration of industries in such places as Cremona, Dalton, and Silicon Valley. Marshall cited three basic reasons. First, Marshall cited the pooled market: "Employers are apt to resort to any place where they are likely to find a good choice of workers with the special skill which they require; while men seeking employment naturally go to places where there are many employers who need such skill as theirs and where therefore it is likely to find a good market" (p. 37). Second, such a center provides specialized products and services, such as hairdressers and film editors in Hollywood: "Subsidiary trades grow up in the neighborhood, supplying it with implements and materials, organizing its traffic, and in many ways conducive to the economy of the material" (p. 37). Third, information flows more easily:

> The mysteries of the trade become no mystery; but are as it were in the air…Good work is rightly appreciated; invention and improvements in machinery, in processes and the general organization of the business have their merits promptly discussed: if one man starts a new idea, it is taken up by others and combined with suggestions of their own; and thus it becomes the source of further new ideas (p. 37-38).

Marshall argued that specialized communities develop many varieties of expertise and that this knowledge flows through the community, leading to new inventions and innovations. A close-knit community fosters expertise and refinements of products and processes, whereas outside influences and demands foster creativity. In a close-knit community there are multiple exemplars of expert practice to learn from. Hearing the latest developments and watching them unfold provides a powerful learning environment. At the same time it is necessary to understand what the outside world is thinking and to develop new ways to meet the demands and opportunities that the outside world offers.

BROWN AND DUGUID'S EXPLANATION FOR THE SUCCESS OF SILICON VALLEY

Brown and Duguid (2000) elaborated on Marshall's third point by developing an ecological metaphor to explain the success of Silicon Valley. They described the Valley as made up of a set of firms and a cross-cutting set of "networks of practice, " which link the different communities of practice

(Wenger, 1998) within each firm to the wider community within the Valley. "Networks of computer engineers, for example, will run through all the firms manufacturing computers" (Brown and Duguid 2000, p. 162). These networks of practice form the connections through which ideas and techniques move through the Valley, because the members of each network have many informal ties to each other. "Knowledge that sticks within firms quickly finds ways to flow between them, as if seeking out the firm with the most suitable complementarity. In such circumstances, as firms keep a constant benchmarking eye on each other, the ecology develops as a whole. Both invention and innovation develop rapidly and together" (p. 165). Further, they argued that "while failure is undoubtedly hard on a particular firm and its employees, it too may be beneficial for the ecology as a whole, providing useful insight into market conditions" (p. 165). They cited the failure of the firm Zilog as seeding the Valley with local-area-network entrepreneurs. Finally, they argued that living in close proximity is essential to the success of the Valley: "In the Valley, people live in and out of each other's pockets, and this helps them see what's doing, what's doable, and what's not being done. This close proximity not only shows how to attack a particular niche, it provides the ability to see a niche before it is visible to most eyes" (p. 168).

CHARACTERISTICS OF KNOWLEDGE-CREATING COMMUNITIES

These views from economics, organization theory, and history of science form a coherent picture about the conditions that lead to invention and innovation. We can synthesize these explanations into a set of seven characteristics found in knowledge-creating communities.

Sharing Ideas

In a knowledge-creating community, the air is filled with ideas and techniques that are exchanged freely, as Brown and Duguid (2000) described Silicon Valley. People are excited to share their ideas and discoveries with others. Everyone has easy access to sources of ideas, such as people and databases, and they contribute ideas to the community in various ways. Different people freely voice their opinions, and feel that they can offer ideas without fear of the consequences. Expertise develops within specialized groups, where people come to know each other's strengths and weaknesses and how to capitalize on the different strengths. They share their tacit knowledge through mentoring and apprenticeship. However, there also are information brokers who communicate across internal boundaries within the community. People carry ideas with them as they move from group to group, which is critical to the spread of ideas throughout the community. Knowledge sharing leads to knowledge creation, because invention involves bringing together different ideas into a coherent new idea. Ideas are taken from different sources and transformed to fit the situation. Because new knowledge is created out of pieces of old knowledge, the widespread sharing of knowledge is critical to the creativeness of a community.

Multiple Perspectives

Sagan (1980) made clear how the different cultural perspectives led to creativity among the Ionians. If a community functions on its own without taking into account the ideas and demands of the outside world, it will tend to become stagnant and uncreative. Multiple perspectives foster creativity in a variety of ways. They raise questions about what is the best approach. They provide different possible solutions to problems from which the best solution can be chosen. They offer the ingredients for new syntheses. Borrowing ideas and techniques from different sources is critical to the invention process. Seeking out different sources from outside the community can foster the generation of multiple perspectives. Likewise, bringing into the community people with different backgrounds and beliefs can provoke stimulating discussion of alternative views. Rather than suppressing different ideas, it is critical to solicit different ideas within the community, so that all may be considered in devising new solutions.

Experimentation

The example of Antonio Stradivari and the other violin-making families of Cremona best illustrates the critical role of experimentation in knowledge creation. The violin makers kept experimenting with different configurations of the elements in their violin design, to see which produced the best sound. Similarly in Silicon Valley there is continual experimentation with new hardware and software ideas. Experimentation is not blind trial and error, but is based on knowledgeable reconfiguring of elements in new patterns that the experimenter has reason to think might lead to improvement. It is important to accurately assess the results of experiments, in order to make sound judgments about which innovations to keep and which to discard. Experimentation leads to progressive refinement of ideas, so that an optimal configuration of elements is achieved. But sometimes it is necessary to start over with a novel design, so that the refinement process does not get stuck in a local maxima, when there are radically different designs that might be more successful.

Specialization

In creative communities people develop different kinds of expertise that are brought together to solve problems and develop new ideas. The essence of specialization is developing deep understanding and skill in an area of interest to the person. People develop the areas in which they are most interested and capable, with the responsibility that they share their expertise with others. By developing diverse expertise, the community can deal with problems and issues that are too difficult for any individual to handle. People take on different roles in the community and each of these roles is valuable to the creative functioning of the community. As Brown and Duguid (2000) described, the different specializations form communities of practice (Wenger, 1998), where knowledge is shared and expertise is highly valued.

Cognitive Conflict and Discussion

It is from the analysis and comparison of different views that new ideas are created. The way that this kind of cognitive conflict is most productive is seen in how the Ionians dealt with the different views brought to them from surrounding cultures. Therefore, it is important that people discuss and argue about ideas without rancor or blame. Arguments must be resolved by logic and evidence, rather than by authority. Ideas are sought from many different sources, particularly ideas that challenge prevailing wisdom. Lampert, Rittenhouse, and Crumbaugh (1996) showed how it is possible to foster productive discussion among fifth-grade students to enhance their abilities to engage in productive argumentation. The students voice different ideas and approaches, and they consider these ideas and opinions in an unbiased way. Respectful listening is important to resolving differences. Discussion leads to knowledge creation by encouraging understanding of different alternatives and how they might be synthesized. Argumentation is crucial to bringing forth different alternatives to consider.

Reflection

To synthesize different views it is important to engage in systematic reflection about ways to improve processes and products. In his description of how the Ionians must have made sense of different gods, Sagan (1980) was describing the reflection process. There are a variety of ways of reflecting about new ideas. One way is to set out criteria for evaluating a particular piece of work, where the goal is to determine how things might be done better in the future. Another way to reflect is to record the process of carrying out work, to compare it to the process involved in other similar ventures. In a similar way, it is possible to compare the products of different efforts to evaluate what are the strengths and weaknesses of each, and how they might be better. The psychological and education literature (e.g., Bransford, Franks, Vye, & Sherwood, 1989; White & Frederiksen, 1998) suggests that reflective consideration helps to recognize global patterns and relationships, which can lead to new syntheses. The pulling together of disparate elements through reflection is crucial to knowledge creation. Furthermore, if the focus is on looking for ways to make improvements, it can support process and product refinement over time.

Synthesis

The culmination of fostering multiple perspectives, argumentation, and reflection is to form new syntheses and inventions that pull together the best ideas and practices. We see this kind of synthesis in the stories of the development of natural science in Ionia and in the development of new products in Silicon Valley. When a community is faced with a problem, the solution does not usually come from a single source. Rather it is cobbled together from past ideas and ways of doing things, from different people's suggestions, from the artifacts and technologies in place, and from ideas and ways of doing things that exist in other communities. In short, communities think and respond to new situations by synthesizing new solutions from bits and pieces that are scattered around in the environment. These are all sources of knowledge that can be of use in dealing with new situations.

Our work over the past few years has focused on classroom learning communities, which are educational models focused on knowledge creation (Bielaczyc & Collins, 1999). In searching for actual examples of such communities, we looked at many different classrooms. Here we describe two settings that share the preceding characteristics, but achieve them in different ways. In both cases the technology tool these classrooms used played a large role. It has specific affordances that support knowledge-creation activities. We also found that teachers in these classrooms themselves operate as a knowledge-creating community. We examine how the mechanisms that foster knowledge creation operate in three areas: tool-based mechanisms, teacher-level mechanisms, and student-level mechanisms.

MECHANISMS TO FOSTER KNOWLEDGE BUILDING IN KNOWLEDGE FORUM

Scardamalia and Bereiter (1991, 1994) developed a model of education they call knowledge-building communities. Knowledge Forum is the name of the computer software they developed, which is used in classrooms that may or may not have adopted the pedagogical model. The essential idea is that students work together to make sense of the world around them and work toward advancing their own state of knowledge and that of the class.

The model involves students investigating problems in different subject areas over a period of weeks or months. As students work, they enter their ideas and research findings as notes in a communal knowledge base. The goal is to engage students in progressive knowledge building, where they continually develop their understanding through problem identification, research, and community discourse. The emphasis is on progress toward collective goals of understanding, rather than individual learning and performance. Scardamalia and Bereiter (1991, 1994) provided the Knowledge Forum environment with a set of seven mechanisms designed to foster knowledge creation among students.

A Public Forum

As the name suggests, Knowledge Forum is built around a public space where ideas are shared among the whole community. Thus the core of Knowledge Forum embodies a basic mechanism to support sharing of ideas. Sagan (1980) put the introduction of writing at the center of the development of science in Ionia. The permanence of the written medium allows members of the knowledge creating community to go back and reread notes, whenever they are confused, or come upon a related idea, or want to cite evidence to support an idea they are developing. By writing their ideas for everyone to see, students participate in a community of ideas. The public forum is designed to provide a place where ideas are visible for everybody to see, so that they can be reflected upon and improved. Knowledge Forum thus enables students to be creative together, but they do not all have to be in one place at the same time. Students can work together to experiment with new ideas, and think and read and communicate with others in an extended discussion over time and space. As students find answers to their questions, they add information to the Knowledge Forum database, so that others can read and learn from them, and even question the reliability of what they added.

Scaffolds

Built into the Knowledge Forum are a set of scaffolds that support students in the inquiry process. The scaffolds address major parts of the process, encouraging students to articulate their theories, formulate their questions, identify things they need to learn, and so on. Thus the scaffolds embody major steps in the inquiry process. The scaffolds and the investigation cycle they embody encourage students to push deeper into any topic. This encourages the development of specialized knowledge, so that students come to be experts in particular domains. Thus when questions arise that call on their expertise, they can work with others to share their knowledge and experiment with novel ideas and solutions to problems.

Build-ons

Discussion and argumentation are fostered by the build-ons embodied in the Knowledge Forum design. Build-ons are designed for students to elaborate on what other students have written. These elaborations might consist of discussions of ideas that others have developed, or conflicts with what is claimed in a note. These elaborations then can serve to clarify ideas or develop new ideas. In both cases discussion is moved forward toward deeper understanding of issues and development of new ideas.

Quotation

Students are encouraged to read others' notes and quote from them. When they quote from another student's note, the quotation appears in italics and a reference is made automatically back to the note that is quoted. The quotation feature encourages students to discuss other students' ideas and make arguments supporting or contradicting their ideas. This fosters both synthesis and reflection on ideas.

Views

By putting notes into different views, it is possible to organize the knowledge in different ways. For example, a knowledge base about dinosaurs might be organized according to the different species, the time sequence in which different types of dinosaurs developed, or the place where their fossils were discovered (Scardamalia, 2004). Thus, the different views allow for multiple perspectives on the domain. This allows students to see how ideas are related to each other from different perspectives, which supports deep understanding and synthesis of ideas.

Rise-Above Notes

The Rise-Above notes are designed to have students pull together the ideas that different students have written about. This synthesis process forces students to reflect on how different ideas are related and how they can best be integrated. At the same time they must consider whether the notes contradict each other and whether some of the information in the notes is wrong. Thus Rise-Above notes foster integration from different sources and synthesis of new ideas.

Publication

When students feel a note makes an important contribution to the collective knowledge base, they can propose the note for publication. This requires that students reflect on their notes and select those that make the most important and creative contributions. An editorial group and the teacher then decide whether to publish the note. At the end of the school year the class may decide on a selection of notes to remain in the knowledge base for classes that come after them.

In the two schools we have looked at, knowledge creation occurred at two levels: among the teachers and among the students. It is striking how the teachers themselves functioned as a knowledge-building community. In both cases they worked to create knowledge about ways to support and improve the functioning of the students' knowledge-building communities. Similarly, at the student level a variety of mechanisms were employed to help the students function as a knowledge-building community. We first consider a middle school in the midwestern United States and second an elementary school in Toronto, Canada, associated with the Ontario Institute for Studies in Education where Scardamalia and Bereiter work.

MECHANISMS FOR KNOWLEDGE BUILDING AT WHITMAN MIDDLE SCHOOL

The first author worked for 2 years with a sixth-seventh-grade team of teachers and students from Whitman Middle School, a small suburban school in the midwestern United States. The four teachers on the team had worked together for several years, and specifically with Knowledge Forum for more than 8 years. The teachers describe their main educational objective as fostering a "learning club," where students view themselves as members of a classroom community whose goal is learning to learn. The first author became interested in working at Whitman because these teachers had sustained their use of Knowledge Forum over 8 years with very little external support. They had also been continually experimenting with ways to help their students in working with Knowledge Forum, and were recognized as innovators by other Knowledge Forum teachers. Beginning in the spring semester of the sixth grade year, she made classroom visits approximately every 6 weeks for a period of 5 days, and collected data from classroom observations, written and online data, and interviews.

The Whitman team had four classrooms of roughly 25 students each, with each teacher specializing in one subject matter area: math, science, language arts, or personal development. Also each homeroom teacher had his or her own class for reading and writing, in which students had many opportunities to develop their individual writing processes and were encouraged to express their thoughts in their own voice. Students moved from one classroom to the next, and hence one subject to another, over the course of a school day.

Each day, on a rotating basis, one teacher would host the Knowledge Forum work. When students came to the designated class, they would spend the 50-minute period working on the Knowledge Forum research unit, rather than the usual subject matter curriculum. Students conducted their research using books from the school and public libraries, ordering relevant videos, searching the Internet, and interviewing experts where possible (through interviews out in the community or bringing specialists into the school). Students gradually learned to manage their own time during the Knowledge Forum period: conducting their investigations offline or working in the Knowledge Forum database.

The four classrooms of the Whitman team had eight computers each for student use, so all students in the designated Knowledge Forum period were able to work on the database at will, sometimes by going on their own to another classroom. Although students worked on their Knowledge Forum research on a class-by-class basis throughout the day, the learning community that the Whitman team worked to build spanned all four classes. The Knowledge Forum database contained the work of all students, and the groups that formed (described later) were based on common interests across all students, rather than within classes of roughly 25 students. The sets of possible interests were chosen from topics determined by the district curriculum.

Over the seventh grade school year, students used Knowledge Forum to support the following research units:

- Fall Term: Global Understanding. Student investigations focused on countries from around the world. Students studied questions such as these: What are important matters that affect how people live and work? How does my country connect with other countries in that region?

- Winter Term: World Religions. Student investigations focused on six major world religions: Buddhism, Christianity, Hinduism, Islam, Judaism, and Taoism. Students studied questions such as these: What are the basic beliefs set forth in this religion? How do the beliefs compare to those of my classmates and me?

- Spring Term: Astronomy and Technology. Student investigations focused on various aspects of either astronomy or technology. Students studied questions such as these: Why do the planets revolve around the Sun? What is the history of the automobile?

Each central research topic was divided into subtopics (e.g., Global Understanding was divided into countries of the world), and students were matched to subtopics based on their top three choices. Most students were matched with their first choice. Each research unit lasted roughly 8 weeks.

Knowledge Building Among the Teachers at Whitman

The four teachers at Whitman functioned as a team, exchanging ideas and supporting each other as they learned to incorporate Knowledge Forum into their teaching. In the middle schools of the district each team had team planning time as well as an individual planning time. There were a number of mechanisms that the teachers at Whitman employed among themselves to function as a knowledge-building community.

Reading Group

Even before the teachers started working with Knowledge Forum, they formed a reading group where they read papers describing Knowledge Forum and its use in different classrooms. The teachers each kept a journal, and would discuss what they had read, and share their emerging thoughts with their team members. They would then discuss different approaches that they might experiment with in their classes. The reading group provided many different perspectives, which formed the basis for them to work out the logistics of how they might use Knowledge Forum. It also gave them the opportunity to share ideas about the kind of culture they wanted to create in their classrooms and the strategies they would use to create a knowledge-building culture among their students.

The Summer Institute

Each year the team attended the Summer Institute for Knowledge Forum that was held in Toronto. There they shared ideas with other teachers who were using Knowledge Forum and talked with the research group at the Ontario Institute for Studies in Education (OISE) that had developed Knowledge Forum. Many of the different perspectives they picked up at the Summer Institute found their way into their classrooms, so that they were continuously renewed as they experimented with different ways to use Knowledge Forum and help students identify their individual ways of learning.

Teaching Experiment

Each time the team taught using Knowledge Forum, they would try different approaches. Sometimes they would have students work on their investigations for several weeks before determining common threads to form
teams, and other times they would start the students off working as inquiry
teams. Sometimes they would have students put together summaries of
what they learned, and other times they would develop a culminating event
to support integration of the ideas. By constantly experimenting the teachers
could reflect on what teaching strategies worked best, at the same time allowing the students to explore different ways of working in Knowledge
Forum.

Researcher Meetings

After the first author had worked with the teachers for a year, they began a
series of meetings after school or on Saturday to reflect on their teaching
practices. They would often discuss strategies that were used by teachers at
other schools, sometimes looking at videos of the practice in other schools
to reflect on these strategies in comparison to their own teaching. They also
watched videos of interviews with their own students explaining what they
thought about learning with Knowledge Forum. These sessions provided
the teachers with a forum to reflect on their teaching approach in the light
of data from other sources.

Presentations

Finally it is important that the teachers presented their work around Knowledge Forum to other teachers in the state and, in some cases, across the
country. By trying to articulate what they were doing and by answering
probing questions by other teachers, they were forced to reflect on and synthesize their practice to address the challenges that come with exporting an
innovation like Knowledge Forum.

Knowledge Building Among the Students at Whitman

The teachers at Whitman developed a number of mechanisms to foster creativity among students. We briefly describe the different ways that they tried
to challenge students to work with knowledge in inventive ways.

No Notes Permitted

When students did research on a topic, such as Buddhism, they were not permitted to use notes from their research when they were writing their entries in the Knowledge Forum database. This was designed to prevent students from copying out what they found in books into the database. Students had to synthesize their own understanding of the topic they were writing about and characterize in their own words what they had learned. They were encouraged by the scaffolds in the system and by the teachers to develop their own theories and questions, and to pursue them through reading and discussions with other students and adults. The emphasis was on students creating their own understanding and expressing it in the tentative voice of a learner rather than repeating the words of an author.

Teaming

Students were grouped in different ways to work on their inquiry. For example, when students created the database on world religions, they were organized into teams of five students, and each team studied one of the six religions. On each team the students were assigned to five different roles (or communities of practice): historian, anthropologist, journalist, politician, and theologian. These roles formed the basis for secondary teams that would work together on specific questions about the interrelations between the different religions (e.g., what the relation is between the origins of the different religions). By working in this jigsaw fashion (Aronson, 1978), students brought ideas from different sources to their online and offline discussions, much as Brown and Duguid (2000) described among the networks of practice in Silicon Valley. This led to more discussion between students and making connections to related ideas (Bielaczyc, 2001).

Interviewing Experts

After students had worked on their research for a while, the students would enlist different "experts" to come to their classes and talk about a topic they were studying. So, for example, a number of people from the community who had special knowledge about each of the religions came to the class to talk and answer questions from the students. By bringing in different views, the students are exposed to multiple perspectives that they must synthesize to create a coherent understanding of the topic.

Mini-lessons

The teachers gave "mini-lessons" to discuss with the students strategies for carrying out their investigations. This typically involved projecting parts of the Knowledge Forum database on a large screen to discuss issues about the student work. The goal was to show students how to dig deeply into topics and pursue questions that arise in their work. These lessons were critical to students learning how to become specialists by engaging in inquiry to deepen their understanding. Sometimes students would be invited to reflect on an important moment of learning in an entry, such as a time when they realized their theory had been wrong, or when a question was raised that pushed their investigation ahead.

Discussion Notes

To synthesize their knowledge, groups of students would work together to create discussion notes addressing some specific question. For example, one discussion note raised the question, "Is there a common link between all religions?" To address such a question, the students had to reflect on what they had learned about all the different religions. Thus discussion notes forced students to bring together the multiple perspectives and the specialized expertise that different students had accumulated in the course of their investigations.

Reflection Notes

As the end of a unit approached, teachers encouraged students to reflect on their journey of learning over the unit. Students would think about their original interest in the topic and what in their background led to this interest. Entering their ideas in reflection notes, they would continue to describe what questions were first raised, theories that directed their search, further questions raised along the way, how their ideas changed, who helped them, times their knowledge was challenged, and other highlights during the study. The reflection notes ended with the raising of more questions, for others interested in this topic or for a student's own future learning.

Culminating Events

At the end of a unit of inquiry there was often a culminating event. For example, in the unit on world religions, the teachers organized a "peace conference" at a 1-day retreat for the students (Bielaczyc, 2001). At the peace conference, mixed groups of students who had studied different religions met together to develop sets of principles that they thought would promote world peace. Then the groups convened to develop a final set of principles based on votes of all the participants. This culminating event encouraged the students to reflect on what they had learned about the different religions, to address a novel problem for students; that is, to synthesize universal principles that might lead to world peace.

MECHANISMS FOR KNOWLEDGE BUILDING AT THE INSTITUTE OF CHILD STUDY

The Institute of Child Study (ICS) is a laboratory school associated with the OISE, which is part of the University of Toronto. As a laboratory school, it is not required to teach all of the standards that are specified in the Ontario Curriculum, although the teachers at the school do attempt to cover the topics specified in the Curriculum. Several years ago two of the teachers in the school started using Knowledge Forum in their teaching: one teacher in a fourth-grade classroom and one in a fifth-and sixth-grade classroom. Because of the proximity to OISE where Knowledge Forum was first developed, they had strong support from the Knowledge Forum research team.

In the 1999–2000 school year three experienced teachers, who had recently joined ICS, agreed to join the other two teachers working with Knowledge Forum. One of the two teachers who had worked with Knowledge Forum in previous years became a teacher-researcher, who supported the other teachers in the project. So there was a group of four teachers using Knowledge Forum, a teacher-researcher supporting them, and a researcher from OISE who worked with the school to help them learn to use Knowledge Forum. One of the new teachers was a first-grade teacher, and this was the first time Knowledge Forum had been used at that level in the school. The other three teachers taught third, fourth, and fifth and sixth grades.

Knowledge Building among the Teachers at the Institute of Child Study

The group of teachers and researchers at the ICS functioned as a knowledge-building community during the course of the year. There were a number of mechanisms that the group employed to foster knowledge creation among themselves (Caswell, 2001; Lamon, Reeve & Scardamalia, 2001; MacDonald, 2001, Messina, 2001; Moreau, 2001; Reeve, 2001).

Reading Group

The teachers and researchers read a number of articles together that gave them different perspectives on the notion of knowledge-building communities and how they can be created. After discussing these articles, they experimented with ways to implement the ideas in the articles into their classrooms. The group met throughout the year and talked about the successes and the problems they were having in implementing Knowledge Forum in their classrooms. These sessions provided an ongoing forum in which to bring up new ideas and discuss what was working.

Teacher-Researcher

The teacher-researcher had used Knowledge Forum for a number of years, so that he was not only technically proficient in the uses of Knowledge Forum, but he also had a wealth of knowledge about effective practices in using Knowledge Forum. He therefore could share ideas with the teachers and provide the kinds of support that they needed as they began working in this new teaching environment.

Experimentation

The group adapted methods from other programs such as the Fostering a Community of Learners (FCL) program (Brown & Campione, 1996) to try out in their classrooms. In particular they modified the "reciprocal teaching" and "crosstalk" procedures from FCL to fit into the Knowledge Forum environment. They collected data on the students from tests and interviews, and systematically reflected on their successes and failures (see later). By experimenting with different ideas and discussing with each other how they were working, the group was able to progressively refine their teaching strategies.

The Summer Institute

Like the teachers at Whitman, the team attended the Summer Institute for Knowledge Forum that was held in Toronto. There they shared ideas with other teachers who were using Knowledge Forum. The different perspectives they picked up at the Summer Institute also found their way into their classrooms, permitting them to experiment with new ideas for teaching with Knowledge Forum.

Calendar of Inquiry

Each teacher used Knowledge Forum as a personal journal to reflect on their teaching and to pose problems they were wrestling with (Reeve, 2001). Both the teacher-researcher and the researcher associated with the group read the journals and discussed with the teachers how to address problems that arose and refine their ways of teaching. The calendar acted to signal problems to the researchers, so that they might meet with the teachers to help them deal with any issues that arose.

Video Journal

To help the teachers reflect on their teaching practice, they made records of class sessions using video (Moreau, 2001). This enabled the teachers to look back on their teaching and study their teaching practices. In this way, they could identify problems, think about different ways of dealing with issues that arose, and systematically reflect on their teaching practice. It also provided a record of how their practice was changing over time, which enabled them to write about the change process in adapting to this new environment.

Knowledge Building Among the Students at the Institute of Child Study

Over the course of the year the teachers and students developed a number of mechanisms to foster knowledge creation among the students. There was a progressive refinement that occurred by which the teachers slowly turned over more and more control to the students. We can best trace this process in the fourth-grade classroom (Messina, 2001), where the teacher had decided to use Knowledge Forum to teach about light, which was part of the Ontario fourth-grade science curriculum. The teacher first broke the 22 students into three groups of seven students, who rotated through the activities of reading materials about light, carrying out hands-on experiments, and working in the Knowledge Forum database. Initially, all students worked in a Knowledge Forum view titled: "What is light and where does it come from?" As the year progressed the teacher moved from this approach, which he referred to as a factory model of teaching, to a specialization model, and from there to a knowledge-building community model. In the course of this progression, there were a number of "inventions" that he and his students came up with to foster creativity among the students.

Varied Topics

The teacher at first had students all working on the same set of issues. However, the students complained that they were all adding the same materials to the Knowledge Forum database and that the groups of seven students they had were too large to work with easily. He realized that to foster more creativity among the students he needed to break them into smaller groups that worked on different topics. So he worked with the groups to develop a set of six different topics, such as "sources of light," "images," and so on. This gave the students more ownership of what they were learning, and at the same time, he allowed the students to flexibly arrange the time they worked and experimented on the different aspects of light. This change marked the transformation from the factory model to the specialization model for the teacher.

Crosstalk

When the teacher broke the students into smaller groups that worked on specialized topics, he introduced a variant of crosstalk, derived from the FCL program (Brown & Campione, 1996). Crosstalk is a procedure where groups of students share their ideas and progress across groups. At these sessions the students discussed their knowledge advances, their experiments, and their problems of understanding with the other students. Sometimes the other students could help explain ideas that a group was having difficulty with. These crosstalk sessions were a valuable tool for sharing ideas among the different groups.

Glossary and Teaching Notes

The teacher found from his analysis of student journals that the students were not reading notes outside the group in which they were working. Therefore, he became concerned that the students were not sharing what they learned about each topic. In a crosstalk session one of the students suggested that they develop a glossary and write teaching notes to help synthesize and explain the knowledge they were gaining to the other students. This was another attempt to increase the sharing of knowledge among all the students.

Light Learnings View

Even with the addition of the teaching notes and glossary, the large number of notes on the screen discouraged students from reading other students' notes. In another crosstalk a student suggested that they use the Rise Above notes to clean up the clutter and bring the key ideas into one coherent view. They decided to label this view the "Light Learnings View" and it was meant to be a synthesis of everything the different groups had learned. They also added new scaffolds to support group learning such as "Our understanding of X" and "What we still need to know." By organizing their knowledge into this new view, students were forced to synthesize the most important knowledge they had gained. It was at this point that the teacher felt they had moved to a knowledge-building community model, because their individual journals showed that they were integrating and organizing their knowledge to reflect the group learning. As the teacher said, "Knowledge did not seem to exist only in the minds of the students, but was something tangible that could be improved upon and/or given to new uses—used to help in the collective knowledge advancement of the class" (Messina, 2001).

Teaching Kindergartners and Parents' Night

There were two events that helped the students reflect on all their knowledge about light. First, at the invitation of the kindergarten, the fourth-grade students put together a program of experiments and explanations of light phenomena. By teaching the kindergartners, students were learning how to make the ideas clear and accessible. Second, near the end of the year, the students invited their parents for an evening, where the class put on a play that included many of their ideas about light and provided posters that embodied the ideas in their Light Learnings View. The students became the teachers and their parents the students.

All of the classes at the ICS have adopted many of these practices. In one case, the 8- and 9-year-old students taught Saturday classes at the Children's Museum in Toronto as part of the museum's hands-on learning program for 2- to 7-year-olds. Parents' Night has been adopted as standard practice among all the classes at the school. For example, one teacher held a garden party, where students instructed their parents using some of the methods employed by the students to learn about gardens and worms, such as creating a garden on land acquired by the school. Basically, the parents took part in a Knowledge Forum session themselves, led by the children. These parent information sessions allow parents to see what gains their children have made by observing their understanding and participation in the communities' goals.

CONCLUSION

The classrooms at the two schools we have described have created environments that embody many of the characteristics we identified in the creative communities where important innovations have been spawned. The teachers at the two schools went out of their way to seek out multiple perspectives by reading and discussing scientific articles describing related innovations. They also attended workshops where teachers and researchers came together to discuss implementation issues surrounding Knowledge Forum. By working with a group of colleagues, they could develop strategies for their teaching, experiment with new approaches, and discuss their successes and failures. This argumentation and sharing of ideas was critical to refining their approaches to teaching with Knowledge Forum. Finally, they made efforts to reflect on their teaching practice and to synthesize the best approaches to teaching based on the data they collected.

Similarly, when working with students, the teachers fostered student creativity in a number of different ways. They encouraged students to specialize in particular areas and share their ideas with other students. This enabled students to gain deep understanding of the topics they studied, which they then taught to others. Furthermore, the students sought out expertise from books, experiments, and outside experts, which brought many different perspectives that the students tried to resolve by discussion and argumentation in Knowledge Forum. By combining their collective knowledge into discussion and teaching notes, they were forced to reflect on their learning and synthesize the knowledge they gained. Finally there were a variety of culminating events, from a peace conference to Parents' Nights, that fostered synthesis and using knowledge in novel ways.

The current move toward a global village is reminiscent of Ionia. People from a wide variety of backgrounds are coming together to share ideas and create new innovations. The classrooms discussed in this chapter show how it is possible to create environments that prepare students to enter into the kinds of knowledge-creating communities that are arising in the global village.

ACKNOWLEDGMENTS

The preparation of this chapter was in part made possible by a grant from the National Academy of Education and the Spencer Foundation to the first author. We thank Myrna Cooney and Mary Jane Moreau for their comments on an earlier draft of the chapter. We also want to thank all of the teachers for their generosity and insights.

REFERENCES

Aronson, E. (1978). *The jigsaw classroom.* Beverly Hills, CA: Sage.

Bielaczyc, K. (2001, March). *Designing social infrastructure: The challenge of building computer-supported learning communities.* Paper presented at the European Computer-Supported Communities of Learning Conference, Maastricht, Netherlands.

Bielaczyc, K., & Collins, A. (1999). Learning communities in classrooms: A reconceptualization of educational practice. In C. M. Reigeluth (Ed.), *Instructional-design theories and models: A new paradigm of instructional theory* (pp. 269–292). Mahwah, NJ: Lawrence Erlbaum Associates.

Bransford, J. D., Franks, J. J., Vye, N. J., & Sherwood, R. D. (1989). New approaches to instruction: Because wisdom can't be told. In S.

Vosniadou & A. Ortony (Eds.), *Similarity and analogical reasoning* (pp. 470–497). New York: Cambridge University Press.

Brown, A. L., & Campione, J. C. (1996). Psychological theory and the design of innovative learning environments: On procedures, principles, and systems. In L. Schauble & R. Glaser (Eds.), *Innovations in learning: New environments for education* (pp. 289–325). Mahwah, NJ: Lawrence Erlbaum Associates.

Brown, J. S., & Duguid, P. (2000). *The social life of information.* Cambridge, MA: Harvard Business School Press.

Caswell, B. (2001, April). *The evolution of inquiry with five knowledge builders.* Paper presented at the annual conference of the American Educational Research Association, Seattle, WA.

Krugman, P. (1991). *Geography and trade.* Cambridge, MA: MIT Press.

Lamon, M., Reeve, R., & Scardamalia, M. (2001, April). *Mapping learning and the growth of knowledge in a knowledge building community.* Paper presented at the annual conference of the American Educational Research Association, Seattle, WA.

Lampert, M., Rittenhouse, P., & Crumbaugh, C. (1996). Agreeing to disagree: Developing sociable mathematical discourse. In D. Olson & N. Torrance (Eds.), *Handbook of education and human development* (pp. 731–764). Oxford, UK: Blackwell.

MacDonald, P. (2001, April). *Knowledge building, from the beginning.* Paper presented at the annual conference of the American Educational Research Association, Seattle, WA.

Messina, R. (2001, April). *Interactive learners, cooperative knowledge building, and classroom inventions.* Paper presented at the annual conference of the American Educational Research Association, Seattle, WA.

Moreau, M. J. (2001, April). *Knowledge building pedagogy and teacher change: One teacher's journey.* Paper presented at the annual conference of the American Educational Research Association, Seattle, WA.

Reeve, R. (2001, April). *The knowledge building lab school: Principles to practice.* Paper presented at the annual conference of the American Educational Research Association, Seattle, WA.

Sagan, C. (1980). *Cosmos.* New York: Ballantine.

Scardamalia, M. (2004). CSILE/Knowledge Forum®. In *Education and technology: An encyclopedia.* (pp. 183-192) Santa Barbara: ABC-CLIO.

Scardamalia, M., & Bereiter, C. (1991). Higher levels of agency for children in knowledge building: A challenge for the design of new knowledge media. *Journal of the Learning Sciences, 1,* 37–68.

Scardamalia, M., & Bereiter, C. (1994). Computer support for knowledge-building communities. *Journal of the Learning Sciences, 3,* 265–283.

Wenger, E. (1998). *Communities of practice: Learning, meaning, and identity.* New York: Cambridge University Press.
White, B. Y., & Frederiksen, J. R. (1998). Inquiry, modeling, and metacognition: Making science accessible to all students. *Cognition and Instruction, 16*, 3–118.

Chapter 4

Enabling Participants in Online Forums to Learn From Each Other

Marcia C. Linn

James D. Slotta

University of California, Berkeley

This chapter reviews the goals and philosophies underlying the design of activities that help students learn from others, examines the role of technology in promoting such opportunities, and suggests principles to guide designers. We identify common design decisions and use research findings to show how these decisions could impact science learning. Technology-enhanced learning environments offer opportunities for those designing collaborative forums to include online discussions, support asynchronous interactions, and study specific curriculum design patterns. These environments support research comparing compelling alternative designs and yield embedded assessments for analyzing impacts. The complex, interacting set of decisions necessary for design of collaborative forums calls for a process of iterative design. We report on a case study involving iterative design of an online discussion to examine the benefit of this process. We synthesize this research in a set of preliminary design principles that are linked to specific features of collaborative forums. We invite others to contribute to this effort by critiquing the principles, adding features, and adding principles.

This chapter reviews the rationale for activities that help students learn from others, examines the role of technology in promoting such opportunities, reports on a case study of iterative design, and offers a preliminary set of design principles. Researchers have identified many aspects of group learning that promote individual understanding and have studied a wide variety of learning environments intended to contribute to science understanding by capitalizing on group learning.

We refer to any opportunity for students to learn from each other as a *collaborative forum*. These include face-to-face discussions, collaborative projects, online discussions, and informal interactions. Those researching collaborative forums argue that these opportunities increase negotiation reflection, and knowledge building. Many argue that scientific research proceeds through a process of argumentation (Keller, 1993; Lemke, 1990; Longino, 1994; Thagard, 1994; Toulmin, 1958).

Brown and Campione (1994) described how communities of learners negotiate meaning and build more coherent understanding. Scardamalia and Bereiter (1992; 1993) described opportunities for participants in a group-learning context to engage in knowledge building and understanding of their own learning, using first the CSILE collaboration software and later the Knowledge Forum software. Collaborative forums can promote effective arguments by motivating individuals to build coherent and cohesive explanations in the process of negotiating meanings with peers (Brown & Campione, 1994; Duschl & Osborne, 2002; Kuhn, 1989, 1992, 1993; Lajoie & Lesgold, 1992). Forums can scaffold individuals to explain their ideas to an audience and therefore get feedback on the coherence and persuasiveness of their message.

Linn and Hsi (2000) called for well-designed group learning to promote the knowledge integration of individual participants and reveal the ideas of students to teachers. Knowledge integration is a process in which students add new ideas to their repertoire of ideas, analyze how the ideas fit together, and build arguments by reorganizing, critiquing, promoting, linking, reformulating, or combining ideas (Linn, 1995). In the process, students compare ideas from varied sources, sort out their ideas, prioritize their thoughts, and typically generate more coherent, normative views. In collaborative forums, students learn new ideas from peers, justify their own views, and critique arguments. Teachers leading these forums get a window on student ideas in-the-making and can add ideas for students to consider. Research suggests that collaborative forums contribute more to the process of adding ideas to the repertoire than to the process of developing a coherent argument, although in some forums, groups develop norms for scientific thinking (Linn & Hsi, 2000).

Papert and his collaborators called for a "constructionism" approach to science learning. They stressed that science students seek coherent understanding of phenomena when they collaborate, reflect on their ideas, and construct artifacts such as computer programs or models to explore their ideas (Bruckman, 2000; Papert, 1980).

Bransford and his colleagues have shown how "anchored instruction" can focus students' efforts on sense making and knowledge building within a compelling, complex context where multiple explanations and ideas can be explored. For example, in the Jasper project, students explore a dilemma involving injured wildlife and develop a plan to provide medical treatment (Cognition and Technology Group at Vanderbilt, 1997).

Researchers advocate collaborative forums to stimulate self-monitoring or metacognition. In collaborative settings, students are called on to explain problems, concepts, and procedures to their peers. These explanations frequently enable peers to recognize flaws or limitations in their reasoning

(Webb & Farivar, 1994; Webb & Palinscar, 1996). Chi and her collaborators demonstrated that students who spontaneously provide what they call "self-explanations" learn more than those who do not (Chi, Bassok, Lewis, Reimann, & Glaser, 1989). Further, when students are prompted to explain texts and materials during learning they also improve their own performance (Chi, deLeeuw, Chiu, & LaVancer, 1994). Researchers have trained students in giving self-explanations, demonstrating the benefits of this approach (Bielaczyc, Pirolli, & Brown, 1995).

Davis (2003a; 2003b) studied the nature of prompts for explanations, finding that overly specific prompts can sometimes derail thinking, whereas more generic prompts have a greater likelihood of eliciting productive explanations. The prompts for explanations provided by peers in a collaborative activity are cast at a relevant level of specificity, have contextual supports that promote reflection, and therefore could resemble the beneficial aspects of generic prompts.

All of these researchers advocate collaborative learning opportunities in science to take advantage of the ideas of peers, to help students guide their own learning, and to reveal how students reason about complex ideas. Taken together, collaborative activities can empower students to formulate more cogent and powerful arguments (Roschelle, 1992). When students engage in well-designed activities, they negotiate meaning with others, critique ideas, build group norms for evidence, construct more powerful representations of their knowledge, monitor their progress, and integrate their ideas. Students potentially both develop more coherent views and learn how others think about the domain.

Researchers have contrasted classrooms where collaboration predominates with those where collaboration rarely arises (e.g. Cohen, 1982, 1994; Johnson & Johnson, 1999; Slavin, 1983). Results of this research reveal that students are more motivated to learn when collaborating with peers than when working independently. Meta-analytic studies also show positive effects of collaboration on attitudes and persistence (Bowen, 2000; Johnson, Johnson, & Smith, 1998; Linn & Clancy, 1992; Springer, Stanne, & Donovan, 1999). These experiences appear to sustain participation in class activities, enabling students to appreciate instructional content that might initially have deterred or eluded them.

The many decisions that go into the design of collaborative activities underscore the need for iterative refinement to improve designs because testing all the combinations is forbidding. Research provides guidance for decision-making but leaves many questions about collaborative learning unanswered. Designers typically create promising approaches and improve them based on user response. Studies of the iterative refinement of collaborative activities generally demonstrate improvement (e.g Linn & Hsi, 2000). These studies suggest that numerous, effective supports for collaborative learning exist. This paper identifies the many decisions that designers face and provides some rationale and background on these decisions. Participants, structure, resources, and assessments all interact to determine the success of a collaborative forum. We discuss the decisions relevant to each of these dimensions and identify interactions among them that shape the design of collaborative forums (see Figure 4.1).

Participants
    Audience—Forum members
    Group and discussion size—Total number of participants and number per forum
    Selection and diversity—Variety of backgrounds of audience
    Duration and pacing—Length and frequency of participant interactions
    Leadership—Type and expertise of moderator
    Expectations—Requirements and rewards for participation
Structure
    Scope—Breadth or depth of the topic
    Curriculum design patterns—Sequence of activities
    Discussion format—Face to face, online, synchronous, asynchronous
    Representation—View or views of the discussion
    Topics and prompts—Instructions and direction during the discussion
    Identity and attribution—Options for identifying participants, leaders, and experts
Resources
    Format—Text, animation, illustration, video, off-line, online
    Timing—Prior to forum, during forum, on demand
    Validity—Normative, opinion, warranted, unwarranted
    Search—Off-line, online, constrained, unavailable
Assessments
    Participation patterns—Frequency, duration, attribution, timing
    Quality of contributions
    Resource use—Frequency, sequence, reuse, interpretation

FIG.4.1. Topics for design decisions in collaborative forums.

PARTICIPANTS

Decisions about participation determine the mix of ideas that individuals in the collaborative forum will encounter and may provide incentives for individuals to contribute. They also shape the norms and standards for consensus building and negotiation that the community endorses. Participants can impose limits on knowledge integration and reinforce non-normative ideas (Linn & Burbules, 1993). We discuss aspects of participation that research suggests deserve attention from designers.

Audience

Audiences for collaborative forums determine the mix of ideas, the available expertise, and the motivation for participation. They vary from well-established groups to informal communities. Audiences include eighth-grade biology classes, girls' clubs, and self-organizing groups whose members complete a project, explore a common interest, or build friendships. In classroom discussions teachers often offer incentives for participation. Discussions among individuals suffering from the same disease, developing expertise in the same hobby, or planning a joint trip tend to be productive and coherent because the topic is personally relevant. Voluntary discussion forums for professional organizations, research groups, or large courses often fail to thrive because participants do not see the value of contributing, and may fear that their ideas will be ridiculed or worry that their efforts will be appropriated rather than rewarded.

Group and Discussion Size

Determining the ideal group size for a collaborative forum depends on the frequency of interaction. To succeed, forums need contributions. In classrooms, face-to-face discussions can involve whole classes or smaller groups. Online discussions offer more flexibility in group size and group composition. Individuals can belong to both small groups and larger groups. Jigsaw approaches can involve groups from diverse geographical areas (Aronson, 1978). Hsi (1997) found that groups of around 15 students were more successful in commenting on others' work than larger or smaller groups. Very small groups did not contribute to the discussion often enough to sustain it, while large groups could not keep track of the whole discussion.

Selection and Diversity

To encourage knowledge integration, diversity of views in a collaborative forum can improve outcomes (Hoadley & Linn, 2000). Hsi (1997) found that groups comprised of individuals from different classes contribute more comments than within class groups. Engaging males and females and individuals from varied cultural groups in the forum enhances the probability of new ideas being introduced to the group. Individuals designing discussion opportunities can also increase diversity by forming groups composed of experts and novices, inviting students to specialize in a topic so they become more expert than their peers, or creating natural variations in expertise by engaging individuals from different geographic regions or with varied ideological views in the discussion.

Classes often use techniques to enable groups to specialize and then tell others (Aronson, 1978). To design expertise into a collaborative forum, Songer (1996) engaged students in a discussion of weather phenomenon and asked each individual to specialize in one aspect of the weather, such as wind, clouds, or a particular extreme weather condition. By increasing the mix of ideas available to each participant this approach increased learning.

Cultural diversity achieves both increased viewpoints and opportunities for underrepresented groups to participate in the discourse of science. Online discussions with incentives for participation typically engage all students in discussion. In contrast, individuals from underrepresented groups, including women and people of color, participate less in science and mathematics discussions than their peers (Sadker & Sadker, 1994). In class discussions, for example, only about 15% of the students participate and a preponderance of comments comes from white males. Hsi (1997) found that over 90% of students participated in the discourse of an online discussion compared to 15% in the classroom. In addition, Hsi (1997) and Hoadley (2004) report that males and females participate equally in online discussion.

Research by Steele (1997) suggests that social settings can invoke and reinforce stereotypes, reducing the likelihood that individuals from certain populations will participate in fields like science. Work by Bargh and Chartrand (1999) on priming demonstrates that subtle perceptions on who belongs in a field or how particular groups behave can have profound implications on social interactions. For example, when primed, individuals of both genders were more likely to view females as dependent and males as aggressive, and responded to strangers based on these views. Agogino and Linn (1992, May-June) reported on groups that become dysfunctional when stereotypes influence interaction patterns. To reduce stereotyping, researchers report benefits from smaller group size and from equating the numbers of individuals from each cultural group (Linn & Hsi, 2000). In addition, moderators can intervene to neutralize stereotyped comments. Students can and do learn from others, but they do not necessarily learn the material intended by instructors. Orchestrating social situations such that science learning occurs and, at the same time, that learners feel valued in the discipline, requires balancing cultural groups and neutralizing stereotypes.

Duration and Pacing

Psychological research demonstrates that distributed practice results in deeper understanding than massed practice, thus promoting knowledge integration. Online discussions support distributed learning because students can revisit the discussion at regular intervals. Online asynchronous forums slow the pace for individual contributions and provide participants with time to think before responding. Research shows that participants in online forums articulate the warrants and justifications for their points of view more than typical face-to-face classroom discussions where the pace and the tempo of the discussion frequently impedes reflection (Hsi, 1997).

Research suggests that the benefits of distributed learning are balanced with the possibility that participants in a discussion will lose interest and stop coming. Ideal durations for discussions appear to be in the range from three to ten weeks when individuals can participate, at minimum, once a week (Hsi, 1997). Often, the duration of a discussion is determined by the time spent studying the topic.

Leadership

Leaders, including teachers, who monitor discussion performance need to keep the discussion focused, reduce stereotypes, showcase normative views, and ensure that all voices are heard. Often, teachers take a leadership role by directing, facilitating, or monitoring the performance of a collaborative forum (Scardamalia, Bereiter, Hewitt, & Webb, 1996). A learning environment or online discussion tool can entice teachers to send messages to small groups while the class progresses in their exploration of the topic or to make online contributions or critiques to individual students. Many studies demonstrate that these interactions vary substantially from teacher to teacher (Slotta, 2004). However, they also show the benefit of teacher intervention on student outcomes (Linn & Hsi, 2000; Stigler & Hiebert, 1999).

Leaders can help support the development of norms and standards for discourse, provide rewards for certain types of contributions, and ensure that the ideas of each participant gain attention in the forum. Some forums have leaders who are experts in the field and can raise issues that others find unfamiliar. Teachers can ensure that students carry out their activities in a context of mutual respect, tutor individuals or small groups on techniques for responding to peers, and tailor the materials to the entering ideas and goals of instruction (Cohen, 1994). Leaders typically develop skills in moderating online activities with feedback from participants. Courses to train leaders have had considerable success (see http://www.metacourse.com/netcourses/approach.html).

Expectations

Designers and users of collaborative forums can establish expectations for the quantity and quality of participation. For example, instructors might require that everyone make three comments in a discussion or assign students to make a contribution and comment on the contributions of others. By establishing the need to comment on contributions of others, leaders can encourage participants to negotiate understanding with peers. Leaders might also require contributions at a certain frequency or of different types, such as questions, elaborations, and evidence-based rebuttals. Research on learning from discussions (Webb, 1995; Webb & Farivar, 1994; Webb & Palinscar, 1996) demonstrates that the roles of individuals in a discussion, including asking questions, getting responses, or offering critiques determine the benefits from the forum. Collaborative forum designers can enhance the information available to participants by setting norms concerning the use of evidence in warrants or claims, by ensuring a diverse set of perspectives, and by expecting participants to justify their contributions. By setting expectations about the participation in a collaborative forum, designers and instructors determine the number of ideas likely to be available to individuals as well as the activity structures that might generate critiques, questions, new ideas, and group norms for understanding.

Summary–Role of Participation

In summary, participation in a discussion can motivate individuals to add ideas, reconsider their ideas, and sustain their efforts to understand a topic. Experts, specialists, leaders, and highly motivated individuals can expand the views and alternative accounts of a phenomenon beyond those held by typical learners. Research suggests that even when individuals come to a discussion with similar kinds of understanding, they spark responses in each other that can increase the total number of ideas available (Hoadley, 2004). The design of effective discussions depends on selecting participants and establishing expectations, but there is no one right answer.

Typically, individuals and teachers report heightened motivation among individuals participating in discussions. Small, intimate discussions provide greater opportunities for individuals to get responses to their own ideas and reduce concerns about appearing foolish (Scardamalia & Bereiter, 1992). Decisions about expectations for contributions to a collaborative forum can increase the cohesion or synthesis in a group. The structure of a discussion, as described in the next section, also impacts the degree of integration and cohesion of ideas.

STRUCTURE

The structures of collaborative forums can help promote knowledge integration and develop student commitments to lifelong learning. Structures determine the intellectual purpose of a collaborative forum and shape the pattern of group work. Researchers have structured discussions around naturally occurring conflicts (Brown & Campione, 1994), contemporary controversies (Bell & Linn, 2002; Linn, 2000), design tasks (Bruckman, 2000; Hoadley, 2004), and critiques (Davis, 2004; Linn, Clark, & Slotta, 2003). In all of these cases, instructors and designers work together to select topics and create resources, environments, tools, or experiments that enable learners to distinguish among alternatives, make sense of information, build their knowledge, and link and connect their ideas.

Scope

The scope of the discussion determines the knowledge integration goal for learners. Open-ended, collaborative forums may result in more ideas but also demand greater support and guidance from the leader than do forums that are more targeted. A very open-ended collaborative experience can create chaos and confusion when learners fail to integrate the ideas (Gordin, Polman, & Pea, 1994; Linn & Hsi, 2000). Benefits from more open-ended forums often arise when the goal is brainstorming.

A highly scripted collaboration can stifle or impede knowledge integration (Eylon & Linn, 1988; Krajcik, Blumenfeld, Marx, & Soloway, 1999). Researchers disagree concerning the ideal scope of a collaborative forum . The degree of independence, autonomy, and flexibility provided to participants in a collaborative forum must be, in the end, a negotiation among a teacher, the students, and the designers.

Curriculum Design Patterns

Central to the structure of a collaborative forum is the curriculum design pattern that students and teachers follow (Linn, Clark, & Slotta, 2003). Curriculum design patterns refer to the series of activities that individuals in a collaborative forum carry out. Curriculum design patterns often reflect the commitments of the designers towards the process of knowledge integration. Thus, individuals develop curriculum design patterns that emphasize the negotiation of understanding, others create curriculum design patterns that emphasize motivation, and others focus on curriculum design patterns that embed discussion in experimentation.

Typically activities in a pattern are orchestrated by some form of inquiry guide (see Figure 4.2). Learning environments such as the Web-based Inquiry Science Environment (WISE) use an inquiry map (see left side of Figure 4.2) to guide students and teachers to perform such activities as gathering evidence, reflecting on sources, articulating a view, critiquing views of others, and summarizing ideas. These activities result in a collaborative project. Considerable research on successful and unsuccessful mechanisms for supporting collaboration suggests some promising curriculum design patterns that can give designers of collaborative forums a headstart.

For example, a curriculum design pattern that balances open-ended and targeted discussion and connects to the overall curriculum has shown success. In this pattern, designers encourage brainstorming and then scaffold the resulting projects so students compare ideas under well-organized conditions. Students might then test these strategies in autonomous projects (Linn, 1980).

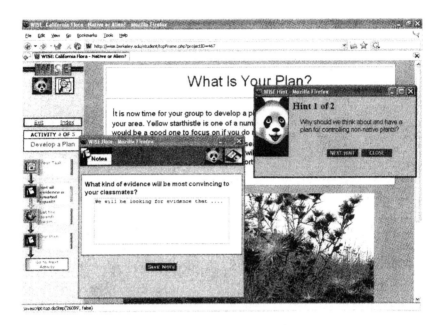

FIG.4.2. A WISE project page, with inquiry map on left, a note, and a hint.

Collaborative forums can also promote the integration of knowledge and the development of more sophisticated ideas, by implementing curriculum design patterns that orchestrate both individual and group work. Hatano and Inagaki (1991) have developed the Itakura method for collaborative forums. They encourage students to generate a list of alternative ideas for a scientific phenomenon presented in class.

They ask each student to select one idea that seems most compelling. Each student defends his or her idea in a whole-class or small-group activity. Individuals provide evidence for their ideas, vote on their predictions, and design a way to test their ideas. The group then discusses the results of the test, reconsiders their ideas, and votes again. Hatano and Inagaki (1991) have shown that this method leads to consensus-building while at the same time helps students seriously consider alternative views. In Japanese classrooms, students actively defend their point of view and often reinterpret experimental evidence to support non-normative views. American students participate in a similar form of classroom learning as researched by Minstrell and Van Zee (2000). In their approach, students generate and reconcile predictions and results.

Clark and Jorde (in press) developed a related pattern while investigating the role of classroom discussion and visualizations in students' understanding of thermal equilibrium. Students have considerable difficulty understanding the topic of thermal equilibrium, frequently confusing tactile information concerning how objects feel with information from measuring the temperature of objects. Students hold multiple views about thermal equilibrium, at times believing that objects in a room may all reach the same temperature and at other times reporting that they do not. Some say, for example, that because a wooden chair feels warmer than a metal desk, clearly the metal desk is cooler than the wooden chair! The WISE Probing Your Surroundings activity helps students consider these alternative perspectives on thermal equilibrium, to sort out their ideas, and to gain a more cohesive perception of the situation. Over a five day period, students make predictions about the temperature of objects in the classroom, use real time data collection to investigate the temperature of these objects, create a graph comparing their predictions, enter the data they collected, and write principles to describe what they think happens when objects are placed in the same surrounding temperature. These principles resemble the viewpoints in the Itakura method.

Students discuss their principles in a collaborative forum. They must enter their principle into the collaborative forum prior to reading the principles from other groups. The discussions in this WISE project become quite lively. Students propose principles that basically say that objects remain at different temperatures in the same surrounding because they feel differently. Other students object to this point of view, illustrating their views by citing compelling evidence from the classroom. Some students reiterate the class-instructed view that objects gain or lose heat energy depending on the temperature of the room. One group explains that objects remaining different temperatures in the same room is "sort of like you are saying that if you put things in the oven for a while they wouldn't get hotter." Others point out that insulation does contribute to how an object feels but not to its temperature. The original writers of the principle introduce the importance of the status of an object as a conductor or an insulator. They explain the view that objects will stay at different temperatures by arguing that insulators and conductors have their own temperatures.

Through exchanges and subsequent activities within this WISE project (e,g,.the use of visualizations) students make substantial progress in understanding the important and complex topic of thermal equilibrium. In particular, Clark (2000) found that students could explain thermal equilibrium situations by warranting their answers with multiple sources from their classroom experience and their discussions with peers. Based on the results from Hoadley (1999) we can conjecture that the discussion contributed to the overall gains along with the other aspects of the activity.

Clark (2000) retested the students several months after they had studied thermal equilibrium, and found that students remained competent on the delayed post-test and perform well on new, challenging problems scored using the same rubric. Contrary to typical instruction, students in the thermal equilibrium unit maintain or exceed their understanding on the delayed post-test. In typical courses, it is common for students' performance on delayed post-tests to be less successful than it was on the initial post-test. This finding is consistent with other results in longitudinal investigations of science projects that include collaboration (Linn & Hsi, 2000).

Clancy et al. (2003) report similar benefits for what they call a gated discussion. In a gated discussion students enter their solution to a complex problem to enter the gate. They then get access to the solutions of others and have an opportunity to critique or incorporate the ideas of their peers.

Discussion Format

Collaborative forums can occur in face-to-face and technology-enhanced formats. Technology-enhanced formats, such as those supported by WISE (shown in Figure 4.2) enable students to use synchronous or asynchronous discussion tools. They also implement the curriculum design patterns mentioned previously such as a gated discussion.

Learning environments expand both research and design of collaborative forums. Learning environments can implement comparison studies of alternative curriculum design patterns, such as those studied by Hoadley (1999) and Hsi (1997). They can also embed assessment tasks and provide researchers with a better understanding of the learning trajectories of the students.

Representation

The representation of a discussion in an online forum can promote knowledge integration by highlighting the ideas under negotiation. Collaborative learning opportunities can represent science as argumentation. Early collaborative opportunities simply allowed individuals to post comments or "notes" on a flat list like a class discussion. Informed by virtual worlds or multiuser domains, a number of researchers built environments where students could enter text and keep track of material according to themes (Bruckman, 1997; Hunter, 1990; Resnick, 1996, 2001). Others have explored concept maps to construct arguments (Baumgartner, 2004; Novak, Gowin, & Johannsen, 1983).

The representation of the argument as a tree, as researched by Hsi (1997) for the Multimedia Forum Kiosk, for example, shows how the representation can shape the behavior of the participants. Although all individuals could participate in any part of the discussion, they were more likely to start a new tree or to continue to participate in a familiar tree than to join an unfamiliar tree. This may reflect the time required to read all the prior comments before contributing to an unfamiliar tree. Starting a new discussion or commenting on an issue raised at the beginning of a discussion means that there is less to consider before contributing. Hsi found that the tree structure demanded too much screen real estate as arguments continued. Hoadley (2004) has sought more economical tree representations.

Researchers have also developed tools for individuals to use to represent their own arguments (Bell, 1998; Bell & Linn, 2000; Lajoie & Lesgold, 1992; Novak, 1990). Tools such as Sensemaker enable individuals to represent connections to warrants and help students distinguish among conjecture, hypothesis, prediction, and evidence (Bell & Linn, 2002). Bell and Linn (2002) demonstrated that students gradually add to their repertoire of images of science as they participate in collaborative activities. This finding resonates with the views of Driver, Leach, Miller and Scott (1995), who introduced argumentation in the science classroom to strengthen the epistemological commitments of science learners. Initially, students often believe that science is a body of facts perhaps based on their experience in learning science. However, they expand their repertoire of views about the nature of science and incorporate images from the popular press and, when encouraged, images from argumentation that occurs in science classrooms.

Representations for discussions have the potential of promoting knowledge integration by capturing the connections among ideas and making them inspectable. The representation tools also shed light on student ideas about argumentation. For example, Burbules and Linn (1991) noted some difficulties in transferring the scientific model of argumentation to science learning. Discussions can squelch normative ideas and also subtly convince atypical science students that their contributions are less worthy. The norms and standards found in the scientific domain are far more extensive than those characterizing classroom science. Furthermore, scientists may warrant their assertions using arrogance and privileged knowledge in ways that fail to promote knowledge integration. Collaborative forums could reinforce a relativistic view of science knowledge rather than strengthening the warrants for arguments.

Topics and Prompts

Researchers have shown the benefit of choosing good topics for collaborative forums. Many collaborative forums, including CSILE, one of the original forums, depend on both compelling topics and either embedded prompts or lists of prompts to help students frame their contributions to the discussion. In the CSILE system, for example, prompts remind students of aspects of argument construction, saying "What I need to know is..." or "My theory suggests..." Prompts help students understand the nature of argumentation and, at the same time, encourage students to engage in meta-cognitive processes by helping them monitor their performance. Effective curriculum design patterns often include the pattern of posing a compelling question, providing epistemological prompts, and encouraging reflection.

Identity and Attribution

The identity of the individual contributing to the discussion helps the participant understand the nature of the contribution. Identifiers can help participants distinguish experts and novices. In addition, individuals have expectations about their peers. As a result, many discussion forums permit individuals to make anonymous or attributed comments. In the CSILE work, the researchers found that students often initially marked their comments as anonymous, but later added their attribution when they discovered that their peers respected the contribution.

Hoadley (2004) examined how students respond to comments attributed to various authority figures, contrasting the contributions of teachers and scientists to an online discussion concerning the nature of the perception of color. In one condition, contributions were attributed to famous historical scientists such as Newton and Kepler who held disparate views about the nature of color perception. In another condition, these same views were attributed to an online guide named Mildred, who acted rather like a teacher. In the "dead scientists" condition, the opposing views of the two contributors were connected to pictures of the scientists and thereby clearly delineated for students. In the Mildred condition, the two different views were both expressed by the same individual, much like a teacher might offer a variety of possible perspectives on a problem as part of a class discussion.

Hoadley (1999) found that students made clear learning gains solely as a result of participating in these discussions, although the gains differed according to the social information presented. Scoring discussions in terms of the ideas held by individuals at pre- and posttest, Hoadley (2004) found that students encountering varied views contributed by a teacher-like participant made about a 14% gain in understanding of the nature of color, whereas students encountering the same comments contributed by Newton and Kepler made about a 25% gain in understanding. To account for these pre-post test differences, Hoadley examined the content of explanations. He observed that students with the teacher-like contributions were less likely to have a productive discussion than individuals whose discussion was supported by comments from Newton and Kepler. Thus, having the social character of the comments articulated and being able to clearly distinguish the two perspectives about the nature of color led to a more effective discussion. Apparently, situating these comments in a rich social context enabled students to sort out the diverse ideas and connect them to their own views.

Summary–Role of Structure

In summary, structuring discussion can enhance success. Research shows that decisions about the scope, expectations for contributions, representations for arguments, and opportunities for reflection impact outcomes from forums. Finding productive design patterns remains an open research area. Structuring the forum offers a chance to promote integration of ideas but can force premature closure or deter creative contributions. Research informs decisions about structure, but successful choices often depend on iterative refinement in the context of use.

RESOURCES

Besides gaining information from participants in a forum, students also can gain ideas and insights from resources available to a collaborative forum. Designers can offer conveners of collaborative forums opportunities to use print, online, video, interactive, and individually-contributed resources. Participants in forums can search for new information, interact with visualizations and modeling tools, and review materials provided by the moderator. Ideally, resources that students encounter for an activity will illustrate alternative views, connect to students' entering ideas, provide personally relevant links to encourage knowledge integration and vary in authenticity to enable students to assess the validity of evidence.

Designing resources to help individuals succeed in a collaborative venture and gain a deep understanding of a complex topic will always require trial and refinement. The designers need understanding of the ideas students bring to the situation, their reading level, the time available, and other factors. For example, Linn, Shear, Bell, and Slotta (1999) found that teachers and disciplinary experts disagreed about the appropriateness of resources in a deformed frogs activity. Scientists believed the project required an understanding of molecular biology. The teacher, aware that the students did not have prior instruction in molecular biology, preferred a project at a more general level of analysis where students contrasted the effect of environmental chemicals with the effect of parasites. The scientists designed resources to illustrate the molecular biology of the parasite impacts and the chemical structure similarities between pesticides and growth hormones in frogs. Pilot testing with a few students in the classroom supported the teacher's view. A discussion at the level of environmental chemicals and parasites could optimally engage all the students. In the classroom trial, students' debates about this topic relied on extensive evidence from experimental studies, although the arguments were not articulated at the level of molecular biology.

Research suggests some criteria for selecting ideas to add to the mix held by students. For example, pivotal cases (Linn, in press) are resources that when added to the curriculum promote knowledge integration. Pivotal cases meet the following criteria: create compelling comparisons; place inquiry in accessible, culturally relevant contexts; provide feedback to support pronormative self-monitoring; and enable narrative accounts of science. Pivotal cases draw attention to a natural experiment with results learners can appreciate and stimulate a search for mechanisms to explain the phenomena. For example, exploring thermal equilibrium, students can contrast how wood and metal feel in a hot car, on a snowy day, and in the classroom to help sort out the role of the temperature objects feel when touched. This case connects to familiar events and enables students to provide personal anecdotes about hot cars, freezers, and ovens.

Format

Considerable research suggests that students pay attention to print, online, multimedia, and interactive materials in distinct ways. Attention, focus, motivation, and depth of understanding all vary depending on format. Visual materials may tap different brain areas than verbal materials. Interactions between format and understanding are not clear-cut. For example, multimedia materials can confuse students by offering too many ideas or enhance understanding by providing ideas that resonate across different learners (Bell, 1998). Recent work comparing diagrams and text suggests that students are more likely to generate self-explanations when using diagrams (Ainsworth & Loizou, 2003). Interactive materials including animations can benefit students if the interactions involve making sense of relevant information, but interactions with electronic games and films often could draw attention to irrelevant information (Hegarty, et al., 1999).

Timing

Participants in a collaborative forum might encounter resources in preparation for the forum, concurrently during the forum, or as a follow-up depending on curricular goals. Typically, collaborative activities occur as part of a larger curriculum. The timing of their introduction depends on the goals for the collaborative undertaking and is orchestrated by a curriculum design pattern. For example, in the Genetically Modified Foods project (Seethaler & Linn, 2004), students benefit from a collaborative forum after conducting experiments to pool results and compare arguments. A collaborative forum might enable students to conjecture about syntheses of the results as well as to interrogate their peers concerning methodological differences between one approach and another. Collaborative forums may fail to encourage synthesis of ideas—just as face-to-face meetings often fail to converge on a common goal.

Validity

Resources vary dramatically with regard to their validity, persuasiveness, comprehensiveness, level of analysis, and accessibility, all of which influence the nature of a collaborative forum. Many science courses seek to help students distinguish among resource available on the Internet. Helping students understand the epistemological characteristics of the resources that they encounter is a crucial aspect of intellectual growth. A mix of resources that vary in their epistemological underpinnings enable students to distinguish among valid and invalid, as well as persuasive and documentary materials. Authorship of resources also determines their effectiveness. Bell (1998) reported that access to a library of resources leads to more sophisticated arguments than when students generate their own evidence in a discussion of light propagation.

In some forums, resources include automatically generated seed comments to start the discussion or provide specific viewpoints. Designers can mislead students by not enabling them to deconstruct the source of seed comments (Hsi, 1997). Designing a topic and accompanying seed comments to clarify the issues and mark the boundaries of the discussion can focus a forum and keep participants on task (Hoadley, 2004).

Search

Providing opportunities for participants in a forum to search for information and link the results of their search to the forum has considerable benefit for adding useful ideas to the discussion and providing students with research skills. When students search for their own information they must pay attention to the epistemological underpinnings of the materials that they locate, distinguish among various types of materials and formats, and make decisions concerning whether the resources they locate are relevant to the topic and will make sense to the audience in the forum (Bell, 1998).

Research in many projects is underway to determine how best to take advantage of search for educational forums. Cuthbert (2002), for example, discovered that both experts and novices could locate appropriate web resources for a science topic, but students had difficulty identifying whether or not the resources they located were relevant. Students also had difficulty making sense of many of the resources, presumably due to their lack of background knowledge. Students will certainly benefit from training in effective search strategies and in making sense of searched materials. Search is a component of technology literacy that collaborative forums might advance.

Summary–Role of Resources

In summary, the design of resources for a collaborative forum can enhance the experience, make learning inefficient, and confuse learners. Designing resources for knowledge integration requires iterative refinement because conjectures concerning which resources will resonate with students often fail. By analyzing student forum contributions designers can identify resources to improve knowledge integration in future uses of the project. When teachers customize projects based on understanding of the backgrounds of their students they generally improve learning outcomes (Linn, Davis, & Bell, 2004).

ASSESSMENT

Collaborative forums provide designers, teachers, and students with a wealth of information. Assessing a collaborative forum can have many goals. First, assessment can help improve the collaborative forum for subsequent users and construct promising curriculum design patterns. Second, assessment can determine what participants learn from the collaborative forum. Third, assessment can clarify the relative value of collaborative forums versus other forms of instruction. Assessments described here respond to the first two questions and are relevant to the third question. The third question involves determining critical competitors to the collaborative forum and making comparisons, a process that is facilitated by using a powerful learning environment that can deliver alternative curriculum designs.

Embedded assessments can inform iterative refinement and also provide evidence of student progress. Collaborative forums, especially those carried out in online settings, provide numerous opportunities for embedded assessments. By embedded assessments, we mean assessments that self-document the effectiveness of a forum by capturing the comments of participants, noting the tempo of activity, documenting which resources are used and when, and characterizing levels of participation. Assessment of knowledge integration can include documenting the variety of ideas that forum participants encounter and analyzing the coherence of arguments.

Besides embedded assessments, traditional assessments can help determine the efficacy of forums. Assessments that comprise part of the larger activity students undertake, such as pretests and posttests, projects, debates, or designs can provide evidence of the benefit of collaborative forums. In cases where a collaborative forum addresses a unique curriculum topic, pretests and post-tests can delineate the benefits of the forum alone (Hoadley & Linn, 2000).

Participation Patterns

To determine whether an online forum has been productive, researchers and instructors typically examine the number of comments contributed, the frequency with which individuals make comments, the tempo of contribution, the attribution of comments, the reading of comments, and the pattern of participation in the commenting space, often distinguishing between individuals who read comments and respond and those who come and read comments but make no contributions themselves. Researchers also can analyze the overall number of ideas contributed to a discussion and the frequency with which responders to ideas raise new issues or critique those ideas. These studies show that frequency of participation varies depending on the scope, topic, resources, and expectations of the forum. Curriculum design patterns impact participation, as do teacher expectations. Analysis may examine both individual and group productivity.

Quality of Contributions

Teachers and designers look at the quality of student work, including the variety and relevance of evidence cited, the fidelity with which participants stick to assigned roles, the quality of comments in the discussion, and the degree of participation and interaction in the discussion to assess progress in knowledge integration and inform iterative design of the curriculum design pattern. Rubrics for the quality of predictions, the number and type of warrants used within explanations, the quality of questions, the number and type of warrants used for critiques, the number of ideas contributed, and the number and type of warrants used in feedback can reflect the researcher's view of the learner. To assess aspects of knowledge integration, researchers document the number of ideas that an individual incorporates, the number of critiques offered, the number of questions asked, the number of questions answered, and the degree of attention to other comments, and the coherence of arguments (Cuthbert, Clark, & Linn, 2002). Researchers have analyzed individual comments for the quality of the ideas, the number of warrants used to characterize the ideas, and the coherence of the viewpoint (Bell, 1997).

Resource Use

Many online forums can document the frequency and duration of student use of resources available online, as well as the interpretation, critique, and perceived relevance of the information. Analyzing resource use enables designers to determine which formats stimulate participants to add ideas to the mix of views and they also review the resources that students ignore

(Hsi, 1997). In some cases, students uncover pivotal cases that advance an argument and communicate them to others. On occasion, these cases rapidly spread through large groups of students and even across collaborative boundaries (Bell, 1998).

Summary–Role of Assessment

Opportunities for students to learn from others require refinement. A project that succeeds in one setting may well fail in another because resources are not aligned with student ideas, because students lack norms and standards for knowledge integration, because students lack experience with the approach, or because topics that appeal to one group may discourage others. To guide iterative refinement and formulate design principles we need powerful assessments of collaborative forums.

Assessment can help designers synthesize promising curriculum design patterns and implement these patterns in a way that supports customization. Design partnerships, cognizant of the complex systemic nature of education are well suited to carry out these research endeavors (Linn, Davis, & Bell, 2004). When teachers customize materials to their own classes, local gains are maximized. Research to date suggests the benefit of customization and the danger of a one-size-fits-all curriculum. Teachers regularly customize instruction even when using relatively unresponsive materials like textbooks. Providing teachers with easily customized and flexibly adaptive materials offers promise for supporting knowledge integration of students, their teachers, and design partnerships.

CASE STUDY: ASSESSING AND REVISING ONLINE PROFESSIONAL DEVELOPMENT DISCUSSIONS

WISE partnerships often employ collaborative forums to help support teachers who adopt our inquiry science materials in the course of professional development programs. Frequently, such programs engage teachers in asynchronous online discussions to provide them with opportunities for peer exchange. The challenge of designing forums so that teachers participate enthusiastically has led to a better understanding of how the various decisions interact. In this case study, we describe a partnership with researchers from the American Physiology Society that engaged in the process of iterative refinement. Each year, a group of approximately 20 teachers is selected by this partnership to participate in a program designed to help them implement science activities in topics of physiology.

We report on the process of refining the collaborative forum. Responding to a lack of participation and peer exchange in our first year (2000-01), we added structure to the forum, improved the available resources, and assessed the performance of participants. These changes resulted in substantial progress.

Version I

In the first version of the Physiology Project (a pseudonym) we provided a learning environment and design framework for the creation of inquiry science activities in topics of physiology. The Physiology Project recruited science teachers from around the country to intern in a physiology laboratory, then developed curriculum activities based on the content knowledge they gained through their internship. These teachers participated in several online forums during the spring and summer months, then gathered for a live workshop at the end of the summer. The collaborative forum was designed to help teachers reflect on important issues of pedagogy and practice, particularly with regard to the use of inquiry and technology. Drawing on the scaffolded knowledge integration framework (Linn & Hsi, 2000), we expected the forum to allow teachers to develop a more coherent understanding through exchange of relevant ideas with their peers.

Participants

A total of 14 teachers participated, ranging in experience from 1 year to 24 years in the classroom, with disciplines including all levels of life science, health, and physical education. Teachers were located in 10 different states. The forum was moderated by the principal investigator for The Physiology Project, who has more than a decade of experience in professional development research, as well as a senior assistant. Both moderators were new to the world of online facilitation, and conducted most of the facilitation activities through e-mail sent either to single participants or else to the whole group.

We allowed one month for each forum. We provided no advance guidance about the expected level of participation. The moderator was available online for e-mail assistance, but did not participate in the discussion and did not contact any teachers proactively.

Structure

We structured the discussion with three discussion topics:

- **Discussion Topic 1: The ideal role of the teacher.** In [the reading], the role of the teacher in an inquiry-based learning situation is described as a facilitator of learning and a resource person... However, in a recent national survey of secondary science teachers, only about a third (37%) viewed themselves as a "facilitator of learning." Another third (32%) described themselves as a "dispenser of knowledge," and the final third (31%) was "undecided" (Becker, 2000). What do you envision as the ideal role for science teachers? How can we move toward that ideal (or how have you worked toward that ideal)? What do you think is the most significant obstacle in teachers taking on this ideal role?

- **Discussion Topic 2: Our perceptions of scientists.** How do you think students' images of scientists influence their attitudes toward science studies? How do teachers' images of scientists influence their approach to teaching science?

- **Discussion Topic 3: Technology in the science classroom.** The use of technology in the classroom is determined by the specific educational goals the teacher has in mind …supporting inquiry, enhancing communication, extending access to resources, guiding students to analyze and visualize data, enabling product development, and encouraging expression of ideas. Which of these uses do you feel is especially important for science education? If possible, give at least one example of how technology has facilitated learning in your classroom.

We set up an online community (see Figure 4.3) to provide participants with a fixed location on the Internet where they could return to examine the developing discussion, particularly any responses that had been made to their own comments.

FIG.4.3. An on-line community to support teachers as they participate in professional development activities, including online discussions and curriculum design.

Resources

Appropriate readings were provided to participants in hard copy, and were expected to serve as references for each of the forums. In addition, moderators and program administrators were available on demand, although no substantial or systematic contact occurred.

Assessment

We analyzed comments as a primary form of assessment. Figure 4.4 provides an excerpt of the first discussion, showing the first 7 of 14 comments made. We found that each participant made only one comment, and only two of 14 comments were made in response to a previous comment. The result was an extremely "flat" discussion, since each participating teacher replied to the discussion with very little attention to or influence from other participants. A result of such a discussion is that many comments are quite similar to one another, with most participants offering the same ideas and failing to notice that they were repeating something their peers had already introduced. Thus, few new ideas are represented by the discussion. Another characteristic that derives from such a limited exchange is that few comments include warrants or supporting evidence, since there is no felt need to justify responses to explain to others.

All 14 comments in this discussion were similar to those excerpted above, suggesting that the ideal role of the teacher would be that of facilitator, with supporting evidence or warrants typically in the form of anecdote from their own teaching experience We coded all three forums in this first year in terms of the number of comments made per participant, the average hierarchical depth of each comment (i.e., how many "levels" deep in the discussion was the comment), the average number of new ideas introduced in each comment, and the average number of warrants per comment.

FIG 4.4

---Teaching and Learning by Inquiry - A.W. (Mentor)
R E P L Y T O T H I S C O M M E N T In chapter 1 and 4, the role of the teacher in an inquiry-based learning situation is described as a facilitator of learning and a resource person... However, in a recent national survey of secondary science teachers, only about a third (37%) viewed themselves as a "facilitator of learning." Another third (32%) described themselves as a "dispenser of knowledge," and the final third (31%) was "undecided" (Becker, 2000). What do you envision as the ideal role for science teachers? How can we move toward that ideal (or how have you worked toward that ideal)? What do you think is the most significant obstacle in teachers taking on this ideal role? ---Teaching and Learning by Inquiry - M.H. (teacher)

FIG 4.4 (cont'd)

REPLY TO THIS COMMENT I thoroughly enjoyed the articles. It certainly makes me reflect on my teaching and feel guilty about areas I need to improve. The ideal role of science teachers should be 90% facilitator and 10% dispenser of knowledge.

Students today want immediate answers to their questions. Internet has spoiled them and also made them lazy. Many of my students don't want to take the time to find the answer to their own questions. I find that I need to give them "some" answers in order to drive them on or for them to not feel so frustrated that they give up and quit.

The main obstacles in moving toward the ideal role is "fear" of releasing control and confidence. These are the driving forces in my fears: 1)How do you come up with questions or demonstrations to excite all 30 students in the class. What do you do with the unexcitables and how do you hold them accountable. 2)How can you provide the materials and the know how to test and answer the questions the students have? The students ask very difficult questions (especially hard to test given the equipment and technology in middle school) 3)What specific content should the teacher prepare and study for to be "ready" for the kids that day. Since we don't know what the students will ask, I need to feel confident enough to guide them and brushed up on specific content. --- Teaching and Learning by Inquiry - W. F. (teacher)

REPLY TO THIS COMMENT The most effective method of teaching At-Risk, incarcerated and non motivated students is for me to take the role of a facilitator. As a facilitator in an inquiry program students are motivated to learn, which was my biggest challenge. Once students are motivated then critical thinking will develop. When students are motivated it will encourage or foster a thirst for knowledge. In addition, to increasing the motivation to learn, students self esteem is also increased by the inquiry method. --- Teaching & Learning by Inquiry - T. R. (teacher)

REPLY TO THIS COMMENT The ideal role for a teacher would be that of a facilitator. This is something that will need to be worked at. Especially when dealing with Junior High students who's lab experience is limited. 2. I feel that one way to move toward this is letting more people know about this method. I had not heard of it before this past October. Definitely more training being available is a definite plus. 3. I feel the most significant obstacle is teachers not wanting to break out of the traditional methods that they have been using to teach. Their comfort zone. Like I said, before this past school year, I had not heard of the inquiry approach for teaching science. It seems to be the latest "bandwagon". From what I have read about it, it appears to be a valid approach and I hope that it is a method that will be long lasting. --- Teaching and Learning by Inquiry - L. J. (teacher)

REPLY TO THIS COMMENT I think the biggest obstacle to teachers becoming facilitators of learning instead of dispensers of knowledge is the standardized tests that require students to memorize a wide variety of science facts so that they can show their legislators that they are proficient at memorizing facts. Teachers are imprisoned by a curriculum that they must design so that their students pass the test. Time constraints do not allow for week long labs. Students get angry if they are asked to actually think. They want instant solutions. --- Teaching and Learning by Inquiry - S. M. (teacher)

REPLY TO THIS COMMENT Regarding Inquiry---I don't care...I've been doing it anyways! I love it, and I have not abandoned everything else to do it! --- Science/Mathematics J. D. (teacher)
REPLY TO THIS COMMENT
I feel the ideal role of teacher is that of a facilitator of learning and a resource person which creates the environment in which inquiry by learning can take place. One of the ways we can move toward this ideal design is offer administrators and instructional leaders training in "learning by inquiry". I feel the most significant obstacles in teachers taking on this ideal role are building principals (instructional leaders) because of public pressure, SAT NINE TESTS, state and municipal regulations, competency frameworks and politics. Some principals following the pacing method to the letter, dis-allowing teachers too much freedom to deviate from their expectations as instructional leaders.

FIG.4.4. (cont'd) Excerpt of Discussion 1, showing the first 7 of 14 comments. All but 2 comments were at the topmost hierarchical level, meaning that they were responses directly to the topic question.

Figure 4.5 presents our findings, showing a common lack of participation (number of comments), lack of interaction (depth of hierarchy), and quality (number of new ideas and warrants). In general, there was approximately 1 comment per discussion offered by participants, at an average hierarchical depth of close to 1, with less than 1 new idea and less than 1 warrant per comment. The number of warrants increased notably in the third discussion, but this is because that topic was related to the ideal use of technology and many teachers cited personal experiences to justify their comments. The bottom row of Figure 4.5 presents a pooled average across all three discussions, showing the limited participation.

Topic number	Number of participants		Comments per participant		Average hierarchical "depth" of comments		Number of new ideas per comment		Number of warrants per comment	
	V I	V II	V I	V II	V I	V II	V I	V II	V I	V II
1	14	19	1.00	2.30	1.14	1.98	0.45	0.92	0.43	1.32
2	17	18	1.25	3.05	1.20	2.56	0.40	.087	0.65	1.03
3	16	19	1.18	2.79	1.31	2.05	0.79	1.13	1.52	1.28
Overall			1.10	2.80	1.22	2.20	0.56	0.95	0.91	1.21

FIG.4.5. Discussion participation and comment quality from version I (V I) and version II (V II) of the forum.

Nevertheless, the ideas contributed to the forum suggested that a more structured experience could benefit participants. We redesigned the forum to promote a greater degree of participation, as well as to strengthen the connections to available resources.

Version II

We revised the curriculum design pattern and changed the expectations for participants. We implemented the new curriculum design pattern using the WISE inquiry map for each of the three discussions. We embedded the discussions within a project-based context. These projects were quite simple, and served mainly to provide explicit instructions, to review resources (we linked directly to the relevant readings), to reflect on the resources, to participate, and to reflect again after the discussions had ended. Figure 4.6 shows one pattern where participants are reminded of the relevance of the readings, before entering the discussion as shown in the right frame of the WISE browser window. In order to clarify our expectations, the following instruction was added to the topic statement for each discussion: "Respond to the questions on the discussion board by clicking on new comment below and sharing your thoughts with your fellow teachers. Respond to AT LEAST two of the comments that have been posted by your fellow teachers." In a concluding activity within each of these WISE projects, teachers reflected on what they had gained from the discussion.

Assessing the Revised Discussions

The design improvements, including new resources, structure with a new curriculum design pattern, and new expectations led to a dramatic increase in participation, interactivity, and productivity. We coded all three discussions for participation level (average number of comments per participant), interactivity (average hierarchical depth of all comments), and productivity (average number of new ideas added per comment, and average number of warrants used in each comment). The results of this coding appear in Figure 4.5.

Figure 4.7 shows an excerpt of the same number of comments for Version II as provided in Figure 4.5 previously. Although this discussion was substantially longer than Version I, we analyzed the same number of comments. Note the increased diversity of ideas, even reflected in teachers' choice of subject titles for their comments, and the apparent level of attention they were now giving to one another's ideas.

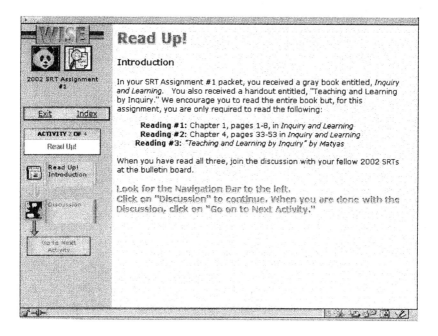

FIG.4.6. WISE projects were created for each of the three discussions to help reinforce the connection to reading materials and provide additional scaffolding for
participant reflections before, during and after the discussion.

FIG. 4.7

Teaching and Learning by Inquiry -A.W. (mentor)
R E P L Y   T O   T H I S   C O M M E N T
In chapter 1 and 4, the role of the teacher in an inquiry-based learning situation is
described as a facilitator of learning and a resource person… However, in a recent
national survey of secondary science teachers, only about a third (37%) viewed
themselves as a "facilitator of learning." Another third (32%) described themselves
as a "dispenser of knowledge," and the final third (31%) was "undecided" (Becker,
2000). What do you envision as the ideal role for science teachers? How can we
move toward that ideal (or how have you worked toward that ideal)? What do you
think is the most significant obstacle in teachers taking on this ideal role?
Respond to these questions on the discussion board by clicking on "new comment"
below and sharing your thoughts with your fellow SRTs. Respond to AT LEAST
two of the comments that have been posted by your fellow SRTs (that is, you should
post at least 3 comments at this bulletin board).
Facilitators of learning - R.E. (teacher)
R E P L Y   T O   T H I S   C O M M E N T

Illinois is not quite as overwhelming in its testing procedures yet, but we have state
and local testing in our district, too. The local testing is very much resented by students and teachers alike. for one thing, once those tests are developed, if something

FIG. 4.7 (cont'd)

new comes along (hot science story), it is difficult to give it class time when you know that it wont be in 'the test'. But, student interest is usually high and they want to discuss it! We don't currently have a 'pacing guide', but when I first taught at this school about 17 years ago, I was handed one for our biology class. I really resented it as it asked me to move along when I knew my students didn't understand certain ideas and test them anyway. Luckily it was eventually discarded. Hopefully this 'testing pendulum' will soon stop its swing towards this over-testing and over-emphasis policy and moderate itself a bit. I dont see how you can be anything but frustrated with the current system and hope you can hang in there till the end of the year :)

Facilitators of Learning - E. S. (teacher)
REPLY TO THIS COMMENT
I understand your dilemma to a certain degree. In New York State we have state mandated courses and final exams. It is a drag to teach to the test. However what is worse is having to teach to the test every quarter and have your test students' results rank your success.
One idea may be to work hypotheses into your already designed labs. Perhaps you could ask your students to predict what might happen in the lab. They might be surprised by the results and could enjoy making a guess about the lab material. A second idea could be to ask students to apply the concept to the real world. For example, in addition to their heavy workload they could be asked to search the web or an electronic database about buffers or solvation, etc. and find out how those things work in living or non-living world. Finally another idea is to ask them to design their own experiments using the same principles or concepts learned in your labs but ask them to propose a prediction based on the concept.

The biggest problem in being a facilitator - R. E. (teacher)

REPLY TO THIS COMMENT

The greatest problem for a teacher who wants to be more of a facilitator is the time involved. Mostly the anticipating what questions will come up, what materials are likely needed and keeping everything running smoothly while students are working at different paces, maybe on different aspects of a problem. It surely serves our students more to run a class in this manner, but the time and organization involved are immense and for many teachers- especially the newer ones, it can be overwhelming. I have been teaching for 17 years and in the 'facilitator mode' I work non-stop all day.

The ideal role for a teacher - R. P. (teacher)

REPLY TO THIS COMMENT □I have a dream of the ideal role of a science teacher. It is definitely more like a facilitator than a dispenser, yet I am not yet sure I should leave the job of dispenser, yet I am not yet sure I should leave the job of dispenser out of the picture. Ideally, I could do a lot better with fewer preps, because of the time it takes to work in the facilitator mode, AND as i have seen in some large, there would be a science teacher facilitator I could turn to- a resource person to help do research on ideas, check out potential problems and help be set up equipment. It is true when students look at a teacher as 'the keeper of all knowledge' they are more like spectators in the classroom and become helpless and

FIG. 4.7 (cont'd)

---

confused when asked to work on a problem.

Response to R. E. - D. (teacher)   R E P L Y T O T H I S C O M M E N T
You make a very interesting point when you say that you work nonstop all day long
when you are the facilitator. Facilitating is hard work! I just had a meeting with one
of the mentors at my high school who has this master plan for facilitating learning
rather than dispensing knowledge. She is convinced it makes teaching so easy because she just sits back and "keeps tabs" on the kids while they do all the work in
the classroom. I have tried some of her methods and quite honestly...it makes me
exhausted by the end of the day!

Facilitating...hard work! - M. B. (teacher)
R E P L Y T O T H I S C O M M E N T
I have to agree with the comment that facilitating is hard work and does take a lot of
energy. It is not something that can (or should) be done every day!

Different paces - L. F. (teacher)   R E P L Y T O T H I S C O M M E N T
I echo your frustration with running a smooth class with kids at different places,
working on more open-ended problems. I know I need to work on better ways to
"shepherd" students through an activity in a way that keeps the class cohesion in
tact. You have some groups that really get into the problem at hand and dive in,
while others zip to the endpoint and announce they're finished. I think if my questioning techniques were better I might be able to get students going on some tan-
gents that might eventually lead them all to a similar endpoint.

Problems - El. H. (teacher)   R E P L Y T O T H I S C O M M E N T
I think that if you do a lot of inquiry based labs you should build up a lot of materials. Is this true or are you constantly buying new stuff? I can usually get enough
time to do labs but like you said it is brain numbing running six different labs at the
same time.

FIG. 4.7 Except from the Version II discussion of the topic

Although the duration of each discussion was roughly constant between the two years, the number of comments increased by almost threefold
(see Figure 4.5). The number of interactions between participants rose cor-
respondingly, with many threads of the discussion going 4 or 5 levels deep,
hierarchically. The average hierarchical depth of a comment was more than
twice that in version I. Finally, new ideas and warrants of ideas rose with
the level of interactivity, as participants felt the need to offer new ideas in
response to their peers, and to justify their comments with insights and experiences from their own teaching.

CONCLUSIONS

Collaborative forums can support a broad range of students as they learn complex topics because every student can receive help and support from peers. Technology-enhanced collaborative forums can extend the repertoire of opportunities for students. Once a collaborative forum has been designed, the forum can be archived and revised. In addition, helpful comments can be reintroduced as seed comments for future discussions. Comparison studies can test designs against each other and identify the most promising approaches. These studies have identified fruitful curriculum design patterns and made these available to authors.

Most designs require trial and refinement to succeed. These studies also spur development of more effective technology-enhanced environments. Technological improvements have improved our forums. For example, many applications enable students to view all the comments made by their peers, without having to open comments individually. Forums often permit participants to include citations or links to comments, and store the links in a database accessible to all participants. Many forums enable participants to search for comments in the forum and find those relevant to their interests. Many applications represent contributions to collaborative forums so newcomers can gain a quick understanding of the overall structure of the discussion and hone in on comments particularly relevant to their current concerns. The multi-media forum kiosk tree structure was particularly effective for this purpose but is not readily implemented using a current browser. In the iterative refinement process, a combination of the technology, the pedagogy, and the classroom opportunities jointly lead to the new designs.

Although forums help students add ideas and encourage students to reflect on their ideas, many questions remain open. For example, we need more guidance on how best to combine collaborative forums with face-to-face discussion, small group work, and other aspects of scientific investigation.

DESIGN PRINCIPLES

The research on collaborative forums suggests several design principles to get partnerships started and to guide refinement:

- Provide students with varied opportunities to engage in scientific discourse, including face-to-face and online forums.
- Enable peers to generate multiple explanations for scientific phenomena. Make sure that all student ideas get articulated.

- Provide representations to encourage critique and review of the range of student ideas. Design prompts to encourage reflection and self-monitoring. These opportunities enable students to practice explaining their opinions or critiquing evidence (Davis, 1998; Davis & Linn, 2000).

- Seek prototypes (Linn & Songer, 1991) and pivotal cases (Linn, in press) to stimulate knowledge integration (Linn & Hsi, 2000).

- Enable students to make predictions and revise ideas regularly. Curriculum design patterns such as gated discussions support this principle.

- Help students to revisit their ideas and reconsider their viewpoints by selecting resources carefully. Select resources that could rekindle the discussion begun in science class.

- Use embedded assessments to refine design patterns and improve design principles.

ACKNOWLEDGMENTS

This material is based upon research supported by the National Science Foundation under Grants 9873180, 9805420, 0087832, and 9720384. Any opinions, findings, and conclusions or recommendations expressed in this publication are those of the authors and do not necessarily reflect the views of the National Science Foundation.

We wish to thank the Computer as Learning Partner, Knowledge Integration Environment, Web-Based Integrated Science Environment, and Science Controversies Online Partnerships and Education collaborators for their helpful and insightful contributions to this research program. Special thanks go to Sherry Hsi, Chris Hoadley, and Doug Clark for contributions on collaborative learning. We also acknowledge the contribution of Marsha Matyas, PhD of the American Physiology Society, whose research contributed to our analysis of professional development discussions. A large body of work conducted by Dr. Maytas, including a professional development program and the development of three WISE projects, will be described in forthcoming publications. Help in the production of this chapter from David Crowell, Scott Hsu, Lisa Safley, and Kathy Lin is much appreciated.

REFERENCES

Agogino, A. M., & Linn, M. C. (1992, May-June). Retaining female engineering students: Will early design experiences help? NSF Directions, 8-9.

Ainsworth, S., & Loizou, A. (2003). The effects of self-explaining when learning with text or diagrams. *Cognitive Science, 27*, 669-681.

Aronson, E. (1978). *The jigsaw classroom.* Beverly Hills, CA: Sage.

Bargh, J. A., & Chartrand, T. L. (1999). The unbearable automaticity of being. *American Psychologist, 54*, 462-479.

Baumgartner, E. (2004). Synergy research and knowledge integration: Customizing activities around stream ecology. In M. C. Linn, E. A. Davis & P. Bell (Eds.), *Internet Environments for Science Education* (pp. 261-288). Mahwah, NJ: Lawrence Erlbaum Associates.

Becker, H. J. (2000). Who's wired and who's not: children's access to and use of computer technology. *The Future of Children, 10*(2), 44-75.

Bell, P. (1997). Using argument representations to make thinking visible for individuals and groups. In R. Hall, N. Miyake & N. Enyedy (Eds.), *Proceedings of CSCL '97: The Second International Conference on Computer Support for Collaborative Learning* (pp. 10–19). Toronto: University of Toronto Press.

Bell, P. (1998). *Designing for students' conceptual change in science using argumentation and classroom debate.* Unpublished doctoral dissertation, University of California, Berkeley, CA.

Bell, P., & Linn, M. C. (2000). Scientific arguments as learning artifacts: Designing for learning from the Web with KIE. *International Journal of Science Education, 22,* 797-817.

Bell, P., & Linn, M. C. (2002). Beliefs about science: How does science instruction contribute? In B. K. Hofer & P. R. Pintrich (Eds.), *Personal epistemology: The psychology of beliefs about knowledge and knowing* (pp. 321-346). Mahwah, NJ: Lawrence Erlbaum Associates.

Bielaczyc, K., Pirolli, P. L., & Brown, A. L. (1995). Training in self-explanation and self-regulation strategies: Investigating the effects of knowledge acquisition activities on problem solving. *Cognition and Instruction, 13*, 221-252.

Bowen, C. W. (2000). A quantitative literature review of cooperative learning effects on high school and college chemistry achievement. *Journal of Chemical Education, 77*, 116-119.

Brown, A. L., & Campione, J. C. (1994). Guided discovery in a community of learners. In K. McGilly (Ed.), *Classroom lessons: Integrating cognitive theory and classroom practice* (pp. 229-270). Cambridge, MA: MIT Press/Bradford Books.

Bruckman, A. (1997). *MOOSE crossing: Construction, community, and learning in a networked virtual world for kids.* Unpublished doctoral dissertation, Massachusetts Institute of Technology, MA.

Bruckman, A. (2000). Situated support for learning: Storm's weekend with Rachael. *Journal of the Learning Sciences, 9*, 329-372.

Burbules, N. C., & Linn, M. C. (1991). Science education and the philosophy of science: Congruence or contradiction? *International Journal of Science Education, 13*, 227–241.

Chi, M. T. H., Bassok, M., Lewis, M. W., Reimann, P., & Glaser, R. (1989). Self-explanations: How students study and use examples in learning to solve problems. *Cognitive Science, 13*, 145–182.

Chi, M. T. H., deLeeuw, N., Chiu, M. H., & LaVancer, C. (1994). Eliciting self-explanations improves understanding. *Cognitive Science, 18*, 439-477.

Clancy, M., Titterton, N., Ryan, C., Slotta, J., & Linn, M. C. (2003). *New roles for students, instructors, and computers in a lab-based introductory programming course.* Paper presented at the Proceedings of the SIGCSE, Reno, NV.

Clark, D. (2000). Scaffolding knowledge integration through curricular depth. Unpublished doctoral dissertation, University of California, Berkeley, CA.

Clark, D. B., & Jorde, D. (in press). Re-explanation of experiential ideas through targeted computer visualizations. *Journal of Research in Science Teaching.*

Cognition and Technology Group at Vanderbilt. (1997). *The Jasper Project: Lessons in curriculum, instruction, assessment, and professional development.* Mahwah, NJ: Lawrence Erlbaum Associates.

Cohen, E. G. (1982). Expectation states and interracial interaction in school settings. *American Review of Sociology, 8*, 209-235.

Cohen, E. G. (1994). Restructuring the classroom: Conditions for productive small groups. *Review of Educational Research, 64*, 1-35.

Cuthbert, A. (2002). *Learning science through the design of passive solar dwellings: Can specialization contribute to improved learning outcomes and design methods.* Unpublished Doctoral Dissertation, University of California, Berkeley.

Cuthbert, A. J., Clark, D. B. & Linn, M. C. (2002). WISE learning communities: Design considerations. In K.A. Renninger & W. Shumar (Eds.), *Building virtual communities: Learning and change in cyberspace* (pp. 215-246). Cambridge, UK: Cambridge University Press.

Davis, E. A. (1998). *Scaffolding students' reflection for science learning.* Unpublished doctoral dissertation, University of California, Berkeley, CA.

Davis, E. A. (2003a). Prompting middle school science students for productive reflection: Generic and directed prompts. *The Journal of the Learning Sciences, 12*, 91-142.

Davis, E. A. (2003b). Knowledge integration in science teaching: Analyzing teachers' knowledge development. *Research in Science Education, 34*, 21-53.

Davis, E. A. (2004). Creating critique projects. In M. C. Linn, E. A. Davis & P. Bell (Eds.), *Internet Environments for Science Education* (pp. 89-114). Mahwah, NJ: Lawrence Erlbaum Associates.

Davis, E. A., & Linn, M. C. (2000). Scaffolding students' knowledge integration: Prompts for reflection in KIE. *International Journal of Science Education, 22*, 819-837.

Driver, R., Leach, J., Miller, R., & Scott, P. (1965). *Young people's images of science.* Buckingham, UK: Open University Press.

Duschl, R. A., & Osborne, J. (2002). Supporting and promoting argumentation discourse in science education. *Studies in Science Education, 39*, 39-72.

Eylon, B. S., & Linn, M. C. (1988). Learning and instruction: An examination of four research perspectives in science education. *Review of Educational Research, 58*, 251-301.

Gordin, D. N., Polman, J. L., & Pea, R. D. (1994). The climate visualizer: Sense-making through scientific visualization. *Journal of Science Education and Technology, 3*, 203-226.

Hatano, G., & Inagaki, K. (Eds.). (1991). *Sharing cognition through collective comprehension activity.* Washington, DC: American Psychological Association.

Hegarty, M., Quilici, J., Narayanan, N. H., Holmquist, S., & Moreno, R. (1999). Multimedia instruction: Lessons from evaluation of a theory-based design. *Journal of Educational Multimedia and Hypermedia, 8*, 119-150.

Hoadley, C. (1999). *Scaffolding scientific discussion using socially relevant representations in networked multimedia.* Unpublished doctoral dissertation, University of California, Berkeley, CA.

Hoadley, C. (2004). Fostering productive collaboration offline and online: learning from each other. In M. C. Linn, E. A. Davis & P. Bell (Eds.), *Internet environments for science education* (pp. 145-174). Mahwah, NJ: Lawrence Erlbaum Associates.

Hoadley, C. M., & Linn, M. C. (2000). Teaching science through online peer discussions: SpeakEasy in the knowledge integration environment. *International Journal of Science Education, 22*, 839-857.

Hsi, S. (1997). *Facilitating knowledge integration in science through electronic discussion: The Multimedia Forum Kiosk.* Unpublished doctoral dissertation, University of California, Berkeley, CA.

Hunter, B. (1990). Computer-mediated communications support for teacher collaborations: Researching new contexts for both teaching and learning. *Educational Technology, 30*(10), 46-49.

Johnson, D. W., & Johnson, R. T. (1999). Making cooperative learning work. *Theory into Practice, 38*, 67-73.

Johnson, D. W., Johnson, R. T., & Smith, K. A. (1998). Cooperative learning returns to college: What evidence is there that it works? *Change, 30*, 26-35.

Keller, E. F. (1993). *Gender and science.* San Francisco: Freeman.

Krajcik, J., Blumenfeld, P., Marx, R., & Soloway, E. (1999). Instructional, curricular, and technological supports for inquiry in science classrooms. In J. Minstrell & E. V. Zee (Eds.), *Inquiry into inquiry: Science learning and teaching* (pp. 283-315). Washington, DC: AAAS Press.

Kuhn, D. (1989). Children and adults as intuitive scientists. *Psychological Review, 96*(4), 674-689.

Kuhn, D. (1992). Thinking as argument. *Harvard Educational Review, 62*, 155-178.

Kuhn, D. (1993). Science as argument: Implications for teaching and learning scientific thinking. *Science Education, 77*, 319-337.

Lajoie, S. P., & Lesgold, A. M. (1992). Dynamic assessment of proficiency for solving procedural knowledge tasks. *Educational Psychologist, 27*, 365-384.

Lemke, J. L. (1990). *Talking science: Language, learning, and values.* Norwood, N.J.: Ablex.

Linn, M. C. (1980). Teaching children to control variables: Some investigations using free choice experiences. In S. Modgil & C. Modgil (Eds.), *Toward a theory of psychological development within the Piagetian framework* (pp. 673-697). Windsor, UK: National Foundation for Educational Research.

Linn, M. C. (1995). Designing computer learning environments for engineering and computer science: The scaffolded knowledge integration framework. *Journal of Science Education and Technology 4*, 103-126.

Linn, M. C. (2000). Controversy, the Internet, and deformed frogs: making science accessible. In *Who will do the science of the future? A symposium on careers of women in science* (pp. 16-27). Washington, D.C.: National Academy Press.

Linn, M. C. (in press). WISE design for lifelong learning-Pivotal Cases. In P. Gärdenfors & P. Johannsson (Eds.), *Cognition, Education and Communication Technology.* Mahwah, NJ: Lawrence Erlbaum Associates.

Linn, M. C. & Burbules, N. C. (1993). Construction of knowledge and group learning. In K. Tobin (Ed.), *The practice of constructivism in science education* (pp. 91-119). Washington, D. C: American Association for the Advancement of Science (AAAS).

Linn, M. C., & Clancy, M. J. (1992). The case for case studies of programming problems. *Communications of the ACM, 35*(3), 121-132.

Linn, M. C., Clark, D. B. & Slotta, J. D. (2003). WISE design for knowledge integration. *Science Education, 87*, 517-538.

Linn, M. C., Davis, E. A., & Bell, P. (Eds.). (2004). *Internet Environments for Science Education.* Mahwah, NJ: Lawrence Erlbaum Associates.

Linn, M. C., & Hsi, S. (2000). *Computers, teachers, peers: science learning partners.* Mahwah, NJ: Lawrence Erlbaum Associates.

Linn, M. C., Shear, L., Bell, P., & Slotta, J. D. (1999). Organizing principles for science education partnerships: Case studies of students' learning about 'rats in space' and 'deformed frogs'. *Educational Technology Research and Development, 47*, 61-85.

Linn, M. C., & Songer, N. B. (1991). Cognitive and conceptual change in adolescence. *American Journal of Education, 99*, 379-417.

Longino, H. (1994). The fate of knowledge in social theories of science. In F. F. Schmitt (Ed.), *Socializing epistemology: The social dimensions of knowledge* (pp. 135-158). Lanham, MD: Rowan Littlefield.

Minstrell, J., & Van Zee, E. (Eds.). (2000). *Teaching in the inquiry-based science classroom.* Washington, DC: American Association for the Advancement of Science.

Novak, J. D. (1990). Concept mapping: A useful tool for science education. *Journal of Research in Science Teaching, 27*, 937-949.

Novak, J. D., Gowin, D. B., & Johannsen, G. T. (1983). The use of concept mapping with junior high school science students. *Science Education, 67*, 625-645.

Papert, S. (1980). *Mindstorms: Children, computers, and powerful ideas.* New York: Basic Books.

Resnick, M. (1996). Beyond the centralized mindset. *The Journal of the Learning Sciences, 5*, 1-22.

Resnick, M. (2001). Closing the fluency gap. *Communications of the ACM, 44*, 3.

Roschelle, J. (1992). Learning by collaborating: Convergent conceptual change. *Journal of Learning Sciences, 2*, 235-276.

Sadker, M., & Sadker, D. (1994). *Failing at fairness: How America's schools cheat girls.* New York: Maxwell Macmillan International.

Scardamalia, M., & Bereiter, C. (1992). An architecture for collaborative knowledge building. In E. De Corte, M. C. Linn, H. Mandl, & L. Verschaffel (Eds.), *Computer-based learning environments and problem solving* (pp. 41-46). Berlin: Springer-Verlag.

Scardamalia, M., & Bereiter, C. (1993). Technologies for knowledge-building discourse. *Communications of the ACM, 36*(5), 37-41.

Scardamalia, M., Bereiter, C., Hewitt, J., & Webb, J. (1996). Constructive learning from texts in biology. In K.M. Fischer, & M. Kirby (Eds.), *Relations and biology learning: The acquisition and use of knowledge structures in biology* (pp. 44-64). Berlin: Springer-Verlag.

Seethaler, S., & Linn, M. C. (2004). Genetically modified food in perspective: An inquiry-based curriculum to help middle school students make sense of tradeoffs. *International Journal of Science Education, 26*, 1765-1785.

Slavin, R. E. (1983). When does cooperative learning increase student achievement? *Psychological Bulletin, 94*, 429-445.

Slotta, J. D. (2004). WISE science teaching. In M. C. Linn, E. A. Davis &
    P. Bell (Eds.), *Internet environments for science education* (pp.
    203-232). Mahwah, NJ: Lawrence Erlbaum Associates.
Songer, N. (1996). Exploring learning opportunities in coordinated net-
    work-enhanced classrooms - A case of kids as global scientists.
    Journal of the Learning Sciences, 5, 297-327.
Springer, L., Stanne, M. E., & Donovan, S. S. (1999). Effects of small-
    group learning on undergraduates in science, mathematics, engi-
    neering, and technology: A meta-analysis. *Review of Educational
    Research, 69*, 21-51.
Steele, C. (1997). A threat in the air: How stereotypes shape intellectual
    identity and performance. *American Psychologist, 52*, 613-629.
Stigler, J. W., & Hiebert, J. (1999). *The teaching gap: Best ideas from the
    world's teachers for improving education in the classroom.* New
    York: The Free Press.
Thagard, P. (1994). Mind, society, and the growth of knowledge. *Philoso-
    phy of Science, 61*, 629-645.
Toulmin, S. (1958). *The uses of argument/* Cambridge, UK: Cambridge
    University Press.
Webb, N. M. (1995). Constructive activity and learning in collaborative
    small groups. *Journal of Educational Psychology, 87*, 406-423.
Webb, N. M., & Farivar, S. (1994). Promoting helping behavior in coopera-
    tive small groups in middle school mathematics. *American Educa-
    tional Research Journal, 31*, 369-395.
Webb, N. M., & Palinscar, A. S. (1996). Group processes in the classroom.
    In. D. C. Berliner & R. C. Calfee (Eds.), *Handbook of educational
    psychology* (pp. 841-873). New York: Macmillan.

Chapter 5

Virtual Reflection: What Teachers Say (and Don't Say) Online About Their Practice

Susan M. Williams
University of Texas at Austin

Gwendolyn Kelly
University of Idaho

Current perspectives on educational reform are based on the premise that the knowledge students need is growing and evolving so rapidly that it is no longer practical for them to memorize a fixed set of facts and skills. Instead, students must acquire flexible knowledge that they can adapt and use as tools for solving a wide range of problems.

These changes in what students are expected to know pose huge challenges for teachers and the school communities in which they work. Assumptions about teaching and learning are dramatically different now compared to the days in which today's teachers were students in elementary or secondary schools or studying teaching in undergraduate teacher education programs. As a result, they may have little understanding of what these new expectations imply about teaching and learning in specific grade levels or content areas. To become successful, teachers, like their students, must acquire more flexible knowledge (Franke, Carpenter, Fennema, Anseli, & Beherend, 1998). Most will need to undergo fundamental changes in their beliefs about the content being learned and about the nature of teaching and learning.

Similarly, changes in what teachers need to know pose huge challenges for teacher education. Recent discussions of in-service teacher education have called for ongoing experiences that take part in the context of teachers' own practice (Cochran-Smith & Lytle, 1999; Franke et al., 1998). These experiences are expected to take the place of the often-maligned in-service workshop and lead to learning that is flexible, self-sustaining, and generative (Franke et al., 1998; Zech, Gause-Vega, Bray, Secules, & Goldman, 2000).

The call for situated teacher learning occurs at the same time that the Internet and the World Wide Web are making possible numerous opportunities for online professional development (Goldman, 2001). Little is known about how teachers make use of these opportunities and the effect they have on teachers' practice. This chapter presents an example of extending the impact of traditional professional development through the use of ongoing computer conferencing to promote teachers' reflection on their practice.

OVERVIEW

This chapter presents a model of professional development we call anchored collaborative inquiry (ACI). The model combines an inservice workshop followed by the simultaneous implementation of a specific standards-based reform in the classrooms of all the participating teachers. The implementation is supported by an ongoing online discussion facilitated by the workshop faculty.

We set the stage for our examination of online teacher discussions by describing the anchored instruction reform implemented by the teachers and the research on student learning that informed its development. Next we describe previous work in teacher professional development by members of the Cognition and Technology Group at Vanderbilt (CTGV) who developed the anchored instruction approach. This work serves as the starting point for our ACI model. We then introduce the ACI model through an example enactment and describe teachers' online reflections as they implement the reform. We conclude with a discussion of the types of preparation that are necessary to capitalize on the promise of online communities to support inservice teacher learning.

Anchored Instruction

Anchored instruction is an approach to instruction developed over the last decade by the CTGV (Bransford, Sherwood, Hasselbring, Kinzer, & Williams, 1992; CTGV, 1999). Throughout its development, the enduring idea behind anchored instruction has been that sustained exploration of realistic, meaningful problems (anchors) leads to learning that is highly valued and likely to be used when needed. Although anchored instruction is discussed in detail elsewhere (cf. CTGV, 1997, 1999), we review several key points here.

Knowledge as Tools

Anchored instruction presents students with complex problems in realistic settings. Before they can solve these problems, students must assemble an impressive array of knowledge and skills, including information about the problem situation, an understanding of important math and science concepts, a solution plan, and the ability to reflect on their own problem solving and level of understanding. By situating learning in the context of meaningful problems, anchored instruction helps students understand the significance of the knowledge and skills they encounter and see how facts and formulas can serve as tools to solve important problems.

Connections With Previous Experience

Students' learning is enhanced when they connect the current task with relevant aspects of their previous experiences. This is a basic tenet of "constructivist" accounts of learning (Cobb, 1994; Piaget, 1952; Vygotsky, 1978). Unfortunately, in today's schools, where teachers and students move frequently and class sizes are large, it is difficult for teachers to be knowledgeable about the previous experience of each student.

As novices, students may fail to see the relationship between a new situation and ones they experienced previously, and teachers are unable to help them make those connections unless they know about them. Anchored instruction is designed to create academically relevant environments that teachers and students can explore collaboratively and refer back to over the course of their time together. These shared contexts can help teachers know which examples to use to help students understand new concepts and vocabulary terms (Johnson, 1987; Sherwood, Kinzer, Bransford, & Franks, 1987).

Opportunities for Meaningful Collaboration

A typical anchored instruction problem has many subtasks with numerous methods for carrying out and evaluating each one. The complexity of these problems makes it valuable for students to work in groups and pool their insights and expertise (Barron, 1991; Vye, Goldman, Voss, Hmelo, and Williams, 1997). Problems that are too complex to be solved by one student can be solved by a group or decomposed into parts with each part solved by an individual. When these parts are reassembled, students must describe and justify their solutions. When the assembled parts are evaluated as a whole, they may not work well together and students will have additional opportunities to collaborate as they negotiate a final solution.

The anchored instruction approach has been used in many diverse content areas including literacy, clinical psychology, and diabetes education. Perhaps the most widely known application is *The Adventures of Jasper Woodbury,* a series of 12 video anchors that support students' learning in problem solving and mathematics (CTGV, 1997). One of the *Jasper* adventures serves as the anchor for the professional development project described in this chapter. We discuss the specifics of the *Jasper* series and this adventure in a later section.

Professional Development and Anchored Instruction

Over the years the scale of anchored instruction research has changed from laboratory experiments to proof-of-concept classrooms to systemwide implementation. As the project changed, so did the understanding of what was necessary to support teaching and learning. At each level, issues were raised that had previously been invisible and research expanded into those areas (CTGV, 1999). In addition to research on student learning, the growing scale of anchored instruction implementations also led to research and collaboration with teachers. In the next paragraphs, we outline the evolution of professional development in anchored instruction using the *Jasper* materials as an example.

Professional development for anchored instruction was initially embodied in teaching materials that presented complex problems in a comprehensive way. The goal was to have the materials themselves "carry" or represent the kinds of classroom interactions that researchers were seeking (Zech et al., 2000). To ensure the completeness of the materials, the development team for each adventure included pedagogical and content-area experts. There was also an advisory board that reviewed each script for accuracy in content as well as balance in issues related to gender, race, and culture. The development process included constant interactions with practicing teachers. As draft versions of each of the adventures were completed, these practicing teachers piloted the materials in their classroom in collaboration with researchers from the CTGV. These initial pilots were design experiments (Brown, 1992), iterative cycles of research and revision that led to final versions of the adventures as well as initial data on the effectiveness of anchored instruction (CTGV, 1997; Van Haneghan et al., 1992).

As the anchored instruction approach evolved, more *Jasper* adventures were developed and eventually published (CTGV, 1997). As part of this effort, the wisdom of practice developed by the pilot teachers and the goals of the research team were codified into a set of teaching videos and manuals that accompanied the adventure videos. These teaching tools provided information about the mathematics, science concepts and vocabulary that were part of each adventure as well as alerts concerning typical student "misconceptions" about the concepts and contexts. Because the videos were distributed on laserdiscs (a new medium at the time) and included computer software, training in the use of technology also became an important part of what teachers needed to know. Researchers and the publisher's staff held frequent in-service workshops to help teachers learn how to use the *Jasper* materials.

These early professional development workshops were consistent with most traditional professional development: Teachers saw the university-based research group as the source for formal knowledge and theory. This included knowledge about the technology, about learning, and about the content area—mathematical problem solving. However, because having middle school students solve complex problems like the *Jasper* problems was unfamiliar to teachers, they also looked to the research group as the source of knowledge about pedagogy. Although teachers learned that each of their students should be allowed to construct his or her own solution to the *Jasper* problems, they assumed that knowledge of how to teach *Jasper* would be transmitted to them and they would attempt to reproduce it exactly as observed in the workshop and teaching video. This understanding of the relationship between knowledge and practice is consistent with what Cochran-Smith and Lytle (1999) called knowledge-for-practice—teachers assume that formal knowledge is generated by others and transmitted to them to be replicated as closely as possible.

Collaborative Materials Development

In 1993, anchored instruction was combined with two other reforms, Fostering Communities of Learners (Brown & Campione, 1994, 1996) and Computer-Supported Intentional Learning Environments (Scardamalia, Bereiter, & Lamon, 1994) to form the Schools for Thought (SFT) project. Although having different foci, each of these reforms shared underlying principles related to student-centered instruction and the active engagement of students in their own learning. The goal of SFT was to work with school systems to restructure the entire school day for grades K–8 (CTGV, 1997; Lamon et al., 1996; Secules, Cottom, Bray, Miller, & CTGV, 1997). The expansion of anchored instruction to new grades and content areas and its combination with the other reforms resulted in the need for additional curriculum units. As part of this change, professional development moved into the knowledge-in-practice mode (Cochran-Smith & Lytle, 1998; Zech et al., 2000) in which researchers collaborated with participating teachers to develop and implement curriculum units in all content areas embodying the principles and procedures of the SFT reforms.

The SFT project represented what McLaughlin, Mitra, and Stokes (2000) called theory-based change, an attempt to put into practice ideas and principles based on theories of cognition and learning. For theory-based change to succeed, teachers must know and understand the theory (first principles) of the reform.

For teachers, the movement of a theory-based reform to the classroom is a difficult process of constructing new teaching knowledge. For the SFT reformers, it became apparent that the focus on codevelopment of curricular materials had not led to an understanding of the underlying principles of SFT (Zech et al., 2000). One of the founders of SFT noted that

> If we developed a set of Schools for Thought curriculum units
> that embodied the deep principles, had assessment built in, formative assessment and pre-, post- kinds of assessment, and work
> with teachers so that they understood those units, and developed

> ways to do those units that reflected trying to go for understand-
> ing that was what we needed to do and that would be sufficient
> for teachers to ultimately understand the principles (McLaughlin
> et al, 2000; For other discussions of curricular materials in
> teacher learning, see Ball & Cohen, 1996; Singer, Marx, Kra-
> jcik, and Chambers, 2000).

Instead of first principles, teachers saw SFT as a set of particular procedures, (e.g., jigsaw, reciprocal teaching, benchmark lessons, etc.). When
necessary, each teacher made adjustments to these procedures based on his
or her own beliefs and established practice, the needs of his or her students,
and the constraints of his or her classroom context. The hybrid versions of
SFT that they constructed sometimes were exemplary; however, often they
were "lethal mutations," versions that unintentionally violated the basic
principles of anchored instruction and the other reforms (McLaughlin et al,
2000).

CONTENT-BASED COLLABORATIVE INQUIRY

Based on the initial SFT experience, researchers revamped their approach to
professional development by engaging teachers in a process of collaborative
inquiry that was grounded in the study of what it means to learn and understand a specific content area. This approach is discussed in detail elsewhere
(Zech et al., 2000). We review several important features here.

Inquiry

The central goal of the collaborative inquiry approach is to engage teachers
in examining their thinking and the thinking of their students as well as the
relationship between their actions and their students' responses. This type
of inquiry is believed to lead to a better understanding of content knowledge, pedagogical content knowledge, and general pedagogical knowledge
(Shulman, 1986; Zech et al., 2000). It is also believed to lead to principled,
flexible change and continued learning (Franke et al., 1998). It bears a family resemblance to action-research, knowledge-of-practice (Cochran-Smith
& Lytle, 1999), practical inquiry (Richardson, 1994), and generative change
(Franke et al., 1998).

Content

It is widely believed that teachers' beliefs, prior experience, and knowledge
play an important role in what they learn (Ball, 1996). For teachers to im-

plement a curriculum involving complex problem solving or mathematical or scientific inquiry, they often need to better understand the nature of inquiry themselves. Helping teachers change their own beliefs about what it means to learn, understand, or do mathematics, science, or other content seems to be an important aspect of impacting students' thinking (Wilson & Berne, 1999). Teachers who participate in professional development experiences designed to enhance their inquiry skills and subject-matter expertise report that they try to create similar learning experiences for their students, were able to model thinking for their students, and evaluate student responses (Kennedy, 1998; Wineburg & Grossman, 1998). SFT teachers initially believed that math is about procedures and rules and that students' understanding can be measured by the extent to which they execute procedures correctly. By having teachers solve problems that require more than just getting the right answer and reflect on their problem-solving process, the SFT professional development team helped teachers deepen their understanding of mathematics and experience new models of teaching and learning (Davies & Zech, 1999).

Collaboration

Collaborative inquiry takes place in a community of peers who are wrestling with similar challenges (Ball, 1996; Franke et al., 1998; McLaughlin et al, 2000; Wilson & Berne, 1999). The knowledge that is constructed in these communities is not fragmented and personal. It involves systematic collection and analysis of data and seeks to account for the experiences and contexts of others. In the case of SFT, for each content area the inquiry community includes teachers at multiple grade levels, representing multiple schools implementing SFT, school principals, and the SFT researchers. Inquiry is ongoing and takes place in multiple contexts: In their classrooms teachers work with the facilitator to develop questions related to student understanding and to collect and analyze related evidence. During in-service meetings teachers discuss their own classroom-based inquiry with teachers from other grade levels and schools to get multiple perspectives on their questions. In school-based meetings, SFT teachers and others not part of the SFT effort meet to investigate questions related to student understanding. The multiple contexts lead to the development and sustainability of communities of inquiry.

Summary

The experiences of SFT researchers and teachers in implementing theory-based change illustrate that implementing a reform involves both assimilation and construction processes as teachers elaborate and adapt what they learn about the reform based on their beliefs and the constraints of their

practice. If teachers focus only on the activity structures and do not understand the relationship of these structures to the first principles of the reform,
they may adapt the activities in ways inconsistent with the reform. Therefore, implementing such reforms requires an ongoing collaboration between
reformers and teachers if the implementations are to be consistent with reformers' goals. Davies and Zech (1999) described this relationship as a
delicate balance between enacting the reforms goals for change and the
need for teachers to be able to construct and evaluate their own versions of
the reform.

In inquiry-based approaches to professional development, teachers
intentionally investigate the formal knowledge generated by others in their
own classrooms and discuss their investigations with colleagues. The availability of resources such as *Jasper* does not lead to learning about anchored
instruction or SFT without the opportunity for implementation and reflective analysis of that implementation including both self-analysis and feedback from others.

ANCHORED COLLABORATIVE INQUIRY MODEL

The essential element of the ACI model is collaborative inquiry in the context of a shared problem. Just as students using the *Jasper* adventures construct and compare their solutions to a *Jasper* dilemma, the teachers in our
in-service groups take multiple perspectives on the problem of implementing the *Jasper* curriculum in their classrooms. By engaging in a dialog with
peers implementing the same reform at the same time, teachers attempt to
make sense of what occurs during the implementation and to enhance their
understanding of how their students learn to solve complex problems. In
this model professional development includes (a) face-to-face meetings to
learn about a reform and collaboratively plan for implementation, (b) individual implementation in each teacher's classroom, and (c) shared reflection via an online conferencing system.

ACI is a hybrid approach combining elements of the traditional face-to-
face in-service workshop and electronic discussions. The traditional workshop gets the learning process off to a rapid start because face-to-face oral
discussions allow a more rapid exchange of information among group
members than written online discussion. In addition, face-to-face conversations set a more informal spontaneous tone that can lead to more open dialog.

Previous research on workshops that take place completely online indicates that a sense of community forms slowly and face-to-face meetings can
be helpful in overcoming a sense of isolation (Goldman, 2001; Williams,
Goldman, Gabella, Kinzer, and Risko, 1999). Face-to-face meetings can
also contribute to a sense of trust among participants essential for those

engaging in challenging, long-term tasks. Participants without a sense of trust are more likely to be guarded in their responses and less likely to engage in a critical examination of their assumptions. On the other hand, participants who do know other participants are more likely to be interested in what their colleagues have to say and to feel an obligation to continue the discussion.

Implementation

Our goal in the ACI model is to enhance the traditional in-service workshop in ways that are consistent with the emerging literature on teacher learning, including the work being done by the CTGV on professional development and anchored instruction. The most effective model is thought to involve follow-up activities, long-term support including coaching in teachers' classrooms, and ongoing interactions with colleagues (Ball, 1996; Putnam & Borko, 1997). This type of professional development is time and resource intensive and is expensive and difficult to implement on a large scale. In testing the ACI model we evaluate the effectiveness of online coaching and interactions for teacher learning. In the following paragraphs, we highlight the features of an implementation of our ACI model, the online data for which are discussed later in this chapter.

The Jasper Reform

The *Adventures of Jasper Woodbury* consists of 12 videodisc-based adventures that focus on mathematical problem finding and problem solving for students in Grade 5 and up. Each adventure provides opportunities for problem solving, reasoning, communication, and making connections to other areas such as science, social studies, literature, and history.

Depending on a teacher's beliefs about teaching and learning, he or she can adapt these materials to create a variety of learning environments. In this chapter, we use the term *Jasper* reform to refer to the use of the *Jasper* adventures in ways that help students learn to construct and solve problems, understand important content, synthesize information, and express themselves proficiently.

In the *Jasper* adventure "Rescue at Boone's Meadow" (RBM), Jasper's friend, Larry, has just taught another friend, Emily, to fly an ultralight airplane. Jasper and his friends discuss his upcoming camping trip to Boone's Meadow. On the trip Jasper finds a badly wounded eagle that needs emergency care. The challenge is for students to determine the fastest way to rescue the eagle and how long that will take. With several routes, two modes of transportation, two speeds, two pilots, fuel, payload, and landing area considerations, RBM has several feasible rescue methods that students must construct and evaluate.

Participants

Twenty-two teachers participated in this implementation. All were practicing teachers in Grades 2 through 8 from school districts in a rural western state. Their classroom settings included a one-room school in a wilderness area serving Grades preschool through 8, a school for Native Americans located on a reservation, and more typical schools in small towns and cities. Although most taught all subjects to an intact class of elementary students, several were responsible for teaching multiple sections of math to middle school students. Participants ranged in experience from 1 year to veteran teachers nearing retirement.

Facilitators

The implementation was led by three facilitators each contributing different kinds of expertise: The first is a university professor in mathematics education with extensive experience in using technology to support teacher and student learning. The second is a university-based researcher interested in the impact of reform-oriented curricula on teachers' and students' understanding. This facilitator was a member of the design team for the *Jasper* adventures with experience in computer programming and training novice computer users. The third facilitator is a classroom teacher who has worked with university researchers on the design and implementation of several reform-oriented curricula, including the *Jasper* series. These facilitators collaborated on the design and implementation of the workshop and moderated the online discussion.

Face-to-Face Workshop

Our implementation of the ACI model began with a 5-day workshop held on a university campus. There were four main goals for the workshop: developing a shared understanding of the *Jasper* curriculum and the theoretical concepts underlying its design, becoming familiar with the technology used for the curriculum and the online conference, collaborating on the development of lesson plans for classroom implementation, and the development of a sense of community among the facilitators and participants.

Teachers were given multiple opportunities to become familiar with the *Jasper* materials and how they might be used. First they assumed the role of students and worked in groups to construct solutions to the *Jasper* problems. Next they brainstormed how they might teach with these materials. They then had the opportunity to view videos of experienced teachers using *Jasper* in their classrooms. Finally, they collaborated with one of the workshop facilitators to teach *Jasper* to a group of children attending a day camp at the university. Rather than just observing, teachers worked with small groups of children so that they could better assess the difficulties that children had during problem solving. After each of these experiences, teachers had lengthy discussions about the relationship between the instructional approach and student understanding.

During the workshop, teachers learned to use the technology required to implement *Jasper* and to participate in the online conference. This included computer-controlled videodisc players and bar code readers that they used daily as part of problem solving. It also included the Internet and the Web-based conferencing software they used daily to post their homework and to collaboratively develop lesson plans. Although all teachers had access at home or school to computers connected to the Internet, they varied widely with respect to their experience. The workshop preparation enabled everyone to get online once they reached home with minimal difficulty.

As part of their homework assignments during the workshop, teachers developed detailed plans for implementing the *Jasper* curriculum in their own classroom in the fall. In addition to plans for activities, teachers were encouraged to focus on how they would assess students' performance during the implementation. With this dual focus on activities and assessments, we hoped to help teachers see connections between their activities and student thinking and learning.

In most cases teachers developed individual plans because they taught different grades or types of students and would be implementing the unit alone; however, planning was not a solitary activity, as teachers were encouraged to comment on each other's plans online and face to face. This planning included a day-by-day outline of activities and assessments, ideas for grouping students, locating videodisc players, and scheduling. In the workshop and online there was much discussion about how this curriculum unit would fit within the school and state-mandated curricula, and teachers worked out elaborate plans for integrating science and literature studies. Lively discussions ensued about how the curriculum might support or interfere with standardized testing performance.

Efforts to establish a sense of community included the development of norms of interaction both online and face to face. Facilitators modeled ways of interacting online including encouraging participants to assist one another with problems. Teachers were encouraged to get to know more about the teaching lives of others through activities in the workshop and after class. Many of the teachers were from out of town and lived on campus or in local hotels while attending the workshop. Social activities were scheduled and teachers often spent time together after class preparing their assignments for the next day.

Individual Implementations

Teachers were asked to teach the same *Jasper* unit in their classrooms during September or October. They could implement the unit in any way they chose. The goal of this simultaneous implementation was to create an anchor for in-depth reflection. Having teachers compare their experiences to those of others teaching students at different grade levels helps them to gain a more global, long-term understanding of student learning (Zech et al., 2000). Having them teach the same materials allowed meaningful comparisons and promoted deeper understanding. Having everyone teaching the unit and interacting online at the same time made it more likely that teachers would get quick responses to their questions from their colleagues, thereby reducing the feeling of isolation that is often a part of both teaching and online learning.

Online Discussion

Between the end of the workshop and the completion of their individual implementations, teachers were asked to post a minimum of five messages to the conference. These included a revised lesson plan with any last-minute changes they made due to the number and type of students in this year's class, any changes to their assessment plans, a reflection following implementation of the unit, and at least two responses to other teachers' postings. The facilitators monitored the conference closely to provide rapid replies to requests for assistance and help maintain the relationships and sense of community that were established at the workshop.

The discussion could be accessed using any Web browser software. It supported asynchronous interaction with notes grouped into threads and threads into various topics of discussion. It was password protected so that teachers would feel more comfortable in sharing negative as well as positive aspects of their implementations.

Rewards for Participation

Participants in the workshop were chosen from a pool of applicants who had Internet access and were willing to attend the workshop, implement the curriculum, and participate in the online discussion. In addition to travel and living expenses for the workshop, they received one continuing education credit for participating in the workshop and another credit for implementing the curriculum. They also received teacher and student materials for one *Jasper* adventure and, after they had completed the minimum online participation, computer software for their classroom.

Teachers' Online Discussion

The results presented here are based on notes posted by teachers and facilitators during the face-to-face workshop and the subsequent implementation phase. Our goal in this analysis is to characterize what teachers reveal about their practice through these postings. We begin by contrasting the contents of the workshop and implementation notes. Then we focus on the interaction among the teachers and the facilitators.

Lesson Plans

After the first day of the workshop, teachers were asked to create and post plans for an interdisciplinary *Jasper* unit to be implemented in September and October of the upcoming year. Our goal in this assignment was to provide practice using the online system and at the same time create a shared database of plans that could be critiqued and revised as teachers became more familiar with the goals of the *Jasper* reform. Lesson plans were expected to include adaptations necessary for working with different grades and ability levels and at least one idea for using RBM in their classroom. Although notes were often much longer, the following entry is representative of the content of the lesson plans posted:

> Rescue at Boone's Meadow offers a nice opportunity to blend a literature unit on survival, with a good quality mathematics project. Some of the literature books that I use with this unit are *Hatchet, My Side of the Mountain, Julie of the Wolves, and Island of the Blue Dolphins*. I divide the class into literature groups and assign one book to each group. The students read the books, do response activities and create a culminating project. The same groups would also work on RBM. This would add some math and problem solving into a unit usually just based on literature. Writing up the group's solution from either the point of view of Emily or Jasper would be a nice way to wrap up the unit.
> —Grace

Lesson planning was abstract and focused primarily on activities relating to the theme of the *Jasper* adventure. Teachers did not mention specifics of their classroom context when planning lessons. Only 2 out of the 22 teachers gave their students' grade level as a consideration for the activities that were planned. Teachers rarely specified adjustments they would make for the ability of students or the length of their class periods. Teachers also frequently failed to mention details of the RBM unit or identify specific learning goals. This was especially true for the mathematical content of the lesson.

Although they were specifically asked to do so, teachers may have failed to mention specifics such as classroom contexts because they were more engaged in planning the interdisciplinary aspects of the lesson. They may have felt it was too time consuming to type these things in, especially for an audience that they would see the next day:

> I'm getting tired of typing this so if you are interested see the
> hard copy that was sent home with you. —Tom

In their role as students in the workshop, teachers may have seen this
type of detailed planning as just another school task they were required to
complete that served no real purpose:

> Dear Debra, What a great idea! Do you plan on doing this lesson
> soon or ever? —Connie

Whatever the reason for these omissions, the postings did not provide
important assessment information about teachers' understanding of the *Jasper* reform and workshop facilitators needed to probe frequently in the face-to-face meetings for more details.

Assessment Plans

During the second day of the workshop, teachers were asked to post their
plans for assessing student learning during the *Jasper* unit. They interpreted
this assignment as a request for summative assessments and frequently
posted the rubrics they would use to give grades on the unit.

> To assess the lesson I would take two grades a day. One would
> be for effort, cooperation, and participation in the group, and the
> other would be for the math skills used and displayed during the
> lesson. These grades would be averaged at the end of the week
> and the students would receive two grades for the lesson. I
> would grade them by observing the groups and marking either a
> plus, check, minus, or a double minus. The check would be
> worth 95%, the check 85%, the minus 75%, and the double mi-
> nus 60%. For exceptional effort a 100% will be given. More as-
> sessment would be done later by having them apply their knowl-
> edge in similar problems or in analogous activities. —Jack

Postings revealed that the Direct Math Assessment (DMA) and other
aspects of the state's testing program heavily influenced the teachers' view
of assessment. The *Jasper* unit was seen as a way of preparing students for
this test and the scoring rubrics from the DMA tests were frequently
adopted as a plan for assessing students' learning.

> I like your idea on using a rubric. I am also considering tying
> this in with the standards for the DMA—a—is the student using
> higher level problem-solving skills and mathematics above
> grade level, is he proficient, adequate, developing, etc. I think
> these problem-solving activities and their justification would be
> very helpful preparation for the DMA. —Kelly

Teachers' plans for summative assessment were very creative and detailed. They planned to assess both individual and group performance and to bring students into the process by having them take part in the creation of the assessment rubric and by having them do self- and peer assessments. In general, teachers were more concerned about students' problem-solving and communication skills and less about the accuracy of their calculations. In keeping with this concern, the most frequent types of assessments planned were observation, daily journals, and presentation.

Implementation Reports

To provide coherence and at least a minimal level of interaction during the implementation phase of the project, teachers were asked to post one note describing their teaching, another describing assessments, and one note describing their reflections on the experience. It turned out to be quite difficult for them to separate their reports into three separate categories and these elements were often combined into multiple notes.

Only one teacher indicated that she had implemented the unit as planned in the workshop. Most did not post revised plans prior to implementation, but their reports indicated changes with the revisions focusing more on math problem solving and *Jasper* and far less on thematically related interdisciplinary activities.

There were several striking differences between the planning notes and those that were posted during implementation. Teachers were now responsible for a group of actual children and now began to incorporate students' ability levels, ages, and social skills into the design of instruction. When contrasted with the previous planning notes, the following entries illustrate how planning in a workshop can be quite different than planning for a real class.

> We are up and running as of Tuesday!!! My class this year is 21 give-or-take. 5 R/R, 9 Title IX, 2 behavior cases, 1 in juvie detention until Oct 10. Piece of cake, right? —Mike

> The 7th grade class is an "accelerated" class. The students are all new to our middle school and come from five different local elementaries. (They) have needed little help with the mathematics, but their social skills/abilities to work together are not as developed. Some of this may be due to the fact that they do not know each other. —Kelly

> I teach a combined class of third and fourth grades, 3 fourth graders are Special Ed., and I have 2 GT for each grade level. I have 6 third graders and 14 fourth graders. I did break my classroom up into different groups, knowing that I would be doing this and wanting to split my GT students, having one in each group. —Penny

> I have 70 minute classes so I had to adjust for that. I taught Pre-Algebra during the same time frame so that I wouldn't get behind the other teachers. —Carol

Although they now included information on students' grade level or ability and their teaching context, many implementation descriptions still lacked important information; for example, teachers provided a list of activities that the class carried out with few details and no evaluation of the success of the implementation. The initial note from our one-room schoolhouse exemplifies this approach:

> Grades 3–6 are working in groups and stated that this was the most fun project they have ever had. They even were working it out during recess. They have used charts, technical math skills, maps, and paragraphs to present their solutions. The older kids are helping with the Kindergarten First graders by drawing maps, compass rose, simple addition and subtraction problems. They have also colored a picture of an eagle. Some of the math skills used were above some of our students. The older ones helped explain and they were also creative in their figuring. The kids will present their solutions today.
> —Sarah/Paige

In contrast to this short note, there were a few teachers whose writing abilities and attention to detail kept everyone logging in day after day to find out how things were going in their classrooms. These exemplary postings brought many aspects of the classroom setting to life and provided a window on both teachers' and students' thinking. Here is a description from one posting that was several typewritten pages in length.

> Day 4 Now with new improved data, each group was to come up with answers to their specific assignment. Yeah right! This was where the glamour of Jasper and his little problem was wearing thin on the maths and the math-nots. Those in the know would write the answer down and not be able (have the vocabulary) to explain what they did to get their answer. Those in the dark; their biggest concerns were bathroom, drink, and recess, (WHEN!) in that order. I finally got around to each group and pretty much worked out their problems in an orderly fashion using a small white board and marker. I left it with them to copy while I went on to the next group. It was like triage, taking care of the most needy problems and letting the rest fester until a more convenient time. Day 5 - A more convenient time - I copied the problems of each group on chart paper and I worked through each problem with the data that they/I had collected from the story on the preceding days. A few more eyes were focused and bright today, but the blank stares of a few were not moved. Day 6 - Tomorrow, we will plot and label the "map" of possible routes for the rescue and time allowing, we will watch

specific sections of the story and consider payload, etc., and in days to come, again consider solutions to Jasper's dilemma. — Randy

Most postings about teaching fell somewhere between the two examples: Teachers gave some indication of their successes and failures but focused primarily on activities.

Assessment Reports

Testing was not a high priority on most teachers' agenda. Their primary goal was to help students solve the *Jasper* adventure. Several teachers apologetically abandoned any formal summative assessment of student learning. They wanted the children to have a positive experience and did not want to "destroy" this by testing. When pressed by facilitators for more information about formative assessment, some teachers responded in frustration:

> I was just trying to deal with the new program, and do what I needed to do with the class. If you are looking for some type of exact information, I would be more than happy to answer any of your questions. I guess I am not quite sure what you want here. —Connie

Other teachers responded with a list of skills they were assessing:

> Each student was assessed on skills involving, time, rate, multiplication, division, repeated addition, subtraction, mapping, and visual observation. As the groups gave their presentation, all math problems had to be clearly written, justified, and logically explained.—Paige

When provided, formative assessment information was embedded in the reports of classroom events. In general, it was vague and unsystematic. Despite their inability to articulate specifics when prompted, teachers were confident of their judgments about student learning.

> I have a lot of evidence and you'll just have to take my word for it!!! I know my students well and I saw them grow mathematically. —Amy

Interaction Among Teachers and Facilitators

Our previous experience in online professional development had under-scored the importance of a sense of community among teachers and facilita-tors (Williams et al., 1999). Without a sense of trust teachers are unwilling to express their true opinions and share difficulties that they are experienc-ing. Teachers in our workshop had become very comfortable with oral dis-cussions, but were more formal when communicating online. The contents of the online conference remained professional and never resembled social banter around the lunch table. However, there was some evidence that teachers' shared experience of implementing their first *Jasper* unit had cre-ated meaningful professional relationships.

> I am so excited that I just had to share with someone. I tried my first day of Jasper with 8th graders today and it was absolutely great! I'll write again when I finish. —Carrie

> This Jasper experience has given us avenues to vent our frustra-tions, share our successes, and empathize with each other over our shortcomings. —Debra

As previously stated, teachers' postings were often report-like and not interactive. These reports rarely included problems with their implementa-tion. The inclusion of a thread called "Requests for Help" and the encour-agement of the facilitators for everyone to post queries and suggestions seemed to encourage some teachers to ask questions and others to respond. Often these responses contained more information about the responding teacher's implementation than was expressed in their reports.

> Necessary vs. Unnecessary information Any ideas out there on how to teach/coach students in the art of taking only what in-formation they need from a situation to solve their problem and leaving the rest? —Randy

> Children improve in this area after the first Jasper episode. After presenting their solutions students enjoy discussing which in-formation was essential and non-essential. This also seems to guide them in future problem solving.
> —Facilitator 1

> I'm thinking what Jill said is correctamundo! I saw an improve-ment in my 6th graders after a day or so. I think it is just a mat-ter of cruisin' through the info and jettisoning the garbage, and they get used to recognizing garbage. —Tom

Teachers' responses to others' reports were always positive. A little over half consisted only of a compliment; the remainder provided feedback by describing something that had occurred in their own classrooms (see last example). No teacher was ever critical in his or her response to another. They rarely asked for further explanation or information.

The three facilitators' postings fell into two categories: Approximately one third were administrative (e.g., announcements and notes of encouragement). The remainder consisted of feedback on teachers' postings. Facilitators attempted to keep the conference going by making sure that all posts by teachers were promptly acknowledged, especially during periods when other teachers appeared to be busy and off line. The content of facilitators' replies was quite different from that of the teachers. Approximately three fourths provided suggestions or requests for more information.

> Your observations sound thorough enough to impress any outside critic. How did the kids do? As well or better than you might expect in a traditional situation? Could you provide some specific evidence for the skeptics? —Facilitator 2

Although sometimes the requests for more information received no replies or met with frustration (as in the case of requests for formative assessment information), these requests helped move the online conference beyond a repository for implementation reports and toward the vision of an anchored community of inquiry.

Evidence for Changes in the Teaching Life of Participants

The time period of our online conference was short and for most teachers it covered only one implementation of the *Jasper* unit. There were few opportunities to try a second *Jasper* unit or *RBM* a second time. Our primarily evidence for change came through reports of "A-ha!" moments posted in the conference. One such moment came as a teacher was in the midst of implementing her carefully prepared lesson and posted the following note in the "Calls for Help" thread.

> You know the old saying about the best-laid plans of mice and men? Well, I thought I had RBM all psyched out according to Bloom's taxonomy, and the sequence of learning according to M. Hunter, and discovered that kids don't approach problem solving in that manner! The more I directed toward a specific skill involved in a sub-problem, the more they wanted to jump in with both feet and tackle the whole big picture. So who can fight city hall? I let them have at it today, and was amazed how much pertinent information they gleaned in one class period. Would you all have done the same thing or should I have stuck to original plans and learning "theories?" —Debra

I think you made the right move. Hunter and Bloom look good on paper, but when you hold them up to the light in the classroom, often times there is but a faint image of reality. —Tom

The Madeline Hunter model is an effective one for direct instruction. But, solving the Jasper Adventures requires the use of a non-directive model — one that is facilitative in nature. What you are trying to do now is develop a method of teaching that is more like coaching than directing. Although it is always frustrating when you find that the skills you have been using effectively for years just don't work well in a new situation it can be very stimulating to have to stretch to build new skills. Keep us updated on the details. We can learn a lot from each other. : --)
—Facilitator 2

For many of the teachers, this was their first attempt to use technology with their students, and to participate in an online discussion (or to even search the Web), and few had tried complex problem solving with their students. In letters to the workshop organizer, these attempts were reported to have an impact on teaching in math and in other areas of the curriculum and professional life.

As a teacher I have come to realize that you can teach sequential skills till you are blue in the face, but it's really the process of thinking, reasoning, and communicating (that helps students) gain confidence as well as skills. —Debra

I am into and growing in the area of electronic communication. This workshop was key in launching me on this journey. —John

Evaluation

By typical evaluation metrics, our implementation of the ACI model was very successful. There was no attrition: All participating teachers attended all meetings at the workshop, all participated in the online discussion, and all implemented the *Jasper* reform. In addition, the level of participation online was more than twice what was required.

The effect of the professional development did not end when the last message was posted to the online conference. Many teachers gave professional development sessions in their own schools to share what they had learned and requested or raised money to buy additional *Jasper* adventures. Teachers involved students' parents in the problem-solving activities, arranged field trips or extracurricular activities related to the curriculum, taught the unit multiple times, or had their students act as experts to teach *Jasper* to students in other classes. Ongoing contact with teachers indicated that they continue to use the *Jasper* materials. Recently, almost 2 years after the workshop, over 40% of the teachers responded to a letter asking if they were interested in obtaining additional *Jasper* materials.

DISCUSSION

Our implementation of the ACI model provides evidence of the types of interactions that might be expected in a facilitated online conference among practicing teachers. We organize our discussion of these results around issues revealed by this implementation.

Shared Context

Teachers need personally relevant activities to encourage interaction in online learning communities. Our results suggest that teachers' sustained and active participation in the online conference was related to the shared context established by the workshop experiences and the simultaneous implementation of the *Jasper* curriculum. Teachers were very goal oriented in their use of the online conference. Notes were always related directly to the implementation. Teachers did not use the forum to initiate social conversations or to engage in professional discussions that were not directly related to the implementation. Notes were only posted during the time period of the implementation, despite the fact that the conference remained available continuously from the beginning of the workshop until a year following the implementation.

These results may appear to be related only to the requirements for course credit or the culture of the community established by the facilitators; however, the data do not support this hypothesis. First, facilitators began discussion threads to share information about grant opportunities, educational Web sites, and other topics of common interest and teachers chose not to participate. An attempt by one teacher to start a discussion on the general topic of assessment received no replies. In contrast, the number of topics specifically related to the implementation that were initiated by teachers was over twice that required. Likewise, the number of replies to these topics was approximately twice the requirements. Thus in our conference, it appears that teachers were responding to a specific learning goal rather than an opportunity to discuss general issues.

Descriptions of Classroom Interaction

Access to descriptions of events in participating teachers' classrooms are critical for facilitators and teachers to carry out collaborative inquiry online. Our frequent requests for formative assessment information during the conference reflected our attempts to gain a window into the classrooms of participating teachers. Typically researchers and teacher educators regularly observe in the classrooms of collaborating teachers. In our project, all participants (both facilitators and other teachers) were completely dependent on the descriptions of the classrooms provided by the teachers themselves.

Adequate information was difficult to obtain from our teachers for several reasons: First, teachers were unaccustomed to articulating how they knew students were learning and what they were learning. When pressed for details, their evidence was likely to be "observation" or "I just know my students" and unlikely to contain any specific evidence of students' work. This is not surprising because neither teacher preparation nor our workshop had prepared teachers to talk about content and student thinking.

Teachers lacked experience in implementing the *Jasper* reform. Therefore, they may have failed to notice and remember important events because their lack of expertise affected what was noticed. Likewise, they may have been unable to accurately evaluate the successes and failures of their implementation without knowing what to look for. Although teachers lacked expertise in the *Jasper* reform, they had acquired well-rehearsed routines of their own for interpreting the classroom and conducting lessons (Leinhardt & Greeno, 1986). These routines may also have affected what was noticed and communicated (Putnam & Borko, 1997).

Text descriptions of the classroom are difficult to create and time-consuming to type. Even the most expert writer may fail to capture the information present in students' facial expressions and posture or the tone of their voice. Teachers may have lacked the writing skills necessary to create rich descriptions. In addition, it is likely that they lacked the time to write detailed reports while they were in the midst of implementing the *Jasper* reform for the first time. Videos of learning activities could provide important details, but it is unlikely that teachers have the necessary video and computer technology to collect the video or the expertise necessary to do the videotaping. Collecting video data is further complicated because teachers may lack enough expertise with the reform to identify which details to videotape and report.

Sustained Dialogue

Participants in online collaborative inquiry need to be able to carry on a sustained dialogue to discuss ideas and integrate information from others into an understanding that grows and develops. Only one third of teachers' postings during the implementation phase of our conference were replies to a previously posted message. The others were reports of various aspects of the implementation. It is possible that teachers viewed reporting as their primarily role despite assignments to respond to other teachers' postings. It is also possible that teachers (and learners in general) are not accustomed to carrying out an extended dialogue about a single idea; that is following an idea from its initial statement to some kind of conclusion (Wilson & Berne, 1999). This kind of interaction was more likely to occur during the face-to-face part of the ACI model than online and we did not make the development of sustained inquiry a specific part of our instruction. Developing this type of interaction is likely to be a difficult learning goal and is likely to significantly extend the amount of time required to establish a productive learning community.

Culture That Supports Critical Dialogue

Developing a culture that supports critical dialogue about practice and ideas is difficult face to face and may be more difficult online. Although teachers enjoy opportunities to learn about ideas and materials related to their work, "the norms of school have taught them to be non-judgmental, and the privacy of teaching has obstructed the development of a critical dialogue about practice and ideas" (Wilson & Berne, 1999, p. 186). Our teachers followed this pattern. They asked no probing questions and did not press for explanations or rationales. Unless a note specifically requested assistance, teachers provided no feedback or suggestions. The primary type of feedback provided was the recounting of analogous situations, (e.g., "I had a similar situation once"). Even this feedback appeared to be supportive and not instructional, (e.g., "I did the same thing" or "I felt the same way").

The built-in privacy of the teaching profession obstructs the development of a critical dialogue, even among colleagues in the same school. The distance associated with online discussion creates further opportunities for privacy, as teachers do not share the same school, curriculum, external assessment, or students, and are therefore unlikely to know even the most surface details of others' teaching context.

Long-Term Interaction

Collaborative inquiry requires a long-term commitment that may be more difficult to maintain in an online community. The current literature indicates that effective professional development for teachers requires long-term support and ongoing interactions with colleagues (Ball, 1996; Wilson & Berne, 1999). At the end of our 4-month test of the ACI model, we believed that we were just beginning to see evidence of changes in teachers' thinking and the online discourse: Some teachers had begun to discuss difficulties they were having in their implementation and ask for feedback. Other teachers reflected on their experiences and indicated that they would teach the *Jasper* materials differently next year. Additional time would have been necessary to nurture this incipient change.

If our learning community had been school based, the shared knowledge and norms might have been maintained. Indeed, there was some anecdotal evidence that teachers participating in the workshop and implementation who worked in the same school or district continued interaction related to the *Jasper* reform offline. For those at a distance, the community ended abruptly within weeks of the last implementation. One participant asked, "I think that Amy and Ed are still checking in. Who else is still there?????" It is also possible that an entirely online school-based learning community might have been unnecessary and less successful as teachers would have other opportunities to interact.

SUMMARY AND CONCLUSIONS

Professional development that attempts to change teachers' beliefs and practice requires a fundamentally different kind of interaction than researching resources, communicating with parents or colleagues, or other ways that teachers use online communication. The professional development model in the study described in this chapter utilized an online discussion as a means of providing support for teachers who were adapting and implementing theoretical and curricular ideas introduced in a summer workshop. The discussion was anchored in the shared simultaneous implementation of a specific reform in teachers' own classrooms and was sustained over the duration of the implementation.

Online discussion was successful in extending support to teachers separated by distance from professional development personnel and encouraging teachers to reflect on their practice in the context of this reform. However, online professional development rooted in teachers' own practice requires some means of sharing what is happening in the classroom with those online. Significant preparation and experience will be necessary to enable teachers or other participants in online learning communities to develop the skills to describe the settings in which they are learning and working and to develop a culture where this type of sharing is the norm.

ACKNOWLEDGMENTS

We would like to acknowledge the outstanding teachers who worked with us during this implementation of the ACI model. We owe much to their expertise and desire to learn new things. We also acknowledge the collaboration of Jill Ashworth, whose experience in teaching *Jasper* and excellent facilitation skills contributed much to this project. The implementation of the ACI model was supported in part by an Eisenhower grant to the second author.

REFERENCES

Ball, D. L. (1996). Teacher learning and the mathematics reforms: What do we think we know and what do we need to learn? *Phi Delta Kappan, 77,* 500–508.

Ball, D. L., & Cohen, D. K. (1996). Reform by the book: What is—or might be—the role of curriculum materials in teacher learning and instruction reform? *Educational Researcher, 25*(9), 6–8.

Barron, B. (1991). *Collaborative problem solving: Is team performance greater than what is expected from the most competent member?* Unpublished doctoral dissertation; Vanderbilt University, Nashville, TN.

Bransford, J., Sherwood, R., Hasselbring, T., Kinzer, C., & Williams, S. M. (1992). Anchored instruction: Why we need it and how technology can help. In D. Nix & R. Spiro (Eds.), *Computers, cognition, and multimedia: Explorations in high technology* (pp. 115–141). Hillsdale, NJ: Lawrence Erlbaum Associates.

Brown, A. L. (1992). Design experiments: Theoretical and methodological challenges in creating complex interventions in classroom settings. *Journal of the Learning Sciences, 2,* 141–178.

Brown, A. L., & Campione, J. C. (1994). Guided discovery in a community of learners. In K. McGilly (Ed.), *Classroom lessons: Integrating cognitive theory and classroom practice.* (pp. 229–270). Cambridge, MA: MIT Press.

Brown, A. L. & Campione, J. C. (1996). Psychological theory and the design of innovative learning environments. In L. Schauble & R. Glaser (Eds.), *Innovations in learning: New environments for education,* (pp. 289–325). Mahwah, NJ: Lawrence Erlbaum Associates.

Cobb, P. (1994). Where is the mind? Constructivist and sociocultural perspectives on mathematical development. *Educational Researcher, 23*(7), 13–20.

Cochran-Smith, M., & Lytle, S. L. (1999). Relationships of knowledge and practice: Teacher learning in communities. In A. Iran-Nejad & P. D. Pearson (Eds.), *Review of research in education* (pp. 249–305). San Francisco: American Educational Research Association.

Cognition and Technology Group at Vanderbilt. (1997). *The Jasper project: Lessons in curriculum, instruction, assessment, and professional development.* Mahwah, NJ: Lawrence Erlbaum Associates.

Cognition and Technology Group at Vanderbilt. (1999). Adventures in anchored instruction: Lessons from beyond the ivory tower. In R. Glaser (Ed.), *Advances in instructional psychology* (Volume V, pp. 35–100), Mahwah, NJ: Lawrence Erlbaum Associates.

Davies, T., & Zech, L. (1999, April). *Professional development for ongoing change.* Paper presented at the annual conference of the American Educational Research Association, Montreal, Canada.

Franke, M. L., Carpenter, T., Fennema, E., Anseli, E., & Beherend, J.
    (1998). Understanding teachers' self-sustaining, generative change
    in the context of professional development. *Teaching and Teacher
    Education, 14*(1), 67–80.
Goldman, S. R. (2001). Professional development in a digital age: Issues
    and challenges for standards-based reform. *Interactive Educational
    Multimedia, 2*, 19–46.
Johnson, R. (1987). *The ability to retell a story: Effects of adult mediation
    in a videodisc context on children's story recall and comprehen-
    sion.* Unpublished doctoral dissertation, Vanderbilt University,
    Nashville, TN.
Kennedy, M. (1998, April). *The relevance of content in inservice teacher
    education.* Paper presented at the annual meeting of the American
    Educational Research Association; San Diego, CA.
Lamon, M., Secules, T., Petrosino, A. J., Hackett, R., Bransford, J. D., &
    Goldman, S. R. (1996). Schools for thought: Overview of the pro-
    ject and lessons learned from one of the sites. In L. Schauble & R.
    Glaser (Eds.), *Innovation in learning: New environments for edu-
    cation* (pp. 243–288). Mahwah, NJ: Lawrence Erlbaum Associ-
    ates.
Leinhardt, G. & Greeno, J. G. (1986). The cognitive skill of teaching. *Jour-
    nal of Educational Psychology, 78,* 75–95.
McLaughlin, M. W., Mitra, D., & Stokes, L. (2000). *Theory-based change
    and change-based theory: Going deeper, going broader.* Unpub-
    lished manuscript.
Piaget, J. (1952). *The origins of intelligence in children* (M. Cook, Trans.).
    New York: International Universities Press.
Putnam, R. T., & Borko, H. (1997). Teacher learning: Implications of the
    new view of cognition. In B. J. Biddle, T. L. Good, & I. F.
    Goodson (Eds.), *The international handbook of teachers and
    teachin.* (Vol. II, pp. 1223-1296). Dordrecht, Netherlands: Kluwer.
Richardson, V. (1994). Conducting research on practice. *Educational Re-
    searcher, 23*(5), 5–10.
Scardamalia, M., Bereiter, C., & Lamon, M. (1994). The CSILE project:
    Trying to bring the classroom into World 3. In K. McGilly (Ed.),
    *Classroom lessons: Integrating cognitive theory and classroom
    practice* (pp. 201–228). Cambridge, MA: MIT Press/Bradford
    Books.
Secules, T., Cottom, C. D., Bray, M. H., Miller, L. D., & the CTGV.
    (1997). Schools for thought: Creating learning communities. *Edu-
    cational Leadership, 54*(6), 56–60.
Sherwood, R. D., Kinzer, C. K., Bransford, J. D., & Franks, J. J. (1987).
    Some benefits of creating macro-contexts for science instruction:
    Initial findings. *Journal of Research in Science Teaching, 24*, 417–
    435.

Shulman, L. (1986). Those who understand: Knowledge growth in teaching. *Educational Researcher, 15,* 4 14.

Singer, J., Marx, R. W., Krajcik, J., & Chambers, J. C. (2000). Constructing extended inquiry projects: Curriculum materials for science education reform. *Educational Psychologist, 35,* 165–178.

Van Haneghan, J. P., Barron, L., Young, M. F., Williams, S. M., Vye, N. J., & Bransford, J. D. (1992). The *Jasper* series: An experiment with new ways to enhance mathematical thinking. In D. F. Halpern (Ed.), *Enhancing thinking skills in the sciences and mathematics* (pp. 15–38). Hillsdale, NJ: Lawrence Erlbaum Associates.

Vye, N. J., Goldman, S. R., Voss, J. F., Hmelo, C., & Williams, S. (1997). Complex math problem solving by individuals and dyads: When and why are two heads better than one? *Cognition and Instruction,* 16 (1) 435–484.

Vygotsky, L. S. (1978). *Mind in society: The development of higher psychological processes.* Cambridge, MA: Harvard University Press.

Williams, S. M., Goldman, S. R., Gabella, M. S., Kinzer, C. K., & Risko, V. J. (1999, April). *Online professional development and mentoring: Initial evaluation.* Paper presented at the annual meeting of the American Educational Research Association, San Diego, CA.

Wilson, S. M. & Berne, J. (1999). Teacher learning and the acquisition of professional knowledge: An examination of research on contemporary professional development. In A. Iran-Nejad & P. D. Pearson (Eds.), *Review of research in education, (Vol. 24,* pp. 173-209). Washington, DC: American Educational Research Association.

Wineburg, S. S., & Grossman, P. L. (1998). Creating a community of learners among high school teachers. *Phi Delta Kappan, 79,* 350–353.

Zech, L., Gause-Vega, C., Bray, M. H., Secules, T., & Goldman, S. R. (2000). Content-based collaborative inquiry: Professional development for school reform. *Educational Psychologist, 35,* 207–217.

Chapter 6

Collaborative Discovery Learning Based on Computer Simulation

Qi Chen
School of Psychology, Beijing Normal University

Jianwei Zhang
Educational Technology Institute, Tsinghua University

Effective learning and knowledge building is achieved through learners' active interactions with their social and physical environment. This study was dedicated to exploring these social and physical interactions by looking at how learners interact with their peers and with a simulated world during scientific discovery learning. In most studies, scientific discovery learning is regarded as an individual scientific reasoning process that involves the generation of hypotheses and testing them against the collected evidence. However, the perspective of social interaction has been overlooked to some extent. This study investigated the influences of peer collaboration and questioning–explanation prompt on simulation-based scientific discovery learning. Peer collaboration had a prominent effect on the discovery outcomes, intuitive understandings, and variable control skills. The influence of the questioning–explanation prompt was less clear, and hence needs to be addressed in depth in future studies.

The most recent developments in learning theory including social constructivism, situated learning, and distributed cognition have converged to regard learning as an active knowledge construction process occurring in socially and physically dynamic contexts. Effective learning and knowledge building are achieved through learners' active interactions with their social and physical environment. From these perspectives, new technologies should be harnessed as powerful tools to enhance understanding, higher order thinking, and intensive social interactions, rather than being merely added in classrooms as media for information transmission. Within the constructivist paradigm, a growing number of studies have focused on scientific discovery learning based on computer simulation (van Joolingen & de Jong, 1997). This study was designed to explore the processes and effectiveness of collaborative discovery learning in a computer simulation environment and to look at how learners interact with their peers and with a simulated world during scientific discovery learning.

Supporting Scientific Discovery Learning in Simulation
Environments

Because computer simulation has the capacity to provide learners with an
exploratory learning environment, it has been regarded as a powerful tool
for scientific discovery learning. Nevertheless, many studies designed to
contrast the effectiveness of simulation-based discovery learning with some
mode of traditional learning found little persuasive evidence in its favor
(see Bangert-Drowns, Kulik, & Kulik, 1985; Carlsen & Andre, 1992). Why
does simulation-based learning that involves learners in active inquiry not
improve learning outcomes more consistently? One explanation lies in the
wide range of difficulties learners may encounter in coping with discovery
learning processes. De Jong and van Joolingen (1998) classified the problems that learners may experience into four categories: (a) difficulties in
handling hypotheses, (b) poorly designed experiments, (c) difficulties in
data interpretation, and (d) problems regarding the regulation of discovery
learning. Despite its potential for stimulating constructive learning activities, it seems that the simulation-based learning environment cannot guarantee effective learning without sufficient support for discovery learning activities. This conclusion was also supported by Lee's (1999) meta-analysis
showing that hybrid simulation involving instructional elements is more
effective than pure simulation for new knowledge acquisition.

Studies have been conducted to help learners with particular strategies.
For example, some researchers developed supportive methods to help students generate hypotheses in simulation-based discovery learning (Njoo &
de Jong, 1993; Quinn & Alessi, 1994; Shute & Glaser, 1990). Others have
examined the issues connected with experimental design (Leutner, 1993),
planning (Tabak, Smith, Sandoval, & Reiser, 1996), explaining the phenomenon, predicting the result (de Jong, Martin, Zamarro, Esquembre,
Swaak, & van Joolingen, 1999), and accessing an appropriate knowledge
base (Lewis, Stern, & Linn, 1993).

On the basis of relevant theories and studies, we (Reid, Zhang, & Chen,
2003; Zhang, 2000; Zhang, Chen, Sun, & Reid, 2004) have hypothesized
that three interrelated main conditions may constrain the effect of scientific
discovery learning: the meaningfulness and systematic nature of discovery
activities and the reflective generalization over the discovery processes.
Three types of learning supports were designed accordingly: (a) interpretative support that helped learners to access relevant knowledge and the development of understanding; (b) experimental support that scaffolded learners in the systematic and logical design of experiments, the prediction and
observation of outcomes, and the drawing of conclusions; and (c) reflective
support that increased learners' self-awareness of the thinking and understanding processes involved in discovery activities that prompted their reflective abstraction and integration. Three experiments were conducted to
investigate the internal conditions by examining the effects of the three

types of learning support. Overall, the results support our main hypotheses, showing that generative meaning making, systematic and logical design of experiments, and reflective generalization constitute three essential conditions for scientific discovery learning. Therefore, learning supports for these three aspects of learning should be taken into account when designing simulation-based discovery learning environments.

The Role of Collaboration in Discovery Learning and Reasoning

In most studies, scientific discovery learning is regarded as an individual scientific reasoning process that involves individuals generating hypotheses and testing them against the collected evidence (Klahr & Dunbar, 1988). Scientific discovery learning as a social process has been relatively ignored. Collaborative discovery is a common and growing practice in science, but has not yet been extensively researched (Okada & Simon, 1997). Li and Chen (2000) compared two ways of cooperatively using computers in learning elementary school geometry. In one mode, the cooperative tool mode, learners in small groups used Windows PaintBrush to explore the area of rectangles. In the second mode, the cooperative computer-assisted instruction (CAI) mode, students used a tutorial CAI program cooperatively to learn the same knowledge. The cooperative tool mode had a significantly greater effect on outcomes related to reasoning ability, geometric knowledge, and motivation to learn than the cooperative CAI mode. The outcomes seem to imply that collaboration combined with open technology tools has more potential to promote explorative learning and higher order thinking.

Among the few studies of collaborative reasoning or discovery are those by Gorman and colleagues (Gorman, 1986; Gorman, Gorman, Latta, & Cunningham, 1984). They studied confirmation bias in a group task on scientific discovery using a rule-discovery 2–4–6 task. Participants were required to find a rule of relationship among three numerals. A set of three numerals, [2, 4, 6], was presented at the initial stage. Participants needed to form their hypotheses of regularity and test them by producing a new set of three numerals and asking the experimenter for feedback. Participants were instructed to use (a) a confirmatory strategy, (b) a disconfirmatory strategy, or (c) a combination of the two. The results showed that groups outperformed individuals and participants in the disconfirmatory condition performed best, followed by those in the combined condition and the confirmatory condition, respectively. Freedman (1992) studied the effect of group versus individual problem solving and the effect of entertaining multiple hypotheses versus a single hypothesis in a rule-discovery task. The groups outperformed individuals, and in the multiple hypotheses condition groups used more diagnostic tests than individuals, which had improved their performance.

In an important study of collaborative discovery learning, Teasley (1995) investigated the role of verbal behavior in fourth-grade students' peer collaborations in accomplishing the spaceship task, which required children to discover how a new mystery key on a spaceship simulation worked. They needed to formulate hypotheses and design experiments to test their hypotheses. The participants were assigned to one of the four conditions. Individuals in the talk alone condition solved the problem alone while talking aloud. Individuals in the no-talk alone condition solved the problem alone without talking aloud. Participants in the talk dyads condition solved the problem with a partner while talking to each other. In the no-talk dyads condition, participants solved the problem with a partner without talking to each other. Participants in the talk dyads condition performed best in the spaceship task, followed by talk alones and no-talk alones, with no-talk dyads performing the worst.

Okada and Simon (1997) explored the processes and effectiveness of individual or dyadic discovery activities using a protocol analysis method. Undergraduate students were asked to discover molecular genetics laws in a computer microworld. Dyads were more successful in discovering laws than were individuals, and dyads participated more actively in explanatory activities (i.e., entertaining hypotheses and considering alternative ideas and justifications). Explanatory activities were effective for discovery only when the participants also conducted crucial experiments. Explanatory activities were facilitated when paired participants made requests of each other for explanation and focused on them.

Discourse Patterns for Mediating Collaborative Learning

Collaborative learning contexts provide opportunities for learners to interact with one another in verbal and nonverbal, paralinguistic ways. It is the quality and patterns of interaction that determine the effectiveness of collaborative learning. In studies of group learning, Webb (1989) consistently found that giving detailed elaborate explanations to others in the group is a strong predictor of achievement.

In a series of studies of peer learning, King (1999) developed a procedure called guided peer questioning, which is a question-asking and answering procedure designed to promote interaction and learning among peers working in small groups. This procedure is guided by structured question "starters" such as, "Why is _____ important?," "How is _____ similar to _____," "What does _____ remind you of? Why?" These open-ended question starters are provided to members of the learning group, who then use the starters to guide them in generating their own specific questions related to the material being studied. A series of studies (King, 1992, 1994; King & Rosenshine, 1993) revealed that when students were taught to ask each other these thought-provoking questions during learning, their questions prompted high-level interaction and learning. Similarly, Coleman

(1998) studied the effect of a scaffolded explanation-based approach in collaborative discussion in classroom settings. During discussion, learners in experimental groups were given prompt cards to guide their questioning activity toward each other. This approach was found to be of great help in promoting learners' understanding of scientific knowledge. However, the learning tasks used in the preceding studies were mainly knowledge acquisition in lecture or text-based context. Could such a reciprocal questioning and explanation approach facilitate collaborative discovery learning based on computer simulation? No study so far has been found that addresses this question.

The Purpose of This Study

Although collaborative discovery learning with simulation is an important topic, relatively few experimental studies have been conducted on this topic. Even fewer studies have been conducted to explore collaborative discovery learning among young learners in schools. Could collaboration function as a type of learning support to facilitate learners' discovery processes as they use computer simulations? How will reciprocal questioning and explanation activities promote discovery learning? This study aims to answer these questions. A peer learning approach was adopted for the study. Explanatory prompt cards were used to guide learners' questioning and explanation activities. Both the effects and the processes were evaluated to reveal the influence of the treatments.

METHOD

The Simulation Learning Environment and Task

The domain chosen for the simulation was floating and sinking, where the learners were required to explore buoyant forces on objects floating or sinking in water. The essential rule governing the size of a buoyant force is Archimedes' law of buoyancy, stating that the size of the buoyant force acting on an object in liquid equals the weight of the displaced liquid. This is the essential physics rule for objects that either float or sink. However, it is difficult for young learners to discover this rule together with the underpinning displacement method in a short time. It is even harder for them to think about the amount of liquid displaced by a floating object in comparison to a sinking object. Therefore, rather than asking the students to discover this essential rule (the ultimate full model) of buoyant forces, this study designed a progressive task (de Jong et al., 1999) for them to explore the relationship between the features of an object and the size of its buoyant force in the circumstances of floating and sinking. The specific task was to discover which one or more of three given factors (shape, mass, and volume of an object) were related to the size of the buoyant force. For objects submerged in water, it is the volume of the object that influences the size of the buoyant force, because the volume of the object determines the volume of the displaced water, which affects the size of the buoyant force. For a floating object, the size of buoyant force always equals the size of its weight. These two forces (weight and buoyant force) balance each other and result in the equilibrium of the object in water. Therefore the mass of the object is the only feature related to the size of buoyant force under this circumstance. Although by nature, Archimedes' law can explain these variable relationships under both floating and sinking circumstances, it should be noted that Archimedes' law was beyond the discovery task in this study.

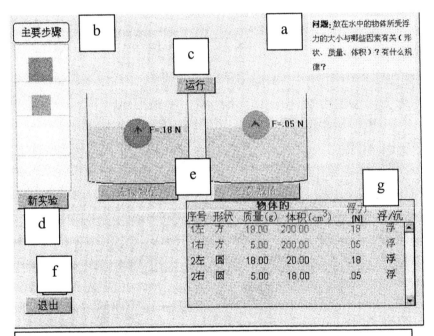

Translation of Figure:
- a. Problem: Which one or more of the factors among shape, mass, and volume influence the buoyant force acting on an object in water?
- b. Main steps
- c. Run
- d. New Experiment
- e. Values on the Left; Values on the Right
- f. Exit
- g. See Table 1.

FIG.6.1. Interface of the simulation software.

The simulation adopted the paired-instance design required learners to construct a pair of experiments at a time, so that they could contrast the outcomes of two instances directly. The simulation started with two floating objects determined by the default parameters of volumes and masses in the program. For all participants, a data sheet was provided on the screen to record the input as well as the value of the output variable in each pair of experiments. For example, as shown in Figure 6.1, a learner first selected two boxes and specified different values for their masses and the same value for their volumes. After running this pair of experiments, he observed that both objects floated, with the sizes of buoyant force of 0.18 Newton and 0.05 Newton, respectively (see Table 6.1).   In addition, a permanent button was prepared to remind learners of the main steps for an experiment. The simulation program was written in such a way that it registered learners' manipulations during the learning processes and wrote a log file for each participant.

TABLE 6.1

The Data Table in the Interface Snapshot

| No. | Features of Objects | | | Buoyant Force (N) | Floating/ Sinking |
	Shape	Mass (g)	Volume (cm3)		
1 left	Box	18.00	200.00	.18	Floating
1 right	Box	5.00	200.00	.05	Floating
2 left	Ball	18.00	20.00	.18	Floating
2 right	Ball	5.00	18.00	.05	Floating

Design

To investigate the effects of peer collaboration and questioning–explanation prompt on simulation-based discovery learning, a 2 (pair or single) X 2 (with or without explanatory prompt) X 2 (floating or sinking) mixed design was adopted to compare the learning effectiveness of learners under four conditions: prompt pairs, no-prompt pairs, prompt singles, and no-prompt singles. The effectiveness in discovering the underpinning rules for floating and sinking objects was contrasted by including floating or sinking as a within-subjects factor. Considering the influence of learners' preexisting physics performance, the achievements on the most recent final physics exam were collected and used as a covariate when conducting analyses of variance (ANOVAs). Log files were used to analyze how learners designed simulated experiments and made the discovery.

Participants

Participants were 44 eighth-grade students from a junior high school in Beijing. The students ranged in age from 13 to 15, with an average age of 13.88. Twenty-one were boys and 23 were girls. The learners were randomly distributed into four groups: prompt pairs (n-12), no-prompt pairs (n-12), prompt singles (n-10), and no-prompt singles (n-10). The overall evaluation of the learners provided by the physics teacher indicated no significant difference among the four groups their physics knowledge and experience with computers.

Assessments

The effectiveness of the discovery learning was assessed from the following perspectives.

Discovered Rules

The participants were required to summarize their discovery when they finished the experiment. As explained earlier in the introduction to the simulation software, this study designed a progressive task asking learners to discover the relationship between the features (shape, mass, and volume) of an object and the size of its buoyant force in the circumstances of floating and sinking. For objects submerged in water, it is the volume of the object that influences the size of the buoyant force. For a floating object, the size of buoyant force equals its weight, which is related to its mass. When evaluating learners' discovered rules, a full score of 3 was given if a participant had clearly stated the exact rules for floating and sinking objects. A score of 2 indicated that the participant had made a general description (e.g., "Mass and volume are relevant to the size of buoyant force") without considering the differences between floating and sinking objects. A score of 1 was given when only one of the related factors (volume or mass) was mentioned. A score of 0 meant that a participant had drawn a thoroughly wrong or irrelevant conclusion.

Intuitive Understanding

Nine multiple-choice questions were designed to measure learners' intuitive understanding, which is regarded as an important goal in scientific discovery learning (see de Jong et al., 1999). Each item depicted a pair of objects with different combinations of shapes, masses, and volumes. Learners were asked to predict how the buoyancies would compare in size. Four of the items were related to buoyancies on floating objects and five were geared to buoyancies on sinking ones.

Variable Control Skills

Variable control (changing one thing at a time) is an important principle in scientific experiments. Unfortunately, learners often vary many variables in one experiment (Glaser Schauble, Raghavan, & Zeitz, 1992; Lin & Lehman, 1999). To examine learners' variable control skills, six items were constructed. One item required learners to describe the principle considerations in designing scientific experiments. Each of the other items showed learners with an instance of experiment (either well-controlled or badly controlled) for them to evaluate.

Evaluation of Learners' Experiments

Surrounding the principle of variable control, we evaluated learners' experiments conducted during the learning process, which had been recorded in their log files. Specifically, we evaluated how learners had made focused examinations of the three variables under floating and sinking conditions. We identified a pair of experiments as having undergone a focused examination of a certain variable (shape, mass, or volume) if that variable was the only variable that was varied in that pair of experiments. For each variable, a full score of 2 was given when it had been examined by at least two pairs of experiments at different levels of the controlled variables (an example is shown in the Appendix). A score of 1 indicated that the variable had been examined by only one pair of experiments or by more than one pair of experiments but at constant levels of controlled variables. Sequentially, a score of 0 meant that no experiment had been focused on this variable at all. Average scores across the three variables were used to evaluate learners' focused examinations under floating and sinking conditions, respectively. This index therefore reflected the distribution of focused experiments across the features and conditions, thus indicating learners' logical and systematic searches in the experiment space.

Procedure

The study took place in a computer laboratory equipped with 50 networked Pentium II computers. The learners were required to accomplish the following tasks in pairs or individually:

1. **Warm-up.** Participants worked with a tutorial version of the simulation program. Three experimenters were present to answer

their questions regarding the program. This stage lasted approximately 10 minutes.

2. **Problem presentation.** The participants were asked to explore which one or more of the factors among shape, mass, and volume are related to the size of the buoyant force on an object either floating or sinking in water. A brief description of the problem was available in the top-right corner of the screen throughout the discovery process.

3. **Exploration.** All participants were reminded that their task was to discover the rules on the basis of sufficient evidence through simulated experiments. Participants in pairs were required to accomplish the task collaboratively and were told that they were to be evaluated as a group. For the prompt pairs and prompt singles, explanatory prompt cards were put in front of their monitors, reminding them of the questions they could request their partners or ask themselves during the exploration processes. These questions included: (a) What's the objective of this experiment? (b) How should the experiment be designed to achieve this objective? (c) What does this experiment mean? (d) How can the experiment support this conclusion? (e) I think the result doesn't support this conclusion, because, and (f) I think this is not the exactly right conclusion, because_____. The participants were required to summarize their discovery at the end of this stage.

4. **Posttest.** The posttests of intuitive understanding and variable control skills were administered immediately after the completion of the exploration in written format. A total of 30 minutes was allotted for this session.

RESULTS

Evaluation of the Rules Discovered by Different Groups

Table 6.2 shows the evaluation results of the discovered rules of different groups. There were relatively few students who had clearly stated the exact rules for floating and sinking objects. The univariate ANOVA using collaboration and explanatory prompt as fixed factors and learners' recent physics scores as a covariate indicated that collaboration had a significant main effect on the discovery outcome, $F(1, 36) = 5.786, p = .021$.

Pairs discovered the underpinning principles more successfully. A clear interaction was observed between collaboration and the covariate, $F(1, 36) = 5.410, p = .026$. To make clear the pattern of the interaction, we aggregated the participants into two groups according to the median of their physics scores. Simple effect analysis revealed that collaboration had a significant positive effect among lower achievement learners, $F(1, 41) = 6.07$, $p = .018$, whereas it had no significant influence on higher achievement learners. The overall attainment of the prompted learners was lower than that for learners without prompts. However, no significant main effect or interaction was observed for explanatory prompt ($p > .10$) in the statistical analysis.

TABLE 6.2

The Discovery Outcomes of Different Groups.

Groups	M	SD
Prompt pairs	1.500	0.905
No-prompt pairs	1.667	0.492
Prompt singles	1.200	1.033
No-prompt singles	1.400	0.843
Total	1.455	0.820

The Intuitive Understanding Test

Table 6.3 indicates the means and standard deviations of learners' intuitive understanding of the buoyant force on floating and sinking objects. The repeated measures multivariate analysis of variance (MANOVA) was implemented using collaboration and explanatory prompt as between-subject factors, floating or sinking as a within-subjects factor, and learners' physics scores as a covariate. There was a marginally significant main effect for collaboration, $F(1, 36) = 3.047$, $p = .089$, indicating that pairs outperformed singles on the intuitive understanding test. A marginally significant interaction was also observed between collaboration and learners' physics achievements, $F(1, 36) = 3.303$, $p = .077$. Simple effect analysis revealed that collaboration had a significant positive effect for higher achievement learners, $F(1, 41) = 8.000$, $p = .007$, but no significant effect for lower achievement ones ($p > .10$). No notable main effect or interaction was observed for explanatory prompt ($p > .10$).

Analysis of Learners' Variable Control Skills

Table 6.4 shows the scores of variable control skills among different groups of learners. The ANOVA using collaboration and explanatory prompt as fixed factors revealed that there was a significant main effect for collaboration, $F(1, 40) = 4.098$, $p = .050$. Pairs demonstrated higher performance on variable control skills. Again, no notable main effect or interaction was observed for explanatory prompt ($p > .10$).

TABLE 6.3

The Means and Standard Deviations of Intuitive Understanding Test.

| Groups | Floating | | Sinking | |
	M	SD	M	SD
Prompt pairs	1.000	0.603	2.000	1.045
No-prompt pairs	2.333	1.303	1.250	1.288
Prompt singles	1.100	0.738	1.500	0.850
No-prompt singles	1.100	0.994	2.100	0.738
Total	1.409	1.085	1.705	1.047

TABLE 6.4

The Means and Standard Deviations of Learners' Variable Control Skills.

Groups	M	SD
Prompt pairs	4.75	1.42
No-prompt pairs	4.83	1.03
Prompt singles	3.30	2.06
No-prompt singles	4.40	1.58
Total	4.36	1.60

Process Analysis

We evaluated learners' experiments conducted during discovery processes using the procedure described in the Method section. The evaluation results concerning learners' focused examinations of the related factors under floating and sinking conditions are reported in Table 6.5. The repeated measures

MANOVA using floating and sinking as within-subjects factor and collaboration and prompts as between-subjects factors indicated that there was a significant main effect for the within-subjects factor, showing that learners had made more focused investigations about buoyant force on floating objects, sphericity assumed $F(1, 36) = 64.342$, $p = .000$.

TABLE 6.5

Learners' Focused Examination of Buoyant Force During Discovery Processes

	Focused Investigation of Floating Objects		Focused Investigation of Sinking Objects	
Groups	M	SD	M	SD
Prompt Pairs	.67	.24	.06	.15
No-Prompt Pairs	.58	.32	.17	.19
Prompt Singles	.83	.33	.00	.00
No-Prompt Singles	.78	.19	.00	.00
Total	.71	.27	.06	.13

A marginally significant interaction was observed between collaboration and floating or sinking condition, sphericity assumed $F(1, 36) = 3.293$, $p = .095$ (Fig. 6.2). Compared to single learners, pairs made more focused investigations on the buoyant force exerted by water on sinking objects, but relatively few examinations for floating objects. Actually, no singles made any focused experiment for sinking objects at all.

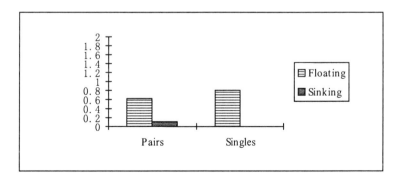

FIG.6.2. Focused examinations of floating or sinking objects made by pairs and single learners.

DISCUSSION

This study examined the effects of peer collaboration and questioning–explanation prompt on simulation-based scientific discovery learning among secondary students. We found that: (a) peer collaboration had notable effects on the overall discovery outcomes and intuitive understanding generated from the discoveries; (b) there were clear interactions between collaboration and learners' physics performance on the overall discovery outcomes and intuitive understanding test, but with different trends; (c) collaboration had positive effects on learners' variable control skills and their focused design of experiments; and (d) no significant main effect or interaction was revealed concerning explanatory prompt.

The Effect of Peer Collaboration on Simulation-Based Discovery Learning

The positive effects of peer collaboration on scientific discovery learning were clearly observed on the overall discovery outcomes, the intuitive understanding test, the variable control skill test. Pairs discovered the rules more successfully, and generated more insightful intuitive understandings on the relationships between the investigated factors and the size of buoyant force under floating or sinking conditions. Hence they could more successfully predict the comparison of the sizes of buoyancies acting on each pair of objects depicted in the intuitive understanding test. These results support the consistent finding that collaborative learners outperformed single learners in accomplishing discovery learning or reasoning tasks (Okada & Simon, 1997; Teasley, 1995). It was revealed by Okada and Simon's (1997) protocol analysis that an important reason why pairs performed better than singles is because pairs participated in explanatory activities such as entertaining hypotheses, talking about alternative ideas, and considering justification more often than singles. It is not because pairs simply had twice as great a chance as singles of getting the right hypothesis, even without active interaction.

Clear interactions were found between collaboration and learners' physics performance on the overall discovery outcomes and intuitive understanding test, but with different patterns. On the evaluation of the discovered rules, collaboration had a significant positive effect for lower achievement learners, but no significant influence for higher achievement learners. On the intuitive understanding test that involved more complex cognitive tasks, collaboration demonstrated significant positive effect for higher achievement learners, but no significant effect for lower achievement learners. The peer collaboration might be helpful to both low- and high-achieving learners, but its effectiveness can be manifest in different levels and aspects of learning.

As far as the discovery process is concerned, in this study, collaboration manifested a positive effect on learners' variable control skills in scientific experiments. Also the index of focused examination of the related features used in this study reflected the distribution of learners' focused experiments across the features and conditions, and hence indicated learners' systematic searches in the experiment space during discovery learning processes. The interaction between collaboration and experiment condition (floating or sinking) manifested that pairs had made more focused experiments for buoyant force acting on sinking objects. Because the default values of the volumes and masses of the objects in the software determine the densities (mass and volume) that are lower than that of water, the simulation software starts with objects floating in water. No deliberate instruction was offered to guide the learners to change the comparisons of masses and volumes to make objects submerge in water, and take both floating and sinking conditions into account. As a result, the learners conducted significantly more focused examinations for floating objects than sinking ones. Pairs made more focused experiments for buoyant force on sinking objects, whereas singles made no focused experiment for sinking objects at all. The result implies that peer collaboration can help learners make more systematic searches in the experiment space and design more crucial and informative experiments during scientific discovery learning. This disagrees with Okada and Simon's (1997) finding that there was no significant difference between pairs and singles on the informativeness and systematicity of experiments conducted during discovery processes.

The Influence of the Questioning–Explanation Prompts

The explanatory prompts used to elicit reciprocal questioning and explanation activities manifested no significant effect in this study. This is inconsistent with Okada and Simon's (1997) conclusion that explanatory activities facilitated by peers' requests had important influence on the effect of discovery, Coleman's (1998) report about the effect of a scaffolded explanation-based approach, as well as King's studies showing that guided peer questioning could help learners in acquiring and understanding knowledge (King, 1992, 1994; King & Rosenshine, 1993).

In this study, the treatments concerning questioning–explanatory prompt included the use of prompt cards reminding of the questions learners could request of each other or ask themselves, and the special instruction to prompt pairs and prompt singles asking them to give attention to the questions on the prompt cards. However, there was no particular procedure to train and coach these learners in asking the questions and giving correspondent responses, as was done in King's research. These treatments might not have guaranteed that the learners, who were young learners from a middle school would follow the explanatory prompt and conduct intensive questioning–explanation activities. This might be one of most important reasons why explanatory prompt did not display any expected significant effect in this study. Chinese students, who are not used to the ways of reciprocal activities, might need particularly more guidance in this aspect. More powerful and clear guidance should be adopted in future studies to investigate the effect of reciprocal questioning–explanation activities as well as its interaction with the mode of collaboration in scientific discovery learning.

Collaborative Discovery Learning in Knowledge-Building Communities

In the past decades, educational researchers have been exploring ways to transform the model of schooling. The practice model of scientists and their community has been recognized as a possible prototype for new learning and teaching practices. However, different researchers look at scientific practices from different perspectives, and thus see different parts of the elephant. Earlier research efforts have been mainly focused on scientific discovery in the laboratory, emphasizing the importance of cultivating skills for scientific thinking and discovery (e.g., scientific discovery learning, experimentation, visualization, making thinking visible, etc.) in schools. Studies using computer-based simulations and microworlds to support scientific discovery learning have been prominently stimulated by this motivation. Recently, researchers have recognized the crucial role of discourse structure in scientific communities, and have started to explore ways to transform schools into knowledge-building communities (Scardamalia & Bereiter, 1994). In a knowledge-building community, learners and their teacher address authentic problems, and produce and continually improve ideas in the form of conceptual artifacts (Bereiter, 2002) of value to a community through transformative and progressive discourse processes. Although our work reported herein and the related studies reviewed in this chapter have embraced social collaboration and interaction in scientific discovery learning, however, they, due to the constraints of the laboratory-focused view of scientific practice, still lack some of the critical features of scientific inquiry in knowledge-building communities. The discovery tasks are often straightforward, rule-based problems that do not require deepening explanations. The inquiry processes and tools are usually prespecified, leaving little space for emergent activities. The evaluations of learning outcomes focus on individual progress instead of community knowledge advancement. Therefore, future research in this field needs to integrate scientific discovery learning into knowledge-building communities and capture the emergent and dynamic nature of collaborative inquiry activities.

CONCLUSION

Nowadays, a growing number of studies have focused on scientific discovery learning based on computer simulation. However, most previous studies in this field focused on individual discovery learning without considering the perspective of social interaction. This study converged scientific discovery learning with collaborative learning to conduct a preliminary experiment in the context of secondary science learning. Peer collaboration was found to have a prominent effect on the processes and outcomes of discovery learning. It can help learners make more systematic searches in experiment space and design more crucial and informative experiments during scientific discovery learning. The influence of the questioning–explanation prompt was less clear, and needs to be addressed in depth in further studies. Future research in this field needs to integrate scientific discovery learning into knowledge-building communities and capture the emergent and dynamic nature of collaborative inquiry activities.

ACKNOWLEDGMENTS

This study was funded by the Tenth Five-Year National Educational Science Plan Project (No.EMB010888). We thank Hongjian Wu for her assistance in the experiment, and Dr. Angela O'Donnell and Dr. Eugenia Etkina for their valuable comments and suggestions.

REFERENCES

Bangert-Drowns, R., Kulik, J., & Kulik, C. (1985). Effectiveness of computer-based education in secondary schools. *Journal of Computer-Based Instruction, 12*, 59–68.

Bereiter, C. (2002). *Education and mind in the knowledge age.* Mahwah, NJ: Lawrence Erlbaum Associates.

Carlsen, D. D., & Andre, T. (1992). Use of a microcomputer simulation and conceptual change text to overcome students' preconceptions about electric circuits. *Journal of Computer-Based Instruction, 19*, 105–109.

Coleman, E. B. (1998). Using explanatory knowledge during collaborative problem solving in science. *Journal of the Learning Sciences, 7* (3&4), 387–427.

de Jong, T., Martin, E., Zamarro, J., Esquembre, F., Swaak, J., & van Joolingen, W. R. (1999). The integration of computer simulation and learning support: An example from physics domain of collisions. *Journal of Research in Science Teaching, 36*, 597–615.

de Jong, T., & van Joolingen, W. R. (1998). Scientific discovery learning with computer simulations of conceptual domains. *Review of Educational Research, 68*, 179–201.

Freedman, E. G. (1992). Scientific induction: Individual versus group processes and multiple hypotheses. In *Proceedings of the Fourteenth Annual Conference of the Cognitive Science Society*. Hillsdale, NJ: Lawrence Erlbaum Associates.

Glaser, R., Schauble, L., Raghavan, K., & Zeitz, C. (1992). Scientific reasoning across different domains. In E. de Corte, M. C. Linn, H. Mandle, & L. Verschaffel (Eds.), *Computer-based learning environments and problem solving* (pp. 345–373). Berlin: Springer-Verlag.

Gorman, M. E. (1986). How the possibility of error affects falsification on a task that models scientific problem solving. *British Journal of Psychology, 77*, 85–96.

Gorman, M. E., Gorman, M. E., Latta, R. M., & Cunningham, G. (1984). How disconfirmatory, confirmatory and combined strategies affect group problem solving. *British Journal of Psychology, 75*, 65–79.

King, A. (1992). Facilitating elaborative learning through guided student-generated questioning. *Educational Psychologist, 27*, 111–126.

King, A. (1994). Guiding knowledge construction in the classroom: Effects of teaching children how to question and how to explain. *American Educational Research Journal, 30*, 338–368.

King, A. (1999). Discourse patterns for mediating peer learning. In A. O'Donnell & A. King (Eds.), *Cognitive perspectives on peer learning* (pp. 87-115). Mahwah, NJ: Lawrence Erlbaum Associates.

King, A., & Rosenshine, B. (1993). Effects of guided cooperative questioning on children's knowledge construction. *Journal of Experimental Education, 61*, 127–148.

Klahr, D., & Dunbar, K. (1988). Dual space search during scientific reasoning. *Cognitive Science, 12*, 1–48.

Lee, J. (1999). Effectiveness of computer-based instructional simulation: A meta analysis. *International Journal of Instructional Media, 26*, 71-85.

Leutner, D. (1993). Guided discovery learning with computer-based simulation games: Effects of adaptive and non-adaptive instructional supports. *Learning and Instruction, 3*, 113–132.

Lewis, E. L., Stern, J. L., & Linn, M. C. (1993). The effect of computer simulations on introductory thermodynamics understanding, *Educational Techology, 33*, 45–58.

Li, M., & Chen, Q. (2000). Comparison of different computer application modes in instruction of primary school geometry. *Chinese Journal of Psychology, 32*, 75–81.

Lin, X., & Lehman, J. (1999). Supporting learning of variable control in a computer-based biology environment: Effects of prompting college students to reflect on their own thinking. *Journal of Research in Science Teaching, 36*, 837–858.

Njoo, M., & de Jong, T. (1993). Exploratory learning with a computer simulation for control theory: Learning processes and instructional support. *Journal of Research in Science Teaching, 30*, 821–844.

Okada, T., & Simon, H. A. (1997). Collaborative discovery in a scientific domain. *Cognitive Science, 21*, 109–146.

Quinn, J., & Alessi, S. (1994). The effects of simulation complexity and hypothesis generation strategy on learning. *Journal of Research on Computing in Education, 27*, 75–91.

Reid, D. J., Zhang, J., & Chen, Q. (2003). Supporting scientific discovery learning in a simulation environment. *Journal of Computer Assisted Learning, 19,* 9–20.

Scardamalia, M., & Bereiter, C. (1994). Computer support for knowledge-building communities. *Journal of the Learning Sciences, 3,* 265–283.

Shute, V. J., & Glaser, R. (1990). A large scale evaluation of an intelligent discovery world: Smithtown. *Interactive Learning Environments, 1*, 51–77.

Tabak, I., Smith, B. K., Sandoval, W. A., & Reister, B. J. (1996). Combining general and domain-specific strategic supports for biological inquiry. In C. Frasson, G. Gauthier, & A. Lesgold (Eds.), *Intelligent tutoring systems* (pp. 288–297). Berlin: Springer-Verlag.

Teasley, S. D. (1995). The role of talk in children's peer collaborations. *Developmental Psychology, 31*, 207–220.

van Joolingen, W.R. & de Jong, T. (1997). An extended dual search space model of scientific discovery learning. *Instructional Science, 25*, 307–346.

Webb, N. M. (1989). Peer interaction and learning in small groups. *International Journal of Educational Research, 13*, 21–39.

Zhang, J. (2000). Scientific discovery learning based on computer simulation: The inner conditions and the facilitative learning support. Unpublished doctoral thesis, Beijing Normal University, China.

Zhang, J., Chen , Q., Sun, Y., & Reid, D. J. (2004). A triple scheme of learning support design for scientific discovery learning based on computer simulation: Experimental research. *Journal of Computer Assisted Learning, 20*, 269-282.

APPENDIX

Focused Examination of Volume: An Example That Was Given Full Score

No.	Shape	Mass (g)	Volume (cm3)	Buoyant force (N)
1 left	Ball	18.00	30.00	0.18
1 right	Ball	18.00	20.00	0.18
3 left	Box	5.00	10.00	0.05
3 right	Box	5.00	400.00	0.05

Chapter 7

Design Principles for Scaffolding Technology-Based Inquiry

Cindy E. Hmelo-Silver
Rutgers, The State University of New Jersey

Reform movements in science education have been urging that students have the opportunity to engage in the practice of scientific inquiry (American Association for the Advancement of Science, 1993; National Research Council, 1996). Teaching students the skills of planning and interpreting experiments is difficult. Students often focus on the doing, obtaining desired outcomes rather than on learning about causes and effects. That is, they often focus on *doing* rather than *learning* (Schauble, Klopfer, & Raghavan, 1991). To learn how to design and interpret the results of experiments, students need appropriate scientific problem-solving experiences and guidance to help shape the experience, model the inquiry process, and encourage reflection. One approach is to simplify these experiences to make inquiry accessible to learners, but an alternative approach is to provide authentic inquiry experiences and scaffold students in dealing with the complexity (Chinn & Malhotra, 2002). In this chapter, I discuss how technology-supported learning environments can provide rich contexts to support learning through problem solving. I present a framework for designing scaffolding in such environments, and in particular, discuss how and why those might be instantiated in technology-based inquiry learning environments. Finally, I relate this framework to the problem of helping students learn through problem solving in the context of scientific inquiry by (a) explaining how this framework was used prospectively to design scaffolding for inquiry learning in the Oncology Thinking Cap (OncoTCAP; Hmelo et al., 2001) and (b) presenting an empirical study of the use of scaffolded inquiry in the OncoTCAP environment.

Open-ended, technology-supported learning environments greatly expand the range of available inquiry contexts. For example, simulations and modeling tools provide opportunities for students to explore phenomena while engaging in a meaningful task. They can provide access to rich and complex phenomena. For example, ModelIt allows students to model various aspects of water quality in local streams (Metcalf, Krajcik, & Soloway, 2000); BGuile provides a rich database of information to allow students to explore microevolution on the Galapagos Islands (Reiser et al., 2002), and GenScope provides a simulation for exploring genetic phenomena (Horwitz

& Christie, 2000). However, just providing the opportunity for inquiry does not necessarily afford deep learning. Scaffolding can allow learners to deal with complexity and successfully learn from problem-solving simulations. Engaging in inquiry provides an opportunity to learn through problem solving (LPS). Students engage in inquiry to learn about content, methods, and epistemology of science, but how does one support students in learning as part of some activity? In addition, ensuring that learning is not forgotten in the process of solving a problem is a major issue for situated learning environments (Bereiter & Scardamalia, 1989). These are important issues for scaffolding learning through problem solving.

LEARNING THROUGH PROBLEM SOLVING: A CONCEPTUAL FRAMEWORK

Constructivist and sociocultural theories suggest mechanisms that might provide support for learning through problem solving (Bereiter & Scardamalia, 1989; Collins, Brown, & Newman, 1989; Lave, Murtagh, & de la Rocha, 1984). From these perspectives, learning occurs through active construction of knowledge, growth of metacognitive strategies, and an enculturation process. This enculturation process means that learners are gradually able to participate in disciplinary practices and adopt disciplinary norms. Thus, learning is socially mediated through common tools, discourse, belief systems, and goal structures. This involves working with others to solve meaningful problems, learning the language of the discipline, and using the tools of practice. For example, in mathematics, that might mean working on complex problems in realistic contexts using calculators and becoming facile with mathematical language and notations (Cognition and Technology Group at Vanderbilt [CTGV], 1997). There are two approaches that researchers take with respect to describing and realizing LPS, part of the general notion of learning by doing—in other words, learning through engaging in activity.

The first perspective is doing for learning. In this perspective, students are engaged in activities that help them to achieve learning goals. For example, the goal may be for students to complete a series of worksheets to learn arithmetic. They "do" the worksheets to learn the math skills. Ng and Bereiter (1991) examined the kinds of goals that students take on in this perspective. Typically, students have task completion goals (just get the task done; learning is incidental), instructional goals (do it to learn what is expected), and knowledge-building goals (do to learn for one's own agenda). Knowledge-building goals are generally not the norm (outside of academia); although this is an ideal, people rarely endeavor to learn without regard to the relevance of the learning to some activity or performance goal (Ram & Leake, 1995). Indeed, Ng and Bereiter (1991) found that task completion goals and instructional goals were most common and knowledge-building goals were quite rare. School activities often engender task completion and instructional goals so that students' goals are to complete the worksheets and other activities; learning is secondary to completing these tasks (Bereiter & Scardamalia, 1989).

The alternative is learning for doing (Hmelo & Guzdial, 1996); that is, to establish a performance goal first (e.g., solving a problem) and to arrange the context such that learning subgoals arise naturally from that task. For example, if students are involved in designing a playground, they need to learn something about geometry to accomplish the task (CTGV, 1997). In this model, the learning subgoals are necessary to accomplish the performance. This is how many learning goals most commonly are generated in everyday life—from the need to achieve some performance or activity goal (CTGV, 1997; Ram & Leake, 1995). In real-world settings, people often learn what they need to know in a just-in-time fashion (Resnick, 1987). In problem-based learning, an approach that originated in medical education, students learn through solving ill-structured problems and reflecting on their experiences. They generate their learning goals in the service of problem solving (Barrows, 1988; Hmelo & Lin, 2000). In the anchored instruction approach, developed at Vanderbilt (CTGV, 2000), video-based scenarios provide goals for the students to learn and use mathematical problem-solving techniques. In all these cases, the goal is not just knowledge building but it is knowledge building for action (Hmelo & Guzdial, 1996).

For the students, the difference between these is in terms of the primary goal: learning versus performance. The former is the traditional focus of school; the latter is the focus of real work (Soloway, Guzdial, & Hay, 1994). In school, however, without the right kinds of support, learning is often forgotten and task completion becomes the goal (Doyle, 1983; Krajcik et al., 1998). The goal in the latter approach is for students to grapple with an authentic problem, learn through the process of solving this problem, and then develop a solution that approaches what an expert might develop. Many tasks afford a rich assortment of potential learning subgoals that allow learners to understand how knowledge is applied (Spiro, Feltovich, Jacobson, & Coulson, 1992). For example, one can learn math through cooking, with the appropriate supports that instill the learning goals to understand fractions. One might learn about principles of physics while repairing a bicycle or designing a roller coaster, provided that appropriate supports for learning are in place.

The challenge is to develop supports for open, complex problems that arise in real practice that (a) lead to successfully solving the problems and (b) support deep learning. In other words, we need to develop support for "doing with understanding" (Barron et al., 1998). To facilitate LPS, the process, supports provided to the student, and context in which the problem solving occurs can all be structured to help students learn through problem solving and inquiry experiences. Students often do not know what process to use, or use an idiosyncratic process (Jeffries, Turner, Polson, & Atwood,

1981; Krajcik et al., 1998; Lave et al, 1984) and unless students perceive that the problem is solvable (with a good process and enough support), a complex problem can diminish motivation more than augment it (Blumenfeld et al., 1991). Because many open-ended LPS environments are technology based, software-realized scaffolding is one approach to providing supports that can enable students to be successful at both learning and problem solving. These are supports provided to a student that define the process such that the student successfully solves the problem and learns in the process.

SCAFFOLDING

Scaffolding is support that (a) enables students to accomplish tasks they could not otherwise do and (b) facilitates learning to succeed even without the support (Collins et al., 1989; Rogoff, 1990; Wood, Bruner, & Ross, 1976). Scaffolding has been used to describe how tutors help students solve problems, how parents teach their children, and how masters teach apprentices a craft (Lave & Wenger, 1991). Well-designed scaffolds help ensure that learners are successful at new tasks and can extend their competences into new areas (Hogan & Pressley, 1997). In general, scaffolding is meant to fade, disappearing over time (sometimes returning at points) so that the learner can succeed without the support. Chi, Siler, Jeong, Yamauchi, and Hausman (2001) defined scaffolding very broadly as any activity that leads students to engage in constructive processing.

Hogan and Pressley (1997) narrowed this definition as they noted the importance of several critical elements in scaffolding scientific inquiry. These include providing help only when needed, establishing shared goals, diagnosing students' understanding, maintaining joint attention, providing feedback, and assisting in internalization. They emphasized providing tailored assistance through use of questioning, prompting, cuing, modeling, telling, and discussing. Peer scaffolding can also play a role in LPS but may require additional support for the collaboration to be effective (King, 1999; O'Donnell & O'Kelly, 1994). These techniques have limitations due to large class sizes and the associated demands on the teacher. Technology can help overcome these limitations to help extend the role of the teacher and enhance LPS. Software-realized scaffolding is a set of technological techniques that provide similar kinds of support.

The literature on cognitive apprenticeship discusses three kinds of scaffolding (Collins et al., 1989; Guzdial, 1994; Hmelo & Guzdial, 1996):

    1. *Communicating process* involves presenting the process to students, structuring and sometimes simplifying the process. Presenting the process to students can occur through modeling or demonstrating a process. Structuring the process means defining the

stages of an activity, whereas presenting it involves explicitly providing the students with the stages of an activity. This can be accomplished by means of checklists, or in software, by menus or screen design such as on-screen forms. These interface elements can help provide target structures that constrain and guide student inquiry (Collins & Ferguson, 1993). This type of support is particularly useful in structuring problem-solving and inquiry processes.

2. *Coaching* refers to providing guidance to learners while they are performing a task. In a traditional apprenticeship, it is the feedback and suggestions that the master provides to the apprentice as he or she is performing the task. This can be accomplished by highlighting critical steps of the process as the student is working on a problem. Coaching can include statements that help frame the problem and articulate inquiry goals (Hogan & Pressley, 1997). In technology, this can be implemented in intelligent tutoring systems or as multiple layers of help that students can use on request (Katz & Lesgold, 1993; White & Frederiksen, 1998)

3. *Eliciting articulation* is asking the students to explain (to themselves or others) to encourage reflection. This can help enhance constructive processing (Chi et al., 2001) and make thinking visible, and therefore, an object for discussion and revision. Generic prompts that ask learners to articulate their thinking lead to significant reflection and subsequent learning (Chi et al., 2001; Davis, 2003). Encouraging reflection helps prepare learners to transfer the knowledge and skills they are learning (Salomon & Perkins, 1989). This may involve asking the students questions, requiring them to keep structured notebooks, or having students work in collaborative groups in which they need to discuss the project they are working on.

Software-realized scaffolding provides scaffolding in technology-based learning environments. Hmelo and Guzdial (1996) described two kinds of software-realized scaffolding: Black-box and glass-box. *Black-box scaffolding* facilitates student performance (more than learning), but is not meant to fade during use of the environment. Black-box scaffolding performs a task in place of the student, usually because learning to perform that goal is determined not to be important for the learning goals of the activity. For example, a statistical calculator for an inquiry environment can be black-box scaffolding if the designers determine that performing computations is not an important learning goal. Black-box scaffolding fades if the student ever performs the activity without the environment. It simplifies the process but does not increase the student's understanding of it.

Glass-box scaffolding facilitates performance and learning, but may fade during use of the environment. It is important for students to understand what glass-box scaffolding is providing so that they eventually internalize functions that glass-box scaffolding provides. This can include several different kinds of supports, including prompts for self-explanations, performance supports that are meant to fade (e.g., a structured editor might fade in favor of a traditional program editor if learning syntax is an objective), collaborative environments, intelligent agents (as coaches), and representations (e.g., column and row headings, prompts for representation elements). Glass-box scaffolding allows students to focus on one set of learning goals before dealing with other, lower level subgoals. Table 7.1 provides examples of black-box and glass-box scaffolding that communicate process, provide coaching, and elicit articulation.

TABLE 7.1.

Examples of Glass- and Black-Box Scaffolding

	Glass-Box Scaffolding	Black-Box Scaffolding
Communicating Process	Apple Guide: Explains what to do to accomplish a task and why.	Menu systems: Do not make evident why items are disabled.
Coaching	ThinkerTools Inquiry: Critics that explain rationale or support inquiry processes (White, Shimoda, & Frederikson, 2000).	Wizards in Microsoft Excel: Accomplish tasks under your direction, but do not tell you how to do them without the coaches—the scaffolding is opaque and not meant to fade.
Eliciting articulation	CSILE: Students choose the metacognitive prompts, which they will then use to label their notes—students understand that this is to help them understand the role of their notes in their learning (Scardamalia et al., 1989).	Summary prompts in Microsoft Word: No explanation for why a summary (and other articulations) are being requested.

Glass-box scaffolding leads to effects of technology; that is, the learner has a "cognitive residue" from the experience (Salomon, 1993). By observing the model of a knowledgeable coach, seeing implicit processes made explicit, and being encouraged to reflect on those processes, the learner is able to construct new knowledge structures and modify existing structures. Black-box scaffolding provides effects with technology; learners can do things that they could not otherwise accomplish. However, once the support is removed, the problem has been solved but the learner has not learned anything about the process. Cognitively, this allows the individual to off-load part of the task and affords higher level accomplishments (Salomon,

1993). For example, by having a computer perform a complex calculation, learners can allocate cognitive resources to understanding why the calculation is being performed. The choice between black-box and glass-box scaffolding is a curricular and design decision, not a technical concern. One uses black-box scaffolding to limit students to an efficient path, one where the search space is constrained and there are few unproductive paths. Glass-box scaffolding may constrain the students' search on some paths and expand their exploration on paths that relate to the intended learning goals.

Emile provides a good example of the use of glass-box and black-box scaffolding (Hmelo & Guzdial, 1996). Emile was an environment designed to support students in learning both physics and programming by building physics simulations (Guzdial, 1994). The student's goal was to build interesting simulations of kinematic phenomena. They referred frequently to their prospective audience as they designed and built their simulations, often adding features based on what their friends might like in their software. The learning subgoals required to meet this high-level performance goal included (a) the physics principles necessary to create a realistic simulation, and (b) the programming knowledge necessary to realize their performance goal. Emile included extensive scaffolding to support students in achieving these goals. Students began programming simulations in Emile by assembling code fragments called actions into complete programs. Students were provided with an extensive library of actions to use in constructing their programs. Each action could be manipulated as a component: saving, copying, and moving into a desired position. Emile also supported fading the scaffolding: (a) Students could choose (by setting a preference) to create their own actions, and (b) students could further choose to edit program lines of code directly rather than manipulate actions. The fading enabled students to explore and learn programming at more sophisticated levels to simulate more advanced physics than was supported by the library. This is an example of glass-box scaffolding that helped structure the process for the learner by providing code fragments that were transparent and could be modified. Emile included black-box scaffolding as well. The code students actually ran was not exactly the code that they had written. Rather, the code was annotated to provide debugging features such as program tracing and stepping. However, the annotations were completely invisible to the students and could not be faded (turned off). Although one could imagine an alternative version of Emile where students could inspect, manipulate, and perhaps even construct their own debugging supports to learn more about debugging, debugging skills were not part of the curricular goals for Emile. Thus, it was sufficient to leave the debugging supports as black-box scaffolding.

The Knowledge Integration Environment (KIE) provides examples of both glass- and black-box scaffolding (Bell & Davis, 2000; Linn & Hsi, 2000; Slotta & Linn, 2000). It provides black-box scaffolding in the form of data that have already been collected, allowing students to focus on making sense of data and using the data to formulate scientific arguments. By directing students to particular sources of information, it constrains students' search and allows them to focus on particular aspects of the scientific inquiry process. They provide support that elicits student articulation to make their thinking visible as well as coaching to support specific activities. The coaching provides students with hints about what they need to do to complete a particular activity, but also why they should be doing it.

White et al. (2000) developed the ThinkerTools Inquiry system that provides scaffolding geared toward general support of scientific inquiry. Their software forms a system of general glass-box scaffolds to support several inquiry tasks: project design, project presentation, and project evaluation. This is accomplished through memory systems such as checklists that communicate elements of the inquiry process and software advisors that provide coaching in the form of advice and modeling the language of inquiry.

In the examples presented, this framework was used retrospectively to describe different approaches to scaffolding. In designing the Phase 2 clinical trial wizard, the glass- and black-box approach was used to prospectively design scaffolding.

SCAFFOLDED INQUIRY WITH THE ONCOLOGY THINKING CAP

Simulations can offer the kinds of experiences that allow students to design studies under different assumptions and compare the results, with support to help shape their experience, model the inquiry process, and encourage reflection (Collins et al., 1989; Kolodner, 1997). Allowing students to simulate experiments and observe the results in real time provides the dynamic feedback needed to enhance their understanding of both the process of experimentation and their knowledge of the domain (Schauble, Glaser, Duschl, Schulze, & John, 1995). Simulations, often designed for experts, may impose excessive demands on those just learning to conduct inquiry and who may have misconceptions about this process. Computer simulations can help students learn about scientific inquiry by communicating important considerations in experimental design and providing feedback in the form of the results of their inquiry. That is, software-based scaffolding can be designed to help the students focus on the relevant aspects of the inquiry process. In particular, glass-box scaffolding can be used to help students learn a systematic process of inquiry, whereas black-box scaffolding can be used to perform tasks in the background that are not relevant to the learning goals. These principles were used to design the Phase 2 Clinical Trial Wizard scaffolds for the OncoTCAP.

OncoTCAP is a simulation tool designed to help professional cancer researchers. Software-realized scaffolding, the Phase 2 Clinical Trial Wizard, was developed to help medical students learn about a specific form of inquiry, clinical trial design. Domain-specific scaffolding is important to use here, because, as Baker and Dunbar (1996) noted, the expert scientist often has a mental schema with slots to be filled with the items needed to determine an experimental design. Glass-box scaffolding was used to communicate the design process and help learners construct these schemas. Black-box scaffolding was used elsewhere in the program to avoid the cognitive burden of statistical computations that might interfere with the main learning goals.

In applying these design principles to OncoTCAP, curricular decisions were made by first considering what an expert needs to know about clinical trial design. This entailed a cognitive task analysis of the domain of clinical trial design to determine how development of a clinical trial design schema could be facilitated through the use of glass- and black-box scaffolding.

Clinical Trial Design

The process of bringing a new cancer drug to market is complex. A drug must go through several stages of testing before it can be available for general use. In the usual paradigm of drug development, Phase 1 of clinical testing involves a small number of patients. Its aim is to identify an acceptably safe dose, the maximally tolerated dose. A Phase 2 trial may be subsequently conducted to see if there is an indication of activity against the disease. This may be followed by a randomized Phase 3 trial to compare the new drug against a standard treatment.

This work focuses on the Phase 2 clinical trial design process. The researchers choose a single dosage and schedule for the drug and specify several requirements for the study characteristics. A design is then chosen to meet those criteria. Typically, the goal is to accurately distinguish subtle effects. Designing Phase 2 trials is complex and students need to learn about the trial design process. To help students understand the subtle aspects of designing clinical trials, the Phase 2 Clinical Trial Wizard was implemented on the foundation of the OncoTCAP simulation.

OncoTCAP provides a comprehensive modeling workbench for experienced cancer researchers. This tool is versatile and can be used to model clinical trials, but its comprehensiveness may impose excessive cognitive difficulty for the novice. Clinical trial design involves knowledge of well-defined designs for testing new drugs. Experienced researchers develop this knowledge through extensive experience spanning numerous clinical trials (Baker & Dunbar, 1996). Designing scaffolds that communicate the slots in the experimental design process is one way to support learners in constructing these schemas.

The Oncology Thinking Cap Software

The core concept underlying OncoTCAP is that tumors are composed of heterogeneous populations of cells and this forms the basis for understanding cancer (Fuji, Marsh, Cairns, Sidransky, & Gabrielson, 1996). OncoT-CAP can model important concepts in cancer research and treatment such as cell cycle control; cell growth, death, and repair mechanisms; mutational processes, treatment characteristics, resistance, and schedules; and genetic characteristics (Day, Shirey, Ramakrishnan, & Huang, 1998). The OncoT-CAP simulation engine provides the means to represent treatment regimen and simulate its effect on tumor growth and normal organ function. The schedule and applications of the drug reduce counts of different tumor cells based on dose and drug definition. The tool is very flexible, but also very difficult to use. The main screen has 20 parameters that need to be set. Setting the parameters themselves is non trivial. Each of these parameters has many options and rules that the user needs to set. This proved quite difficult for novices. In a usability study, Ramakrishnan, Hmelo, Day, Shirey, and Huang (1998) found that students had a great deal of difficulty creating a cell property in OncoTCAP, but that when asked to do the same task with scaffolding that communicated the process of setting the property, they reliably improved their performance. The Clinical Trial Wizard created a special-purpose interface that "black-boxed" many of these parameters, allowing the users to consider only those relevant for clinical trial design, and only at the times at which they need to be considered.

OncoTCAP provides two different ways of displaying the simulation. These two representations allow learners to explore the simulation from the perspective of an individual patient or the population of patients. In the Cancer Patient Simulator (CPS), the interactive simulation of tumor cell growth is shown by means of a graph of the number and characteristics of tumor cells in a single patient (Fig. 7.1). The relative cell counts of the different cell types are shown in different colors. The event window shows different clinical and simulation events such as simulation start, diagnosis, tumor spread, treatment, and death.

The Multiple Patient Simulator (MPS), shown in Figure 7.2, runs the same simulation as the CPS over many patients. While the simulation is running, the MPS window shows a dynamic tally of the number of patients simulated, the number of responses, cures, and deaths. At the end of the simulation, the MPS window displays the clinical event history for any selected patient. The patient histories can be browsed, and a selected patient history can then be displayed in the CPS, showing the ordinarily invisible details of cancer subpopulation sizes over time. The MPS and CPS are the two main representations used for displaying simulation results in the Phase 2 Clinical Trial Wizard.

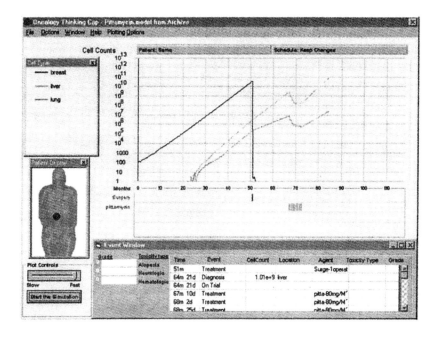

FIG.7.1. Cancer Patient Simulator.

Phase 2 Clinical Trial Wizard

From earlier usability studies, it was clear that the OncoTCAP software was too complex for medical students (Ramakrishnan, et. al., 1998). Among the aspects of trial design that are important, some are not obvious to novices. The more obvious elements of a Phase 2 clinical trial design include:

- Background information about the disease being treated.
- Information on the drug being tested, including the results of pre-clinical and Phase 1 testing.
- Criteria for including or excluding patients.
- Dosage, treatment schedule, and treatment duration.
- Choice of clinical measurement endpoint.

Students may be aware that the elements in this first list are important but not know how to operationalize them. Students may not consider other elements that are part of an expert schema, including:

- Conditions under which the drug dosage is to be modified as a result of toxic side effects
- Conditions under which the patient will stop receiving the experimental protocols

- Operational characteristics needed for determining how many patients will be included in the study, and of that group, how many
responses need to be observed to conclude that the drug should be
studied further.

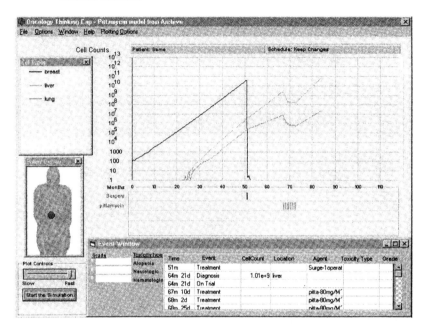

FIG.7.2. Modified Multiple Patient Simulator summarizes the results of the simulation and allows students to examine individual patient event histories.

The Phase 2 Clinical Trial Wizard was developed to help scaffold student learning about trial design without dealing with the complexity of the
underlying simulation environment. Thus, the wizard is a form of black-box
scaffolding for OncoTCAP as it allows the users to learn about clinical trial
design without dealing with the complexities of the underlying modeling
tool. A *Wizard* in a computer program is a set of simple screens that walk
the user through a complex cognitive task. The screens were designed to
help communicate the trial design process in terms of the Phase 2 clinical
trial design schema. By presenting these elements, the wizard is also providing glass-box scaffolding to help explicitly communicate the clinical
trial design process. In particular, the issue of toxicity is an important issue
in trial design and the conditional rules that deal with toxicity (dose modification and deciding when to remove patients from treatment altogether) are
difficult to understand, and failure to understand them has serious consequences. Thus curricular decisions were made based on (a) what experts

need to know and (b) important aspects of the design process that novices have difficulty understanding.

By differentiating the task into multiple subtasks, the cognitive load required to complete the task is reduced. Thus, the glass-box scaffolding helps make the task manageable while focusing the learner's attention on semantically important elements of the clinical trial design process. The wizard provides support for running the simulation in three ways. First, it makes the learner aware of the expected elements in the Phase 2 Clinical Trial Wizard by the contents of the various screens. Second, the wizard structures inquiry by allowing learners to concentrate on one subtask at a time. The screens of the wizard allow the learner to easily navigate from one subtask to another as needed. Third, much of the complexity of the simulation environment is reduced as the wizard uses a simplified interface to (a) transparently generate the input needed to run the simulation and (b) present only the relevant results to the learner.

The computer-supported clinical trial design and interpretation process can be divided into four components (Fig. 7.3). The first component is the Introduction screen, which describes the objective of the wizard and the information the user will need to provide in the rest of the screens. The second component consists of a set of four well-defined steps, represented in screens that lead the user through the subtasks. In these computer screens, the user specifies the Schedule, Dose Modifications Due to Toxicity, Off-Treatment Criteria, and Statistical Criteria. The Statistical Criteria screen black-boxes the computational procedure that takes the user's statistical criteria and produces an optimal design. The third component is the Summary, in which the user's trial design from Steps 1 through 4 are summarized in natural language, and from which the user can initiate the clinical trial just designed by clicking a button. The MPS, which actually runs and displays the results of the clinical trial, forms the fourth component of the process. Learners can navigate between various screens in the wizard using simple buttons. The MPS has a Back to the Wizard button to return to the wizard screens to revise their design and run a new trial. It is important to note that although the wizard models and communicates the design process, additional scaffolding was provided through the collaborative classroom activity structure. The facilitator and other students can help elicit reflective articulation (see Hmelo, Nagarajan, & Day, 2000, for additional details). In the next section, I report the results of using this software in a classroom design experiment.

METHODS

In the research reported here, students used the Phase 2 Clinical Trial Wizard using a model of breast cancer and a hypothetical drug, Pittamycin.

Participants

The participants in this study were 24 fourth-year medical students who were divided into six groups of four students each. This was part of the class requirement for a clinical elective in cancer medicine.

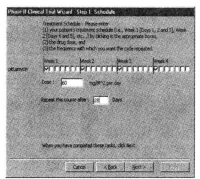
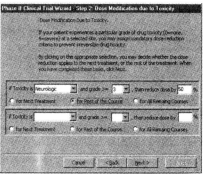

Step 1 of the Clinical Trial Design Wizard: Defining the dose and schedule

Step 2 of the Clinical Trial Design Wizard: Modifying the dose due to toxicity

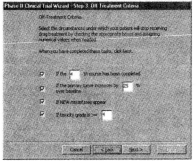
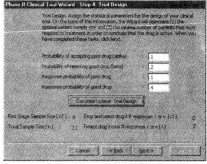

Step 3 of the Clinical Trial Design Wizard: Deciding when individual patients will be taken off-treatment

Step 4 of the Clinical Trial Design Wizard: Setting the statistical parameters

FIG. 7.3. Phase 2 Clinical Trial Wizard.

Procedure

Prior to the computer session, students collaboratively developed a research plan for a Phase 2 trial of the hypothetical drug, Pittamycin. Students were given laboratory and Phase 1 trial results. This information included the maximum dose that was tolerated by patients and the types of toxicities that were observed (impaired neurological function and blood formation). Subsequently, each group of students worked collaboratively at a computer for a 2-hour session. The students first used the wizard to design and simulate the Phase 2 trial they had designed before coming to the lab. The author facilitated the learning process by (a) asking students to summarize their initial proposal, (b) helping them with any interface problems they had and ensuring that they understood relevant software features, (c) asking them to justify their changes, and (d) encouraging them to reflect on what they learned from this experience.

The goal of this exercise was for students to create clinical trial concept sheets, which are short summary plans for testing a new drug. The concept sheet is a brief summary of the research design and implementation. It contains sections such as objectives, eligibility criteria, study design, treatment plan, treatment modifications, and definitions of study endpoints. Students received a one-page instruction sheet that specified what should be included. Students worked on this task in their groups. The groups completed their first concept sheet before using the software and a second draft post simulation.

Data Sources

Each run of the wizard generated a printout of the group's design. These design summaries contained all the characteristics the students specified: the dosage and schedule, any conditional rules for dose modification and removing patients from treatment, and the statistical considerations. In addition, students printed out the results of the simulation that represented their group's final design. Group and individual learning were assessed using data from two sources: (a) group clinical concept sheets pre- and post software use, and (b) individual critiques of a flawed concept sheet. For the investigators to assess individual learning, students critiqued a flawed concept sheet. This was a proposal to test another hypothetical drug that was active against lung cancer. The concept sheet was 1.5 pages long including instructions. The students were asked to list any problems that they found and for each, explain why it was important. The critiquing task was completed after students wrote the first draft of their concept sheet in groups and after the simulation.

RESULTS

Collaborative Simulation Activity

The six student groups ran an average of 8.67 simulations during their sessions. The students' first simulation run was an implementation of their initial proposal. For the majority of the groups, their initial dosage and drug schedule was consistent with the maximum tolerated dosage identified in the Phase 1 trial information they received. The wizard constrained students to specifying the dosage and scheduling more completely. Five of the six groups' pre computer session concept sheets discussed monitoring patients for toxicity, but none of the six initial concept sheets specified dose modifications if toxicities were observed. In the first run through the wizard, when students reached the screen where they could set conditional rules for dose modification, students in all the groups expressed surprise. In each session, the students initially skipped these rules in their first attempt, and thus remained consistent with their original design. They were less surprised when they encountered the screen that required them to specify off-treatment criteria. Although only two of the groups' concept sheets contained vague specifications for off-treatment criteria, students seemed to understand the importance of setting these criteria.

Finally, students specified the statistical characteristics of the trial design. The program then computed the number of patients needed and the number of responses that would allow them to conclude that the drug had some clinical activity and was worthy of further study. The facilitator tried to elicit student understanding of these statistical considerations, but this remained a murky area for the students.

Following this, students simulated running the trial they had designed. The MPS summary displayed the results of the simulation and included information about patient responses, deaths due to tumor, and deaths due to drug toxicity. The students closely watched the cumulating results. They were able to view a survival plot that allowed them to see the increase in median survival time. This helped students appreciate the therapeutic effect of the treatment. In addition, they observed that along with any responses they observed, there were often many patients that died due to drug toxicity. Their perusal of individual patient records, particularly in the first few runs, led students to a deeper understanding of (a) the types of toxicity that occurred, (b) how long they took to resolve, and (b) why responses tended to occur fairly early in the treatment process.

This concern with toxicity led all groups to add dose modification rules in their second design. The dose modification screen was an important focus for student discussion about the nature of different types of toxicity (Hmelo, Nagarajan, & Day, 2002). For example, students noted that neurologic toxicity caused very severe consequences (i.e., death of brain tissue) and only resolved slowly, whereas toxicity that impaired the body's ability to make new blood cells resolved quickly and was treatable. Thus, students tended to be conservative about dose modification for brain toxicity and would severely reduce the dose. They were more liberal in tolerating hematologic toxicity, which reflects current oncology practice. Thus the scaffolding provided a focus for students as it modeled an important aspect of the trial design process.

The groups changed an average of 19.17 (SD = 6.57) variables over the course of their simulation trials. The most frequent types of changes were in the category of dose modification (M= 9.33, SD = 4.68). The next most frequent were variables involving conditional rules: when to remove patients from treatment (i.e., because the drug did not help or was posing life-threatening toxicity) and when to modify the dosage because of drug toxicity (M = 5.00, SD = 1.83 for off treatment; M = 4.83, SD = 2.27 for dose modification). These latter two are particularly interesting because initially the students only had very vague ideas about how to deal with contingencies until they were faced with making decisions about them in the wizard. The students did not make any changes in the statistical portion of the wizard.

Group Assessment of Learning

The group pre- and postconcept sheets were coded for the 24 elements of the Phase 2 clinical design schema described earlier. In the postcomputer session concept sheets, all groups modified their initial design to include specific dose modification rules and stop-treatment rules. They also specified their statistical parameters more completely, suggesting that students were constructing more elaborate trial design schemas. This was consistent with the scaffolding provided by the wizard. The conditional rules (dose modification and off-treatment criteria) and statistical characteristics were either not fully specified or not considered in the initial trial designs, but were included after students were made aware of these factors in the wizard.

The pre- and postconcept sheets were coded for the components needed for a complete trial design. The mean score for the initial trial design was 14.83 out of a possible 24 points (SD = 4.07). The students improved on their post research proposals to a mean of 19.83 (SD = 1.55, $t(5)$ = 2.89, p < .05). Table 7.2 shows descriptive statistics for the different aspects of the clinical trial schema. The results indicate that students improved in their specification of dose and schedules and application of dose modification rules. This is consistent with the locus of changes that students made during the trial. Although students made changes to off-treatment criteria, this was not reflected in an improvement on the postconcept sheet assessment. This may have occurred because, in response to the wizard, students realized that the conditions that they were thinking about as off-treatment criteria could be reconceptualized as dose modification rules.

TABLE 7.2

Group Concept Sheet Scores by Schema Slot

Schema Slot	Max	Pre		Post	
		M	SD	M	SD
Background information	4	3.33	0.75	3.33	0.75
Participation criteria	3	2.00	0.58	2.50	0.96
Dose and schedule*	3	2.50	0.41	2.92	0.19
Dose modification**	3	0.67	1.11	2.83	0.37
Off-treatment	3	1.50	0.96	1.83	0.90
Statistics	8	4.67	2.56	4.67	2.56
Response criteria	1	0.83	0.37	0.92	0.19
Total	25	14.83	4.07	19.83	1.55

*$p < .05$ for improvement pre to post.
**$p = .005$ for improvement pre to post

Assessment of Individual Learning

Tested individually, students became better at critiquing the flawed clinical concept sheets. There were 20 components missing from the concept sheet used in the assessment. The mean number of missing components identified by students was 4.67 ($SD = 3.25$) after the initial design, and 6.92 ($SD=2.60$) after the computer session, a significant improvement, ($t(23) = 2.96, p < .05$). This effect was largely a result of improved knowledge of how to plan the treatment (including conditional rules for modifying dosages and taking patients off treatment). Because the students spent much of their time engaged in adjusting the treatment plan, this is where we expected to see the greatest effect. None of the students mentioned dose modification in their critique before using the software but after the simulation session, 84% of the students discussed dose modification criteria, $t(23) = 9.8, p < .001$. There was no improvement in the students' understanding of the statistics, which was to be expected because this aspect of trial design was largely black-boxed and not a focus of discussion.

DISCUSSION

New approaches to teaching and learning stress the importance of teaching scientific inquiry in the context of authentic problems that integrate both the inquiry process and subject matter learning (CTGV, 2000). However, LPS can be extremely difficult for novices and requires additional support to help them manage the complexity. Scaffolding students' scientific inquiry using a simulation is a promising approach. The notion of glass-box scaffolding was used in designing the software. The forms that comprised the wizard helped the students specify the study characteristics and opened up the processes of clearly specifying the dose, schedule, and conditional rules, thus communicating the Phase 2 trial design process. Reflective articulation was elicited as part of the activity structure in which the facilitator encouraged students to explain their thinking. The learning outcome results suggest that the glass-box scaffolding left students with effects of the scaffolding as they internalized particular aspects of the inquiry process. Those aspects that were black-boxed (i.e., the statistical aspects) were not internalized.

Understanding how students learn through solving authentic problems and engaging in inquiry is an important aspect of developing learning environments that support constructive activity. LPS helps motivate learners and enables them to construct deep understanding and transferable knowledge and skills (Guzdial et al., 1996). Trying to support problem solving and inquiry while maintaining a focus on learning is an important issue for designers of learning environments. This chapter tackled that issue by focusing on the kind of scaffolding support that can be provided by using the metaphors of glass-box and black-box scaffolding to describe ways of supporting learning and performance. Deciding what kind of support to provide depends on the learning goals being emphasized. Black-box scaffolding is used to allow the learner to complete a task and allow cognitive resources to be concentrated on higher level goals. Glass-box scaffolding allows the learner to look inside the support being provided, understand what the support is, and understand why it is needed. Research is needed to continue to evolve a theory of learning through problem solving to further elucidate and rigorously test design principles for scaffolding learning environments.

ACKNOWLEDGMENTS

I am indebted to Mark Guzdial for many conversations about scaffolding and for our collaboration on the theoretical development presented in earlier work. I am grateful to Roger Day, Sailesh Ramakrishnan, and Bill Shirey for the opportunity to work with them on OncoTCAP project and the Clinical Trial Wizard. The work on OncoTCAP was supported by an NIH R-25 grant to Roger Day. This chapter is dedicated to the memory of my father, who was my first science teacher.

REFERENCES

American Association for the Advancement of Science. (1993). *Benchmarks for science literacy*. New York: Oxford University Press.

Baker, L. M., & Dunbar, K. (1996). Problem-spaces in real-world science: What are they and how do scientists search them? In G. Cottrell (Ed.), *Proceedings of the Eighteenth Annual Conference of the Cognitive Science Society* (pp. 21–22). Mahwah, NJ: Lawrence Erlbaum Associates.

Barron, B. J. S., Schwartz, D. L., Vye, N. J., Moore, A., Petrosino, A., Zech, L. (1998). Doing with understanding: Lessons from research on problem and project-based learning. *Journal of the Learning Sciences, 3/4,* 271–312.

Barrows, H. (1988). *The tutorial process*. Springfield: Southern Illinois University Press.

Bell, P., & Davis, E. A. (2000). Designing Mildred: Scaffolding students' reflection and argumentation using a cognitive software guide. In B. Fishman & S. O'Connor-Divelbiss (Eds.), *Fourth International Conference on the Learning Sciences* (pp. 142–149). Mahwah, NJ: Lawrence Erlbaum Associates.

Bereiter, C., & Scardamalia, M. (1989). Intentional learning as a goal of instruction. In L. B. Resnick (Ed.), *Knowing, learning, and instruction: Essays in honor of Robert Glaser* (pp. 361–392). Hillsdale, NJ: Lawrence Erlbaum Associates.

Blumenfeld, P. C., Soloway, E., Marx, R. W., Krajcik, J. S., Guzdial, M., & Palincsar, A. (1991). Motivating project-based learning: Sustaining the doing, supporting the learning. *Educational Psychologist, 26,* 369–398.

Chi, M. T. H., Siler, S. A., Jeong, H., Yamauchi, T., & Hausman, R. G. (2001). Learning from human tutoring. *Cognitive Science, 25,* 471–533.

Chinn, C. A., & Malhotra, B. A. (2002). Epistemologically authentic inquiry in schools: A theoretical framework for evaluating inquiry tasks. *Science Education, 86,* 175–218.

Cognition and Technology Group at Vanderbilt. (1997). *The Jasper project: Lessons in curriculum, instruction, assessment, and professional development*. Mahwah, NJ: Lawrence Erlbaum Associates.

Cognition and Technology Group at Vanderbilt. (2000). Adventures in anchored instruction: Lessons from beyond the ivory tower. In R. Glaser (Ed.), *Advances in instructional psychology* (Vol. 5, pp. 35–100). Mahwah, NJ: Lawrence Erlbaum Associates.

Collins, A., Brown, J. S., & Newman, S. E. (1989). Cognitive apprenticeship: Teaching the crafts of reading, writing, and mathematics. In
L. B. Resnick (Ed.), *Knowing, learning, and instruction: Essays in
honor of Robert Glaser* (pp. 453–494). Hillsdale, NJ: Lawrence
Erlbaum Associates.

Collins, A., & Ferguson, W. (1993). Epistemic forms and epistemic games:
Structures and strategies to guide inquiry. *Educational Psychologist, 28,* 25–42.

Davis, E. A. (2003). Prompting middle school science students for productive reflection: Generic and directive prompts. *Journal of the
Learning Sciences, 12,* 91–142.

Day, R., Shirey, W., Ramakrishnan, S., & Huang, Q. (1998, April). *Tumor
biology modeling workbench for prospectively evaluating cancer
treatments.* Paper presented at the 2nd IMACS International Mul-
ticonference: CESA'98 Computational Engineering in Systems
Applications, Tunisia.

Doyle, W. (1983). Academic work. *Review of Educational Research, 53,*
159–199.

Fuji, H., Marsh, C., Cairns, P., Sidransky, D., & Gabrielson, E. (1996). Genetic divergence in the clonal evolution of breast cancer. *Cancer
Research, 56,* 1493–1497.

Guzdial, M. (1994). Software-realized scaffolding to facilitate programming for science learning. *Interactive Learning Environments, 4,*
1–44.

Guzdial, M., Kolodner, J. L., Hmelo, C. E., Narayanan, N. H., Carlson, D.,
Rappin, N. (1996). Computer support for learning through complex problem-solving. *Communications of the ACM 39 (4),* 43-45.

Hmelo, C. E., & Guzdial, M. (1996). Of black and glass boxes: Scaffolding
for learning and doing. In D. C. Edelson & E. A. Domeshek (Eds.),
Proceedings of ICLS 96 (pp. 128–134). Charlottesville, VA:
AACE.

Hmelo, C. E., & Lin, X. (2000). Becoming self-directed learners: Strategy
development in problem-based learning. In D. Evensen & C. E.
Hmelo (Eds.), *Problem-based learning: A research perspective on
learning interactions* (pp. 227–250). Mahwah, NJ: Lawrence Erlbaum Associates.

Hmelo, C. E., Nagarajan, A., & Day, R. S. (2000). Effects of high and low
prior knowledge on construction of a joint problem space. *Journal
of Experimental Education, 69,* 36–56.

Hmelo, C. E., Nagarajan, A., & Day, R. (2002). "It's harder than we
thought it would be": A comparative case study of expert–novice
experimentation. *Science Education, 86,* 219–243.

Hmelo, C. E., Ramakrishnan, S., Day, R. S., Shirey, W., Brufsky, A., Johnson, C. (2001). The Oncology Thinking Cap: Scaffolded use of a
simulation to learn about designing clinical trials. *Teaching and
Learning in Medicine, 13,* 183–191.

Hogan, K., & Pressley, M. (1997). Scaffolding scientific competencies within classroom communities of inquiry. In K. Hogan & M. Pressley (Eds.), *Scaffolding student learning*. (pp. 74-107). Cambridge, MA: Brookline Books.

Horwitz, P., & Christie, M. A. (2000). Computer-based manipulatives for teaching scientific reasoning: An example. In M. J. Jacobsen & R. B. Kozma (Eds.), *Innovations in science and mathematics education* (pp. 163–192). Mahwah, NJ: Lawrence Erlbaum Associates.

Jeffries, R., Turner, A. A., Polson, P. G., & Atwood, M. E. (1981). The processes involved in designing software. In J. R. Anderson (Ed.), *Cognitive skills and their acquisition* (pp. 255–283). Hillsdale, NJ: Lawrence Erlbaum Associates.

Katz, S., & Lesgold, A. (1993). The role of the tutor in computer-based collaborative learning situations. In S. Lajoie & S. Derry (Eds.), *Computers as cognitive tools* (pp. 289–318). Hillsdale, NJ: Lawrence Erlbaum Associates.

King, A. (1999). Discourse patterns for mediating peer learning. In A. M. O'Donnell & A. King (Eds.), *Cognitive perspectives on peer learning* (pp. 87–117). Mahwah, NJ: Lawrence Erlbaum Associates.

Kolodner, J. L. (1997). Educational implications of analogy: A view from case-based reasoning. *American Psychologist, 52,* 57–66.

Krajcik, J., Blumenfeld, P. C., Marx, R., Bass, K. M., Fredricks, J., & Soloway, E. (1998). Inquiry in project-based science classrooms: Initial attempts by middle school students. *Journal of the Learning Sciences, 3/4,* 313–350.

Lave, J., Murtagh, M., & de la Rocha, O. (1984). The dialectic of arithmetic grocery shopping. In B. Rogoff & J. Lave (Eds.), *Everyday cognition: Its development in social context* (pp. 67–94). Cambridge, MA: Harvard University Press.

Lave, J., & Wenger, E. (1991). *Situated learning: Legitimate peripheral participation*. Boston: Cambridge, University Press.

Linn, M. C., & Hsi, S. (2000). *Computers, teachers, peers: Science learning partners*. Mahwah, NJ: Lawrence Erlbaum Associates.

Metcalf, S. J., Krajcik, J., & Soloway, E. (2000). Model-It: A design retrospective. In M. J. Jacobson & R. B. Kozma (Eds.). *Innovations in science and mathematics education* (pp. 11–46). Mahwah, NJ: Lawrence Erlbaum Associates.

National Research Council. (1996). *National science education standards*. Washington, DC: National Academy Press.

Ng, E., & Bereiter, C. (1991). Three levels of goal orientation in learning. *Journal of the Learning Sciences, 1,* 243–271.

O'Donnell, A. M., & O'Kelly, J. O. (1994). Learning from peers: Beyond the rhetoric of positive results. *Educational Psychology Review, 6,* 321–349.

Ram, A., & Leake, D. B. (1995). Learning, goals, and learning goals. In A. Ram & D. B. Leake (Eds.), *Goal-driven learning* (pp. 1–37). Cambridge, MA: MIT Press.

Ramakrishnan, S., Hmelo, C. E., Day, R. S., Shirey, W. E., & Huang, Q. (1998). The integration of a novice user interface into a professional modeling tool. In C.G. Chute (Ed.) *Proceedings of AMIA 98* (pp. 678-682). Bethesda, MD: AMIA.

Reiser, B. J., Tabak, I., Sandoval, W., Smith, B., Steinmuller, F., & Leone, A. (2002). BGuILE: Strategic and conceptual scaffolds for scientific inquiry in biology classrooms. In S. M. Carver & D. Klahr (Eds.), *Cognition and instruction: Twenty-five years of progress* (pp. 263–306). Mahwah, NJ: Lawrence Erlbaum Associates.

Resnick, L. B. (1987). Learning in school and out. *Educational Researcher, 16*(9), 13–20.

Rogoff, B. (1990). *Apprenticeship in thinking.* NewYork: Oxford, University Press.

Salomon, G. (1993). No distribution without individual cognition: A dynamic interactional view. In G. Salomon (Ed.), *Distributed cognitions* (pp. 111–138). New York: Cambridge, University Press.

Salomon, G., & Perkins, D. N. (1989). Rocky roads to transfer: Rethinking mechanisms of a neglected phenomenon. *Educational Psychologist, 24,* 113–142.

Scardamalia, M., Bereiter, C., McLean, R. S., Swallow, J., & Woodruff, E. (1989). Computer-Supported Intentional Learning Environments. *Journal of Educational Computing Research 5,* 51-68.

Schauble, L., Glaser, R., Duschl, R., Schulze, S., & John, J. (1995). Students' understanding of the objectives and procedures of experimentation in the science classroom. *Journal of the Learning Sciences, 4,* 131–166.

Schauble, L., Klopfer, L. E., & Raghavan, K. (1991). Students' transition from an engineering model to a science model of experimentation. *Journal of Research in Science Teaching, 28,* 859–882.

Slotta, J. D., & Linn, M. C. (2000). The knowledge integration environment: Helping students use the Internet effectively. In M. J. Jacobson & R. B. Kozma (Eds.), *Innovations in science and mathematics education: Advanced designs for technologies of learning* (pp. 193–226). Mahwah, NJ: Lawrence Erlbaum Associates.

Soloway, E., Guzdial, M., & Hay, K. E. (1994). Learner-centered design: The challenge for HCI in the 21st century. *Interactions, 1*(2), 36–48.

Spiro, R. J., Feltovich, P. J., Jacobson, M. J., & Coulson, R. L. (1992). Cognitive flexibility, constructivism, and hypertext: Random access instruction for advanced knowledge acquisition in ill-structured domains. In T. M. Duffy & D. H. Jonassen (Eds.), *Constructivism and the technology of instruction: A conversation* (pp. 57–75). Hillsdale, NJ: Lawrence Erlbaum Associates.

White, B. Y., & Frederiksen, J. R. (1998). Inquiry, modeling, and metacognition: Making science accessible to all students. *Cognition and Instruction, 16,* 3–118.

White, B. Y., Shimoda, T. A., & Frederiksen, J. R. (2000). Facilitating students' inquiry learning and metacognitive development through modifiable software advisors. In S. Lajoie (Ed.), *Computers as cognitive tools II: No more walls* (pp. 97–132). Mahwah, NJ: Lawrence Erlbaum Associates.

Wood, D., Bruner, J. S., & Ross, G. (1976). The role of tutoring in problem solving. *Journal of Child Psychology and Psychiatry, 17,* 89–100.

eStep as a Case of Theory-Based Web Course Design

Sharon J. Derry
University of Wisconsin–Madison

This chapter explains the design of eSTEP, an innovative, experimental Web-based course in the learning sciences[1] for preservice teachers. I describe instructional approaches that integrate interactive study of classroom video and learning science text, supported by an online multimedia environment called a Knowledge Web (KWeb), with collaborative lesson design, supported by an online environment for problem-based learning (PBL). I also address the question, Why do it that way? Although the answer includes a number of practical considerations, this chapter focuses largely on how theory about learning and transfer is reflected in course activities and the Web site that the eSTEP team designed to support them. The theoretical question addressed is how to make the conceptual systems (e.g., learning sciences) taught in college truly useful in students' future professional lives (e.g., teaching). This chapter reflects several years of thinking about this problem and about course and Web site designs for transfer.

For purposes of grounding this discussion, I consider both learners and practitioners as people experiencing a social and physical learning environment through cognitive processes of recognition and pattern matching that are essentially perceptually based. From this perspective, I believe that professors and managers of large, professionally oriented courses will make the ideas they teach useful for their students' later practices to the extent they can create course designs that cause students to repeatedly mesh (e.g., Glenberg, 1997) patterns of activation associated with conceptual systems taught in courses with families of perceptual patterns resembling events learners will experience in practice. I think of these learned meshings, which I call *conceptual/perceptual fields*, as potential future patterns of activation. To help students be able to bring perceptual/conceptual fields to bear on practice, they must also be meshed with cognitive patterns repre-

---

[1] The term *learning science* refers to current scientific theory and findings concerning student learning and development in informal and formal educational settings.

senting useful planning heuristics (Suchman, 1987) that can guide later re-flective, adaptive action in practice. I argue that this complex form of pat-tern meshing is most likely to occur when learners are motivated, through learning environment design—which includes material, social, and facilita-tion structures—to actively use course concepts to develop and evaluate multiple goal-based plans in the context of studying a library of cases that realistically represent a range of patterns that will be experienced in the field of practice. My chapter further elaborates this view.

THE ACTIVITY FIELD HYPOTHESIS

This theoretical framework, which is guiding and evolving with our work, assumes existence of a continuously organizing *activity field*, a complex system of cognitive activation representing human experience of an activity that can be thought about and analyzed at the individual or group level. The *learning activity field* is a virtual "space" where, when instruction is well-designed and facilitated, cognitive patterns activated by more perceptual aspects of instruction (e.g., video study) mesh with interpretive patterns generated through more conceptually based aspects (e.g., text study) as well as "embodied" patterns of planning and problem solving (Glenberg, 1997) representing authentic professional activity. This concept of mesh within a dynamic cognitive field is related to Clancey's (1997) ideas about percep-tual-conceptual organization and coupling.

Conceptual/Perceptual Mesh

Although all forms of learning probably promote both perceptual and con-ceptual activation, some forms, such as study of video, are regarded as more perceptual, whereas others, such as reading or explanation, are typically more conceptual. The challenge of instructional design is to create activity fields in which learners repeatedly mesh conceptual knowledge with per-ceptual visions of practice to which those concepts apply.

Repeated meshing is important. To illustrate this point, consider the following: Students in sixth-grade mathematics often manifest an opera-tional rather than a relational view of equality, and the future teacher must learn to recognize a range of perceptual patterns through which students reveal this developmental phase. Behavioral patterns demonstrating opera-tional or relational views vary widely, but share family resemblance (Wittgenstein, 1953). Not all possible patterns can be experienced during instruction, but if a sufficient number of patterns are experienced, such as through video study, new patterns within a family might later be appropri-ately identified by a human perceptual system even if never seen before.

However, pattern activations are only meaningful if they simultaneously activate concepts relevant to practice.

Importance of Planning Activity

The activity field hypothesis suggests that for many forms of professional practice, including teaching, an important mechanism promoting both mesh and transfer is adaptive planning in action. That is, "perceptualized" concepts learned in a course must become useful tools for guiding practice, not just passive interpretive lenses (Kozulin, 1998). This idea is based partly on current theory and research on event perception (Zacks & Tversky, 2001), which suggests that events of professional practice are experienced as unfolding, nested goal-based plans—basically cause-and-effect structures—that are adapted in action (Suchman, 1987). As an example of a nested plan, consider that a teacher in an inquiry science classroom may ask students questions with the immediate goal of surfacing current understandings, a proximal goal of challenging misconceptions if detected, and a longer range goal of preparing students to participate meaningfully in an inquiry science experience. Hence, our teacher education courses attempt to promote meshing of perceptualized learning science concepts to professional activity, through discussions that employ those concepts as a cause-and-effect language of goal-based planning. The validity of this argument is supported by Dewey (1933), Schon (1983), and Lemke, (2002).

Entering Student Characteristics

In addition, as the substantial body of research studying the effects of prior knowledge on learning documents, what students bring to the instructional environment is also important. As a whole, we characterize the learning activity field as a generalized cognitive *attitude*, a representation of experience that includes not only patterns of activation representing organization and meshing of perceptual and conceptual experience with general plans for future action, but also the prior attitudes, feelings, beliefs, and dispositions that learners activate during the learning activity. As part of the learning activity field, these neural patterns can exert biasing influences on professional learners' goals, on what they perceive, and on how such perceptions support learning new conceptual systems. Such biasing cognitions may be either compatible or incompatible with the conceptual and planning material being taught, and so may either help or hinder learners' receptivity and ability to "see" and operate using concepts being offered. For example, if a teacher-learner tends to believe that a child's environment is mostly responsible for whether a child learns, that teacher may easily learn to see and plan in terms that help engineer that environment, but may have more difficulty learning to see and develop the child as a self-determining cognitive agent.

Understanding and challenging or building on such cognitive attitudes is part of the instructional design problem.

Social Interaction

Much social interaction can occur within learning environments, including online ones. Students in our courses discuss readings, participate in collaborative lesson study, and engage in small-group lesson design projects. The activity field within a learning environment is both highly influenced and revealed by social interactions, which can be studied for how such interactions promote meshings that may or may not relate to targeted learning goals. Following Wertsch (e.g., Wertsch & Kazan, 2003), we view social interaction online as a dialectical struggle to mesh learners' perceptual and prior-knowledge activations that occur within the course's activity field with the language (e.g., learning science concepts) of a new semiotic community they are asked to appropriate, within task and social structures imposed by the course. There is the struggle of using learning science terminology to help articulate and represent thoughts to others in the class; and there is the struggle of trying to mesh personal understandings with signs for ideas and goals, expressed in learning materials and assignments and by others. Beyond this problem of understanding and being understood in the course context—as Greeno's (2001) analysis reminds us—there are social achievements related to being able to carry course ideas and practices into the future professional social problem-solving environment. Thus, the learning activity field must also help students activate and mesh patterns of social interaction, including attitudes and behaviors that will support carrying forward and sustaining practices advocated by the course. From the goals of classroom participation to sustained participation in professional practices, learning is a very complex form of social coordination involving such issues as status, competence, agency, and personality within social environments (Clancey, 1997; Greeno, 2001). By focusing on the learning activity field revealed through social discourse as a dependent variable, research may uncover ways that group composition, activity design, tool design, and forms of facilitation work together online as factors that help or hinder achieving desired forms of mesh through social learning (e.g., Chernobilsky, Hmelo-Silver, & DelMarcelle, 2003; DelMarcelle & Derry, 2003).

Summary

In very brief summary, the basic idea is that instructional design for useful conceptual learning should attend to the activity fields created through learners' participation. To promote transfer, learning environments must create fields characterized by mesh between families of perceptual patterns representing events of practice and the conceptual systems taught in their courses. There should also be mesh with causal structures that can guide reflective action in practice, and dispositions and beliefs that support conceptual thinking during practical activity. Here, we propose that such learning fields are likely to be produced if learners are motivated, through "designed" social interaction, to use and combine concepts in developing and evaluating multiple goal-based plans in the context of varied authentic situations that are presented perceptually, as with video study. By conceptualizing activity fields as virtual complex systems that can be described and manipulated, we open the door for new ways of thinking about such ideas as transfer and authenticity. For example, rather than judging the authenticity of a classroom learning activity in terms of its physical match to a professional environment, one might ask whether the learning activity fields and professional activity fields match in critical ways.

TOWARD A DEEPER UNDERSTANDING OF MESH

An Event-Perception Analysis

A typical way of thinking about professional education is that it helps learners acquire conceptual systems (e.g., the learning sciences) that can flexibly be assembled and imposed as interpretive lenses on events of practice (e.g., classroom teaching), to guide and inform it (e.g., Spiro, Feltovich, Jacobson, & Coulson, 1992). Presumably, such flexible cognition increases the professional's power to see multiple possible interpretations and solutions, leading to better decision making. However, a relevant concern not addressed in many such analyses is how the events of professional practice, on which conceptual systems are flexibly imposed, are naturally segmented and structured by the physical world, including the physiological systems of human event perception. This issue is important, for event perception in professional environments is a cognitive and physical process strongly influenced by the "bottom-up" mechanisms of human perception that have evolved to reflect how humans interact with events in situ. We argue that instructional designers should give more consideration to how humans connect with their environment through the meshing of perceptual patterns triggered by the environment and those triggered by conceptual memories learned through courses.

In classroom teaching, the professional landscape teams with hundreds of complexly interwoven events occurring simultaneously in three-dimensional space and continuously over time. The teacher at the center must refine, select, edit, and impose order on what would otherwise be an overwhelmingly complex experience. Fortunately there are features of the physical world that form patterns and gestalts, and human perceptual systems have evolved means of taking advantage of them. Zacks and Tversky (2001) synthesized a large body of literature concerned with perception of events in a dynamic environment. Events as perceived tend to be structured by certain objective physical properties, such as change in an actor's behavior or direction of movements, and have beginnings and endings that are reliably detected across observers. These perceived patterns very often correspond to chunks of activity representing systems of physical causality: For example, an agent (e.g., the teacher) acts on objects (e.g., writes on a transparency) with particular, usually multiple, physical consequences (e.g., a display appears and students stop talking and look toward it). There is evidence that such episodes are perceived as objects that have parts (agent, action, ground, direction) and are themselves parts of hierarchical event structures (Zacks & Tversky, 2001). For example, the transparency event is part of a larger daily activity that is a part of a lesson that has particular event outcomes in the context of a larger instructional unit and course, all associated with learning goals and expected outcomes for students.

Although events are perceptually cued by objective physical properties and individuated on the basis of physical properties of motion and causality, they may also activate conscious meaning through mesh with prior knowledge. Teachers interpret events, drawing inferences about classroom plots, students' understandings and motives, problem-solving processes, and so on. Many researchers and theorists have noted that the ordinary language that people use to talk about, and draw inferences regarding, the meaning of events is shaped by physical properties of events themselves and reflects how the human body interacts with them. For example, Zacks and Tversky (2001) suggested that the basic syntactic and semantic structures of all languages reflect the hierarchical and causal nature of events. Highly regarded theorists such as Hofstadter (2000) and Lakoff and Johnson (1980) proposed that all thinking is fundamentally analogical and metaphorical (terms used interchangeably), grounded in our embodied experiences with the environment. Informal professional discourse about teaching practice thus reflects a universal human tendency to interact naturally with events as physically structured and perceived. This is why teachers *cover*, *skip*, *skim*, *go through*, *go over*, and *throw around* the ideas they teach.

This viewpoint has implications for professional education. One is that practitioners' comfort with a new conceptual discourse, such the learning sciences, will likely be tied to how naturally that language maps to events in the world of work. Those involved in teacher education are well aware that teacher-learners often expect and gain little from the theories to which their curricula expose them (Simon, 1992). Scientific theory talk might be too far removed from the events of classroom practice, either because the foundations of educational science were not historically grounded in classroom practice in the first place, or because even grounded theories have evolved away from practice through out-of-classroom professional discourse (e.g., talks and discussions at academic conferences, in journals, in university classrooms). If theory is not well matched to student teachers' perceptions of the kinds of events it is supposed to explain, it will not be used, especially if teacher-learners are immersed in classroom experiences while studying.

However, an event that can informally be described as the teacher presenting material and students receiving it can also be seen as the teacher talking in a way that uses instructional tools and artifacts that help direct students' attention to what is most important for them to process. An instructional objective is characterized, not merely in everyday terms as a goal to cover material or pass a test, but as a goal of helping students construct understanding of important concepts in a way that will help them transfer that understanding into new situations within communities of practice outside of school. These sentences are examples of using learning sciences terms in a way that maps naturally on event perception, but that expands and deepens it in useful ways. Note that most terms that mesh natural events to the science of learning are also metaphors. Also note that these metaphors serve as tools in teaching; that is, they serve useful functions, such as describing goals for teaching and learning and actions, including mental ones, for achieving them. Teachers who understand the metaphors of learning science can unpack them further for deeper insights into the causal nature of instructional goals and actions, including hidden "thinking" actions that facilitate goal achievement.

In sum, this drives home the point that which learning science concepts taught in education courses, as well as the way they are taught, should respect the shape of the perceptual landscapes of practice. Such concepts must not only make sense metaphorically in helping teachers describe a complex professional world that is structured by event perception, but also serve as useful tools for flexible goal-based planning and action within that world.

Instructional Design for Enhancing Mesh

In recent years, many researchers and educators have proposed innovative designs for learning environments that strengthen the connection between the conceptual world of classrooms and real-world practice. Some examples include cognitive flexibility hypertext systems (Spiro, Feltovich, Jacobson, & Coulson, 1992), PBL (Barrows, 1988; Koschmann, Glenn, & Conlee, 1999), understanding by design (Wiggins & McTighe, 1998), and contrasting cases instruction (Schwartz & Bransford, 1998). All of the aforementioned methods can be characterized as proposals for creating forms of conceptual mesh that we see as necessary for conceptual transfer, and we have in fact incorporated all of them into our work. However, we believe that each of these approaches, at least in the versions implemented so far, is in some sense incomplete in that it has dealt with only part of the mesh that needs to occur within the learning activity field. Some proposals focus on connecting practice with planning; others center on creating mesh between conceptual analogies and the landscape of event perception, or on the connection between the learning of new concepts and prior knowledge. In our work we have borrowed from and adapted these approaches, creating and testing hybrid blends of them in an attempt to motivate more complex forms of mesh within the learning activity field. In the following sections we describe how we have adapted and blended several of these approaches in the context of an experimental online course.

A Course Experiment

For several semesters, my colleague Cindy Hmelo-Silver and I have collaboratively designed, taught, and studied learning within two courses for preservice teachers at UW-Madison and Rutgers. The two courses, called the eSTEP (Elementary and Secondary Teacher Education Project) courses, have similar goals: to help preservice teachers acquire useful knowledge of learning science concepts. The courses employ similar methods consistent with the AFH viewpoint. Briefly, these methods include integrated study of learning science text and video cases of lessons, coordinated with small-group projects involving adaptive lesson design following a PBL format (Barrows, 1988; Hmelo-Silver, 2002).

The courses must be adapted to the different sites and student populations. For example, the UW-Madison course is taught to a socially cohesive cohort of upper division students who have completed their majors and been selected into a competitive secondary teacher education program. The Rutgers students are not in a cohort, are in earlier stages of their degree work, are considering teaching as a career, and enroll in a learning science course as a prerequisite to applying for admission to either elementary or secondary teacher education. An example of a required adaptation is that UW students are mostly grouped by disciplinary major and they study and design lessons for secondary students, whereas Rutgers students work in interdisciplinary groups and study in both elementary and secondary contexts.

Partly to reduce the time and resources necessary to separately develop eSTEP for the particular needs of two different populations of users, partly to address a number of practical considerations, and partly to obtain standardization and control for our research, we built a common Web site to support both courses. In both courses, most of the students' time is spent in extended (2–3 week) facilitated small-group PBL activities in which they acquire (through integrated text and video study) learning science concepts as they design assessments and learning activities. Although students may continue to attend some classes to hear occasional lectures and meet face-to-face with their groups, much of their individual and collaborative work takes place and is submitted online through the course Web site (eSTEP-Web.org), which guides individual students and groups through steps for completing each problem. This Web site illustrates much of what about our course is theory-based design, and is described next.

Components of the Course Web Site, eSTEPWeb.org

The main parts of the course Web site, eSTEPWeb.org, are:

1. The "Knowledge Web," a multimedia online resource that is used during lesson design and includes two integrated networks:
   a. The Case Library, (see Fig. 8.1), a digital library of stories of real lessons in real classrooms and representing the landscape of practice.
   b. The theories net, a hypertext book containing conceptual knowledge from the learning sciences and representing the conceptual landscape.
2. PBL Online: A site including step-by-step scaffolding and tools to help groups carry out authentic lesson design tasks

I explain these Web components in greater detail, simultaneously elaborating on the theoretical issues related to their design and describing instructional activities that make use of them.

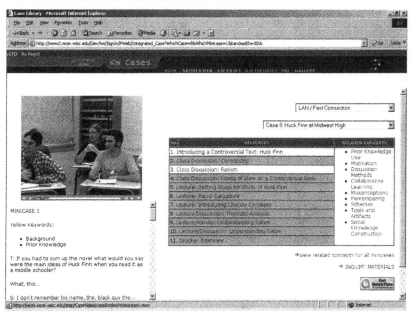

FIG.8.1. A web page from the Case Library.

The eSTEP Knowledge Web

This discussion draws a distinction between two kinds of domains: the highly perceptual domain of professional practice (e.g. mechanical engineering, medical practice, classroom instruction, etc.) versus the highly conceptual domain of classroom subject-matter knowledge through which practices should be understood and interpreted (e.g. physics and art for architecture, biological sciences for medical practice, learning psychology for teaching). The eSTEP Knowledge Web (KWeb for short) is a multimedia hypertext resource on the www that contains materials related to both practitioner and conceptual domains and that is explicitly designed to support instruction that has the goal of creating mesh between them.

The Case Library: A Landscape of Practice

Our case library is a flexible instructional resource that represents the perceptual landscape of practice. It currently contains 11 cases for five subject disciplines and is growing. Although cases vary in how they are designed, a typical case in our collection is a story about learning and instruction in an actual classroom setting. A typical case's components include approximately 15 to 20 minutes of edited video plus supplementary materials, such as teacher commentary, examples of student work, class handouts, test scores, information about school context, and so on. Our cases range from examples of problematic classroom instruction that could be improved (redesign cases) to examples of exemplary instruction we would like for students to emulate (adaptation cases). Most cases lie somewhere in between.

To enable instructional flexibility we edit video footage in a way that captures major to-be-taught themes in small segments of video called minicases. In eSTEP, cases are collections of such minicases; however, when desired, minicases can also be extracted from their larger case contexts and reassembled into different groupings for instructional purposes. For example, a lecture or other presentation for the eSTEP course might use an assembly of minicases, drawn from various case contexts, that illustrates a course topic, such as social knowledge construction or teaching for transfer.

How the technology itself shapes conceptual analysis is illustrated by our rule of thumb for minicase size: A video less than 2 minutes long can be downloaded quickly with a fast connection and, if downgraded in quality, with a 56K modem. Hence, the 2-minute (or less) minicase was born. Yet our experience indicates that this is a good grain size for illustrating meaningful and complex instructional events that require complex interpretations using multiple concepts.

The Theories Net as a Conceptual Landscape

The theories section of KWeb currently consists of about 100 densely inter-
linked web pages that contain explanations and other instruction for selected learning sciences concepts. These pages are intertwined and linked
with the more then 100 minicase segments in the case library that illustrate
varied instances of learning science concepts at work in the classroom.
Hence, while viewing any case or related minicase in the KWeb cases library, the user can easily link to relevant learning science concepts in the
theories net. For example, from a case on the teaching of *Huckleberry Finn*,
shown as Figure 8.1, one can access a range of learning science concepts in
the theories net, which can be combined in various ways to help interpret
the case. Also, on every learning science page within the theories net, there
are links, not only to other related concept pages, but also to minicases
within the library that illustrate that page's learning science concept. This is
shown in Fig. 8.2, where the page on social knowledge construction contains a list of minicases from the case library that illustrate a range of situations in which that concept is experienced in the domain of practice.

   Designing the conceptual structure for the theories network proceeded
as a rational historical and conceptual analysis of the learning sciences domain. Our analysis uncovered significant theoretical intermingling: Similar
but subtly different ideas with similar names are claimed by different theories. A good example is the term *constructivism,* which is uncomfortably
shared by the sociocultural, sociocognitive, and information processing
theories and is used in reference to both instructional methods and theories
of learning. Also, there was considerable historical confounding of theoretical knowledge. For example, the body of knowledge that is often taught and
represented as information processing theory presents concepts derived
from early versions of the theory side by side with those derived from later
versions. Hence, from the student's perspective, one idea may seem to be
explaining phenomena in very different ways, a situation that frequently
leads to serious misconceptions that must be challenged, such as the idea
that information processing psychology is synonymous with a behavioral or
passive "knowledge-transmission" perspective. Designing the theories net
taught us firsthand that learning sciences in instructional contexts is an ill-
structured domain with numerous sources of messiness.

   We needed a pragmatic structural metaphor for setting up the site and
specifying relationships among concept pages and minicase nodes in the
network. Such structures facilitate navigation and serve as tools for constantly updating and maintaining a Web site, but they impose constraints on
domain representation that we must be able to live with. We chose a loose
family metaphor, such that every page, or node, in the theories net is linked
with other nodes in the web that are designated as its ancestors, parents,
children or "other relatives." The theories net is organized as three inter-
linked idea families: Cognitive Theory, Sociocultural Theory, and Cross-

Theory Ideas. The Cognitive Theory family has two main branches: Information Processing and Sociocognitive (Developmental) Theory. Each idea family and its main branches also have several major family branches. As an aid in navigation, the family metaphor helps prevent disorientation in hyperspace (Diaz, Gomes, & Correia, 1999), because from any entry point within the theories net the user can identify the major theory and idea families to which that page belongs. The family metaphor also supports site maintenance very adequately: When a new node is added, only its parents and relatives need be specified, then its position in the network with respect to all other nodes is automatically generated. And, although the family relationships metaphor is an apparent hierarchy at superordinate levels, it is a loose family metaphor that affords creation of partially nondirectional graph structures specifying complex interrelationships among pages (i.e. there can be three or more parents, and relational links can be either directional or nondirectional). Thus, the structure is valid for representing complex, conceptually messy domains.

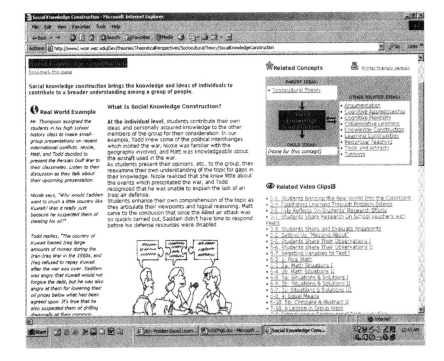

FIG.8.2. A page from the Theories Net.

Instruction With the eSTEP Knowledge Web

In designing our KWeb, we adopted a number of proposals and ideas from CFT, a theory of advanced knowledge acquisition for ill-structured domains. In particular, we designed the KWeb to support two forms of hypertext instruction suggested by R.J. Spiro (personal communication, 2002): domain criss-crossings and small multiples. We use these strategies to create mesh between the conceptual analogies of the learning sciences and the perceptual landscape of practice. These strategies attempt to compact experience and so are expected to accelerate development beyond what might be accomplished through traditional instruction combined with field-based professional placements.

Domain Criss-crossings and Small Multiples

We combine domain criss-crossings with the small multiples strategy. Small multiples is an exercise in which students are guided as they repeatedly blend together different concepts in different combinations in the process of developing alternative complex interpretations for a single case. For example, one student might critique a teaching video case from a sociocultural perspective using the concepts of authenticity, tools and artifacts, social context, mentoring, and identity development. Another student might offer an alternative but equally valid and coherent interpretation of the same video that blends sociocognitive and information processing ideas, such as metacognition, attention, prior knowledge, misconceptions, and disequilibrium. The pros and cons of the different interpretations could be discussed. The purpose is to guide students in studying a large number of varied real-world cases that represent the landscape of practice contexts in which those concepts are to be "perceptualized." For example, a course lecture or assignment might require students to view a large number of minicases illustrating a variety of ways the concept *transfer* is found in the domain of practice. The strategy is intended to help students develop patterns of understanding representing varied ways in which practice is meshed with key subject-matter concepts. Video cases are usually preferred, because perceptual processes stimulated while watching an activity on film show significant overlap with those stimulated during physical participation in an activity (Gibson, 1979; Zacks & Tversky, 2001).

Domain criss-crossings are combined with the small multiples strategy, in which students are asked to repeatedly mesh concepts, in different blends, to a single case. The purpose is to provide students with practice in "perspectivity" (e.g. Goldman-Segall, 1998), and to encourage habits of mind associated with "cognitive flexibility" (e.g., Feltovich, Spiro, Coulson, & Feltovich, 1996). Depending on the sophistication of the students and the difficulty of the subject matter, the multiples approach may begin with activities in which students examine complex cases but consider multiple themes sequentially. For example, students in eSTEP may be asked to "see" a minicase, first as an example of knowledge construction, then as an example of classroom management, and finally as an example of formative evaluation. From this strategy of sequential viewing, instruction proceeds to a more advanced phase in which students are scaffolded in constructing and evaluating more complex interpretations that combine and recombine multiple concepts.

Case-based Learning With the KWeb: Learning Theory

What type of learning does the criss-crossing and small multiples activities afford? Our way of thinking is that examining many cases as examples of learning science concepts creates overlapping idea "families" (Derry, 1996), assemblies of meshed conceptual/perceptual fields. Instruction creates, within students, memory patterns associated with various concepts and their contexts. Through criss-crossing and small multiples instruction using a video case library, the students' memory representations are gradually enriched, differentiated, and expanded with exposure to varied perceptual presentations of concepts. Hence, for each student individually or the class as a whole, the conceptual/perceptual field associated with a concept such as transfer increases in its range of real-world application.

Students are not expected to recall specifics of cases used in instruction, because a process of pattern meshing occurs in which both constructive and reconstructive memory processes promote active memory change over time, leading to integration, abstraction, and loss of case details. We believe this process tends to strengthen memory and later perception for situational aspects that tend to occur repeatedly across contexts and cases with family resemblance.

Our view of case-based learning can be contrasted with that of Kolodner and Guzdial (2000), for example, who assumed memories of cases encountered remain basically intact. From their perspective, cases represent possible templates for thought, old friends that, if learned, might later be recalled, adapted, and combined to guide thinking in a new situation. The belief is that new events in the real world will trigger a "reaching backward" (Salomon & Perkins, 1989) to find relevant cases in memory, which are then used to guide current behavior. From our viewpoint, the reaching backward is triggered by pattern matching with the environment, which activates a conceptually rich memory *schema*, as that term in used is the tradition of Bartlett (1932), representing a meshed perceptual/conceptual cognitive field.

eSTEP PBL Online

Returning to the description of eSTEP components, this section describes the online PBL environment we have developed. The KWeb, as described earlier, is used both independently and in conjunction with PBL online. The purpose of PBL is to help students acquire domain knowledge, usually scientific knowledge, in the context of solving real-world problems based on real-world cases. Originally developed for medical education (Barrows, 1988), PBL has made its way into many other types of classrooms, including K–12 classrooms. What we know about this method is largely gleaned from wisdom of practice, both from its developer, Howard Barrows, and from the widespread PBL community that uses this method and has begun to conduct research on it. In this community there is a standard PBL procedure, and some members feel strongly that it should not be changed. This procedure takes students through a facilitated small-group, student-centered process in which students discuss and "solve" a problem case (e.g., a case of medical diagnosis) as they fill out a whiteboard that has been structured to facilitate their inquiries. In filling out the whiteboard, students proceed through stages in which they observe facts in the case, formulate hypotheses, identify learning issues for further investigation, conduct research, and revisit and discuss hypotheses until a problem solution is reached. The main purpose of this activity is to learn about a conceptual scientific domain that underlies a real-life problematized case.

The purpose of PBL in eSTEP is to promote meshing of perceptualized learning science concepts to visions of future professional activity, through discussions that employ those concepts as a cause-and-effect language of goal-based instructional planning. Originally, eSTEP PBL problems were face-to-face small-group activities supported by the KWeb but carried out primarily in classrooms. The eSTEP team decided that PBL should go online for a number of reasons (Steinkuehler, Derry, Hmelo-Silver, & DelMarcelle, 2002). First, we wanted to distribute some of the facilitation responsibility to the system and the students themselves, lightening the responsibility for teacher assistants, who often lack experience with this complex instructional method. Second, the eSTEP community is growing, and an online system facilitates larger course management. It makes the site more scalable for professional development, enabling us to offer distance education courses. Finally, the online environment facilitates data collection and analysis for our research on professional learning and transfer.

The eSTEP PBL system supports either online small-group instruction or a hybrid model in which students meet face-to-face in small groups during class and then extend their work outside of class through online interaction. In both online and hybrid models, students are guided by a human facilitator (typically a teaching assistant), and are required to complete and submit individual and group artifacts, products related to and documenting various stages of instructional design, through the online system. The online system collects and displays data on student performance and affords detailed monitoring of work by individuals and small groups, permitting detailed (and powerful) formative assessment of individuals and groups throughout the course. This is both a bane and benefit of online courses, for this monitoring capability makes them powerful learning tools that place substantial performance demands on both students and instructors (O'Donnell, 2002).

Although they can be set up in different ways by the course manager, eSTEP instructional design activities in PBL typically involve a phase of individual study and preparation, followed by a phase of facilitated small-group design work, followed by a final phase in which the individual analyzes, extends, and reflects on the group's work and how much the individual gained from it. These phases are scaffolded online by the eSTEP system, which guides students through a series of steps. The number of steps and required activities for each step may vary from problem to problem, as desired by the course manager or designer.

Example eSTEP PBL activity

Here we describe one of the activities created for the Fall 2002 course at UW-Madison, which took students through a 4-week, nine-step design challenge. All students in this course completed two PBL activities online. The example to be described is the second activity that was completed by the English majors. Similar design problems were created for students in secondary science, mathematics, social studies, and foreign language.

When students entered the eSTEP PBL system to start their design challenge, they saw a "sidewalk" with nine steps, each associated with a particular due date for completion (see Fig. 8.3). Each student began the task by clicking on Step 1, which opened a page of instructions and a design problem appropriate to that student's academic teacher certification area. The design problem for English majors, studying *Huckleberry Finn* at Midwest High is shown in Figure 8.4. Previously, each student had been assigned to a small discipline-based work group that was maintained in this problem activity and throughout the course.

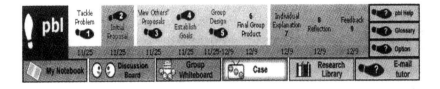

FIG.8.3. The eSTEP sidewalk.

FIG. 8.4

Teaching "Controversial" Texts

Teachers who address controversial and sensitive topics through literature studies take a risk and sometimes meet disapproval from parents, administrators, students, even colleagues. The case you will study as part of your STEP PBL activity is based on the English classroom of a popular high school teacher, Mr. H, who is now in his fifth year of teaching. For the past several years Mr. H has gone out on a limb in teaching a controversial seven-day unit based on *The Adventures of Huckleberry Finn*. A "classic" in American literature, this book is taught in many high schools. However, over the years it has also appeared on several lists of banned books, due to its controversial racial content.

    The video case, Huck Finn at Midwest Hi, is based on a high school honors English class that is being audited by one student who is the only African-American student in the classroom. You will see video based on the first four days of instruction, although the unit continued for about seven days. In this unit, Mr. H poses the question for the class, "Should the book be banned?" Throughout the unit, Mr. H and his students approach the issue from multiple perspectives, connecting what they are discussing to their own environment and simultaneously delving deeply into important literary concepts, such as satire, which are fundamental to intelligent reading and social criticism. Thus, the instructional goals for the unit pertained to critical thinking about a controversial social topic, as well as development of domain-specific expertise in the field of English literature.

    Mr. H's discourse style, teaching and assessment methods, and choices for how to handle various topics and issues in this classroom environment should be of interest. Through reading, questioning, and discussion Mr. H and his students seem to reach a higher level of understanding, although (as noted in Mr. H's interview), not all ideals are achieved. However, by the end of the book, students ironically see Mark Twain as one of history's greatest opponents of racism, and a brilliant writer who was able to deal with the issue at a time when few other writers would or could.

    Notice there are yellow "keywords" placed throughout the video. These keywords are based on Mr. H's own description of how he thought about his teaching when he viewed and helped edit the video.

Your Group's Task

    Carefully study the video case of Mr. H's classroom plus the inquiry materials related to the case, in order to develop ideas for how you would teach a similar unit. Your group's task is to follow the online PBL steps (based on the Wiggins and McTighe approach to instructional design) in planning a 1-2 week unit focusing on race and diversity issues present in this novel, *or a different novel of your own choosing which also focuses on race or diversity issues*. You may also choose to plan your instruction for a very different teaching context. For example, you may develop ideas for teaching in a rural high school, in middle school, in a racially heterogeneous classroom, or in a non-honors classroom. The choice of teaching context, as well as which novel you use, is your group's decision.

    Watching the video case closely is important. As you are watching, identify some learning science principles that are (or are not) at work in the video and that may be influencing the success of the instruction. Some questions you will wish

to think about while watching the video case and in discussions with your group
include:
-What do you think the teacher is trying to accomplish?
-How does he know his students are achieving what he intends for them?

-Why is he teaching as he does and how successful are his instructional
activities?
Following examination of the video case, your group will follow the PBL
steps to generate proposals for goals, assessments, and instructional activities for a
similar unit of instruction. You may use the case to inform your own unit plan, or
you may also have different ideas that you would like to put forward. During your
PBL activity, your group will articulate: 1. the enduring understandings you hope
your students will achieve, 2. how you will use assessment to insure those understandings are acquired, and 3. the activities and methods of instruction and class-
room/discourse management you will employ. Your approaches should be framed
and justified in learning science terms when possible.
While designing your unit, think about the following in relation to the case:
-Can you build on what seemed to work for Mr. H?
-What changes would you make and why?
-What types of assessments did Mr. H use and what would you use to
evaluate your own teaching and your students' progress?
-Which of Mr. H's instructional activities would you include and what
would you do differently?
The information you enter into your eSTEP PBL online notebook and the Group
Whiteboard should provide a synopsis of your individual and group thinking on
these kinds of issues.

FIG.8.4.(cont'd) A design challenge for English majors.

Like design problems for other disciplines, the English problem referenced and linked to a particular video case in the eSTEP video library, a
classroom story that students were asked to analyze in preparation for their
design work (Fig. 8.1). Students were asked to draw lessons and ideas from
the case under study and then apply those lessons and ideas by working
with their group to design or redesign a similar type of instruction. All design problems for all disciplines required students to warrant their instructional designs through learning science research. This research was facilitated by availability of the eSTEP KWeb (Fig. 8.2) and other online research resources integrated with the eSTEP PBL system.

PBL activities required students to apply a process of "backward design" leading to the creation of a "group product," a plan for an instructional unit. The unit to be developed in the English teachers' groups (see
their problem) was to employ a controversial text of the students' choice
and address instructional objectives related to themes of equity and diversity (similar to the case the students were required to study), as well as literary topics, such as satire. Students learned about backward design through
readings in the KWeb and an assigned text, *Understanding by Design*

(Wiggins & McTighe, 1998). Adhering to the steps in their PBL "side-walk," students first completed their reading assignments and studied their case, entering their thoughts and reflections about the case into an online notebook (see Fig. 8.5). After completing initial assignments by the date due, students were at Step 4, where they joined their group of 4 or 5 other students and began group design work. Groups were allowed to choose whether to work online at all times or whether to supplement online work with face-to-face meetings during class. Most groups continued to meet face to face occasionally.

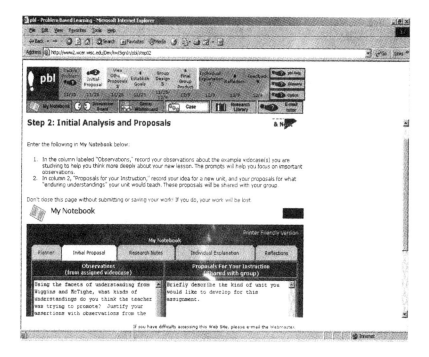

FIG.8.5. The PBL site at Step 2, showing part of individual student notebook with prompts.

During group design, Steps 4 through 6, the preservice teachers were scaffolded through a process in which they first carefully considered what "enduring understandings" their unit would teach. Next, they developed ideas for how they would assess their students, to determine whether goals for understanding were being acquired. Finally, they worked together to design goal-related activities. Each step in the process involved submission and discussion of the various teacher-learners' ideas for goals, assessments, and activities. Ideas were refined online through discussion and voting, with ideas receiving the strongest group support becoming part of the final group product. Group activity was supported online by a group whiteboard (Fig.

8.6) and a supplementary discussion board. As shown in Figure 8.6, the whiteboard contained sections (marked by "tabs") for each stage of the groups' work. For example, during the design of assessments the group members were in the assessment section of the group whiteboard. During each major phase of the group activity, such as the assessment s design phase, students entered their "proposals" for what the group's design should include, plus a justification for their proposals, onto the group whiteboard. Students also used the group whiteboard to view and comment on others' proposals and justifications, read comments about their own proposals, and modify their own proposals in response to group feedback. Students controlled what the system put into their final product with a voting mechanism through which proposals receiving group support were included.

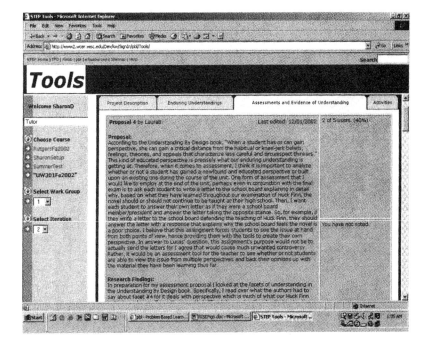

FIG.8.6. Part of a group whiteboard (viewed from the facilitator's system).

Thus, the group whiteboard "forces" students to design an instructional unit, thinking about assessments and activities in a certain order and in terms of how they would lead to enduring understandings. Thus the group whiteboard represented the course manager's epistemological commitments regarding what kinds of goals, knowledge and evidence the course manager wanted students to consider and discuss during learning. Parenthetically it is noted that the group whiteboard in eSTEP PBL is a general tool that allows course managers to change these commitments from problem to problem and course to course, by altering the number of tabs, tab headings, and instructions to learners within each tab.

On completing the group product—a justified plan for an instructional unit specifying goals, assessments, and activities—individual students completed Steps 7 through 9 individually. In Step 7 individual students wrote their own critique and analysis of the group product. In Step 8 students reflected on their learning, and in Step 9, they provided anonymous feedback on the activity and site. A teaching assistant facilitated all steps online. Each teaching assistant in the fall course managed four small groups of about five or six students each.

Students' Ratings of eSTEP PBL Activities and Site Tools

There were two instructional design PBL activities in the fall course at UW-Madison, similar to the one described earlier. Based on a class size of 60 and a response rate of about 97%, the following ratings of components of the two PBL activities (Table 8.1) and the system tools used during the PBL activities (Table 8.2) indicate that although there is room for improving the design of eSTEP PBL, the activities were valued and generally well received. Several patterns in these responses can be observed. First, from PBL-1 to PBL-2, there was a substantial increase in student satisfaction. This is likely due to a number of factors, including student and teaching assistant experience with the method and system, as well as the use of discipline-specific cases and problems in PBL-2 (rather than the generic instructional design scenario grounded in a case on design-based instruction in a science class, which was employed in PBL-1). Second, a decrease in ratings for teaching assistants likely reflects a deliberate fading of scaffolding. Because teaching assistant were trying to decrease their involvement in student work, it is not surprising that students perceived their input as less important. Finally, it is notable that the most rewarding activities for students were those involving collaboration rather than individualized work. Also, a highly rated tool was the hypertext information resource, the eSTEP KWeb.

Although a few students' comments reflected a struggle with technology (this type of comment is becoming less common with increasing availability of high-speed Internet connections), characteristic quotes from students, taken from their reflections about the experience, are positive.

- This lesson that we have designed as a group is definitely something I could see myself using down the road when I have my own classroom. I feel it is a well thought out lesson that can be easily modified to meet the needs of whatever type of class "make-up" that I may have.

- I will attempt to use this method when creating lesson plans for next semester. I think it is a valid model that helps the teacher keep objectives clear and plan meaningful activities which cater to the objectives.

- I would use the unit itself. It was a good final product. I would also use this method of creating lesson plans.

- The plan that we made up as a group will be something that will be extremely useful for me as a teacher. I also learned the value of input from others' viewpoints on the same unit because you are able to see different perspectives that can give you some new and different ideas.

TABLE 8.1

Students' Ratings of Phases of eSTEP PBL Activities.

"How much did you learn from the following activities?"
Scale= 1 (*Nothing*) to 5 (*A lot*)

Activity	PBL 1 Rating	PBL 2 Rating
Overall PBL activity	3.80	4.35
Initial proposal	3.35	3.70
View others' proposals	4.24	4.33
Establish goals	3.84	4.19
Group design	3.94	4.38
Final group product	3.73	4.08
Individual explanation	3.91	3.84
Reflection	3.72	3.88
Interaction with group	4.28	4.37
Interaction with teaching assistant	3.06	2.87

With future refinement, we are confident that online design activities in the eSTEP PBL site will prove to be an important and successful addition to current approaches to teacher preparation.

TABLE 8.2

Students' Rating of eSTEP Tools

How well did the following tools work?
Scale=1 (*Very poorly*) through 5 (*Very well*)

Tool	PBL 1	PBL 2
Cases	3.58	4.02
Case-related concepts	3.75	4.22
Notebook—Initial proposals	3.64	4.05
Notebook—Research notes	3.66	4.02
Notebook—Individual evaluation	3.91	4.16
Notebook—Reflections	3.84	4.18
Group whiteboard	3.75	4.16
Group discussion	3.65	4.07
Research library	3.58	4.21
Knowledge Web (hypertextbook)	4.29	4.50
PBL help	3.27	3.45
Worked examples	3.07	3.46

CONCLUDING COMMENTS

The research reported in this chapter is about making the conceptual systems taught in college classrooms useful to students' future professional lives. Toward this end, my colleagues and I are designing and evaluating new kinds of learning environments that combine video with online learning technologies, evaluating these designs in theory-based studies within laboratory settings and in the context of online courses in the science of learning, offered for future teachers. Our experimental instruction engages preservice teachers in video study to help them acquire perceptual familiarity with events they will encounter in classrooms. Through integrated text study, learners mesh this perceptual knowledge with a system of concepts associated with the science of learning. Through planning and design problems, learners connect this meshed perceptual/conceptual knowledge with systems of thought about actions that help manage classrooms. Our future research will continue to seek better designs for learning and will test ideas about the relative value of these instructional components and how they should be integrated, sequenced, and facilitated.

Future work will also test the AFH, a theory of learning and learning environment design that is introduced in this chapter and evolving with this work. This theory posits existence of a continuously organizing virtual activity field, a complex system of cognitive activation representing human experience during learning. The research questions we will address using our Web-based course are the following: Do learning environments that integrate text and video study with collaborative design produce evidence of productive activity fields? Can evidence of more or less productive activity fields be causally linked to important learning objectives, such as sophisticated, spontaneous use of learning-science concepts in authentic teaching tasks? Can manipulation of learning environment characteristics, such as facilitation, online tools, and activity design, predictably vary learners' activity fields?

ACKNOWLEDGMENTS

This work was supported by Grants #REC-0107032 and #REC-0115661 from the National Science Foundation. The views expressed are not endorsed and may not represent the views of the foundation. The ideas in this chapter build on work and discussions with Cindy Hmelo-Silver, Rand Spiro, David Woods, Matt Del Marcelle, Joan Feltovich, Constance Steinkuehler, Chris Fassnacht, Kate Hewson, Anandi Nagarajan, Ellina Chernobilsky, Mary Leonard, and John Stampen.

REFERENCES

Barrows, H. (1988). *The tutorial process*. Springfield: Southern Illinois University Press.

Bartlett, F. C. (1932). *Remembering: A study in experimental and social psychology*. Cambridge, UK: Cambridge University Press.

Chernobilsky, E., Hmelo-Silver, C. E., & DelMarcelle, M. (2003, April). *Collaborative discourse, tools, and activity in online problem-based learning*. Paper presented at the annual meeting of the American Educational Research Association, Chicago.

Clancey, W. J. (1997). *Situated cognition: On human knowledge and computer representations*. Cambridge, UK: Cambridge University Press.

195

DelMarcelle, M., & Derry, S. J. (2003). *A reflective analysis of instructional practice in an online environment.* Unpublished manuscript.

Derry, S. J. (1996). Cognitive schema theory in the constructivist debate. *Educational Psychologist, 31,* 163–217.

Dewey, J. (1933). *How we think.* New York: D. C. Heath.

Diaz, P., Gomes, M. J., & Correia, A. P. (1999). Disorientation in hypermedia environments: Mechanisms to support navigation. *Journal of Educational Computing Research, 20,* 93–118.

Feltovich, P. J., Spiro, R. J., Coulson, R. L., & Feltovich, J. (1996). Collaboration within and among minds: Mastering complexity, individually and in groups. In T. Koschmann (Ed.), *CSCL: Theory and practice of an emerging paradigm* (pp. 25–44). Mahwah, NJ: Lawrence Erlbaum Associates.

Gibson, J. J. (1979). *The ecological approach to visual perception.* Boston: Houghton-Mifflin.

Glenberg, A. M. (1997). What memory is for. *Behavioral and Brain Sciences, 20,* 1–55.

Goldman-Segall, R. (1998). *Points of viewing children's thinking.* Mahwah, NJ: Lawrence Erlbaum Associates.

Greeno, J. G. (2001). *Students with competence, authority and accountability: Affording intellective identities in classrooms.*, Retrieved 12/7/2004, from http://www.collegeboard.com/about/association/academic/2000_2001_scholars.html

Hmelo-Silver, C. E. (2002). Collaborative Ways of Knowing: Issues in Facilitation. In G. Stahl (ed.) *Proceedings of CSCL 2002* (pp. 199-208). Mahwah, NJ: Lawrence Erlbaum Associates.

Hofstadter, D. (2000). Analogy as the core of cognition. In J. Gleick (Ed.), *The Best American Science Writing 2000* (pp. 116-144). New York: HarperCollins.

Kolodner, J. L & Guzdial, M. (2000). Theory and practice of case-based learning aids. In D. Jonassen and S.Land (Eds), *Theoretical foundations of learning environments* (pp. 215-242). Mahwah, NJ, US: Lawrence Erlbaum Associates.

Koschmann, T., Glenn, P., & Conlee, M. (1999). Theory presentation and assessment in a problem-based learning group. *Discourse Processes, 27,* 119–133.

Kozulin, A. (1998). *Psychological tools.* Cambridge, MA: Harvard University Press.

Lakoff, G., & Johnson, M. (1980). *Metaphors We live by.* Chicago: University of Chicago Press.

Lemke, J. L. (2002, October). *Keeping learning alive: Multiple timescales in the social organization of learning.* Paper presented at the International Conference of the Learning Sciences, Seattle, WA.

O'Donnell, A. (2002, December). *Facilitating online learning: A view from the facilitator.* Paper presented at the Invitational Conference on

What We Know and Need to Know About Facilitated Online Learning for TPD, Madison, WI.

Salomon, G., & Perkins, D. N. (1989). Rocky roads to transfer: Rethinking mechanisms of a neglected phenomenon. *Educational Psychologist, 24,* 113–142.

Schon, D. A. (1983). *The reflective practioner: How professionals think in action.* London: Temple Smith.

Schwartz, D. L., & Bransford, J. D. (1998). A time for telling. *Cognition and Instruction, 16,* 475–522.

Simon, R. L. (1992). *Teaching against the grain: Texts for a pedagogy of possibility.* New York: Greenwood.

Spiro, R. J., Feltovich, P. J., Jacobson, M. J., & Coulson, R. L. (1992). Cognitive flexibility, constructivism, and hypertext: Random access instruction for advanced knowledge acquisition in ill-structured domains. In T. M. Duffy & D. H. Jonassen (Eds.), *Constructivism and the technology of instruction: A conversation.* (pp. 57-75). Hillsdale, NJ: Lawrence Erlbaum Associates

Steinkuehler, C. A., Derry, S. J., Hmelo-Silver, C. E., & DelMarcelle, M. (2002). Cracking the resource nut with distributed problem-based learning in secondary teacher education. *Journal of Distance Education, 23,* 23-39.

Suchman, L. A. (1987). *Plans and situated actions.* New York: Cambridge University Press.

Wertsch, J. V., & Kazan, S. (2003, November). *Saying more than you know in instructional settings.* Paper presented at the Coupling Theories of Learning and Research on Practice Workshop, Champaign-Urbana, IL.

Wiggins, G., & McTighe, J. (1998). *Understanding by design.* Alexandria, VA: Association for Supervision and Curriculum Development.

Wittgenstein, L. (1953). *Philosophical investigations.* Oxford, UK: Blackwell.

Zacks, R., & Tversky, D. (2001). Event structure in perception and conception. *Psychological Bulletin, 127,* 3–21.

Chapter 9

Collaboration in Computer Conferencing

Jerry Andriessen
Utrecht University, Netherlands

We have been experimenting with Web-based electronic conferencing at the Educational Science Department of Utrecht University for a period of nearly 10 years now. Obstacles such as insufficient participation, low quality of messages, and integration of CMC into a course have been overcome and many of our students now appear actively engaged with knowledge construction activities (Veerman, 2000). Although we may have succeeded in organizing interesting computer conferences, things are missing relating to the affordances of computer conferencing for collaborative learning. It seems that at the level of individual courses we have reached limits we cannot move beyond. To understand this problem and its possible solutions, in this chapter we discuss some of our data concerning the role of computer conferencing in higher education.

The main conclusion of this chapter is that productive use of computer conferencing for learning purposes in the context of current higher education requires participants (students and teachers) to have more knowledge of collaboration. We are currently witnessing (at least in the Netherlands) a gradual shift in thinking about learning and education, which is traditionally taken as a process of individual knowledge acquisition by transmission from expert knowledge, toward more collaborative and project-based forms of learning. It is a slow change with many dangers of failure, and we do not know much about the success factors. One main assumption, as a result of our research, is that the main obstacle for the success of any collaborative learning task is in the design of the curriculum; that is, if collaboration is not implemented as a necessary and important learning activity, it will not survive in the classroom. This integration of new learning is reflected in the conceptions about learning objectives of the participants in the educational activity system, and in the roles and responsibilities of participants, including the place of technology. A corollary of this idea is that causes of problems of using collaborative technology are not only in characteristics of the new technology, but also, and more important, in the new forms of collaboration it permits.

This chapter is organized as follows. First, we present a review of research on computer conferencing. We then provide an overview of our use of computer conferencing in regular courses that we have been engaged in during the past. In the second part, we describe our research findings. We investigated the role of argumentation in computer conferencing and the relationship among task focus, argumentation, and constructive discussion. We also examined how messages in a computer conference are thematically linked to each other, and if instruction can affect this linking. The nature of explicit personal reference between messages in an electronic forum is also examined from a social perspective. Finally, we examine participation profiles of participants in a 6-month course in which all decisions had to be made by the participants themselves.

The three parts of this chapter presents an explanatory framework for these results, both from a theoretical and didactical perspective. This framework supposes that the educational paradigms in which collaborative learning is used in practice evolve from use in knowledge transmission to use in knowledge negotiation, presumably though a number of intermediate stages. In different scenarios, specific learning goals, and theoretical viewpoints on learning, characterize these different stages and the didactical methods that are applied. It is argued that an advanced use of computer-mediated commication (CMC) requires more advanced educational paradigms. The evolution through the stages can be characterized as increasing awareness of the goals of a learning situation and of the means to meet these goals. This evolution has to be supported by appropriate educational design. Computer conferencing (CC) as in constructive discussions, knowledge building, or community building can only be fruitfully used in contexts where users are in advanced stages and contexts of awareness of learning.

RESEARCH WITH COMPUTER CONFERENCING

In CC, two or more persons participate in an electronic conference about a certain topic, called a forum. The conference is asynchronous; that is, participants do generally not contribute at the same time. They communicate by sending electronic messages that typically are displayed in a list (called a thread) visible to all participants. The topic could be a question or a controversial statement devised by a teacher, containing some crucial issues pertaining to a course or a text to study. Students can react to the initial statement and then to each other. Under ideal circumstances, an interesting discussion may develop. The role of the instructor in discussions may vary among observer, social worker, group therapist, expert on demand, organizer, and many other roles (Mason, 1991). Discussions can be constrained or not with respect to duration, timing, types of answers, and conclusions.

CC may be envisaged as a slow discussion, offering participants much time for reflection and pondering, during which they may take appropriate notice of everything that has been said before. CC offers an educator a potentially interesting means to make students broaden and deepen their insights about important issues and to monitor progress at a relatively slow pace. For a researcher involved in actual educational practice, it is relatively easy to arrange discussions to obtain large databases with examples of constructive and less constructive communication, on the basis of different initial statements, moderator roles, and collaborative arrangements.

The use of electronic discussions in educational settings seems a promising way of promoting reflection and learning by communication and argumentation. To date, mainly single-case exemplars of such discussions have been published, often with an important role for the instructor. At the current stage, analyses of such discussions still have to establish accepted frameworks that specify the complex interactions between domain knowledge type, student knowledge (about the domain and about discussion and collaboration), student attitudes, and characteristics of the resulting discourse.

From a rhetorical perspective on academic learning, academic education can be framed as an ongoing argumentative process (Petraglia, 1997). It is the process of discovering and generating acceptable arguments and lines of reasoning underlying scientific assumptions and bodies of knowledge. The purpose of collaborative discussion tasks is to have students externalize, articulate, and negotiate alternative perspectives, inducing reflection on the meaning of arguments put forward by peers and experts.

It is believed that collaborative learning is particularly achieved when students are presented with conflicts, engage in argumentative processes, and manage to produce a shared interpretation of information or arrive at a shared problem solution (e.g., Baker, 1996; Doise & Mugny, 1984; Erkens, 1997; Petraglia, 1997; Piaget, 1977; Savery & Duffy, 1996). In argumentation, students can give prominence to conflict and negotiation processes, critically discuss information, elaborate on arguments, and explore multiple perspectives. Knowledge and opinions can be (re)constructed and coconstructed and expand students' understanding of specific concepts or problems. Thus, argumentation can be seen as an important mechanism for fruitful discussions and the production of constructive activities.

In effective collaborative argumentation students share a focus on the same issues and negotiate about the meaning of each other's information. Incomplete, conflicting, doubted, or disbelieved information is critically checked, challenged, or countered on its strength (is the information true?) and its relevance (is the information appropriate?), until finally a shared answer, solution, or concept arises. However, generating effective argumentation in educational situations requires participants to deal with many constraints. First of all, adequate focusing is important for grounding and understanding messages. Students have to initiate and maintain a shared focus of the task. They have to agree on the overall goal, descriptions of the current problem state, and available problem-solving actions (Roschelle & Teasley, 1995). Failure to maintain a shared focus on themes and problems in the discussion results in a decrease of mutual problem solving (Baker & Bielaczyc, 1995; Erkens, 1997). Second, assessing information critically on its meaning, strength, or relevance depends on many factors, such as the (peer) student, the role of the tutor, the type of task, the type of instruction, and the selected medium (Veerman, Andriessen, & Kanselaar, 2000). Key problems that can inhibit students from engaging in critical argumentation are that students tend to believe in one overall correct solution or show difficulties with generating, identifying, and comparing counterarguments and with using strong, relevant, and impersonalized justifications (Kuhn, 1991). In addition, students' exposure of a critical attitude can be inhibited because of socially biased behavior. For example, students may fear loss of face (e.g., in front of classmates), going against dominant persons in status or behavior (e.g., a tutor), or what other people think (e.g., you are not a nice person).

To support and optimize students' engagement in argumentative dialogues for collaborative learning purposes, CMC systems provide new educational opportunities. Text-based and time-delayed communication can be beneficial to keep track and keep an overview of complex questions or problems under discussion. Text-based discussion is by necessity explicit and articulated. A history of the discussion can be used to reflect over time on earlier stated information. Moreover, in CMC systems, students lack physical and psychological cues such as physical appearance, intonation, eye contact, group identity, and so on, which sometimes leads to democratizing effects (Kiesler 1986; Rutter, 1987; Short, Williams & Christie, 1976; Smith, 1994; Spears & Lea, 1992; Steeples et al., 1996). Critical behavior, therefore, may be less biased toward a tutor or a dominant peer student than in face-to-face discussion. However, it is unclear how the use of a CMC system, and which characteristics of such a system, relate to effective argumentation for collaborative learning purposes. The research reported in this chapter attempts to identify some of the necessary characteristics.

COMPUTER CONFERENCING AT UTRECHT UNIVERSITY

In our department we have been experimenting with electronic discussions for the past 6 years. Our initial purpose as teachers was to look for added value to our course by using CC, in terms of deeper insights, motivation, and course efficiency. From a theoretical viewpoint, our interest was in knowledge co-construction; that is, participants' attempts to arrive at shared understanding of concepts by explaining ideas, discussing alternatives, and arguing viewpoints (Roschelle & Teasley, 1995; Scardamalia & Bereiter, 1994). In addition, we wanted to analyze the content of the discussions to find out in what way constructive discussions and learning could emerge form certain arrangements, and in what ways such discussions could be supported. All data reported were obtained in actual courses with regular students. In the next sections we discuss some examples of what we tried to do, followed by a discussion of some relevant experiences and lessons learned.

As we work with regular students who are in general not used to seriously employing CC for learning purposes, one of the major obstacles was getting students to effectively use the medium. When we started it was not even very clear what effective use would mean. It was obvious that we needed our students to experience added value and to have as few technical problems as possible. Therefore we decided to build a Web site, and to integrate use of the Web with the rest of the course. One problem appeared to be that although we gradually succeeded in adding meaningful learning experiences for the students, this also required students to spend more time on a course. Not many students are prepared for this, for various reasons. One effect is that we tend to lose about 20% of our students during the first weeks of a course.

The context in which our experiences with CC were taking place was a series of courses for advanced students in the Department of Educational Sciences, aiming at the study of learning with new media. The topic of the courses, and the fact that they all were coordinated by the first author of this chapter, allowed us to arrange them relatively independently from the rest of the curriculum, to make use of the Internet as much as possible, according to the following main principles:

- Students are responsible for their own activities and participation and are expected to support each other. Teacher time is limited and we do not want to set a standard of high teacher involvement in terms of hours spent on a course. Teachers intervene as infrequently as possible, only to provide structure and guidance, not answers or evaluations. Students are encouraged to say what they think, and not to feel ashamed about things they do not know or do not express clearly.

- The courses are on new media, but the actual topic is education and learning. Integrated use of new media is attempted: Educational use of new media needs to be experienced as much as possible rather than read about.

- The use of specific applications of new media is carefully tuned to task purpose. We prefer open tasks, in which there are many correct solutions and many ways to arrive at a result. We foster collaboration, argumentation, and use of discursive media.

These principles were applied in three different courses. Table 9.1 gives a comprehensive list of the discussions and the frequency of participation in one of the courses in 1998. The discussion forums were part of a Web site in which other types of activities and information (software, instructions, background texts, etc.) were provided. In our opinion, Table 9.1

presents satisfactory results in terms of student participation and evaluation of the activities. Of course, improvements on details and functionality are possible.

Student Reactions to Computer Conferencing

Our evaluations of students' reactions have been informal. Most students indicated they found it useful and instructive to participate in theoretical discussions and that this increased their understanding. Some indicated it even stimulated them to look for additional information. Most students acknowledged that participation was most useful if it was prepared for by reading the relevant texts. Some individual students thought the discussions were not always very deep. One student viewed discussions mainly as a means to keep students busy.

Some students judged the discussions as too theoretical; others said that the discussions are too much about students' own experiences. Many students claimed that too many questions remain and not enough conclusions are reached. Only a few students thought these discussions helped to develop a personal viewpoint. Half of the respondents indicated a preference for face-to-face discussions in addition to electronic ones. Many also indicated a need for more information from a tutor.

All students indicated they learned more from the collaborative discussions than from learning by themselves. The discussions require attention and clarity, and to see other viewpoints and insights helps understanding. Others help to keep learning going. It matters who is participating in a particular discussion. One student preferred independent study because relying on others' responses takes too much time.

Asynchronous discussions were preferred over synchronous discussions. Students liked the possibility to reflect longer, and some indicated the relative anonymity induces them to really say what they think. One student suggested starting theoretical discussions asynchronously, but having a synchronous conclusion session.

Students' opinions of the role of the moderator were mixed. This clearly is a controversial issue. Some think that the presence of the moderator should be more prominent and that he or she should intervene more often. The moderator should summarize, conclude, and ask questions to deepen discussion, and has to provide content-related feedback during the discussions. Some students indicated they wanted to know if their ideas were correct or not. Only a few students mentioned the danger of a moderator bringing a discussion to a standstill.

TABLE 9.1

Available Forums in the 1999 Course and Their Participation per Week by 30 students[a]

Name	Description	N[b]	Rating[c]
Theoretical forums (compulsory)	A discussion about theoretical issues (formulated as questions or discussible statements) derived by the tutor from course texts. Sometimes moderated. The purpose of these discussions is to deepen understanding of theoretical matters. These discussions last 2 weeks and are then closed. In 1999 there were three discussions of this type every 2 weeks, for a total of 14 for the full course. Students could choose one and were to contribute at least two substantial messages each week. In addition, a long list of expert consultants (mostly scientists from all kinds of disciplines) is available, who can be contacted with specific questions. It is possible for students to propose new discussion themes, but this hardly ever happens. A discussion is closed and then commented by one of the instructors on a different Web location. Example: For the study of learning processes, phenomenography offers a more promising research approach than instructional design, intelligent tutoring systems, or instructional psychology.	48[d]	8.0
Applied forums (compulsory)	A discussion on practical issues (picked by the tutor) on the basis of the literature and the student's own intuitions and experiences. Sometimes an instructor who attempts to provide structure and motivation moderates a discussion. There are three such forums, and students have to actively participate in one forum of their own choice. The purpose of these discussions is to promote reflection on the relations between theory and practice. These discussions last 2 weeks and are then closed. It is possible for students to propose new discussion themes, but this hardly ever happens. A discussion is closed and then commented by one of the instructors on a different location. Example: Human tutors are better adapters to student learning styles than intelligent tutoring systems.	47[d]	7.8

TABLE 9.1 (cont'd)

Name	Description	N^b	Rating^c
Read threads	On the basis of questions or statements formulated by the instructional team, students are requested to post at least 2 serious contributions during the full course to a discussion on general issues related to the use of media in education. In 1999 there were two such forums, and students were free to propose additional ones, however, this has not happened. Examples: (1) Interactive learning should be a crucial aspect of educational design of courses in social sciences. (2) Learning with new media equals adaptive instruction.	5.1	6.2
Course organization	These serve all kinds of purposes. The most important one is the forum in which the instructors post announcements on new assignments, changing course plan, and the consequences of failing technology. Students are expected to consult this forum on a daily basis.	2.7	6.8
Comprehension forum	Serves for students to discuss their problems with understanding the literature with each other and with the instructors.	1.9	6.0
Practice forum	A number of teachers from secondary schools participated in the 1999 course and were invited to propose some issues and ask questions to the students about their own practice with the implementation and use of new media.	3.1	6.0
News forums	Relevant conferences, Web sites, and texts. Also, there is the evaluation forum, for students to post their experiences with the course, and to propose alternatives and solutions for all kinds of problems experienced.	17	7.7
Helpdesk	For all kinds of problems involving technical matters.	2.7	5,6

TABLE 9.1 (cont'd)

Name	Description	N[b]	Rating[c]
Stock Exchange	Requests for new topics and themes and meetings with or without tutors. Tutors are to oblige a student request, for example, to give a lecture about intelligent tutoring systems, if at least 5 students support the request.	0.2	5.6
Visual Basic	Programming help desk.	2.8	6.2
Bar and café	There is a bar (asynchronous) and a coffee shop (synchronous), where students and staff can meet for informal chat.	7.4[1]	5.3
Total (week)		171	

[a]The number of students in the course decreased by about 20% during the first weeks
[b]Mean number of contributions each week
[c]Student evaluation of a discussion type on a 10 point scale
[d]An average of 9 students participate in each discussion of this type, the number sums up three discussions

---

[1] Only for asynchronous contributions

All students indicated they like to receive information from experts. This helps them to understand the concepts involved. It can also be interesting to compare reactions to the same questions from different experts. However, most students did not consult any expert even once. They indicated hesitations to write and a lack of time as the main reasons for this. Furthermore, experts did not always react promptly. When experts reacted, their messages were not interpreted, but simply pasted into the discussion.

When reported in research studies (e.g., Goodfellow & Manning, 1999; Tolmie & Boyle, 2000), student evaluations of electronic learning groups give a consistent picture. Some of the students are very happy with these new developments, but another group, just as big, prefers traditional education. Most students want more tutor feedback, for structure as well as for content evaluation. Although, in our case at least, students have many opportunities to take initiative, and tutors are mainly reactive here, hardly any initiative is found. For example, students barely pose any questions about the source texts to the tutors. We do not think this is a feature of electronic discourse or even of collaborative learning. It is a feature of traditional, tutor-based educational contexts. Students participate in compulsory parts of a course, and although they tend to dislike most things that are compulsory, they tend to acknowledge their usefulness afterward, even when inappropriate. The responses of our students indicate involvement and understanding, but lack of shared purpose (Tolmie & Boyle, 2000).

RESEARCH QUESTIONS

How can the discussions in the electronic forums be characterized? To what extent do we have constructive, interesting, argumentative, or simply good discussions? Many questions can be asked, and our approach is to ask seemingly simple questions, from different theoretical viewpoints. Discussions can be explained from quite different angles (see, e.g., Baker, 1999, for constructive argumentation), and we feel that theoretical insights are complete enough to be able to present and explain a clear picture of what is happening. In the next sections we present five analyses that attempt to clarify some main characteristics of these electronic discussions:

Study 1

1. To what extent are these discussion content related? In what way can they be called constructive? Does this relate to argumentation?

2. To what extent are discussions focused? On what does this depend?

3. To what extent are messages connected in terms of personal reference? Does this depend on the content of a message, or the individual posting the message, and are there developments over time in this respect?

Study 2

4. To what extent are messages connected in terms of content? Can the type of discussion or the rules of discussion affect connectedness?

Study 3

5. To what extent do individuals differ in terms of their responsibility for a discussion?

The first three analyses involve the same 28 theoretical and applied forums of the electronic conferences that were discussed previously. The second study (Analysis 4) concerned the same course 1 year later. The third study involves an analysis of a different course (Analysis 5).

STUDY 1

The purpose of this study is to characterize students' discussions with respect to the relations among focusing, argumentation, and collaborative learning in progress. Two content-related focus categories reflect students' focus on the task and learning goals: (a) a focus on the meaning of concepts, and (b) a focus on the application of concepts. In addition, students' focus could be on task strategy issues (planning how to start the task, time management, how to carry out the task), social issues, and so on. Furthermore, six types of dialogue moves are included in the analyzing system: statements, acceptances, conclusions, checks, challenges, and counterarguments. Although all these categories may embody elements of argument, only (a) check questions (e.g., "What do you mean by"), (b) challenges (e.g., "How can you justify that") and (c) counterarguments (e.g., "I don't agree on the issue of") are considered as argumentative dialogue moves.

Students' discussions can be viewed as collective information networks in which content can change dynamically and grow by the production of constructive activities: messages in which content-related information is added, explained, evaluated, summarized, or transformed. Adding information means that an input of new information is linked to the discussion. Explaining information means that earlier stated information is, for example, differentiated, specified, categorized, or made clear by examples. Evaluations are (personally) justified considerations of the strength or relevance of already added or explained information. In transforming knowledge, already stated information is evaluated and integrated into the collective knowledge base in such a way that a new insight or a new direction transpires that can be used to answer questions or solve problems. Summarizing means that already given information is reorganized or restated in such a way to reflect the main points of the discussion. The production of constructive activities is regarded to signal collaborative learning in process and is related to the concept of knowledge-building discourse (Scardamalia & Bereiter, 1994). In this research, all content-related messages are analyzed on types of constructive activities. Each message was coded once, as one (or none) of the following constructive activities: (a) addition, (b) explanation, (c) evaluation, (d) transformation, and (e) summary.

Content of Forums

Table 9.2 presents a summary of the results of this analysis. These results are presented in more detail elsewhere (Veerman, 2000). Veerman, Andriessen, and Kanselaar (in press) compared these data, using the same classification system, with synchronous chat discussions and discussions using Belvedere (Suthers, 2001), and this allowed considering the number of content-related messages and the number of constructive activities (explanations) in CMC as relatively high. However, argumentation is low, especially challenges and counters. Moreover, we do not find transformations or summaries. Remember the student evaluations earlier indicated that students expected the tutor to be responsible for this.

TABLE 9.2

Number and Kinds of Messages Generated in Forums From Veerman (2000) Study

Total number of discussion forums analyzed	28
Average number of messages per discussion (2 weeks)	34
Average number of words per message	120
Total number of messages analyzed	952
Number and percentage of content-related messages	30 (88%)
Number of non-content-related messages (focused on task strategy, social issues, etc.)	4 (12%)
Focus of content-related messages per discussion forum	
meaning of concepts	14 (47%)
application of concepts	16 (53%)

TABLE 9.2 (cont'd)

Argumentativeness of content-related messages per discussion forum	
Not argumentative (statements, acceptances, etc.)	21 (71%)
Checking information	7 (23%)
Challenging information	1 (3%)
Countering information	1 (3%)
Constructiveness of content-related messages per discussion forum	
Not constructive	8 (27%)
Constructive	22 (73%)
Types of constructive messages per discussion forum	
Additions	7 (30%)
Explanations	11 (50%)
Evaluations	2 (10%)
Summaries	1 (5%)
Transformations	1 (5%)

The results of this study caused us to be quite positive about the usefulness of electronic conferences. Although the conferences are mainly used to explain rather than to argue, they are very much content focused. At this point, also considering the results from student evaluations, our conclusion is that this type of discussion characterizes students seriously trying to discuss things they are not very familiar with. The next analysis concerns the focus of these discussions.

Focus of Discussions

Although the discussions were characterized to be much on-topic, topics can be defined at various levels of generality. For example, one discussion was about the statement made by Laurillard (1993): "Teaching is a rhetorical activity." General topics are teaching, rhetorical, and activity. More specific topics include teaching experience, types of activities, motivation, involvement, teaching materials, mediation, argumentation, and so on. In this study, a more specific topic definition was applied, which allowed examining (a) the breadth (number of topics and arguments) and depth (number of contributions for a topic or about an argument) of discussion threads, and (b) references to other topics and arguments in the discussion threads.

All discussions were about a general topic mentioned in the problem statement. However, analysis of more specific topics (van der Pol, 1998) revealed the opposite: The number of specific topics increased with time, and students did not return or refer to specific topics discussed earlier. In addition, discussions seldom arrived at a conclusion. Recall some students in the earlier evaluation also remarked about this. This aspect of discussions is characterized in Figure 9.1. The picture on the left matches the results of the topic analysis.

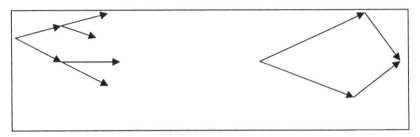

FIG.9.1. The left picture characterizes a discussion in which topics disperse. The picture on the right shows topics that merge toward a conclusion.

Further analysis showed that students did not very often react to each other, in terms of references to other topics. They merely appeared to explain their own contributions on the basis of a question (check) by someone else. Moreover, students seldom directly reacted to tutors. Suggestions by tutors about the plan to proceed and criteria to keep in mind were often completely ignored.

At this point, it seems that interpretations in the previous section were too optimistic with respect to the constructiveness of explanations and additions in the discussions. It seems that our discussions elaborate in terms of breadth, but do not go deeper and do not arrive at integration or a conclusion. This process seems to be characteristic of brainstorming and it may be that students need help, more time, different motivation, or more knowledge and skills, to engage in deeper discussions. In the next section, we look at the degree to which students referenced one another's comments. It may be that connectivity among students may promote greater depth in the discussions.

Personal Reference

Effective collaboration requires awareness of the process of collaboration in which students are engaged. For example, it would be good for collaboration if students in their messages explicitly referred to other students, and not only to their messages. Brand (1999) examined students referring to each other's messages from a s~cial viewpoint, regarding the manner in which messages referred to each other, and whether explicit reference to a specific individual's messages increased or decreased during participation in several discussions over a 13-week period. The idea was that, as in every collaborative group process, over time some people would be better recognized as to the importance of their contributions to the discussion, reflected in more explicit references to their messages.

First, the referential density of a discussion was computed as the percentage of explicit personal references to messages in a discussion. This was computed for three types of reference: explicit naming of the author, repetition of parts of the message, and use of personal or referential pronouns. A referential density of 1 for a discussion means that on the average, a message by a participant is explicitly referenced to once during the 2-week period of a discussion.

Figure 9.2 displays the results. As can be seen, referential density was uniformly low, a message generating an average of about 1 personal reference in a discussion. In addition, the personal reference density for individual participants varied between 3.67 and 0.4; that is, for the most referenced participant, each message that this participant contributed elicited an average of 3.67 explicit reactions. In case of the least referenced participant, each message was referred to only 0.4 times.

Second, we attempted to identify characteristics of core messages in a discussion; that is, messages that are referred to with a frequency above the average (in this case, 4 references or more). To this end, the following variables were examined: (a) contributor (regular student, part-time, working, tutor), (b) Gender, and (c) type of discussion (theoretical vs. applied).

A total of 18 discussions were analyzed, each discussion lasting 2 weeks. In all of these discussions together, 17 core messages could be identified, 14 of which were posted during the first week of a 2-week discussion. There were no differences between discussions that started during the first, third, or fifth week in the frequencies of core messages. Women produced twice as many core messages as men. There were no other significant differences.

Whereas the previous analyses showed characteristics of content relations between messages, this study examined these relationships from a different angle. It seems to show that there are no discernible changes of personal status over time. The number of core messages in the discussion, (i.e., messages that are referred to relatively very often) is very low, and this number does not change over time. In addition, it seems that messages in which the contribution of another student is personally acknowledged are quite rare as well, and we also see no developments over time. Discussion groups change every 2 weeks, which could be a possible explanation for this result. It may be interesting to examine what happens when collaboration is extended over a longer period.

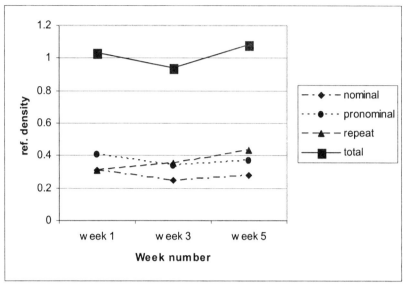

FIG.9.2. Development of three types of personal reference between messages over time (6 parallel discussions, 5 weeks).

STUDY 2: INTERVENING TO INCREASE CONNECTIVITY

The connections between different messages seem to cause the topic structure of electronic discussions to expand, with the result that often newly added knowledge will just keep floating on its own, without being further refined or elaborated. This results in different pieces of knowledge coexisting in the discussion without ever being confronted. The lack of specific comments on earlier messages could be a general problem in electronic discussions for educational purposes: Veerman (2000) found there were hardly any transformational activities in electronic discussions and Wan and Johnson (1994) found there were no integration messages, although both are essential to learning and to building a shared knowledge base.

The specific research question for this study (van der Pol, 2001) was: "Is it possible to create more and better connections between messages in electronic discussions by means of task-specific instruction?" The choice for task-specific instruction was a practical one, because changes in the interface (with the purpose of creating a more natural form of connecting and learning in electronic discussions) were not yet possible.

Twenty-five third-year educational science students have been discussing in one of three different conditions for contributing to discussions, designed to stimulate them to connect more and relate better to each other's messages: a) to contribute in the form of explicit replies to a previous message, or b) to contribute summaries of previous discussion, and c) to compose more and shorter messages. The messages in every condition were scored according to their level of connectivity, which could be any of the following (hierarchical) categories: no connection, association, checking, elaboration, and convergence. The control group consisted of 10 discussions on identical topics that were held the year before with different students.

There were significant differences among the three conditions in terms of connectivity, measured as the proportion of elaborations, F (2, 22) = 6.247, p = .003. Table 9.3 displays the differences among conditions. There were hardly any messages that were scored as converging different contributions in the discussion.

TABLE 9.3

Connectivity of Messages as a Function of Condition

	N Forums	N Messages	% Replies	% Connect[a]
1. Reply (Weeks 1–4)	10	341	.77	.47
2. Summarize (Weeks 5–8)	10	308	.69	.34
3. Short messages (Weeks 9–10)	5	212	.80	.38
M	25	861	.65	.40
M previous year[b]	10	280	.65	.37

[a]Corrected for replies to the moderator
[b]Only discussions with identical topics were taken into account

The variable with the most influence on the level of connectivity between messages appeared to be the topic of discussion. Two classes of topics were compared: discussions about the book used in the course, and broader discussions, which involved relating personal experience, the same book, articles, and combinations between them. Discussions in the first group displayed a significantly higher level of connectivity, F (2, 22) = 6.172, p < .007. This effect can be interpreted as the influence of common ground. A discussion topic with a fixed reference point (the book) appears to help connecting to each other's messages. Making a good connection to a message demands a good understanding of the ideas involved, and the effort of interpretation is reduced when some degree of common ground has been achieved. This supports the idea that grounding is a natural and gradual process in communication: With less common ground more information checks are found. The amount of checking, in turn, is moderately positively related to the level of connectivity (correlation = .439, α = .10). This is promoted in Condition 3, where more and shorter contributions were requested, which in turn increases the amount of replies. With high common ground, Condition 1 gives the best results for connectivity. These results can be interpreted as indicating that connectivity can be stimulated, but the appropriate way to do this depends on the level of common ground.

We conclude that this study helped to better understand what actually happens in a discussion. Although the number of messages that summarize or converge a discussion is very low, indicating that the level of a discussion can still be substantially raised, the characteristic that has a significant effect on the elaboration of a discussion is the degree to which a discussion is grounded. Multiple discussions over time on topics from the same book gradually achieve more connectivity, presumably because of increasing familiarity with the reasoning of the author, especially when participants are explicitly asked to reply to each other's contributions. It seems that students have to learn how to react coherently, and that grounding in these electronic discussions is a slow process, which has to be studied more deeply (Baker, Hansen, Joiner, & Traum, 1999; Clark & Schaefer, 1989). Furthermore, checking and explicit replying may increase connectivity, checking being an indication of attempts to achieve common ground, and replying may serve elaboration.

STUDY 3: KNOWLEDGE NEGOTIATION

Some conclusions from the previous analyses concern the importance of grounding and the apparent lack of development in the sense of personal reference. Can such developments be observed in discussions over a longer period? A small group ($n = 10$) of serious and experienced students volunteered to be part of a long-term experiment. The original plan was to collaboratively produce a review of a theoretical textbook on constructivism (Petraglia, 1997). The assignment to produce a review (to be published!) was a pretext, based on the idea that this could be a way of advanced students joining the ranks of serious researchers to study electronic communication. The group was aware of this, and the participants agreed with the general constraint that all communication was supposed to take place electronically and publicly on a discussion forum. The role of the tutor was not defined at the start, and there was no plan. The original intention was to carry on for 3 months, for a couple of hours each week, but the process took much more time, and currently, 2 years after the start of the course, 4 students are left working to produce a text, communicating both orally and electronically. The analyses that are presented here involve the first 6 months of this process. The participants had to decide, organize, and plan many things, and they did not succeed in all respects. Van de Groep (2000), who was one of the participants of the course, undertook a study in which he examined the extent to which individual participants contributed to various aspects of the group process. To this end, first, the 34 different discussion threads were categorized and the frequency of the individual contributions to each class of discussions were counted. Figure 9.3 shows the landscape of general discussion themes over the first 6 months. The sizes of the peaks indicate the number of contributions.

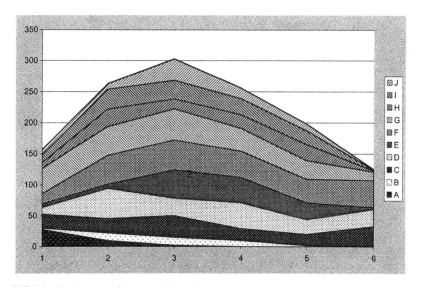

FIG.9.3. Landscape of themes of the discussions over six months.

The following classes of discussion forums were distinguished:

- Social: Explicitly for chatting, not related to group tasks.
- Texts: Forums in which participants contributed texts for the final product.
- Ccourse: Theoretical discussions about the authenticity of the course.
- Cmoderate: Theoretical discussions about moderating electronic discussions.
- Cbook: Theoretical discussions about the book to review.
- Org-write: Negotiations about the organization of the writing task.
- Org-course: Negotiations about the organization of the course.
- Other: Other discussions.

Concerning themes, Figure 9.3 shows that from the start of the group, participants were very concerned with the issue of the role of the moderator. They decided to alternate and evaluate the moderator role every 2 weeks. One important task of this role was to regulate the group process in terms of tasks, but also to support the social process, with encouragement as well as intervention when things went the wrong way. Immediately, it became clear that not every participant was equally involved in each part of the process, as can be easily seen from Figure 9.4, where the relative participation of individuals is displayed. Very soon organization problems emerged, and the nature of the course, both at the level of theory (Is this negotiation?: Ccourse) as well as practice was extensively discussed (Org-course).

The peak at the very end, after 6 months, shows that the organization question remained and was not answered satisfactorily. Division of tasks, and taking up the responsibility of carrying out a task within reasonable time constraints, remained a problem for the group. Individual expectations differed and many of these differences only appeared during discussion, sometimes when explicitly addressed, but more often implicitly as silence and delays. At the end, 4 participants remained active (C, D, F, & G).

FIG.9.4. Individual participations over six months.

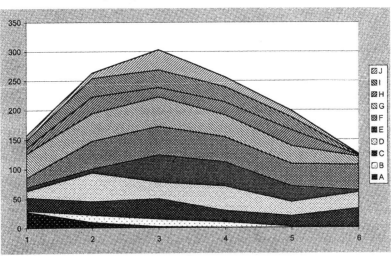

Participant A was only active at the beginning, but left the group after 2 months. Participant B lasted a bit longer, but was never very active. Participant E was very active during months 3 through 5, when most text production for the assignment took place. Participants H and J contributed selectively.

Although participants differed to some extent concerning the distribution of their individual activities across themes, every participant contributed the most messages to organization discussions, and then to content-based discussions.

One of the core activities of the group was supposed to be engagement in content-based discussion. Although organization of the group process and writing were obvious tasks to focus on, the main goal of the course, as explained at the beginning, involved the construction of theoretical knowledge about conceptions of constructivism and learning, triggered by the text to read. This activity (Cbook) mainly took place during the third month, and was followed by a discussion about the authenticity of the current course (Ccourse) in months 3 and 4. After that, all content-based discussion faded out and discussion on organizational matters and text production took over.

The next step in the analysis was to arrive at a characterization of the group activities. To this end, the level of activity of each message was classified (Hansen, Dirckinck-Holmfeld, Lewis, & Rugelj, 1999; Heeren & Lewis, 1997). Based on ideas formulated by Leontiev (1978) it is supposed that these levels coexist at the same time but the focus of activity may be at different levels:

- Intentional: A participant focuses on motives, desires, needs, and values. It is the level of global orientation that gives meaning to human processes. Practically it means that a participant indicates and explains his or her intentions, for example to reach a shared understanding. This is supposed to be a major activity for grounding, especially during the initial stages

- Functional: Activity is oriented to specific conscious goals in the context of motives. It is the level of organizational planning and problem solving to achieve (intermediate) goals.

- Operational: The level of practical conditions of actions. It is the level of practical routines required to carry out conscious, purposeful actions at the functional level.

Figure 9.5 clearly shows that the activity of the participants was mainly at the operational level, especially without enough expression of motives. In other words, discussion focused on the result, and not on the personal reasons to achieve this result. This result can be compared to that of Study 1, in which it was shown that students tend to focus on practical application of knowledge as often as on meaning. This study provides an enlarged picture of this: Students are struggling with what to do and on how to achieve that goal, whereas the reasons for the activities (discussing personal views on concepts) are not negotiated enough.

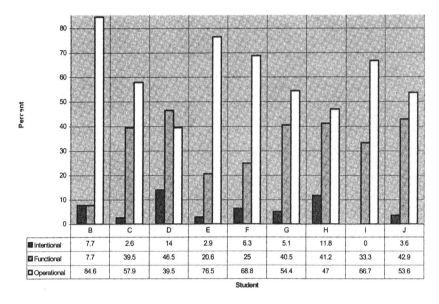

	B	C	D	E	F	G	H	I	J
■ Intentional	7.7	2.6	14	2.9	6.3	5.1	11.8	0	3.6
▧ Functional	7.7	39.5	46.5	20.6	25	40.5	41.2	33.3	42.9
□ Operational	84.6	57.9	39.5	76.5	68.8	54.4	47	66.7	53.6

Student

FIG.9.5. Individual differences in activities for all discussions.

A more general conclusion is that the task seems too hard for our students. First, it may be too difficult for most students to produce a review of
a theoretical text. Although it was made clear from the start that theoretical
discussions were more important than the actual product that was required,
the group took their main task as producing a review. This product orientation was necessary to give ground to their efforts. Second, to facilitate the
process at the level of course organization, it would have been possible for
a tutor to provide more structure and task division. Participants had problems with focusing on task organization and engaging in theoretical discussions at the same time. However, it would be hard to organize the roles of
individual participants during different phases of the process, as these roles
are an outcome of the group process itself. Needs of learners change over
time, and roles may develop as a function of that change. Third, these and
other problems seem not to be at the level of motivation (at least for most
participants) or even planning of tasks, but at the level of actually getting
things done until they are finished. Although the electronic communication
mode was clearly slowing down this process, the main problem was collaboration itself, represented as a lack of explicit attention to goals and motives. The result of this was a lack of grounding of the discussion at these
levels, which may have caused problems at the operational level.

DISCUSSION

The studies that we presented showed a number of characteristics of electronic collaboration in CMC. Study 1 showed that participants in discussion forums engage in content-based discussions that are explanatory rather than argumentative, individual contributions are not very much linked to one another, and students do not often explicitly refer to each other's messages. Study 2 showed that the connectiveness of individual contributions can be affected by instruction, but that there was an important effect of the degree of grounding or familiarity of the content to be discussed. Study 3 showed that students tend to focus on planning and problem solving rather than on personal motives, which causes a lack of common ground, which in turn renders the existence of individual differences in the amount, the timing, and the focus of individual contributions as problematic. Moreover, this focus on planning and problem solving did not result in efficient organization of the process. To put it bluntly, students did not effectively collaborate to reach their goals.

Electronic communication is still a new kind of activity for students, and it seems to offer more possibilities for collaboration and learning. The development of effective collaboration takes time, but Study 3 showed that more time does not lead to better collaboration. There are many things students need to learn to engage in fruitful discussions. It seems that most of these results are not due to characteristics of the electronic medium, but that the medium affords new ways of working for which participants lack the appropriate knowledge and skills.

The question now arises what can be done about that. We could explain to students that it is important to argue more, and to provide an "argumentation in electronic dialogue" course to help them acquire the skills needed. We can tell students to connect to previous messages and to explicitly focus on the topic and on coherence. One main problem is that to do that effectively, students need to understand the topic of discussion sufficiently. Traditional education does not get them even that far. We could explain to students that it is important to acknowledge and value each other's contributions, which may be new to them. But do we have the knowledge and time to train students who seem to be motivated enough, to assume responsibility for a complex group process, for which not everyone has the same expectations, in all skills required to carry out several subparts of the process? In addition, being open about your personal goals and motives is something that seems crucial for effective knowledge negotiation, but requires a level of group safety that is not found in ordinary university education. Finally, the requirement to monitor group processes is something that not many university students, nor their teachers, seem to be capable of (Veerman, Andriessen, & Kanselaar, in press). It is obvious that these issues should be taken up at a more general level than that of a single course. There are more ways to collaborate, according to different goals, each requiring different skills to develop. It seems that education in general should more explicitly aim for developing students' insight into the constraints of different collaboration settings.

A Pedagogical Framework for Advancing Effective CMC

The system of secondary and higher education in most countries is not designed for meeting the needs of current and future learning. It functions as transmitting domain-specific content, within a strictly specified period, and compares learner results at the end of a period in terms of explicit evaluation marks. This system works as a selection mechanism rather than fostering learning. Any system that is designed for learning rather than selection must be able to allow flexible individual learning periods and should allow evaluation based on what individuals do rather than by comparing them (Versloot, 2000). In addition, current educational systems have severe problems with the incorporation of collaborative learning tasks. Evaluating learners on the basis of their performance in collaborative and/or project-based tasks, if not impossible, then at least imposes an additional workload on teachers, which far exceeds their regular hours.

Figure 9.6 is taken from a text by Stahl (2000) and depicts a tentative, and probably incomplete, framework of processes involved in learning as a process of collaborative knowledge building (Brown & Campione, 1994; Lave, 1991; Pea, 1993; Scardamalia & Bereiter, 1999). Figure 9.6 attempts to model the mutual (i.e., dialectical) constitution of the individual and the social as a learning process (Brown & Duguid, 1991; Lave & Wenger, 1991). Starting in the lower left corner, it shows the cycle of personal understanding. The rest of the figure depicts how personal beliefs that we become aware of in our activity in the world can be articulated in language and enter into a social process of interaction with other people and with our shared culture. This culture, in turn, enters into our personal understanding, shaping it with ways of thinking, motivational concerns, and diverse influences. Personal cognition and social activity can only be separated artificially, as in a model like this designed for analysis.

Figure 9.6 helps to understand the problem of current education from the viewpoint of learning processes: Current education is designed (if anything) for personal understanding and not for social processes involved in knowledge building. The result is that, if one tries to implement a CMC-based education course into regular education, one deals with participants who are used to learning for personal understanding and who have no experience with other processes involved in knowledge building.

What can be supposed is that CMC, given the appropriate and appropriated tools, allows social knowledge building, something traditional education can never achieve. Nevertheless, participants in current education work with the conceptions and expectations of traditional education, while more and more often being subjected to collaborative tasks and tools. This is a serious problem not easily overcome, and solving it involves all participants in educational activity, including the redesign of the curriculum. The goal of redesign is to develop skills for personal understanding, shared understanding, and social knowledge building, which are interdependent processes, but at the same time can be taken as the basis of a sequence of educational goals that each require advanced awareness about collaborative learning. The framework we are about to present describes three idealized scenarios for education to proceed through, starting from where education currently is supposed to be.

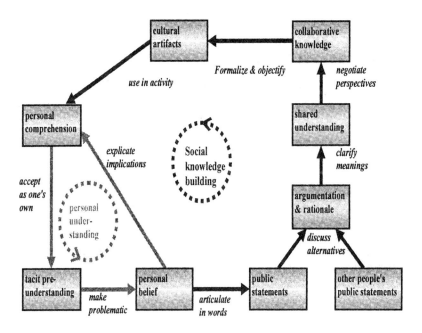

FIG.9.6. Knowledge-building processes (Stahl, 2000).

Pedagogic Scenarios

Andriessen and Sandberg (1999) proposed three basic pedagogic scenarios that together represent important dimensions of pedagogic stances and choices. A pedagogic scenario describes an educational arrangement in which the conceptions of the users are characterized with respect to underlying pedagogic goals. These conceptions define the roles users (teachers and learners) play in a collaborative learning task. The idea that we develop here is that the three scenarios also constitute an evolution users should go through to become successful knowledge builders, characterized by the ability to engage in all processes depicted in Figure 9.6. This evolution has to be educationally designed to change user conceptions. Conceptual change involves collaborative learning, and not domain knowledge and skills. Changing conceptions means making users aware of their roles during different types of collaboration, and those played by others, by designing specific collaboration arrangements. In such collaboration arrangements, the concerted design of task, software environment, and support aim at gradually increasing awareness of collaborative roles by appropriate experience and reflection. It should be noted that to reach these goals, more research about collaborative learning is very much needed.

Scenario 1: Transmission

This is the view that knowledge can be more or less directly transmitted to students through a system of lectures, textbooks, and testing. This scenario reflects the production and transmission of universal, objective knowledge, and the diminishing of local, subjective, and personal knowledge (Ball, 1997). The transmission view most closely matches traditional education. Transmission scenarios favor closed assignments with criteria determined by the instructor. The ideal learning environment is one with an inspiring tutor teaching with clear demonstrations, expositions, narratives, arguments, and examples. Collaboration between students is motivated by efficiency criteria: It will be used if a fixed learning result is attained faster or cheaper. Transmission is about achieving personal understanding of what experts mean.

Characterizing current education as knowledge transmission is not doing justice to the fact that in reality many different approaches exist, differing in goals, content matter, and didactical strategy. Also, it is not clear whether transmission, as the transfer of expert knowledge from teacher and text to a student, is the best way to develop personal understanding. It seems efficient to process large amounts of declarative knowledge from books by trying to understand the most important ideas in the text, and to be able to summarize them and to reproduce them on test occasions. Also, teacher feedback on these activities, on the basis of answers to questions or solutions to problems, seems an effective way of understanding what the teacher, as representative of the expert community, thinks is important. Cognitive learning theory is able to explain such learning quite well (Anderson, 1995). As long as the right conditions are created for understanding information and producing explanations, it is possible that misconceptions are repaired and personal knowledge is transformed to incorporate new insights.

The problem with transmission is in the expectations it generates of learners, which make transmission unsuitable as an approach to collaborative learning. At best, in transmission, collaboration may support participants in trying to understand each other's ideas, by explanation and comprehension processes. Argumentation is mainly considered as a reasoning process, in which learners try to articulate strong and relevant arguments and warrants, to arrive at an approved conclusion. This best case is not very often achieved, as the results discussed in this chapter have shown. Learners expect answers from teachers for almost every problem they encounter, and these problems are understood as problems of personal understanding. Someone who understands sufficiently does not need to collaborate. Learners do not develop collaborative learning skills because of this expectation, and because the transmission scenario does not include approaches and goals that treat collaboration as a serious vehicle toward acquisition of personal learning goals. In transmission, knowledge of collaboration is not sought, and will for the most part be the result of modeling and learning by discovery.

However, the design of specific collaboration arrangements would be possible from a transmission perspective. In the sphere of transmission, such collaboration arrangements would be scripted, focusing on acquisition of domain knowledge (O'Donnell, 1999). Another characteristic of transmission-based collaboration would be its task specificity, because the success of the collaboration in transmission depends on the attainment of domain-specific knowledge. This may be a reason why problems of transfer and authenticity typically occur in such scenarios (Bereiter, 2002; Laurillard, 1993; Petraglia, 1997). Furthermore, one would expect such collaborations to be most successful for students who already have high domain knowledge (Palincsar & Herrenkohl, 1999; Webb & Farivar, 1999).

Scenario 2: Studio

In a studio scenario users learn how to collaborate with others by encouraging, scaffolding, and critiquing each other, while sharing information in a safe environment. This should allow them to learn how to reach shared understanding. The main assumption here is that responsibility for learning should reside more with the student. The more constructive efforts a student undertakes, the more he or she will learn. In the current approach, students also need the skills to collaborate with the purpose of personal understanding of information. Now they should learn that different collaboration tasks may involve different forms of peer learning, and that participant roles in this process may require different skills.

In a studio, group tasks are designed for which it is necessary to collaborate with different partners for different reasons. Tasks could be designing and carrying out a research project, preparing project presentations, evaluating research reports, or modifying a software environment (White, Shimoda, & Frederiksen, 2000). Information is distributed between partners, and all information is necessary to accomplish the task. Some partners are more expert than others in certain areas, other partners are good at raising questions, others are good strategic advisors, or investigators, planners, reasoners, debaters, and so on. This is what we mean by roles. Roles can be assigned, or users can choose their own role to play. Users learn to play roles, they have to learn which roles are useful for which task, they have to know their own strong and weak points in this respect, and they have to learn what it takes to play a role well. Finally, users have to be able to assess group performance, evaluate to what extent the collaboration between group members was successful, and determine how to improve on that.

Technology could provide a space where these activities can be carried out. Users should be able to work on task documents, organized around a possible sequence of subtasks (Schwarz, Neuman, Gil, Ilya, 2003). They need cognitive maps to display information in different ways (Suthers, 2001). They need a tool to organize their work. They need role advisors who propose what to say next and may give strategic advice on demand (White et al., 2000). Finally, they need a metaphor for an environment in which all these activities can be authentically carried out. This could be a MOO-type environment (e.g., a building or town setting) in which artificial agents try to disturb or support collaboration. Educational design has to focus on finding innovative ways of promoting user reflection on their own communication, collaboration, and learning in this environment.

Learning in a studio setting fosters development of metacognitive knowledge and domain-independent skills. One such skill is argumentation. Argumentation in a studio has to be taken as arguing to learn, not as learning to argue, as in transmission (Andriessen, Baker, & Suthers, in press; Veerman, 2000). This eventually should lead to a student having acquired the flexibility of knowing how to learn in new situations. The role of instruction in this scenario is to provide tools and opportunities for learning, commenting, and coaching; creating room for collaborative learning, and interactive learning; providing feedback; supporting finding and evaluating information; creating flexible environments; and so on. Learning goals are still assumed to be fixed and well defined, and to be individual. Only the way to reach the learning goal is flexible and allows for student initiative in determining through which means the goal is to be reached.

Scenario 3: Negotiation

From a rhetorical perspective on academic learning, education can be framed as an ongoing argumentative process (Petraglia, 1997). It is the process of discovering and generating acceptable arguments and lines of reasoning underlying scientific assumptions and bodies of knowledge. From a sociocultural perspective on education, students should acquire practice and expertise in this activity, through sustained and, to some extent, guided efforts in meaning negotiation. However, little is known about what it takes to make such things succeed.

Negotiating implies individuals communicating and debating points of view to reach agreement or understanding. In a knowledge negotiation scenario, the focus is on producing collaborative knowledge during this proc- ess. The most important difference between studio and negotiation scenar- ios involves the change of focus from the individual as the learning entity in a studio to the group as the learning unit in negotiation. This means that individuals in a negotiation scenario are supposed to assume responsibility for the functioning of the group as a whole.

Negotiation happens in learning groups engaged in knowledge-building activities (Bereiter, 2002; Brown & Campione, 1994; Scardamalia & Bere- iter, 1994): creating new knowledge by sharing and negotiating content. All professional practices have found their current shape by long-term interac- tion and negotiation processes (Brown & Duguid, 1991). Participating in professional groups implies the ability to understand the important debates and problems and to use the right language to examine and influence ongo- ing discussion. Learning in the negotiation scenario essentially is learning to produce and comprehend discourse. The difference with seemingly simi- lar activities in transmission is that discourse in negotiation is aimed at pro- fessional discourse, including its normative, social, and political dimen- sions.

In a collaborative learning situation in a negotiation scenario, partici- pants mutually support each other to produce ideas as much as possible. This requires a safe social environment that supports new knowledge con- stitution, and allows various organizations and inspections of old and new information. Support should focus on community building and knowledge building. In addition, technology should work with community models, in which various contributions are assessed and evaluated with respect to pa- rameters of the effective sharing and creation of knowledge by the group. Users should have easy access to external information on the Web, which includes information of different quality and status. Storage and retrieval of information (knowledge management) is a crucial aspect of this process. All tool support has to be available on demand.

The Evolution From Transmission to Negotiation

When confronted with a negotiation scenario in a transmission context, both students and teachers may feel lost. Students complain about the vagueness of assignments and the lack of explicit guidance, whereas teachers complain about their lack of control of the learning situation. Apparently, the transi- tion induced in such cases is too abrupt to be smoothly adopted by the stu- dents as well as the teachers. Therefore, we have to investigate the way students as well as teachers can be guided in a process of change, by gradu- ally moving from transmission to negotiation.

The progress from knowledge transmission to knowledge negotiation can be taken as a gradual evolution during which mastery of a previous phase is required to move to the next phase. Each phase has its own goals and learning results, and offers more possibilities for collaboration, at the same time requiring more insight into and experience with collaborative learning. Collaboration arrangements have to be explicitly designed to allow users to collaborate according to their pedagogic scenario, at the same time making them reflect on further options allowed in the next phase. New educational design approaches are needed here. The further users advance toward knowledge building, the more constraints they are able to deal with, and the more responsibility and insight by users can be expected.

As an example, in a pioneering study on moving the teaching of proofs from a knowledge transmission scenario to a negotiation scenario (Schwarz & Glassner, in press), designers, teachers, and students first began to solve problems in geometry in a knowledge transition mode (without taking into consideration the motives of the learners). The teacher then moved to a studio mode by giving new activities (designed by a designer according to the teacher specifications) in which problem solving served as a device for being convinced of the correctness of conclusions. Teacher and students reflected then on what they did (to convince the other, to raise an ambiguity, to explain a surprise, etc.). Teachers and students then interacted with a designer for choosing new activities to understand more about proofs. The creation of new activities was in fact a process of modification to manipulate learners' motives and goals.

The study by Schwarz and Glassner (in press) was done with extraordinary teachers, though. Other preliminary studies indicate that to change conceptions about learning, teachers must be empowered through the help of designers who can translate intentions for specific learning scenarios into "real activities" and point out the constraints that some choices of tasks may put on the realization of the curriculum. As suggested in Schwarz and Glassner (in press), in multiple cycles of curricula in which teachers and designers are engaged in the creation of a series of activities, the activity of the teachers becomes progressively more autonomous.

CONCLUSION

In this chapter, we showed some of the characteristics of current electronic discussions in higher education. We think the discussions that we obtained rate among the more successful implementations of CMC in this context. Nevertheless, we feel much more can be achieved if a carefully designed approach to educational practice in terms of educational scenarios is implemented.

Our ideas as they have been presented still remain at the level of intentions. Even in transmission not much collaboration is designed in practice. In our descriptions of scenarios, not all details of the complex processes students are engaged in are well known or articulated enough. Projects that test some of these ideas are underway, and when results appear, more details can be provided.

The most important message of this chapter is that new learning has to be designed and needs more careful study. Changing educational practice has to be an engineered approach, in which goals change as a function of the scenario in which users are engaged. If the goal of education is personal understanding, maybe any scenario will do as long as it is properly designed. Results in this case will depend on the appropriate interplay of individual and task situation characteristics. However, if the goal of education is shared understanding, transmission is not good enough. Design of learning arrangements in which awareness of collaboration is raised and encouraged are then a necessary requirement.

REFERENCES

Anderson, J. R. (1995). *Cognitive psychology and its implications.* New York. Freeman.

Andriessen, J., Baker, M., & Suthers, D. (Ed.s). (in press). *Arguing to learn: Confronting cognitions in computer-supported collaborative learning environments.* Dordrecht, Netherlands: Kluwer.

Andriessen, J. E. B. & Sandberg, J.A.C. (1999). Where is education heading and how about AI? *International Journal of Artificial Intelligence in Education, 10,* 130–150.

Baker, M. (1996). *Argumentation and cognitive change in collaborative problem-solving dialogues.* (COAST Research Rep. No. CR-13/96). France.

Baker, M. (1999). Argumentation and constructive interaction. In J. Andriessen & P. Coirier (Eds.), *Foundations of argumentative text processing.* (pp. 179–202). Amsterdam: Amsterdam University Press.

Baker, M., & Bielaczyc, K. (1995). Missed opportunities for learning in collaborative problem-solving interactions. In J. Greer (Ed.), *Proceedings of AI-ED 95 - 7th World Conference on Artificial Intelligence in Education* (pp. 210–218). Charlottesville VA: Association for the Advancement of Computing in Education.

Baker, M., Hansen, T., Joiner, R., & Traum, D. (1999). The role of grounding in collaborative learning tasks. In P. Dillenbourg (Ed.), *Collaborative learning: Cognitive and computational approaches* (pp. 31–63). Oxford, UK: Pergamon.

Ball, G. (1997). *Constructivism in educational technology.* Unpublished manuscript, Utrecht University, Department of Educational Sciences, Utrecht, Netherlands.

Bereiter, C. (2002). *Education and mind in the knowledge age.* Mahwah, NJ: Lawrence Erlbaum Associates.

Brand, M. (1999). *Leren als sociaal proces in een universitaire, CSCL omgeving* [Learning as a social process in academic CSCL situations]. Unpublished master's thesis, Utrecht University, Utrecht, Netherlands.

Brown, A., & Campione, J. (1994). Guided discovery in a community of learners. In K. McGilly (Ed.), *Classroom lessons: Integrating cognitive theory and classroom practice.* (pp. 229–270). Cambridge, MA: MIT Press.

Brown, J. S., & Duguid, P. (1991). Organizational learning and communities of practice: Toward a unified view of working, learning, and innovation. *Organization Science, 2.* 40–57.

Clark, H. H., & Schaefer, E. F. (1989). Contributing to discourse. *Cognitive Science, 13,* 259–294.

Doise, W., & Mugny, G. (1984). *The social development of the intellect.* Oxford, UK: Pergamon.

Erkens, G. (1997). *Coöperatief probleemoplossen met computers in het onderwijs: Het modelleren van coöperatieve dialogen voor de ontwikkeling van intelligente onderwijssystemen* [Cooperative problem solving with computers in education: Modeling of cooperative dialogues for the design of intelligent educational systems]. Utrecht, Netherlands: Brouwer Uithof.

Goodfellow, R., & Manning, P. (1999, March). *Expert, assessor, co-learner—Conflicting roles and expanding workload for the online teacher.* Paper presented at CAL99; London.

Hansen, T., Dirckinck-Holmfeld, L., Lewis, R., & Rugelj, J. (1999). Using telematics for collaborative knowledge construction. In P. Dillenbourg (Ed.), *Collaborative learning: Cognitive and computational approaches* (pp. 169–196). Oxford, UK: Pergamon.

Heeren, E., & Lewis, R. (1997). Selecting communication media for distributed communities. *Journal of Computer Assisted Learning, 13,* 85–98.

Kiesler, S. (1986). The hidden message in computer networks. *Harvard Business Review, 64,* 46–58.

Kuhn, D. (1991). *The skills of argument.* Cambridge, UK: Cambridge University Press.

Laurillard, D. (1993). *Rethinking university teaching: A framework for the effective use of educational technology.* London: Routledge.

Lave, J. (1991). Situating learning in communities of practice. In L. Resnick, J. Levine, & S. Teasley (Eds.); *Perspectives on socially shared cognition.* (pp. 63–83). Washington, DC: American Psychological Association.

Lave, J., & Wenger, E. (1991). *Situated learning: Legitimate peripheral participation.* Cambridge, UK: Cambridge University Press.

Leontiev, A. N. (1978). *Activity, consciousness, personality.* Englewood Cliffs, NJ: Prentice Hall.

Mason, R. (1991). Moderating educational computer conferencing. *DEOSNEWS 1*(19).

O'Donnell, A. M. (1999). Structuring dyadic interaction through scripted cooperation. In A. M. O'Donnell, A. M., & King, A. (Eds.). *Cognitive perspectives on peer learning* (pp. 179-196). Mahwah, NJ: Lawrence Erlbaum Associates.

Palincsar, A. S., & Herrenkohl, L. R. (1999). Designing collaborative contexts: Lessons from three research programs. In A. M. O'Donnell & A. King (Eds.) *Cognitive perspectives on peer learning.* (pp. 151–178). Mahwah, NJ: Lawrence Erlbaum Associates.

Pea, R. (1993). The collaborative visualization project. *Communications of the ACM, 36*(5), 60–63.

Petraglia, J. (1997). *The rhetoric and technology of authenticity in education.* Mahwah, NJ: Lawrence Erlbaum Associates.

Piaget, J. (1977). *The development of thought: Equilibration of cognitive structures.* New York: Viking Penguin.

Roschelle, J., & Teasley, S. D. (1995). Construction of shared knowledge in collaborative problem solving. In C. O'Malley (Ed.), *Computer-supported collaborative learning.* New York: Springer-Verlag.

Rutter, D. R. (1987). *Communicating by telephone.* Oxford, UK: Pergamon.

Savery, J., & Duffy, T. M. (1996). Problem based learning: An instructional model and its constructivist framework. In B. Wilson (Ed.), *Constructivist learning environments: Case studies in instructional design* (pp. 135–148). Englewood Cliffs, NJ: Educational Technology Publications.

Scardamalia, M., & Bereiter, C. (1994). Computer support for knowledge-building communities. *Journal of the Learning Sciences, 3*, 265–283.

Scardamalia, M., & Bereiter, C. (1999). Schools as knowledge building organizations. In D. Keating & C. Hertzman (Eds.), *Today's children, tomorrow's society: The Developmental health and wealth of nations.* (pp. 274–289). New York: Guilford.

Schwarz, B. B., & Glassner, A. (in press). The blind and the paralytic: Fostering argumentation in social and scientific domains. In J. Andriessen, M. Baker, & D. Suthers (Eds.), *Arguing to learn: Confronting cognitions in computer-supported collaborative learning environments.* Dordrecht, Netherlands: Kluwer.

Schwarz, B. B., Neuman, Y. and Gil, J., & Ilya, M. (2003). Construction of collective and individual knowledge in argumentative activity: An empirical study. *Journal of the Learning Sciences, 12,* 219-256.

Short, J., Williams, E., & Christie, B. (1976). *The social psychology of telecommunications.* New York: Wiley.

Smith, J. B. (1994). *Collective intelligence in computer-based collaboration.* Hillsdale, NJ: Lawrence Erlbaum Associates.

Spears, R., & Lea, M. (1992). Social influence and the influence of the social in computer mediated communication. In M. Lea (Ed.), *Context of computer mediated communication.*

Stahl, G. (2000). A model of collaborative knowledge-building. Retrieved from http://www.cis.drexel.edu/faculty/gerry/publications/conferences/2000/icls/icls.pdf, 12/1/04.

Steeples, C., Unsworth, C., Bryson, M., Goodyear, P., Riding, P., Fowell, S., Levy, C. (1996). Technological support for teaching and learning: Computer-mediated communications in higher education (CMC in HE). *Computers & Education, 26*(1–3), 71–80.

Suthers, D. D. (2001). Towards a systematic study of representational guidance for collaborative learning discourse. *Journal of Universal Computer Science, 7,* 254–277.

Tolmie, A., & Boyle, J. (2000). Factors influencing the success of computer mediated communication (CMC) environments in university teaching: A review and case study. *Computers & Education, 34,* 119–140.

Van de Groep, J. A. H. (2000). *OnderhandelingsOnderwijs: rollen van studenten in een elektronische discussie* [Negotiative education: Roles of students in an electronic discussion]. Unpublished masters thesis; Utrecht University, Dept. of Educational Sciences, Utrecht, Netherlands.

van der Pol, J. (1998). *Argumentatie in elektronisch gevoerde discussies en het effect van verschillende manieren om een discussie op te zetten* [Argumentation in electronic discussions and effects of different ways of designing them]. Unpublished manuscript, Utrecht University, Dept. of Educational Sciences, Utrecht, Netherlands.

van der Pol, J. (2001). *Aansluiten in electronische discussies* [Connecting in electronic discussions]. Unpublished masters thesis, Utrecht University, Dept. of Educational Sciences, Utrecht, Netherlands.

Veerman, A. L. (2000). *Computer-supported collaborative learning through argumentation.*, Retrieved from http://www.library.uu.nl/digiarchief/dip/diss/1908992/inhoud.htm, 12/1/04.

Veerman, A. L., Andriessen, J. E. B., & Kanselaar, G. (2000). Enhancing learning through synchronous discussion. *Computers & Education, 34*(2–3), 1–22.

Veerman, A. L., Andriessen, J. E. B., & Kanselaar, G. (in press). Question asking and collaborative argumentation in academic education. *Instructional Science.*

Versloot, B. (2000). *Een andere facilitering van de leerfunctie* [A different facilitation of learning functions]. In K. Stokking, G. Erkens, B. Versloot, & L. van Wessum (Eds.), *Van Onderwijs naar Leren* (pp. 299–312). Leuven/Apeldoorn: Garant.

Wan, D., & Johnson, P. M. (1994). *Experiences with CLARE: A computer supported Collaborative environment.* Paper presented at the 1994 ACM Conference on Computer Supported Work, Chapel Hill, NC.

Webb, N. M., & Farivar, S. (1999). Developing productive group interactions in middle school mathematics. In A. M. O'Donnell & A. King (Eds.), *Cognitive perspectives on peer learning.* (pp. 117–150). Mahwah, NJ: Lawrence Erlbaum Associates.

White, B. Y., Shimoda, T. A., & Frederiksen, J. R. (2000). Facilitating students' inquiry learning and metacognitive development through modifiable software advisers. In S. P. Lajoie (Ed.), *Computers as cognitive tools*, (Vol. 2, pp. 97–132). Mahwah, NJ: Lawrence Erlbaum Associates.

Chapter 10

Planning and Coordinating Activities in Collaborative Learning

Gijsbert Erkens, Maaike Prangsma, and Jos Jaspers
Utrecht University, Netherlands

This chapter focuses on the way collaborating students coordinate and adjust their activities to the processes of knowledge construction and problem solving. In the COSAR project we study the relationship between dynamics of interaction on the one hand and learning and problem solving on the other within the framework of computer-supported collaborative writing. A groupware program (TC3) has been developed that combines a shared text editor, a chat facility, tools for generating and organizing ideas, and private access to information resources to encourage collaborative distance writing. The program is meant for pairs of high school students (16–18 years old) working together on argumentative essays in Dutch. The assignment was to choose a position pro or contra a current topic (cloning or organ donation) and to write a convincing argumentative text. The texts had to be based on recent Internet newspaper articles and commentaries.

We are investigating what dynamics of interaction could explain the learning experiences and appropriation processes activated by collaborative tasks. Overall coordination and planning of the writing activities on a metalevel frequently occurred, but did not prove very influential on the argumentative quality of the shared text. However, we found that coordination and discussion of specific content of goals, knowledge, and formulation positively influenced the argumentative quality of the final product. From these results we conclude that shared knowledge construction is an essential part of collaborative learning—both on a metacognitive level and on a specific content level. Our analyses of the students' chats and activities during collaboration showed that the coordinated activity was realized through complex interaction between task strategies, cooperative intentions, and communication processes, giving rise to processes like activation, grounding, focusing, checking, and argumentation. First, collaboration requires students to activate their knowledge and share information and resources. Second, they need to establish a common frame of reference (grounding) to communicate and negotiate their individual viewpoints and inferences. Third, students use focusing to maintain a shared topic of discourse and to repair a common focus when noticing a focus divergence. Fourth, by checking new information with knowledge that was coconstructed, the students guard the coherence and consistency of their collective knowledge base. Finally, a process of explicit argumentation should lead to agreement on the task strategies to be followed and the inferences to be made.

Recent educational research reemphasizes cooperative or collaborative learning. This emphasis follows a reformulation of learning as a social process of enculturation by recent constructivist or situated learning views on cognition and instruction (Cognition and Technology Group at Vanderbilt, 1994; Duffy & Jonassen, 1991). In the constructivist approach of learning collaboration plays a central role. The idea that authentic learning only occurs in collaboration with others has become "the central pillar of constructivist orthodoxy and is the one on which practically every other principle is dependent to some extent" (Petraglia, 1998, p. 77). The Vygotskian tradition views peer collaboration as an intermediate stage in the developmental process of internalization of social activities. The (social) learning environment should support the learner in constructing his or her own knowledge and skills. Learning—both inside and outside school—is seen as advancing through collaborative social interaction, and through social construction of knowledge in a process of participation in a community of learners (Scardamalia, Bereiter, & Lamon, 1994).

However, these assumptions give rise to at least as many questions (Van der Linden, Erkens, Schmidt, & Renshaw, 2000). How are new knowledge and insights formed during collaborative learning? Which roles do the participants play in these shared processes of knowledge construction? How and why are roles assigned and tasks distributed by the members in a collaborative group? When do collaborating students need to challenge each other's ineffective strategies and misconceptions? How are confrontations and conflicts resolved and what influence does the resolution have on the learning processes? Do students differ in collaborative skills and activities? In short, what dynamics of interaction could explain the learning experiences and appropriation processes that collaborative task situations supposedly activate? To answer these questions, more research on the interaction processes of collaborative learning is needed (Cohen, 1994; Kumpulainen & Mutanen, 1999).

In the first section of this chapter we present a review of research and theoretical viewpoints on processes of planning and coordination in collaborative learning and writing. Next, we discuss our analyses of collaborative discourse and actions with regard to these processes in episodes of explicit argumentation. The third section focuses on methodological considerations for studying discourse in collaborative learning. Here, we also introduce MEPA, a computer program developed for qualitative and quantitative analysis of collaborative dialogue protocols. In the final section we argue for a theoretical model of planning and coordination in collaborative learning.

Learning Processes During Collaboration

In natural educational settings we can specify a collaborative learning situation as one in which a small group of two or more students work together to fulfill an assigned task within a particular domain of learning to achieve a joint goal (Cohen, 1994). In natural collaboration, the collaborating partners must have a common interest in solving the problem at hand. Furthermore, they should be mutually dependent on the information, resources, tools, and cooperative intention or willingness of the partner(s) to reach their (shared) goals. Collaboration can only be fruitful and be searched out in a natural way if the participants have complementary abilities, information, and willingness (Erkens, 1997).

Mutuality is a necessary condition for natural collaborative learning situations: a positive interdependence and equal opportunity of participation in the interaction. Under these conditions of mutuality, coordination of task strategy and of the constructive activities to achieve a shared understanding of the problem are crucial aspects of collaborative learning. In earlier research we found that this coordination is realized by a complex interaction among task-related strategies, cooperative intentions, and communication processes during collaboration. In the collaborative learning situation the learning results will be influenced by the type of task, the composition of the group, the common goal or task product, the complementarity in expertise of the participants, the resources and tools available, and the educational climate. To achieve the common goal, the collaboration partners will have to coordinate their activities and their thinking. Real collaboration requires a common frame of reference to be able to negotiate and communicate individual viewpoints and inferences. Furthermore, shared understanding of the problem at hand, a joint problem space (Roschelle & Teasley, 1995), or a collective landscape of concepts (Erkens, Andriessen, & Peters, 2003) must be constructed and a problem-solving strategy has to be agreed on.

After reviewing research on the learning activities that may be stimulated by the dynamics of the interaction between the participants in the collaborative learning situation, we now think that there may be three main processes: activation of knowledge and skills, grounding or creating a common frame of reference, and negotiation or the process of coming to agreement. Specific activities can be distinguished within these three processes:

1. Activation of knowledge and skills

    a.   Initiating (taking initiative in the task interaction).

         ·   Degree of participation: equality or asymmetry in contributions between the participants.

         ·   Proposing topics of discussion: initiating topics of discourse, taking control of the task strategy.

b.   Articulation of knowledge and information.

         ·   Explicating and verbalizing: making ideas and knowledge explicit for the other and oneself.

         ·   Organizing and structuring: (re)structuring ideas and knowledge for communicative purposes.

c.   Exchanging knowledge and information.

         ·   Sharing information and resources: making one's own information and knowledge accessible.

         ·   Seeking or asking for information: seeing the other as source of information.

We assume that the collaborative learning situation—simply by its shared goal directness and the interactive situation—stimulates processes of taking initiative in the interaction, encourages the verbalization and thus (re)structuring of knowledge (situated articulation; Brown, Collins, & Duguid, 1989), and promotes the exchange of information and resources (Teasley and Rochelle, 1993). In short, collaboration stimulates the activation and exchange of task-related knowledge and information and thus stimulates a shared task orientation.

2. Grounding (creating a common frame of reference)

a.   Tuning.

         ·   Adapting to the level of understanding of the partner: taking into account possible future misunderstandings of the other, for example, by proactive clarifications.

b.   Checking.

         ·   Checking exchanged information in relation to the existing knowledge structure: asking for clarification if new information conflicts with knowledge already (co)constructed.

c.   Focusing.

         ·   Mutual control of focus and topic of discussion: checking if contributions refer to the same topic of discourse and attempting to amend divergence in this respect.

d.   Co-construction.

         ·   Complementing knowledge and skills of the partner: adding to the shared knowledge structure, helping the other to verbalize his or her ideas.

Collaborative communication requires that the students acquire a common frame of reference to allow them to communicate and negotiate their individual viewpoints and inferences. Grounding is a process characterizing all communication (Clark & Brennan, 1991; Clark & Schaeffer, 1987). For communication to be successful, we need to make sure that we understand each other. By back channeling (confirming, nodding, acknowledgments, etc.), communicating participants can signal their understanding. By tuning, participants try to adapt to the perceived level of understanding of their collaborative partners. By focusing, students try to maintain a shared topic of discourse and repair a common focus if they notice a focus divergence. By checking new information with regard to the knowledge that was coconstructed, the students guard the coherence and consistency of their collective knowledge base (Erkens, 2004). In coconstructing the participants collaboratively add to this shared knowledge base by complementing each other's contributions (Van Boxtel, 2000). In short, by processes of grounding students maintain the consistency of their collective, commonly understood knowledge base of concepts and relationships between them. Mutual understanding is a necessary condition for communication and hence for collaboration. However, understanding each other's perspective is not the same as agreeing on one perspective.

3. Negotiation and coming to agreement

    a.   Explanation.

           ·   Elaboration, explanation and accounts: giving elaborations to clarify an idea or position, giving explanations to support and emphasize relations between concepts.

    b.   Argumentation.

           ·   Discussion, persuasion, and criticizing: giving arguments pro or con to convince the partner of a position.

           ·   Comparing and evaluating: comparing arguments pro and con and weighing their relative importance.

    c.   Coming to agreement.

           ·   Deciding and according: controlling the process of coming to an agreed on, shared decision.

In collaboration the participants also need to come to agreement about task strategies, relevant concepts, and relationships. They try to change the other's viewpoint to arrive at the best way to solve the task at hand or at a definition of concepts acceptable for all. In this process they try to convince the other by elaborating on their point of view, giving explanations, giving justifications, and providing accounts (Antaki, 1994). A process of explicit argumentation should lead to agreement on the task strategies to be followed and on the inferences to be drawn (Baker, 1999). Alternatives need to be deliberated and compared to each other, and a joint decision has to be made on which alternative to use (Di Eugenio, Jordan, Thomason, & Moore, 2000). In (neo-) Piagetian theory the resolution of the social-cognitive conflict between participants is seen as the most crucial factor for learning in collaborative learning situations (Doise & Mugny, 1984). In our opinion, however, it is in fact the paradox of collaborative learning: the assumption that students learn from arguing, criticizing, and conflict versus the necessity of reaching consensus for collaboration to advance.

From our research we believe that the need to coordinate activities—in other words, to come to a common goal, a common task strategy, and the construction of a shared knowledge base—is crucial for solving the collabo-rative task at hand. In the first place, this need for coordination stimulates the activation of knowledge and the initiative to share this private informa-tion or knowledge. Second, the need to coordinate not only necessitates transfer of information, but also a common frame of reference to understand each other's perspective. Third, agreement on a common line of reasoning should be reached. In fact this accounts for the difference between obtain-ing mutual understanding ("I understand what you mean") versus obtaining a common understanding ("I agree with what you mean"). Whereas mutual understanding (grounding) can be seen as a cooperative prerequisite for all communication, and thus also for collaborative learning situations, coordi-nation of activities and agreement on a common line of reasoning is neces-sary for successful collaboration. Furthermore, one may assume that col-laborating students will need to coordinate their activities on three levels of thinking and action: the task content level (concepts and procedural skills), the metacognitive level (task strategy and monitoring), and the sociocom-municative level (interpersonal relations and interaction).

COLLABORATIVE ARGUMENTATIVE WRITING

Writing texts of any length is a complex process consisting of several inter-related subprocesses, each with its own dynamics and constraints (Rijlaars-dam & Van den Bergh, 1996). We conceptualize writing argumentative texts mainly as a knowledge construction and problem-solving task (see also Galbraith, 1999). In this open task, various units of information must be generated, selected, collected, related to each other, and organized in a consistent knowledge structure. Furthermore, the writers need to solve the problem of convincing the reader, by finding a persuasive arrangement of arguments and counterarguments. This involves a number of skills, for in-stance in social, cognitive, rhetorical, and cultural domains.

The main advantage of collaborative writing, compared to individual writing, is the possibility of immediate feedback. Argumentation in itself, according to Stein, Calicchia and Bernas (1996), facilitates learning because it necessitates searching for relevant information and using each other as a source. Furthermore, the discussion generated by the activity makes the collaborators verbalize and negotiate many issues: representations, purpose, plans, doubts, and so on. Collaborating writers need to test their hypotheses, justify their propositions, and make their goals explicit. This may lead to progressively more conscious control and increased awareness of the processes (Giroud, 1999). Previously mentioned, every collaborative learning participant may ask for argumentation processes to convince other participants of a line of reasoning or task strategy to achieve an agreed-on decision. So it is with collaborative argumentative writing as well. However, it is important to note that the arguments used in the process of collaborative coordination may be very different from the arguments that are used in the text.

Planning Argumentative Texts

Theories of writing (Hayes & Nash, 1996) generally distinguish three types of activities in the writing process: planning (generating, organizing, and linearizing content), formulating or translating (writing the text), and revising. In planning an argumentative text, arguments need to be generated and ordered according to the position defended and the intended readers. Unlike storytelling, the contents of an argumentative text cannot be ordered chronologically, but will rather be organized in, for instance, argument clusters. Hence, the contents need to be linearized before the ideas can be put into writing, and again when the text needs to be reorganized. Linearization, therefore, is an important activity in argumentative writing (Levelt, 1989). Research at our department showed that a deliberate division between the idea organization phase and the linearization phase during planning leads to improved quality of the argumentative text (Coirier, Andriessen, & Chanquoy, 1999). Apparently, translating the conceptual representation of ideas into linear text is a crucial problem in producing argumentative texts.

A large amount of research has been concerned with *preplanning*, which refers to planning activities that occur before the actual writing of the text. This research has shown that preplanning can have a favorable effect on text quality, but also that inexperienced writers rarely preplan (Andriessen, Coirier, Roos, Passerault, & Bert-Erboul, 1996). Moreover, due to lack of knowledge of the issues concerned, preplanning in novices—when it does occur—is often no more than superficial brainstorming: not much more than simple content activation on the basis of the terms used in the assignment. Bereiter and Scardamalia (1987) found this to be true for children. Torrance, Thomas, and Robinson (1996), likewise, found little idea generation based on rhetorical demands during preplanning for adult undergraduates (relative novices), but more based on a simple content activation model. Also, the number and originality of ideas in the draft did not correlate with time spent on preplanning. Preplanning for writing informational or argumentative texts, however, largely consists of searching, reading, and annotating information sources.

Lacking preplanning skills, support of *online planning* becomes especially important for inexperienced writers. Online planning consists of the monitoring activities performed during writing based on set goals, ideas, expectations, and strategies. These activities direct the process of knowledge construction during writing. Online planning activities, unlike preplanning, are generally linked more strongly to the local organization of the text. Preplanning in experts is concerned more with broader issues like setting goals and determining overall organization and genre. In earlier research, the transition from preplanning to writing was found to be a stumbling block. Kozma (1991), Scardamalia and Bereiter (1985), and Schriver (1988) all found positive effects of instruction on preplanning for the amount or the quality of preplanning, but not for the quality of the final text. Transitional processes—linearization and translation—might be causing these problems.

In collaborative writing, reflecting on such transitions becomes a natural process, and thus collaboration can give support during writing. When writing a shared text, the partners need to agree both on the content and the ordering of the text. Furthermore, the use of resources needs to be coordinated and discussed. It seems that this type of forced discussion leads to better results. In previous research, in which college undergraduates selected arguments and produced an argumentative text while collaborating in a groupware environment, differences in the argumentative discussion were found to correlate with the representation of the source material. It was found that in a task in which the arguments appeared as pictures, more inferences were needed to determine the usefulness of the information. The students discussed more new arguments in the chat discussion and more new arguments in their common argumentative text (Andriessen, Erkens, Overeem, & Jaspers, 1996). Having to put the pictures into words must have helped. Thus, the constructive activities of organizing, linearizing, and translating into the shared text need to take place in mutual deliberation, necessitating verbalization and reification of ideas. This negotiation, leading to shared knowledge construction and a common task strategy, takes place in the collaboration dialogue between the partners (Erkens, Andriessen, & Peters, 2003). The expectation is that a higher frequency of mutual coordinating activities in the dialogue results in a more consistent, shared knowledge structure and in a better solution; that is, a better argumentative text (also see Baker, 1999). Furthermore, computer support for content generation, organization, and linearization will help to make these planning activities explicit and negotiable. These two assumptions are investigated in the COSAR project.

THE COSAR PROJECT

In the last 3 years of college preparatory programs, Dutch schools are expected to provide opportunities for students to do increasingly independent research to prepare them better for university studies. Active learning, knowledge construction, and working collaboratively are seen as important aspects of the curriculum. The computer-supported collaborative writing environment developed in the COSAR project was meant to fit within this curriculum, as the information and communication technology (ICT) involved can emphasize both the constructivist and collaborative aspects through its active and interactive nature.

Computer and telematics-based environments seem especially suited for collaborative learning by the variety of possibilities they possess: They may integrate multimedia information sources, data processing tools, and systems of communication (time and place independent) in one single working environment (Bannon, 1995; Van der Linden et al., 2000).

Computer-supported collaborative learning (CSCL) systems are assumed to have the potential to enhance the effectiveness of peer learning interactions (Dillenbourg, 1999). As for the role computers play with regard to education, the focus is on the construction of computer-based, multimedia environments, open learning environments that may give rise to multiple authentic learning experiences (Cognition and Technology Group at Vanderbilt, 1994). The cooperative aspect is mainly realized by offering computerized tools, which can be helpful for collaborating students in solving the task at hand (e.g., the CSILE program of Scardamalia et al., 1994; the Belvèdere program of Suthers, Weiner, Connelly, & Paolucci, 1995). These tools are generally one of two kinds: task content related or communicative. Task-related tools support the performance of the task and the problem-solving process (Teasley & Rochelle, 1993). Communicative tools give access to collaborating partners, but also to other resources like external experts or other information sources via the Internet. The function of the program is in this respect a communication medium (Henri, 1995). Programs that integrate both functions are generally known as *groupware*, programs that are meant to support collaborative group work by sharing tools and resources between group members and by giving communication opportunities within the group and to the external world. In complex, open problem-solving tasks students will have to decide when and where to use the task related and communicative tools and resources during the process of collaboration within the groupware environment. Furthermore, they will have to coordinate the use of shared tools and discuss their application.

In the COSAR project (which stands for COmputer-Supported ARgumentative writing) we studied the relationship between characteristics of interaction, and learning and problem solving within the framework of electronic collaborative text production (see owkweb.fss.uu.nl/cosar).

A groupware program (TC3: Text Composer, Computer Supported & Collaborative) was developed that combines a shared text editor, chat boxes, and private access to internal and external information sources to foster collaborative distance writing. The main screen of the program displays several private and shared windows. TC3 consists of the following main windows (see Fig. 10.1):

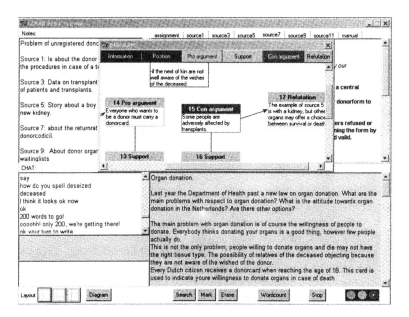

FIG.10.1. Screen dump of the collaborative writing environment TC3 (translated from Dutch).

1. Information (upper right): The task assignment, sources, and TC3 operating instructions can be accessed within one private window in a tabbed format. Sources were divided evenly over the students. Each had different sources. The content of the sources cannot be copied or pasted.

2. Notes (upper left): A private notepad where each partner can make personal, nonshared notes.

3. Chat (lower left): The lower chat box is for the student's current contribution, and the other shows the incoming messages of his or her partner. Every typed letter is immediately sent to the partner via the network, so that both boxes are WYSIWIS: (What You See Is What I See). The scrollable window holds the discussion history.

4. Shared text (lower right): A text editor (also WYSIWIS) in which the shared text can be composed while taking turns, and a turn-

taking device. Information in notes, chat, chat history, and shared text can be exchanged via copy and paste functions.

5. Diagrammer (upper center): A preplanning and online planning tool for generating, organizing, and relating information units in a graphical knowledge structure. This tool is conceptualized to the students as an argumentative concept map, a graphical summary of the pro and con arguments in the paper.

6. Outliner (not depicted in this figure): Tool for linearization of content. This tool is conceptualized to the student as producing a meaningful outline of the paper, and as in the diagrammer, the student is required to have the information in the outline faithfully represent the information in the text when it is handed in. Both planning windows are WYSIWIS.

The program keeps a log file of all actions in the separate windows and the chat discussion history. This log file can be used to literally replay all keystrokes and thus the full collaboration between the students. The log file can also be used to construct an activity and chat dialogue protocol for analysis.

EXPERIMENTS IN THE COSAR PROJECT

In the COSAR project we have done two studies with the TC3 collaborative writing environment. In the first study 49 pairs of students from two college preparatory high schools wrote one or two argumentative texts on the topics of cloning and organ donation in the basic TC3 environment without the two planning tools. The evaluation of the students showed that, although they criticized technical flaws and drawbacks of the program (mainly in the first session), they were rather satisfied with this way of CSCL. In a second study, with 120 students from six different high schools, we experimentally varied the planning tools to determine the effect of sharing these tools on the argumentation in the discussion and on the resulting argumentative text. We expect that using various ICT tools during collaborative planning will lead to better coordination in coconstructive activities and, therefore, to qualitatively better texts. It is expected that the effects of the Diagrammer will mainly concern the consistency and completeness of the argumentation of the text. Using the Outliner should result in a better and thus more persuasive argumentative structure. Our central question is this: how do students coordinate their activities, resources, and knowledge to come to a joint product? In this chapter we will discuss results from the first experiment regarding this question.

Research Questions

We examine whether task coordination in the chat discussion relates to the quality and argumentative structure of the resulting common argumentative text. As we assume argumentation to be a crucial aspect of collaborative coordination, we are specifically interested to find out how students argue and come to agreement, and about what type of topics. Does argumentation between the students have a positive effect on the collaboration and the quality of jointly made text?

In this chapter we discuss results of four research questions in the context of the first study in the COSAR project:

1. What types of writing activities and strategies do the students discuss to coordinate their activities in writing an argumentative text?
2. How do the types of writing activities and strategies discussed by the students relate to the quality and argumentative structure of the resulting text?
3. How do students argue and what types of topics are discussed?
4. Are number and type of argumentation episodes related to the quality of the argumentative texts?

In the next section we discuss the design of the experiment and the method of analysis we are using to study the coordination of the collaborating students during planning and writing the argumentative texts. In the following section we present results on the research questions. We give some examples of chat dialogues and of the qualitative patterns we are looking for with regard to argumentation episodes mentioned in the third and fourth question.

Participants and Assignment

The participants were 49 pairs of students (16–18 years old, college preparatory high school) working together in writing argumentative essays in Dutch based on given information sources. The assignment was to choose a position pro or contra a current topic (cloning or organ donation) and to write a convincing argumentative text addressed to the Minister of Welfare, Public Health, Culture. The texts had to be based on recent articles and commentaries from well-known Dutch newspapers, recently published on the Internet, and accessible within the program. The final texts had to count 600 to 1,000 words and were graded anonymously by the students' teachers. Each partner worked at his or her own computer and, wherever possible, partners were seated in different classrooms.

Method of Analysis

Process-oriented research in general is very laborious work and consists of two types of analyses in sequence: (a) single-case analyses of protocols of the processes, and (b) comparison of quantitative or qualitative characteristics of the processes in the protocols that have been analyzed. If several process protocols need to be compared, this can be an enormous task. We try to reduce the effort of protocol analysis by using a computer program, Multiple Episode Protocol Analysis (MEPA), developed at the University of Utrecht. The purpose of MEPA is to offer a flexible environment for creating protocols from verbal and nonverbal observational data, and annotating, coding, and analyzing these (see Fig. 10.2 for a screen dump of MEPA). Examples of suitable data within educational research are class discussions, collaborative discussions, teaching conversations, think-aloud protocols, e-mail forums, electronic discussions, and videotape transcriptions. The setup of the program is multifunctional in the sense that one can develop both the coding and protocol systems within the same program, as well as directly analyze and explore the coded verbal and nonverbal data using several built-in quantitative and qualitative methods and techniques for analysis. MEPA can execute frequency and time-interval analyses; generate cross tables with associative measures; perform lag-sequential, interrater reliability, visual, word frequency, and word context analyses; and carry out selecting, sorting, and search commands. It also provides some aids for inductive pattern recognition. MEPA uses a multidimensional data structure, allowing protocol data to be coded on multiple dimensions or levels, differentiating on event and episode variables. To minimize the work associated with coding protocols and to maximize coding reliability, MEPA contains a programming module allowing the user to code the protocols automatically (to a large extent) using structured if–then rules.

The chat discussion data (easily temporarily selectable from the full action log files) and the argumentative papers were coded on several dimensions using MEPA. The chat data were initially divided into utterances based on use of the Enter key (used by the students to move one or more messages into the chat history). The utterances were divided into subunits if each subunit represented a different message and thus required a different categorization. The main utterances were split automatically, using about 330 if–then rules. The chat utterances were coded on two dimensions: task acts and discourse episodes. The two dimensions represent the task content and communicative levels in the discourse. In this chapter we discuss results on the task content level—as they refer to the writing strategies the students use to write their argumentative essays—and on the communicative level with regard to argumentation episodes.

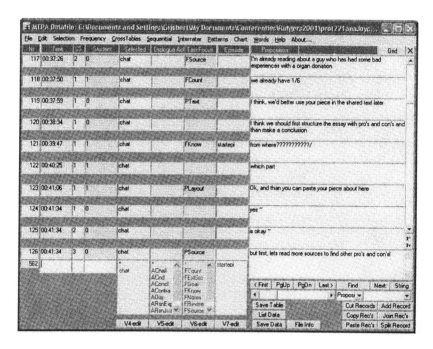

FIG.10.2. Screen dump of the MEPA program (translated from Dutch).
Analysis of Chat Discussion and Argumentative Texts

Task Acts: Discussion Of Writing Strategy. Task acts label the task-related content of the utterances in the chat discussion. Each task-related episode receives a single coding. A total of 20 task acts categories of writing strategies are distinguished (see Table 10.1). The three main levels of categorization are planning (metacognitive level), formulating (executing level), and nontask (social and technical level). Categories refer to discussion of the writing goals, sources, notes, knowledge, text, layout, revision, turn taking, and overall coordination (interrater agreement Cohen's kappa = .74 and .75).

Discourse Episodes: Episodes Of Argumentation. Argumentation episodes are defined as episodes in the chat protocols in which a specific topic is discussed, where both students participate, and in which a reason, justification, or a pro or con argument is used to convince the partner of a statement or position. Topics of discussion of argumentation episodes could be categorized in five types, collapsing the task act categorization in main categories (see Table 10.2). Teams of two raters checking each other's coding coded argumentation episodes. Interteam agreement of two pairs of raters on two chat protocols was satisfying (88% and 98%) resulting in Cohen's kappas of .85 and .73.

TABLE 10.1

Coding Definitions for the Task Acts (Chat Dialogue)

Task Acts	Code	Explanation of Term
Planning		Expressions concerning the task, not the details of the literal text
Plan layout	PLayout	Concerning global layout of the paper, form, and structure
Plan coordination	PCoord	Concerning coordination over time: propose global actions
Plan alternate turn	PTurn	Coordinate turn taking
Plan goals	PGoals	Specifying product goals or criteria relating to task demands
Plan source	PSource	Concerning use of information sources
Plan external source	PExtSrc	Concerning use of external source material (books or others)
Plan knowledge	PKnow	Use of previously learned information, ideas, own experiences
Plan text	PText	Roughly planning the text and discussion of global content
Plan notes	PNotes	Planning to make or making notes, coordinating use of notes
Plan revise	PRevise	Propose and coordinate revision of the text
Formulate task		Concerns the text itself: discussing the specific contents
Formulate goals	FGoals	Concerning verification of meeting task demands
Formulate count	FCount	Concerning checking the number of words written thus far
Formulate source	FSource	Pass contents of an internal source, discussion over contents
Formulate external source	FExtSrc	Pass contents of an external source to the other, summarized
Formulate knowledge	FKnow	Discuss original ideas, opinions, and knowledge
Formulate text	FText	Propose and discuss additions of specific text
Formulate notes	FNotes	Discuss notes; specific content of sources written in the notes
Formulate revise	FRevise	Discuss revision of specific text
Nontask		
Nontask program	NTProg	About technical aspects of TC3 program
Nontask social	NTSocial	Not task-related chat; social talk and small talk

TABLE 10.2

Coding Definitions for the Argumentation Episodes (Chat Dialogue)

Argumentation Episode	Code	Explanation of Term
		Topic of argumentation concerning:
Subject matter	Sub-jBeg	Task content concepts and relationships (cloning or organ donation)
Metacognitive	Meta-Beg	Task strategy and planning of the writing process
Cooperation	Coop-Beg	Cooperation between participants, proposals of task division, actions
Technical	TechBeg	Nontask matters of technical, program-related topics
Else (Social)	ElseBeg	All other non-task-related topics, mainly social

TABLE 10.3

Coding Definitions for the Quality Measures of Argumentative Texts (Essays)

Quality Measure	Scale	Explanation of Term
		Scoring rules regarding:
Textual structure	1–10	Formal text characteristics: introductory, middle, concluding parts? Title, references to used information sources, and so on.
Audience focus	1–10	Is the reader taken into account? In clarification of terms, correct addressing, explanation, and so on.
Segment argumentation	1–10	Number of statements of position, arguments or reasons, pro and con, supports and refutations within each segment or alinea.
Overall argumentation	1–10	Global argumentative structure in the text: position stated, supported by arguments pro and refutations of arguments con; vice versa for alternative positions.
Mean score	1–10	Mean of quality measures 1–4.

Essays: Quality of Argumentative Texts. The argumentative papers were coded on separate scores (see Table 10.3) for formal textual structure; ability to empathize with the reader as audience (audience focus); and quality of the argument in each segment (segment argumentation) as well as in the text as a whole (overall argumentation). The separate scores can also be combined in an overall grade or mean score. This grading of argumentative quality was done separately and blind to the grades the teachers gave following their own criteria. Interrater agreement on five papers by two raters varied between 74% and 87% on these categories, resulting in satisfying Cohen's kappas between .69 and .79.

RESULTS

In our analyses we examine whether task coordination in the chat discussion relates to the quality and argumentative structure of the resulting common argumentative text. Furthermore, some examples of argumentative episodes of coordinated action on a communicative level in the chat protocols are presented and related to the argumentative quality of the texts.

1. Types Of Writing Activities And Strategies Discussed. Our first question concerns the types of writing activities and strategies the students refer to coordinate their actions in collaboratively writing an argumentative paper.

Table 10.4 presents mean percentages and standard deviations of the task act episodes in 49 chat discussion protocols. On the whole, planning was done more often than formulating (47% vs. 36%), whereas non-task-related episodes occurred the least frequently (17%). After planning the text (13%), planning coordination was the most frequent (9%), followed by planning turn taking for writing (6%) and planning the use of sources (6%). Relatively few episodes were spent on planning goals, planning the use of one's own knowledge, and planning revision. Even fewer episodes were used for planning the use of external sources, planning the layout, and planning the use of the private notes.

For formulating, the highest percentages of episodes were used for revising (10%) and formulating text (9%). Formulating one's own knowledge, formulating knowledge from the supplied sources, and spending time tracking the number of words written in the shared text occurred in 4% to 5% of the episodes. Small percentages of the episodes were spent formulating goals, formulating information from external sources, and formulating material from the notes. In the nontask category by far the most episodes were spent on social chat (12%). Students spent 4% of the episodes discussing problems with the program.

No significant differences in the distribution of types of writing activities and strategies in the chat protocols were found between students from the two schools that participated in the experiment. Also, no differences in writing strategies were found for the two topics students were asked to write about: cloning and organ donation. No differences between boys and girls were found either.

TABLE 10.4

Mean Percentages of Task Acts (Writing Activities and Strategies) Discussed in the Chats (N = 49)

Task Acts %	M	SD	Task Acts %	M	SD
Planning	46.66		Formulate task	36.47	
Plan layout	1.69	1.47	Formulate goal	2.77	1.45
Plan coordination	9.34	3.65	Formulate count words	3.80	2.30
Plan alternate turn	6.53	3.35	Formulate source	4.55	3.01
Plan goals	2.04	1.58	Formulate external source	1.13	1.31
Plan source	5.81	2.60	Formulate knowledge	4.88	3.32
Plan external source	0.85	1.03	Formulate text	9.01	3.66
Plan knowledge	2.52	1.73	Formulate notes	0.41	0.57
Plan text	12.71	3.98	Formulate revise	9.92	5.87
Plan notes	1.74	1.62	Nontask	**16.85**	
Plan revise	3.43	1.85	Nontask program	4.34	1.92
			Nontask social	12.51	5.94

2. Relationship Between Writing Strategies Discussed And Argumentative Quality Of The Text. The second research question asks how types of writing strategies discussed by the students relate to the quality and argumentative structure of the resulting text. In a correlation analysis between percentages of task acts and scores of text quality we have found that, contrary to our expectations, the discussion of planning activities on a metacognitive level in general does not relate to the quality of the resulting text. Only a few significant correlations were found (see Table 10.5). More discus-

sion on global coordination matters (plan coordination) is in fact negatively related and leads to lower scores on audience directedness (Pearson $r = -.25$) and the argumentative structure in the text segments ($r = -.25$). Planning to find information in the sources (plan source) is negatively related to these measures in a similar manner ($r = -.24$). Only planning the use of one's knowledge and ideas, that is, asking the other person's opinion and ideas about the topic (plan knowledge) leads to better argumentative structure in the text segments ($r = .24$).

TABLE 10.5

Pearson Correlations Between Task Acts % and Quality Measures of Argumentative Texts ($N = 49$)

Task Acts	Textual Structure	Audience Focus	Segment Argumentation	Overall Argumentation	Mean Score
1. Planning					
Plan layout	.10	-.08	-.10	-.08	-.07
Plan coordination	-.11	-.25*	-.25*	-.08	-.20
Plan alternate turn	-.13	.03	-.20	-.07	-.10
Plan goals	.03	-.08	.01	-.04	-.04
Plan source	-.07	-.15	-.24*	-.23	-.23
Plan external source	-.11	.07	.20	-.06	.02
Plan knowledge	-.01	.04	.24*	.07	.10
Plan text	.05	.18	.14	-.05	.08
Plan notes	.01	-.15	-.11	.04	-.06
Plan revise	-.10	.16	.21	.05	.11

TABLE 10.5 (cont'd)

2. Formulate task					
Formulate goals	.06	.34**	.17	.16	.24
Formulate count	-.03	-.13	-.17	-.05	-.12
Formulate source	.01	.00	-.01	-.03	-.01
Formulate external source	-.02	.00	.11	.08	.06
Formulate knowledge	.27*	.39**	.23	.23	.34**
Formulate text	.15	.30**	.37***	.21	.31**
Formulate notes	-.18	-.02	-.09	.01	-.06
Formulate revise	.11	.13	.21	.14	.18
3. Nontask					
Nontask program	-.08	-.28**	-.25*	-.10	-.21
Nonask social	-.20	-.37***	-.35**	-.19	-.34**

* p < .10, ** p < .05, *** p < .01.

On the executing level, however, more positive relationships are found. More specific discussion of the goal of the paper that has to be written (formulate goal) results in texts with a better audience focus ($r = .34$). Discussion of specific content of one's own ideas and knowledge and those of the partner (formulate knowledge) leads to texts with better quality on all scores, especially textual structure ($r = .27$) and audience directedness ($r = .39$). Also, discussion of the formulation of specific content in the text (formulate text) correlates with higher quality of audience focus ($r = .30$) and better argumentative structures in the paragraphs or segments ($r = .37$).

Asking and talking about specific information in the sources does not influence text quality. Discussion about revision of the text, on a planning level as well as on a formulating level, does not clearly correlate with the quality of the text, although a small positive (not significant) correlation with the argumentative quality of segments was found ($r = .21$). As expected, discussion of nontask matters, like the computer program itself or social talk, were negatively related to the quality of the resulting text. More nontask chat discussion resulted in lower audience focus and less argumentative structure in the text segments.

We may conclude that coordination of specific content of goals, knowledge, and formulating text (formulate goals, formulate knowledge, and formulate text) between collaborating students is more important than overall coordination and planning of the writing activities (plan activities). Furthermore, on the basis of these results we assume that shared knowledge construction—that is, discussing and thereby coordinating knowledge on a metacognitive (plan knowledge) as well as on a specific content level (formulate knowledge)—is an essential part of collaborative text writing that influences the argumentative quality of the text.

3. Argumentation Episodes In The Chat Protocols. The analyses described previously gave us some idea of the type of writing activity the students discuss on a metacognitive (planning) and executive (formulating) level during the process of collaborative argumentative writing, and how these discussions of writing strategies relate to the quality of the written text. Still, we do not know how students go about coordinating their writing activities and strategies on a communicative level. How do the collaborating students succeed in their coordination (exchange, negotiation, and coming to agreement) in the computer-mediated dialogues? For the third and fourth research questions we conducted a further qualitative analysis for a (random) selection of the chat dialogues focusing on episodes of arguing.

An example of argumentation is shown in Table 10.6: a brief episode by two male students working on a text on organ donation after about 3 hours. The columns in the table (left to right) show protocol line number, time from start, sequence number, actor (student) task act categorization (for code definitions see Table 10.1), argumentation episode code (for code definitions see Table 10.2) and chat text string. The fragment starts with one of the boys asking whether they already have a title for the text and after his partner's response asking whether they should use a nicer one (509–512).

TABLE 10.6

Argumentation Episodes in Chat Protocol of Two Students (Both Male).

Line	Time	Sq.	Actor	Task Acts	Argumen- tation Episodes	Dialogue
509	2:57:34	2	1	Ftext	MetaBeg	by the way, do we have a title?
511	2:57:35	2	0			organ donation
512	2:57:47	1	1	Fknow		that's what I meant shall we think of a nicer one
513	2:57:57	1	0			How very creative
514	2:58:06	1	0			what do you have in mind
515	2:58:32	1	1	Pcoord		mmmmmmm...let me think
516	2:58:48	1	1	Ftext		How about....everything you ever wanted to know about organs!!! ~
518	2:59:53	1	0	Fgoals		We are not writing an essay on organs, ~
519	2:59:56	1	1			Just kidding.
520	2:59:56	2	1			I know I meant it as a joke.
521	3:00:30	1	0			ha ha
522	3:00:30	2	0		Stop	but we give our opinion so that should be clear in the title
544	3:05:00	2	0	PAlt	CoopBeg	if you give the text to me, then I will read through it first, ~
545	3:05:12	1	1			lets do it!!!!!!!
546	3:05:12	2	1			ok, ~
547	3:06:04	1	0	PKnow		you can ~
548	3:06:04	2	0			read whilst I type and ~
549	3:06:04	3	0		Stop	if you have any comments send them to me
557	3:06:06	1	1	FText	MetaBeg	are you going to do the title as well or do we have one already
558	3:06:25	6	0			just organ transplantation~
559	3:06:25	7	1	FText		we should also something in the title with donation and transpl.
560	3:06:50	1	0			if we can't think of anything else in the mean time
562	3:07:20	1	0			or with waiting lists ~
563	3:07:27	1	0			because our conclusion is that it must be shortened, ~
564	3:07:27	2	0	FText		or maybe with donor register
566	3:08:01	1	1	FText		waiting list is only a part of it I think
567	3:08:23	1	1			what do you think of donating and transplanting organs
568	3:08:54	1	0		Stop	all right

When his partner asks for clarification, and after a joking answer, student 0 explains that he thinks the title should have a reference to the position they take (521). The argumentation episode stops there and they do not come to an agreement. Other topics are discussed in the chat; the fragment includes an argumentation episode about task division (544–549), and the problem of the title re-enters the discussion initiated by student 1 after 5 minutes, starting a new argumentation episode. They agree on the fact that the current title (organ transplantation) is not good enough and next they discuss the alternatives (adding "donation" proposed by student 1 versus adding "waiting lists" proposed by student 0). Student 1 gives the contra argument that shortening the waiting lists is only a part of the problem (563). In the end, after a pause of almost 1 minute, student 0 accepts the title proposed by student 1 by typing "all right" and the episode ends (568). Although the argumentation is not very elaborated or deep, the fragment shows that, for collaboration to proceed in a coordinated and mutually acceptable way, arguments need to be resolved. The issue of the title had not been solved yet and was bound to be reopened. Furthermore, the fragment shows that students do not argue for the sake of arguing. As soon as an acceptable agreement can be reached, it is taken. In general, argumentation episodes are rather short—5 to 10 utterances on average.

Another example of the necessity of coming to agreement is illustrated in an episode of a chat protocol of two other students (male and female) in Table 10.7 (for code definitions, see Table 10.1 and Table 10.2). It is an example of arguing about subject matter, in this case the position the students want to defend. Although the students are not obliged to write a text about a position that reflects their own opinion, students in general try to come to an agreement about a common position to defend, but also about other content matter, such as general opinion, the interpretation of factual information, and controversial issues. Although arguments about subject matter are not very frequent in the protocols, they seem to be very important. The collaboration seems to develop in a more disorganized fashion if the students do not reach a mutual commitment on matters of content. In almost all protocols the question "What position should we take?" is the first to be asked after reading the information sources. Sometimes this problem is resolved pragmatically ("Let's be for the position, it seems easier"). In other cases, as in the example in Table 10.6, a more or less elaborated argumentative debate develops early on in the protocol. In the fragment student 1 (the girl) opposes the idea of being an organ donor herself ("how egotistically it may sound"; 122–123). When student 0 (male) gives his point of view (124), the girl after joking, makes a reopening in stating that she might change her ideas later (129), that is, in a few years time when she has become more social. After an interruption with a cooperation argument, and after rereading some sources on donor registration, student 1 reconsiders her position and changes her point of view ("so I'm in favor"; 158).

TABLE 10.7

Subject Matter Argumentation in Chat Protocol of Male and Female Students

Line	Time	Sq.	Actor	Task Acts	Argumentation Episodes	Dialogue
119	00:24:12	2	1	FSource	SubjBeg	if you haven't completed a donor registration form, ~
121	00:24:35	1	1			your family can decide for you.
122	00:24:35	2	1	FKnow		I never want to lose my organs, ~
123	00:25:05	1	1			no matter how egotistically it may sound
124	00:24:59	1	0			I always think, you don't notice a thing when you're dead.
127	00:25:41	1	0			so as far as I'm concerned they can have my organs.
125	00:25:05	2	1			you're too good for this world
128	00:25:41	2	0			maybe I am
129	00:25:51	1	1			maybe, I will think differently in a few years time
130	00:25:51	2	1			i would be more social
136	00:26:38	2	0			that is not important when you're dead, ~
138	00:27:02	1	0			whether you are social or not.
137	00:26:53	1	1			nice statement
139	00:27:02	2	0		Stop	I know
142	00:27:29	1	1	PSource	CoopBeg	I am reading more sources, ~
143	00:27:40	1	1	PCoord		what are you doing at the moment
144	00:27:40	2	1			kick ass
145	00:27:43	1	0	PSource	Stop	I'm reading the sources as well
146	00:27:59	1	1	FSource	SubjBeg	in source 1 it says that you need to register, ~
147	00:28:24	1	0	FText		and I wonder whether the text should perhaps be on whether or not to register donors.
149	00:28:47	1	1			you read the first bit
152	00:28:50	2	0			already done so, ~
155	00:29:04	2	1			you're right. ~
156	00:29:19	1	0	FSource		that's how they are trying to prevent losing possible donors.
158	00:29:28	1	1	FKnow	Stop	so I'm in favor

The protocols show that arguing is a crucial process for managing coordination, and that it is necessary to come to an agreement. Arguments are found in the protocols about every aspect of the task and about many nontask matters as well. So, an interesting question might be whether arguments occur the most on the topics that we think matter. What topics do the students argue on? For this last question we have collapsed the task act categorization into five major topics: subject matter, metacognitive, cooperation, technical, and other/social.

As shown in Table 10.8 the students generally engage in about 19 argumentation episodes, ranging from 12 to 42 different episodes in the protocols. About half of these argument episodes are about metacognitive matters: the task and writing strategy. Matters of cooperation and task division occur in 19% of the argument episodes; 6% and 14% are discussion about nontask topics, technical or social. Only 8% of the arguments are related to the subject matter of the task: cloning or organ donation. These percentages are similar to the distribution of the comparable task acts. So, the topics that the students need to discuss, to give reasons for, or to give justifications for do not differ from those in the chat as a whole.

4. Relationship Of Argumentation Episodes With The Quality Of The Argumentative Texts. Table 10.9 shows the correlations between the argumentation episodes and the quality measures of the resulting texts. The number of argumentation episodes is not related to the quality measures of the texts. However, arguing about subject matter has a positive effect on the quality of the resulting text, especially concerning the focus on the audience. Furthermore, from these results it is clear that real argumentation about metacognitive decisions has a positive effect on the argumentative structure of the text paragraphs. This is remarkable, as we found that discussing metacognitive planning activities in general were not related to these quality measures (see Table 10.5). Although the students seem to discuss the task often on a meta-cognitive planning level, only explicit argumentative discussion and trying to come to an agreement about these matters have a positive relationship with the resulting text quality. Explicit argumentative discussion about the cooperation between the participants themselves has no clear positive relationship to text quality. Technical and other nontask debates are negatively related to almost all quality scores as expected.

We also analyzed whether equal contribution in the interaction is necessary for optimal collaboration. To this end we have measured the asymmetry of contribution in the argumentation episodes (as the absolute difference between the percentages of contributions of the two students). We only found small negative, mostly nonsignificant correlations between asymmetry in participation in the argumentation episodes and the quality of the resulting texts. Equality in contribution does not seem to be a very important factor in this collaborative writing task, although we should add that in general only small deviations from equal participation were found in these protocols (M asymmetry = 11.1–20.9 %, SD = 10.48–26.10%).

TABLE 10.8

Mean Percentages of Topics Argued About in Argumentation Episodes, Standard
Deviations, Range, and Mean Number of Argumentation Episodes Found in the
Chat Protocols (N = 34)

Argumentation Episodes	M	SD	Minimum	Maximum
Number	19.2	7.41	12	42
Subject matter	8.3%	5.84%	0%	23.1%
Metacognitive	50.9%	13.11%	26.3%	71.4%
Cooperation	19.3%	13.59%	0%	43.7%
Technical	6.5%	3.94%	0%	13.6%
Other (social)	13.8%	13.03%	0%	52.6%

TABLE 10.9

Pearson Correlations Between Argumentation Episodes and Quality Measures of
Argumentative Texts (N = 34).

	Textual Structure	Audience Focus	Segment Argumentation	Overall Argumentation	Mean Score
Number of argumentation episodes	-.29	.22	.13	.03	.06
Subject matter	.21	.37**	.16	.16	.27
Metacognitive	.11	-.02	.47***	.12	.18
Cooperation	.12	.08	.08	.28	.19
Technical	-.24	-.04	-.34*	-.21	-.23
Other (Social)	-.14	-.33*	-.52***	-.36**	-.42**

$*p < .10$, $** p < .05$, $*** p < .01$.

CONCLUSION

In the chats of collaborating students—writing an argumentative paper in a computer-supported environment—discussion of planning writing activities on a metacognitive level is more frequent than discussion of the specific contents of knowledge, goals, or the text itself. Still, we found that coordination and discussion of specific content of goals, knowledge, and formulating text have a positive influence on the argumentative quality of the texts. Overall coordination and planning of the writing activities on a metalevel seems less important for the quality of the text, unless it is accompanied by reasons, explanations, and justifications as in argumentation. Talking about the coordination process itself too much even has a negative effect on the final text, possibly because collaborating partners start talking about coordination itself when the collaboration between them fails. Furthermore, on the basis of these results we can conclude that shared knowledge construction—coordination of knowledge in the discussion, both on a metacognitive and on a specific content level—is an essential part of collaborative text writing. Discussion and sharing of knowledge result in a higher argumentative quality of the text. When we focus on the process of arguing and coming to agreement, it turns out that about half of the argument episodes are on metacognitive matters: the task and writing strategy. Other topics of argumentation are matters of cooperation and task division and nontask topics, such as technical aspects of the computer environment or social interests. Only 8% of the argumentative episodes are related to the subject matter of the task: cloning or organ donation. We concluded that the topics that the students need to discuss, give reasons for, or give justifications for do not differ from those in the chat as a whole. Arguing about subject matter, however, showed a positive effect on the quality of the resulting text. Analyses of the chat protocols showed that students regularly re-enter topics of argumentation when they do not succeed in coming to agreement. This seems especially important in content, knowledge, and opinion-related subject matter. Mutual commitment on a shared position apparently needs to be stated. Furthermore, it is clear that real argumentation about metacognitive decisions has a positive effect on the argumentative structure of the text. Explicit argumentative discussion about the cooperation between the participants themselves is not clearly positively related to text quality. As expected, technical and social debates or argumentation were negatively related to almost all quality scores of the resulting texts. Equality of contribution does not seem to be a very important factor in this collaborative writing task, although we should add that in general we only found small deviations from equal participation in the protocols.

Argumentation can be seen as a crucial part of coordination in collaboration in the sense that participants try to change each other's point of view. In argumentation, participants at first do not agree and try to convince each other to come to an agreement. However, coming to an agreement may succeed or fail. By its nature, arguing can have positive and negative effects in collaborative learning: constructive effects for shared knowledge building and cooperation on the one hand, and contradictory effects for knowledge construction and disruptive effects on collaboration on the other hand. In fact, this reflects the paradox in our assumptions on collaborative learning: learning from arguing, criticizing, and conflict versus the necessity to reach consensus for collaboration to advance. This paradox makes it hard to specify pedagogical consequences: How can we stimulate the explication of argument and discussion, and at the same time assume the necessity to agree in collaborative learning? An important distinction needs to be made here between argumentation for reaching agreement and argumentation for convincing the partner of one's own opinion, or even enforcing one's beliefs. Making students aware of this distinction might partly resolve this paradox. Perhaps tools like the diagrammer—in which the argument structure is visualized, made explicit, and open for discussion—can support argumentation of content in the dialogue between students, and at the same time externalize the necessity of shared commitment to one position. A similar effect could be expected for some metacognitive aspects with regard to the outliner tool. We hope to show these effects in our analyses of students collaborating in argumentative writing in the TC3 environment with support of these tools. In those protocols we expect to find better coordination, more elaborated argumentation, and more explicit coming to agreement.

ACKNOWLEDGMENTS

The research reported in this chapter was made possible by a grant from the Dutch Scientific Organization (NWO-project 575-33-008). The analyses to answer research questions 1 and 2 were assisted by Joyce van Berlo in her master's thesis. The analyses to answer research questions 3, 4, and 5 were assisted by Tobi Boas, Nicolette van der Meijden, Chris Phielix, and Jan-Willem Schoonhoven as a research project in a second-year methodology course.

REFERENCES

Andriessen, J. E. B., Coirier, P., Roos, L., Passerault, J. M., & Bert-Erboul, A. (1996). Thematic and structural planning in constrained argumentative text production. In H. Van den Bergh, G. Rijlaarsdam, & M. Couzijn (Eds.), *Theories, models and methodology in writing research* (pp. 237–251). Amsterdam: University Press.

Andriessen, J. E. B., Erkens, G., Overeem, E., & Jaspers, J. (1996, September). *Using complex information in argumentation for collaborative text production.* Paper presented at the First Conference on Using Complex Information Systems (UCIS'96), Poitiers, France.

Antaki, C. (1994). *Explaining and arguing: The social organization of accounts.* London: Sage.

Baker, M. (1999). Argumentation and constructive interaction. In J. E. B. Andriessen & P. Coirier (Eds.), *Foundations of argumentative text processing* (pp. 179–203). Amsterdam: University Press.

Bannon, L. J. (1995). Issues in computer supported collaborative learning. In C. O'Malley (Ed.), *Computer supported collaborative learning* (pp. 267–283). Heidelberg, Germany: Springer-Verlag.

Bereiter, C., & Scardamalia, M. (1987). *The psychology of written composition.* Hillsdale, NJ: Lawrence Erlbaum Associates.

Brown, J., Collins, A., & Duguid, P. (1989). Situated cognition and the culture of learning. *Educational Researcher, 18,* 32–41.

Clark, H. H., & Brennan, S. E. (1991). Grounding in communication. In L. B. Resnick, J. M. Levine, & S. D. Teasley (Eds.), *Perspectives on socially shared cognition* (pp. 127–150). Washington, DC: American Psychological Association.

Clark, H. H., & Schaeffer, E. F. (1987). Collaborating on contributions to conversation. *Language and Cognitive Processes, 2,* 19–41.

Cognition and Technology Group at Vanderbilt. (1994). From visual word problems to learning communities: Changing conceptions of cognitive research. In K. McGilly (Ed.), *Classroom lessons: Integrating cognitive theory and classroom practice* (pp. 157–201). Cambridge, MA: MIT Press.

Cohen, E. G. (1994). Restructuring the classroom: Conditions for productive small groups. *Review of Educational Research, 64,*1–35.

Coirier, P., Andriessen, J. E. B., & Chanquoy, L. (1999). From planning to translating: The specificity of argumentative writing. In J. E. B. Andriessen & P. Coirier (Eds.), *Foundations of argumentative text processing* (pp. 1–29). Amsterdam: Amsterdam University Press

Di Eugenio, B., Jordan, P. W., Thomason, R. H., & Moore, J. D. (2000). The agreement process: An empirical investigation of human–human computer mediated collaborative dialogs. *International Journal of Human–Computer Studies, 53,* 1071–1075.

Dillenbourg, P. (1999). Introduction: What do you mean by "collaborative learning"? In P. Dillenbourg (Ed.), *Collaborative learning: Cognitive and computational aspects* (pp. 1–19). New York: Pergamon.

Doise, W., & Mugny, G. (1984). *The social development of the intellect.* New York: Pergamon.

Duffy, T. M., & Jonassen, D. H. (1991, May). Constructivism: New implications for instructional technology? *Educational Technology,* 7–12.

Erkens, G. (1997). *Coöperatief probleemoplossen met computers in het onderwijs: Het modelleren van coöperatieve dialogen voor de ontwikkeling van intelligente onderwijssystemen* [Cooperative problem solving with computers in education: Modeling of cooperative dialogues for the design of intelligent educational systems]. Unpublished doctoral dissertation, Utrecht University, Utrecht, Netherlands.

Erkens, G. (2004). Dynamics of coordination in collaboration. In J. L. van der Linden & P. Renshaw (Eds.), *Dialogic learning: Shifting perspectives to learning, instruction and teaching* (pp. 191-216). Dordrecht, Netherlands: Kluwer Academic.

Erkens, G., Andriessen, J. E. B., & Peters, N. (2003). Interaction and performance in computer supported collaborative tasks. In H. Oostendorp (Ed.), *Cognition in a digital world* (pp. 225–251). Mahwah, NJ: Lawrence Erlbaum Associates.

Galbraith, D. (1999). Writing as a knowledge-constituting process. In M. Torrance & D. Galbraith (Eds.), *Knowing what to write: Conceptual processes in text production* (pp. 139–159). Amsterdam: Amsterdam University Press.

Giroud, A. (1999). Studying argumentative text processing through collaborative writing. In J. E. B. Andriessen & P. Coirier (Eds.), *Foundations of argumentative text processing* (pp. 149-179). Amsterdam: Amsterdam University Press.

Hayes, J. R., & Nash, J. G. (1996). On the nature of planning in writing. In C. M. Levy & S. Ransdell (Eds.), *The science of writing* (pp. 29–55). Mahwah, NJ : Lawrence Erlbaum Associates.

Henri, F. (1995). Distance learning and computer mediated communication: Interactive, quasi-interactive or monologue? In C. O'Malley (Ed.), *Computer supported collaborative learning* (pp. 145–165). Heidelberg, Germany: Springer-Verlag.

Kozma, R. B. (1991). The impact of computer-based tools and embedded prompts on writing processes and products of novice and advanced college writers. *Cognition and Instruction, 8,* 1–27.

Kumpulainen, K., & Mutanen, M. (1999). The situated dynamics of peer group interaction: An introduction to an analytic framework. *Learning and Instruction, 9,* 449–475.

Levelt, W. J. M. (1989). *Speaking: From intention to articulation.* Boston: Bradford Books.

Petraglia, J. (1998). *Reality by design: The rhetoric and technology of authenticity in education.* Mahwah, NJ: Lawrence Erlbaum Associates.

Rijlaarsdam, G., & Van den Bergh, H. (1996). The dynamics of composing—An agenda for research into an interactive compensatory model of writing: Many questions, some answers. In C. M. Levy & S. Ransdell (Eds.), *The science of writing* (pp. 107–125). Mahwah, NJ: Lawrence Erlbaum Associates.

Roschelle, J., & Teasley, S. D. (1995). Construction of shared knowledge in collaborative problem solving. In C. O'Malley (Ed.), *Computer-supported collaborative learning* (pp. 69-97). New York: Springer-Verlag.

Scardamalia, M., & Bereiter, C. (1985). The development of dialectical processes in composition. In D. Olson, N. Torrance, & A. Hildyard (Eds.), *Literacy, language and learning: The nature and consequences of reading and writing* (pp. 307-329). New York: Cambridge University Press.

Scardamalia, M., Bereiter, C., & Lamon, M. (1994). The CSILE project: Trying to bring the classroom into world 3. In K. McGilly (Ed.), *Classroom lessons: Integrating cognitive theory and classroom practice* (pp. 201-229). Cambridge: MIT Press.

Schriver, K. A. (1988, April). *Teaching writers how to plan: Which planning heuristics work best?* Paper presented at the meeting of the American Educational Research Association, St. Louis, MO.

Stein, L. S., Calicchia, D., & Bernas, R. S. (1996). *Understanding and resolving arguments: Do compromise instructions help?* Chicago: University of Chicago, Eastern Illinois University.

Suthers, D., Weiner, A., Connelly, J., & Paolucci, M. (1995). Belvedere: Engaging students in critical discussion of science and public policy issues. In J. Greer (Ed.), *Artificial intelligence in education* (pp. 266-273). Charlottesville, VA: AACE.

Teasley, S., & Rochelle, J. (1993). Constructing a joint problem space: The computer as tool for sharing knowledge. In S. P. Lajoie, & S. J. Derry (Eds.), *Computers as cognitive tools* (pp. 229-257). Hillsdale, NJ: Lawrence Erlbaum Associates.

Torrance, M., Thomas, G. V., & Robinson, E. J. (1996). Finding something to write about: Strategic and automatic processes in idea generation. In C. M. Levy & S. Ransdell (Eds.), *The science of writing* (pp. 189-205). Mahwah, NJ: Lawrence Erlbaum Associates.

Van Boxtel, C. (2000). *Collaborative concept learning.* Unpublished doctoral dissertation, Utrecht University, Utrecht, Netherlands.

Van der Linden, J. L., Erkens, G., Schmidt, H., & Renshaw, P. (2000). Collaborative learning. In P. R. J. Simons, J. L. van der Linden, & T. Duffy (Eds.), *New learning* (pp. 37-55). Dordrecht, Netherlends: Kluwer Academic.

Chapter 11

Historical Reasoning in a Computer-Supported Collaborative Learning Environment

Jannet van Drie

Carla van Boxtel

Jos van der Linden

Utrecht University

INTRODUCTION

A computer-supported collaborative learning (CSCL) environment is a learning environment in which a large amount of information can be accessed easily, and in which knowledge can be shared and coconstructed through communication and joint construction of products. It is believed that these characteristics make CSCL an environment with potential to provoke and support the construction of knowledge (Lethinen, Hakkarainen, Lipponen, Rahikainen, & Muukonen, 2001). However, using a CSCL environment is no guarantee of productive student interaction or positive effects on learning. Research on collaborative learning has shown that meaningful learning is related to the quality of the interaction processes (Van der Linden, Erkens, Schmidt, & Renshaw, 2000). This relationship can be studied by taking into consideration the specific characteristics of the domain of study and the co-constructed nature of knowledge.

The main focus of the research described in this chapter is the domain-specific content of the student interaction in a CSCL environment. We are especially interested in the domain of history and more specifically on the improvement of historical reasoning within an inquiry task. Historical reasoning implies that students situate historical phenomena in time that they describe and explain historical phenomena, distinguish processes of change and continuity, consider the trustworthiness and value of sources, and support their viewpoint or opinions with arguments. Reasoning within the domain of history also involves the use of historical concepts with which historical phenomena can be described and explained.

Another, and complementary, way to study the relationship between student interaction and meaningful learning is to put into focus the co-construction of knowledge. In recent years, especially from a sociocultural perspective on learning, the joint and situated construction of meaning through communication and the role of mediational tools have been emphasized. When students work on a common task, mutual understanding must be created and sustained continuously (Roschelle, 1992). Research has shown that the need to coordinate activities can provoke valuable learning processes. Knowledge can be coconstructed through the integration of ideas or through productive argument, questioning, and exploration. Several researchers showed the importance of asking and answering of questions (e.g., King, 1990; Webb, 1991) and argumentation to resolve controversy (e.g., Brown & Palincsar, 1989; Dillenbourg, Baker, Blaye, & O'Malley, 1995). Furthermore, student interactions can differ from each other in the amount of co-construction. A student interaction in which one of the students is dominating, or that shows unproductive dispute or the accumulation of ideas without critical challenges, is not believed to be valuable for learning (Mercer, 1995).

How can we elicit student interaction that reflects historical reasoning and co-construction in a CSCL environment? The design of the task and the tools that are available can be considered important factors that affect the quality of the student interaction (O'Donnell, 1999; Palincsar & Herrenkohl, 1999; Van Boxtel, 2000). We focus in this chapter on the design of the task. We present a small-scale study in which we compared the interaction of students working together on different historical inquiry tasks. In our study we distinguish effects with and effects of computer-supported collaborative learning (Salomon & Perkins, 1998). The effects with are to be found in the interaction between the students during the accomplishment of the task. The effects of are to be found in the residues of the collaborative activity, such as the group product that is jointly constructed and the individual learning outcomes that are reflected in the participation of students in new situations. Lethinen, et al., (2001) stated that until now research on CSCL hardly focuses on learning outcomes.

Next, we first elaborate on the term *historical reasoning*. Second, we discuss the potential of inquiry tasks to provoke and support collaborative historical reasoning. Then we describe the method of our study and the instruments we used to analyze the quality of the student interactions and the learning outcomes. The results section contains the results of the analyses of the student interaction, the quality of the group products, and the individual learning outcomes. Finally, we summarize our findings and make some recommendations for future research, especially about tools that might be helpful in supporting historical reasoning.

HISTORICAL REASONING

The research project described in this chapter focuses on the domain of history in upper secondary education. Different concepts are used to describe the aim of history education. Perfetti, Britt, and Georgi (1995) and Roderigo (1994) used the term historical literacy, whereas Spoehr and Spoehr (1994) and Husbands (1996) used the term *historical thinking* and others use the term *historical consciousness* (e.g., Goegebeur, Simon, de Keyser, van Dooren, & van Landegem, 1999; Jeismann, 1997; Von Borries, 1997), or *historical reasoning* (Kuhn, Weinstock, & Flaton, 1994; Leinhardt, Stainton, & Virji, 1994). The terms historical literacy and historical consciousness refer to a more general ability and attitude, whereas the terms historical thinking and historical reasoning stress the actual activity of the students. In this research project we use the term *historical reasoning*. We prefer this term because it stresses the activity of students: Students not only have to acquire knowledge of the past, but they have to use this knowledge while interpreting phenomena from the past and the present. Moreover, it refers to verbally explicated reasoning, in speech or in writing. Historical reasoning can thus been seen as the activity of students by which historical consciousness is expressed. Moreover, the active role of students is in line with (socio-) constructivist theories about learning, which argue that knowledge is not transmitted or passively received, but actively constructed (Brown, Collins, & Duguid, 1989; Duffy & Jonassen, 1992) and mediated by the use of language and tools (Wertsch, 1991). Especially in history education, a long, strong tradition of transmitting historical knowledge exists.

We define historical reasoning as describing, explaining, or judging phenomena of the past with the use of historical concepts. Using historical concepts is important, because an important goal in history education is that students can use "the language of history". We distinguish six aspects of historical reasoning, on which we elaborate next.

Situating Historical Phenomena in Time

History education aims at the development of the ability to create a historical context to interpret traces of the past or contemporary phenomena. Setting phenomena into a historical context requires that students have an idea of when certain phenomena took place and in which chronological order. This chronological order of events is also important to discern aspects of change and continuity and to explain historical events. Furthermore, it requires that they can use the language of time, such as dates, centuries, and names of periods (e.g., Antiquity, Middle Ages, and modern times). Students must learn to think about the past from the perspective of the past itself, and not to judge past actors solely by present standards. The failure to grasp the nature of historical context is an important source of pupil misunderstanding (Husbands, 1996). Although not perfectly possible, empathy, role taking, and the change of perspective within a distant time frame are essential in history education. In addition, the practice of contextualized thinking is not only important in history education; it also helps to understand people different from us or people in different situations in our own time.

Describing Phenomena From the Past

History deals with events, structures, developments, and persons in the past. An important aspect of historical reasoning is the description of phenomena from the past. History education aims at the construction of images and descriptions of the past that are carefully grounded in reliable traces of the past, such as documents, pictures, artifacts, and oral accounts. In history lessons new images are constructed and existing images are transformed.

History has its own language to describe phenomena. Some concepts are drawn from other disciplines, whereas others are more specific to the study of history, or used in everyday life. Historical phenomena are described and analyzed with concepts from several disciplines, such as sociology, anthropology, philosophy, economics, and politics (e.g., class, democracy, parliament, capitalism). The concepts that are drawn from other disciplines are mostly used within the context of different themes of the history curriculum and also in the curriculum of other subjects, such as geography and economics. Although most of these concepts are very abstract, the fact that students come across the terms more than once may stimulate students to give meaning to the concepts. Some historical concepts are specific and limited to a specific historical period and students come across them only a couple of times (e.g., feudalism and pharaoh). History thus uses many concepts that are not known by students and that are difficult to learn because there is only a limited opportunity to give meaning to the concepts.

Some historical concepts are the product of historians and not known by students, whereas others are grounded and used in everyday life. Problems may arise, however, because although the students are familiar with the term of the concept, the term may refer to a different phenomenon. Our present world differs from the world of the past. Church in the Middle Ages is something different than a church in our present Western society and trade in Antiquity differs from trade in our present time. Students must learn to describe an unknown reality with known terms. Students often interpret a concept on the basis of their knowledge of the present time. Misunderstanding through anachronism can easily develop. Students must differentiate between the present meaning of concepts and the meaning of concepts used in a specific historical context (Carretero & Voss, 1994).

Describing Change and Continuity

A very central aspect of historical reasoning is the recognition and description of processes of change, such as the spread of Christianity, the collapse of the communist system in Russia, or the emancipation of women. According to Stearns (2000), the main purpose of history is to understand the phenomenon of change over time. Historical change is a multifaceted subject. It can occur in very different areas of society, such as political systems, technologies, fundamental beliefs, and family life. Historians often make a distinction among political, economical, social, and cultural changes. Studying historical changes raises not only the question of what changed, but also of what stayed the same and what caused the change (see the next section). Focus on continuity helps to interpret the historical change: to see what the impact of the change is, and how the change came about, (e.g., suddenly, gradually, or more long term). For students it is important to realize that it is not a matter of black and white. During a change other aspects of society can stay the same. Historical change and continuity can occur at the same time. In studying information about the past, students have to be able to recognize aspects of change and continuity and to use historical lexicon and analytical tools to describe changes.

Explaining Historical Phenomena

In reasoning about historical phenomena, explaining the phenomena by searching for causes and consequences is important. The study of causality within the domain of history has been both important and controversial (Voss, Ciarrochi, & Carretero, 2000). It has been important because ascertaining how antecedent conditions possibly play a role in producing historical events presumably adds to our understanding of history. It has been controversial because causation in history does not involve simple cause–effect relationships. Instead, there are many actions and events that occur over time, which may play a role in producing historical events. Furthermore, a distinction can be made between immediate and long-term causes, and between manifest events and latent events (i.e., long-term developments), such as population shift or climate change (Spoehr & Spoehr, 1994). So, a historical event cannot be explained by one single cause: Political and economical causes, personal motives, and acting interact with each other in a complex way.

Jacott, López-Manjón, and Carretero (2000) mentioned two different theoretical models of explanation in history. The intentionalist model conceptualizes historical explanation basically in terms of human actions, attributing a great importance to the particular motives, intentions, and beliefs of the agents involved. The structural model of explanation is based on the relationship between a set of conditions (e.g., economic, demographic, social, political, religious, etc.) that constitute social reality. Results from several studies show that students tend to explain historical events from the intentionalist, personalistic point of view (Carretero, Jacott, López-Manjón, and León, 1994; Halldén, 1986; Voss, Carretero, Kennet, & Ney Silfies, 1994). In a study conducted by Carretero, Jacott, and López-Manjón, (1997), novices and experts were asked to explain four historical events by ranking six different type of causes in order of importance (political, economic, ideological, personalistic, remote, and international policy). The results showed that nonexperts attributed greater importance to personalistic causes. Experts tend to vary the importance given to different causes according to the historical event in question. They do not attribute the same influence to political, economic, ideological, and other causes, but consider each event in its own context.

Taking Into Account the Trustworthiness of Sources

Information about the past is acquired by very different historical sources, such as all kinds of written documents, images, and objects. Historical sources often contain complementary, but also contradicting information about historical phenomena. Therefore, students cannot simply combine the contents of several documents into a single representation (Rouet, Britt, Mason, Perfetti, 1996; Wineburg, 1991). They first have to recognize the conflict and then compare and weigh the different accounts and their specific arguments. In this process they should

- Carefully select information.
- Evaluate this information in the context of who wrote it and for what purpose.
- Determine how the document relates to other documents.
- Coordinate and resolve inconsistencies.

This requires that a student must acquire specific knowledge about document characteristics and methods to evaluate the trustworthiness of sources. Adequate reasoning with and about documents is especially important for writing an argumentative essay. In an argumentative essay, students have to present a personal point of view on a certain historical issue that is based on information from and the trustworthiness of the different historical sources.

Supporting a Personal Point of View With Arguments

In reasoning about history problems students are also asked to evaluate past phenomena, acts of persons, and sources. Presenting an own point of view on a historical issue is more than giving just an opinion. The implication of that would be that one opinion is as good as the other and that grading such opinions is a purely subjective exercise. Within history an opinion can be viewed as an expression of historical reasoning and this is only as good as the evidence and arguments used to support this opinion (Spoehr & Spoehr, 1994). We therefore prefer to use the term personal point of view, instead of opinion. A coherent description of phenomena and taking into account the historical context, the possibility of multicausation, and the trustworthiness of sources all contribute to the construction of a convincing argumentation of that point of view.

Finally, we have to take into consideration that reasoning about history in the way just described is difficult, especially for students in secondary education. According to Spoehr and Spoehr (1994) the hardest part of historical thinking and reasoning is learning to anticipate counterarguments, to weigh alternate explanations for the phenomena being explained, and to be able to explain why one interpretation seems preferable to others.

The Social and Situated Nature of Historical Reasoning

The study of history is an ongoing discourse about the interpretation of the past. Tools such as concepts, traces of the past, narratives, and analytical schemes that are provided by the cultural, historical, and institutional settings in which students participate and that are available in a specific situation always mediate historical representations. Historical reasoning is a social activity, although it can take place in situations with more or less interaction. Reasoning that is mediated by social interaction occurs in a situation in which agents shape each other's actions through verbal or computer-mediated, spoken, or written communication. Especially collaborative reasoning within the domain of history may contribute positively to the competency of historical reasoning, as it can provide students with the opportunity to discuss historical phenomena, concepts, and sources.

Historical Inquiry Tasks

In an inquiry task students have the opportunity to construct their own knowledge, with the assistance of others and with the available mediational means. We confine ourselves to historical inquiry tasks in which the students, in pairs, write a text based on the study of several historical sources. Although writing tasks are regularly used in history education, collaborative writing does not often occur. As stated earlier, we believe collaborative learning to be a powerful means to enhance reasoning about historical issues. The main advantage of collaborative writing, compared to individual writing, is the possibility of receiving and giving immediate feedback (Giroud, 1999). The discussions generated by the writing task make the collaborators verbalize and negotiate many things, such as representations, purposes, concepts, arguments, text structure, plans, and doubts. This may lead to increased awareness of and more conscious control over the writing and learning processes (Gere & Stevens, 1989; Giroud, 1999).

Research has shown that the study of multiple historical sources to write a text can result in a deep understanding of historical phenomena (Perfetti, et al., 1995; Rouet, et al., 1996; Voss & Wiley, 1997; Wiley & Voss, 1996). In a study on developing understanding while writing essays in history, Voss and Wiley (1997) compared the writing of three kinds of texts: a narrative, a history, and an argumentative essay. They concluded that students who wrote an argumentative essay are likely to construct more causal models than students who wrote a narrative or a history and that writing an argumentative essay enables more knowledge transformation. In addition to this research, we were interested in the effect of several types of inquiry questions. Within the domain of history, three types of inquiry questions can be distinguished: descriptive, explanatory, and evaluative questions. For example, we can ask the question of what kind of weapons were used during World War I (descriptive), what can be considered causes of World War I (explanatory), or whether only Germany can be blamed for the war (evaluative). Describing, explaining, and evaluating are important aspects of historical reasoning. It is likely, however, that students who try to answer a descriptive question do not spontaneously discuss explanations or give their own viewpoint. Explaining and evaluating, on the other hand, both require a description of what is explained or evaluated. In a pilot study (Van Drie, 2000) in which students had to explain the American fear of communism in the 1950's, we saw that especially when the students discussed which cause was most important (which is an evaluation) historical reasoning occurred. Evaluating historical phenomena seems to enhance a more thorough way of historical reasoning, because it requires deep understanding, a clear description of what has to be evaluated, and adequate argumentation.

The purpose of the study presented here was to investigate the influence of the type of inquiry question on the interaction between students and on the learning results. We compared two types of inquiry questions: an explanatory question and an evaluative question. We expected that the type of inquiry question would affect the way in which students reason about history. Students in the explanatory condition were expected to talk more about explanations than the students in the evaluative condition. The students in the evaluative condition were expected to talk more about their opinion and supporting arguments than the students in the explanatory condition, but not at the cost of describing and situating phenomena in time, because those forms of historical reasoning are needed to formulate and support an opinion. Furthermore, we expected that more historical reasoning and a more thorough way of historical reasoning in the evaluative condition would also be reflected in better learning outcomes.

METHOD

The aim of this study was threefold: first, to investigate what kind of student interaction is provoked by a historical inquiry task in a CSCL environment; second, to get more insight into whether the type of inquiry task (explanatory vs. evaluative) affects the quality of the interaction and learning; and third, what kinds of problems students face while performing the task at hand. The outcomes on these questions will form the basis for follow-up studies in which we will compare different tools for supporting historical reasoning in a CSCL environment. Before we can design supporting tools we first have to gain insight into the quality of students' reasoning about history. In the next section we first describe the learning environment and task we used and second the design of the study.

Learning Environment and Task

The students worked in a computer-supported learning environment for collaborative text writing: TC3. This name stands for Text Composer, Computer Supported, and Collaborative (see Erkens, Prangsma, & Jaspers, chap. 10, in this volume). Students work one to a computer, physically separated from their partner. They communicate by means of a chat facility, and a shared text, which they can edit through taking turns. In addition to these communicative facilities, they each have access to a private notepad and to different information sources. The students were presented with a historical inquiry task, which involved studying historical sources and writing a text of approximately 750 words on a given question. Students were given a 5-hour maximum for work on the task. For this research project a task was constructed concerning changes in the behavior of the Dutch youth in the 1950's and 1960's. Different types of sources were used, such as descriptive texts from textbooks, interpretations of historians, photos, tables, and interviews. The sources were divided between the two collaborating students, so they each had different sources. For both the students two texts were added with general information about the 1960's. The task was improved through the comments of two experts on history education and the comments and the performances of two first-year social science students who had accomplished the task. The topic of the task was only familiar to the students in a general way; they did not receive any instruction about the topic in advance.

Design

Partcipants of the study were 20 students from a history class in upper secondary education at preuniversity level (16 and 17 years of age). The students worked in 10 randomly assigned pairs. The students had some experience with historical inquiry tasks and with collaborative learning. The pairs were randomly assigned to one of the two conditions, five pairs in each condition. In the explanatory condition, students were asked to explain the changes in behavior of the youth in the 1950's and the 1960's. In the evaluation condition, they were asked to judge whether the changes in behavior of the youth in these years were revolutionary or not. Five dyads worked in the explanatory condition and five dyads in the evaluative condition.

Considering the interaction process we expected differences in how the students reasoned about history. The explanatory condition was expected to contain more interaction about explanations, whereas the evaluation condition was expected to contain more interaction on taking a point of view and arguments to support their viewpoint. We expected the same amount of interaction for both condition on the following aspects: situating in time, description, changes and evaluation of sources. Furthermore, we did not expect any differences in the task focus, nor in the amount of co-construction. On the level of texts, we hypothesized that the texts in the explanatory condition would contain more explanations but a less explicit viewpoint as the evaluative texts. The texts in the evaluation condition were expected to contain as much description of change and continuity as the texts in the explanatory condition but fewer explanations. Finally, we expected more individual learning gains in the evaluation condition, because in this condition the students participated in a more thorough way of historical reasoning.

Analyses

Interaction Analyses

To analyze the interaction processes we used Multiple Episode Protocol Analysis (MEPA); see http://edugate.fss.uu.nl/mepa). MEPA offers a flexible environment for the qualitative and quantitative analysis of collaborative dialogue protocols. The interaction in the chat protocols was coded on the level of utterances. The chat protocols were analyzed on three dimensions: task acts, historical reasoning, and co-construction. Furthermore, we analyzed the use of historical concepts in historical reasoning.

First, utterances were coded on the dimension of task acts, which are described in Table 11.1. Five main categories were distinguished: utterances related to the content of the task at hand (coded task) and to procedures to perform the task (coded procedure), talk about the technical functioning of the computer program (program), social talk (social), and greetings at the start or end of a working period (greetings). The categories task and procedure were coded in subcategories, which are described in Table 11.1. Interrater agreement was satisfactory and ranged between .77 and .85 (Cohen's kappa).

Second, the utterances coded in the first step as historical reasoning were analyzed in more detail, for we were especially interested in which way students reasoned about history. Based on the earlier description of aspects of historical reasoning, we discerned six aspects: (a) situating historical phenomena in time, (b) describing the past, (c) describing changes and continuity, (d) explaining the past, (e) discussing the trustworthiness of the source, and (f) presenting a viewpoint and supporting this with argumentation. Because using domain-specific concepts is important for the quality of reasoning, we made for each of the six categories a distinction in two subcategories: using historical concepts and without using historical concepts. However, this distinction does not give any information on which concepts are used. We selected six concepts, which we thought to be central to the subject studied, and counted how often these were used in the chat protocols. The selected concepts were:

1. Democratization: Process in the 1960's in which the society became more democratic, as the people demanded more direct participation in politics, companies, organizations, schools, and so on.

Individualization: Development in Dutch society in the 1960's, in which the interests of individual people became more central and people became more focused on individual rights and needs.

2. Nozem: Name for a subgroup of young people in the 1950's, mostly from the working class, who were hanging around the streets and loved rock and roll, motorbikes, and so on.

3. Provo: Movement of young people who wanted to discuss the welfare society and provoked the authorities through all kinds of playful actions. They were mainly centered in Amsterdam.

4. Depolarization: In the first half of the 20th century Dutch society was strictly divided in socioreligious groups (Protestants, Catholics, Socialists, and Liberalists), which are referred to by the term pillarization, or compartmentalization. In the 1950's and 1960's this system broke down by processes such as individualization, democratization, and secularization. This process is called depillarization.

5. Second women liberation movement: Second wave of the women liberation movement, which took place in the 1960's and 1970's (the first wave was around 1900 and focused mainly on the right to vote).

Interrater reliability between two judges was measured over two randomly chosen chat protocols (in total 343 utterances) and reached .69 (Cohen's kappa).

Third, to measure degrees of co-construction while reasoning historically, we focused on the extent to which students reasoned together and built on each other's contributions (Kumpulainen & Mutanen, 1999; Van Boxtel, 2000). We first divided the historical reasoning utterances into episodes. An *episode* is defined as a meaningful sequence of utterances about one of the six aspects of historical reasoning; such as an episode consisting of eight utterances in which the students discuss one of the causes of the changes in the behavior of the youth. For each episode we decided to what degree it reflected coconstructed reasoning. We considered episodes as coconstructed reasoning when both participants equally contribute to the reasoning. Furthermore, we distinguished the category individual reasoning, in which only one participant contributes, and dominated reasoning, in which one student dominates the reasoning and the other only gives a small contribution. For the analyses of this aspect we did not count the number of episodes, but instead, we measured the number of utterances within the episodes. In this way it is taken into account how many utterances are part of the episode, for the episodes differ in length. Interrater reliability on four randomly chosen protocols (112 episodes) reached .95 (Cohen's kappa).

TABLE 11.1

Coding Definitions Task Acts

Category	Description and Examples
1. Task	1. Expressions concerning the content of the task
1.1 Historical reasoning	1.1 Discussion of the historical content of the task, including the content of the historiclal sources • Do you know when depillarization started? • I think the 1960s revolutionary, because a lot changed during that period.

TABLE 11.1 (cont'd)

1.2 Text construction	1.2 Concerning the construction and structure of the text
	• Shall we start with an introduction, follwed by a paragraph about the chages in the 1960's?
1.3 Text revision	1.3 Discussion of revision or addition of specific text
	• We need to add something about the influence of TV in this part.
	• We have written twice about the influence of Provo, we should delete one of them.
1.4 Goal	1.4 Concerning verification of meeting task demands
	• We should state something about the changes in the behaviour of youth, for that was the task.
1.5 Information	1.5 Concerning the use of the information sources (not discussing the content of the source)
	• I have an interesting source about Provo.
	• How many sources do you have?
1.6 Tool	1.6 Concerning the construction of the tool
	• We have to add another argument contra, for we hardly have any.
	• Evaluating the content of the task, the tool, or the text.
	• This task is difficult!
	• The conclusion is badly written.
1.8 Word count	1.8 Concerning checking the number of words written
	• We already have 700 words.
	• Still 150 words to go.
2. Procedure	
2.1 Approach	
2.2 Evaluation	
2.3 Turn-taking	
2.4 Coordination	
2.5 Planning	2.5 Concerning coordination of time
	• We should start writing the text tomorrow.
	• We have three lessons to finish the assignment.

TABLE 11.1 (cont'd)

3. Social	4. Concerning topics not related to the task or the program, but with a social function • Did you see that movie on TV last night? • Can you say hello to Astrid?
4. Starting and closures	5. Greetings at the beginning or end of a working session • Hi Monique, how are you today? • We have to stop now, see you tomorrow. •
5. No code	6. Utterances not coded as one of the previous categories

Text Analyses

The collaboratively written texts were scored on six aspects of historical reasoning. In Table 11.2 the different items of the text analyses are described. Compared to the aspects mentioned earlier, we did not use the aspect description of the past, because it proved to be hardly possible to distinguish this aspect in the text from the other aspects. Instead we decided to add the use of historical concepts as one of the items.   On each aspect of historical reasoning two or three items were constructed, focusing both on amount and quality. Each item was scored on a scale from 1 to 3. Two judges independently scored the texts. Initially, the proportion of agreement on 10 texts was 59%, which we considered agreeable for assessing texts that are highly interpretative. The scores were subsequently discussed until agreement was reached between both judges.

Pretest and Posttest

The pretest and the posttest consisted of eight items. In the items, different aspects of historical reasoning are reflected. The pretest and posttests questions were the same; we only used different historical sources, (e.g., a different picture or source). The reliability of the eight post test items .73 (Cronbach's alpha), which is satisfactory for a test with open questions.Two judges scored the tests. The interrater reliability on 10 randomly chosen pretests and 10 posttests varied between .62 and .94 (Cohen's kappa). Table 11.3 summarizes detailed information of the test at the item level.

TABLE 11.2

Items of Text Analyses

Aspects of Historical Reasoning	*Items of Text Analyses*
1. Time	1.1 How many time references are given? 1.2 Are the time references correct?
2. Change	2.1 How many changes are mentioned? 2.2 Are the changes described correctly? 2.3 Is a differentiation in changes given (i.e., continuity, impact of the change, suddenly, gradually, etc.)?
3. Explanation	3.1 How many explanations are given? 3.2 Are the causes described correctly? 3.3 Is a distinction made between the impacts of the different causes?
4. Sources	4.1 Did the students use their own words for describing information of the sources? 4.2 Is a distinction made between different historical interpretations?
5. Point of view	5.1 Does the text give a clearly formulated point of view, which includes argumentation? 5.2 What is the quality of the argumentation?
6. Concepts	6.1 How many different historical concepts are explicitly used? 6.2 Are the concepts correctly used? 6.3 How many different methodological concepts are explicitly used (i.e., causes, change, trustworthiness, etc.)?

RESULTS

The results of the analyses are described in this section. First we discuss the results on the interaction process in the chat protocols, after which we discuss the results on the texts written and the individual learning outcomes. In the description of the results we compare the two conditions: the explanatory inquiry task and the evaluative task. Comparison between the two groups on the results of the pretest showed no difference in scores, $t(18) = .35, p = .73$.

Interaction Processes in the Chat

Task Acts

Students performed different activities within the learning environment, for example reading sources, writing the text, writing notes, and chatting. The mean length of the chat was 572 utterances (SD = 274.53). As described earlier, we analyzed the chat protocols on different dimensions. The chat protocols were first analyzed on the level of task acts, which gives information about what kind of chat discussions were provoked by the given inquiry task. Table 11.4 shows the mean frequencies and the percentages of the task acts discussed in the chat protocols. From Table 11.4 we can conclude that the students' work focused on the task.

TABLE 11.3

Description, Maximum Score, Agreement and Interrater Reliability of Items in the Pre- and Posttest.

Question	Descriptions of the items	Aspect of historical reasoning	Maximum score	Interrater agreement in %	Cohen's Kappa
1	Association task¹	Concepts	16	85	.84
2	Situating historical phenomena in time	Time	10	– ²	– ²
3	Situating photos in time	Time	10	90	.89
4	Describing changes in the 1950's and 1960's	Change	6	95	.94
5	Giving causes for the changes	Explantation	12	70	.62
6a	Selecting information from a source	Source	2	80	.70
6b	Evaluating trustworthiness of a source	Source	2	85	.78
7	Taking and argumenting a point of view	Viewpoint	4	80	.76
8	Giving descriptions of six concepts	Concepts	12	82	.72

¹Association task: task in which students are asked to give associations on the 1950's and the 1960's in a mind map.

² Multiple-choice items. The answers were correct or false.

About 72% of the utterances were directly related to the task, of which 32% were about procedures and 40% about the task itself. The chat was often used to coordinate the activities: About 20% of the utterances were related to this aspect.

About 13% of the utterances contained historical reasoning. As the high standard deviations show, the chat discussions differed a lot among the pairs; especially the amount of social talk: from 4% to 40%.

Historical Reasoning

Second, we were interested in how students reasoned about history, and whether and how there were differences between the students who worked on the explanatory question and on the evaluative question. We therefore analyzed the utterances coded as historical reasoning in more detail. We discerned six aspects of historical reasoning and also coded whether historical concepts were used in the reasoning. The results are presented in Table 11.5.

TABLE 11.4

Mean Frequencies, Standard Deviations, and Mean Percentages and Standard Deviations of Task Acts in the Chat Protocols ($N = 10$)

Task Acts	Frequencies		Percentages	
	M	*SD*	*M*	*SD*
Task	206.50	76.14	39.28	11.77
Historical reasoning	61.10	36.41	13.42	9.50
Text construction	25.40	11.43	4.76	2.11
Revision	51.90	36.30	9.03	4.40
Goal	11.70	6.27	2.32	1.35
Information	13.20	10.04	2.09	1.34
Evaluation	21.60	10.07	4.10	1.61
Word count	21.40	14.42	3.55	2.15
Procedure	179.50	77.30		7.51
Coordination	115.10	57.28	32.77	6.40
Task approach	10.70	7.29	20.60	1.88
Planning	15.60	8.88	2.35	3.31
Turn taking	27.30	27.86	3.45	2.51
Evaluation	11.30	7.83	4.24	1.36
			2.21	
Program	31.90	25.05	5.24	3.12
Social	117.50	134.43	16.22	12.72
Greetings	35.40	18.10	6.30	1.37
No code	0.70	1.89	0.20	0.42
Total utterances	572.00		274.53	

Table 11.5 shows that all aspects of historical reasoning occurred in the chat while performing this inquiry task. However, additional analyses showed that not all types of reasoning were used by all 10 dyads; the chat protocol of only one dyad showed all types of reasoning.

TABLE 11.5

Mean Frequencies and Standard Deviations for Aspects of Historical Reasoning for the Two Conditions ($N = 10$)

Aspects of Historical Reasoning	Explanatory question		Evaluative question		
	M	SD	M	SD	p
Time	3.60	4.93	6.60	5.37	.38
Concepts	3.00	4.24	3.20	3.42	.94
No concepts	0.60	1.34	3.40	3.29	.14
Description	6.20	4.21	20.00	20.46	.18
Concepts	4.00	2.35	11.80	9.50	.14
No concepts	2.20	2.95	8.20	13.44	.36
Change	11.20	7.29	14.60	11.74	.60
Concepts	6.60	6.27	6.40	4.62	.96
No concepts	4.60	6.69	8.20	9.42	.51
Explanation	12.20	6.61	1.00	1.41	.02*
Concepts	7.80	6.02	0.80	1.30	.04*
No concepts	4.40	1.82	0.20	0.45	.00*
Source	7.00	4.30	8.20	8.23	.78
Concepts	2.20	2.17	2.80	4.76	.80
No concepts	4.80	3.96	5.40	4.04	.82
Viewpoint	0.20	0.45	31.60	14.76	.01*
Concepts	0.20	0.45	29.60	14.21	.01*
No concepts	0.00	0.00	2.00	3.08	.22

*$p \leq .05$.

Almost all dyads gave descriptions of the past, talked about the changes that occurred in the 1960's, and discussed the historical sources, although on a small scale. Six dyads talked about the aspect situating in time. The aspects explanation and point of view also did not occur in all the chats. The students who worked on the explanatory question talked a lot about explanations, whereas the students who worked on the evaluative question frequently discussed their point of view. A t test for independent samples showed that the difference in the amount of talk about explanations was significant, $t(8) = 3.71$, p $\leq$ .05, as was the difference in the amount of talk about viewpoint $t(8) = 4.75$, $p \leq .01$. So, as we expected, the students who had to explain the changes of the youth in the 1960's, talked significantly more about explanations and the students who had to evaluate whether the changes were revolutionary or not discussed significantly more about their viewpoint. This latter type of talk did not go at the expense of other types of reasoning because the students in the evaluation condition talked as much about change as the students in the explanatory condition. For the other aspects of historical reasoning no differences were found.

Furthermore, we analyzed whether and how students used historical concepts when constructing historical reasoning. Historical concepts were used most of the time, except when they discussed and evaluated the historical sources. The episodes in which students discussed their point of view almost always contained historical concepts. Additional analyses focused on the use of the six concepts that were considered central to the subject of the task, which were democratization, individualization, nozem, Provo, depillarization, and second women liberation movement. The concepts nozem and Provo were most frequently used and were also used by almost all the dyads. Most of the dyads did not explicitly use the concepts democratization, individualization, and second women liberation movement at all. Most often the concepts were used in an implicit way; only occasionally, was the meaning of a concept explicitly explained.

TABLE 11.5

Mean Frequencies and Standard Deviations for Aspects of Historical Reasoning for the Two Conditions ($N = 10$)

Aspects of Historical Reasoning	Explanatory question		Evaluative question		
	M	SD	M	SD	p
Time	3.60	4.93	6.60	5.37	.38
Concepts	3.00	4.24	3.20	3.42	.94
No concepts	0.60	1.34	3.40	3.29	.14
Description	6.20	4.21	20.00	20.46	.18
Concepts	4.00	2.35	11.80	9.50	.14
No concepts	2.20	2.95	8.20	13.44	.36
Change	11.20	7.29	14.60	11.74	.60
Concepts	6.60	6.27	6.40	4.62	.96
No concepts	4.60	6.69	8.20	9.42	.51
Explanation	12.20	6.61	1.00	1.41	.02*
Concepts	7.80	6.02	0.80	1.30	.04*
No concepts	4.40	1.82	0.20	0.45	.00*
Source	7.00	4.30	8.20	8.23	.78
Concepts	2.20	2.17	2.80	4.76	.80
No concepts	4.80	3.96	5.40	4.04	.82
Viewpoint	0.20	0.45	31.60	14.76	.01*
Concepts	0.20	0.45	29.60	14.21	.01*
No concepts	0.00	0.00	2.00	3.08	.22

*$p \leq .05$.

We provide an example of both occasions. In the first example, Astrid and Mark discuss the meaning of the concept nozem. The first part of this fragment took place after 52 minutes, the second part after 1 hour and 17 minutes.

Excerpt 1. An example of discussing the meaning of historical concepts

1	Astrid	Do you know what a nozem is?
2	Mark	I have seen the word in the novel "Ik, Jan Cremer". I think it is a sort of nerd or loser, but I am not sure. It was also used as a term of abuse.
3	Astrid	Thank you.
4	Mark	Again, what was a nozem?
5	Astrid	Nozems were boys between 16 and 18 years old, mostly only lower educated and from lower social-economical background. They protested against abuses, but they were no criminals. Because they were bored they sometimes provoked, especially the police.

In the first part of Excerpt 1, Astrid asks what a nozem is. Mark uses his own prior knowledge to explain the concept and refers to a novel he has read. Although he says he is not quite sure, Astrid accepts the explanation. They do not search the sources to find a better description. After some time, Mark does not feel sure about the meaning of the concept nozem and asks Astrid. In the meantime, Astrid has read about nozems and is able to provide a more elaborate description. Astrid and Mark explicitly discuss the meaning of the concept.

The second fragment shows an example in which the meaning of a concept is not explicitly discussed. Eric and Lisa reason about changes in the sixties and discuss the process depillarization. They use the concept in order to describe the change in behavior of the youth. They relate the concept to the process of secularization (although this term is also not explicitly used).

Excerpt 2. An example of implicit use of historical concepts

1	Eric	It is about the youth who still go to church, but who start to ask themselves whether God exists.
2	Lisa	Oh.
3	Eric	The children of the fifties did not ask themselves these kinds of questions.
4	Lisa	Oh, then it is a clear change, I think.
5	Lisa	Yes, because in the fifties and the sixties there is also depillarization.
6	Eric	Yes, I have also read about that.

Did the students reason collaboratively while reasoning about the past? Table 11.6 shows the amount students reasoned together or individually. It is shown that most historical reasoning reflected coconstructed reasoning for both the conditions. Individual reasoning also occurred regularly, reasoning dominated by one student not so often. The students in the evaluative condition showed more coconstructed reasoning compared to the students in the explanatory condition. A t test for independent samples revealed that this difference is significant, $t(8) = 2.92, p \leq .05$. Therefore, the students who worked on the evaluative inquiry task showed significantly more coconstructed reasoning compared to the students who worked on the explanatory inquiry task.

TABLE 11.6

Mean Frequencies and Standard Deviation of Degree of Co-construction in Historical Reasoning (N = 10)

Degree of Co-construction	Explanatory question		Evaluative question		
	M	SD	M	SD	p
Co-constructed reasoning	21.20	8.93	50.60	27.26	.05*
Dominated reasoning	4.80	5.63	11.00	7.87	.19
Individual reasoning	14.40	7.16	20.40	17.24	.49

$*p \leq .05$

Next, an example of a co-constructed historical reasoning is given. Paula and Wendy, who participated in the evaluation condition, discuss whether they think the 1960's were revolutionary or not.

Excerpt 3. An example of co-constructed historical reasoning

1	Paula	But what is our opinion?
2	Wendy	To start with, what is your opinion?
3	Paula	The sixties were revolutionary.
4	Wendy	Why?
5	Paula	Because the consequences are still noticeable now.
6	Wendy	Okay, that is true.
7	Paula	But it already started in '50.
8	Wendy	That's true too, but that's got little to do with the

	revoltionariousness, so the sixties were indeed revolutionary!?
9 Paula	If you think so too.
10 Wendy	Yes, sure I do too.
11 Paula	Okay.
12 Wendy	Which arguments pro are we going to use?
13 Paula	That young people became a group, and that they had their own opinion.
14 Wendy	The depillarization went on strongly.
15 Paula	Yes, and the consumptive society arose.
16 Wendy	People started to think more flexible about sex, which meant greater freedom for young people.
17 Paula	Yes, young people had more freedom anyway, because of their being financially independent they were able to leave their parents more early and they were independent of their parents.
18 Wendy	Exactly.
19 Paula	Okay.

In this example Paula and Wendy discuss their point of view on the question whether the 1960's were revolutionary or not. In this reasoning historical concepts are used, (e.g., depillarization). Paula and Wendy coconstruct their meaning on this subject. First, they talk about which point of view they are taking, and whether they both agree on this. They ask questions that elicit elaboration, such as "What is our opinion?" "Why?" and "Which arguments pro are we going to use?" They both, in turn, add arguments to support their meaning, and they build on the reasoning of the partner, as is shown in lines 16 and 17.

The Texts

The collaboratively written texts were scored on aspects of historical reasoning. The results for the two conditions are presented in Table 11.7.

The texts showed all aspects of historical reasoning. The texts contained many (correct) descriptions of the time in which certain phenomena took place and of the changing behavior of the youth. The students of both groups did not score so high on giving explanations. Although some texts contained a reasonable number of explanations, the quality of these explanations was often low, and did not contain aspects such as the importance of the causes. When we look at differences between the two conditions we see that the texts that were produced in the evaluation condition showed a higher quality of historical reasoning compared to the texts that were produced in the explanatory condition. This difference is significant $t(8) = 2.63, p \leq .05$. As in the chat, the scores on the aspect viewpoint were significantly higher in the evaluative condition, $t(8) = 7.12, p \leq .001$. However, although the students in the explanatory condition talked more about explanations in the chat, they did not score significantly higher on this aspect in the text produced.

TABLE 11.7

Maximum Scores, Mean Scores, and Standard Deviations on Aspects of Historical Reasoning in the Text in Two Conditions and the Results of t Tests for Independent Samples ($N = 10$)

	Maximum Score	Explanatory Question		Evaluative Question		
		M	SD	M	SD	P
Time	6	5.00	1.00	5.40	.89	.52
Change	8	5.40	.89	6.20	.84	.18
Explanation	8	4.20	1.64	3.40	.89	.37
Source	5	2.40	1.52	3.80	1.10	.13
Viewpoint	6	2.20	.84	5.40	.55	.00*
Concepts	9	6.20	.45	6.20	.84	1.00
Total score	42	25.40	3.58	30.40	2.30	.03*

*$p \leq .05$.

Of the six central concepts, the concept of Provo was most often used in the text, followed by nozem and depillarization. Democratization, individualization, and second women liberation movement were hardly used and they were only used by a few of the 10 dyads. These results correspond with the way the concepts were used in the chat. The text also contained other historical concepts that were less central to the task, such as Second World War, industrialization, welfare, and rock and roll. On the average the dyads used 15 to 19 different historical concepts. They also used several methodological concepts, such as cause, consequence, fact, and change. On average they used 5 or 6 concepts. The historical concepts were most often used correctly, although some descriptions were somewhat vague or incomplete.

Individual Learning Outcomes

Did the students individually learn from this inquiry task? The results of the pretest and the posttest are presented in Table 11.8.

TABLE 11.8

Mean Scores and Standard Deviations of the Pretest and the Posttest and

Results of a *t* Test for Paired Samples (N = 20)

Items	Pretest		Posttest		
	M	*SD*	*M*	*SD*	*p*
1. Association task[1]	7.05	2.99	10.11	3.53	.00*
2. Time (phenomena)	6.55	1.50	6.75	1.80	.62
3. Time (photo)	5.65	2.06	6.30	1.75	.10
4. Change	2.85	0.93	3.15	1.31	.25
5. Explanation	1.80	1.36	3.60	2.06	.00*
6. Source	1.95	1.14	2.90	1.12	.02*
7. Viewpoint	1.90	1.12	1.85	0.99	.88
8. Concept definitions	6.05	2.24	7.10	2.34	.09
Total score	34.40	7.40	41.55	9.25	.00*

* $p \leq .05$
[1] $n = 19$

From Table 11.8 it can be concluded that the students did learn from the inquiry task. The total scores on the posttest improved significantly compared to the pretest. Analyses on the level of the different items showed that in the posttest the students' scores were significantly higher on the following items: association task, explanation, and the use of sources. The results on the association task showed that the students' ability to give correct associations on the 1950's and 1960's increased significantly. By correct associations we mean that the given association is correctly related to the 1950's or the 1960's. For example, the first man on the moon is related to the 1960's and not to the 1950's. Additional analysis was carried out on the association task. We investigated whether the associations were abstract or concrete. In the pretest the percentage of abstract associations was 54.60 (on a total of 163 associations); in the posttest this percentage was 72.03

(on a total of 211 associations). Thus, the students were not only able to give more correct associations; the use of abstract associations also increased reasonably. Detailed analyses showed that the highest increase was related to the concepts nozem (pretest: 2 times mentioned; posttest: 10 times), Provo (3 and 12), and depillarization (1 and 16).

Although the students did not significantly improve on the total score of the concept definitions, additional analyses for each concept showed that students improved significantly on two concepts: nozem, $t(19) = 3.32$, $p <$ .01 and Provo, $t(19) = 2.13$, $p < .05$. The scores on the concepts of democratization, depillarization, and second women liberation movement did not show a significant difference, whereas the score on the concept of individualization significantly decreased, $t(19) = 2.35$, $p < .05$).

TABLE 11.9

Mean Scores and Standard Deviations of the Posttest in Two Conditions and the Results of t Tests for Independent Samples ($N = 20$)

Items	Explanatory question		Evaluative question		
	M	SD	M	SD	p
1. Association task	9.44	4.22	10.70	2.87	.45
2. Time (phenomena)	6.60	1.90	9.90	1.79	.72
3. Time (photo)	6.40	1.71	6.20	1.87	.81
4. Change	3.20	1.40	3.10	1.29	.87
5. Explanation	4.10	2.47	3.10	1.52	.29
6. Source	2.50	1.35	3.30	0.67	.11
7. Viewpoint	1.70	1.06	2.00	0.94	.51
8. Concept definitions	7.00	2.31	7.20	2.49	.85
Total score	40.60	10.15	42.50	8.70	.65

*$p \leq .05$.

In Table 11.9 the scores on the posttest are compared for the two conditions. For the results on the posttest we expected that the students in the evaluation condition would show more overall learning gains. Besides, we expected that students in the explanatory condition would score better on the item explanation, and that the evaluation condition would score higher on the item viewpoint. Contrary to our expectations we did not find any differences between the two conditions on the results of the posttest, as is shown in Table 11.9.

CONCLUSIONS AND DISCUSSION

In this chapter we presented the results of our study on historical reasoning in a CSCL environment. For this study, pairs of students were presented with an inquiry task, in which they had to study multiple historical sources to write a text. Two types of inquiry conditions were compared: a condition with an explanatory question and a condition with an evaluative question. Analyses focused on the interaction process, more specifically on domain-specific reasoning and the co-construction of knowledge, the collabora-tively written texts, and individual learning outcomes. First, we summarize our general findings on the analyses on student interaction in the chat and the learning outcomes. Then we discuss the differences between the two conditions. Finally, we describe the tools that can be made available in the CSCL environment and that may stimulate and support collaborative his-torical reasoning.

Analyses of the collaboratively written texts and the chat protocols showed that the inquiry task presented in this study elicited historical rea-soning. All aspects of historical reasoning occurred in the text and in the chat. When reasoning historically, the students usually used historical con-cepts in a correct way. The larger part of the historical reasoning episodes was coconstructed by both students. However, our analyses also showed some weak aspects of the student interaction in the chat. First, only 13% of all the utterances contained historical reasoning. Second, not all dyads showed all aspects of reasoning. For example, students hardly discussed the time in which phenomena took place. Although some dyads gave explana-tions for historical phenomena or gave a point of view, these were often of poor quality or not well supported with arguments. Third, the meaning of historical concepts was hardly explicitly negotiated. This makes it difficult to evaluate whether the students really understood the concepts they used. Furthermore, more abstract concepts, such as democratization, individuali-zation, and second women liberation movement were hardly used.

The results on the posttest indicated that the students did learn from the inquiry task. The students were, compared to the pretest, more able to give explanations, evaluate the trustworthiness of sources, and give defi-nitions of the concepts nozem and Provo. Furthermore, the students im-proved significantly on the association task. They were not only able to give more correct associations, but also more abstract associations. Thus, after completing the inquiry task the students had a broader conceptual frame-work on the subject studied. Comparing the results of the chat, the text, and the posttest, it can be concluded that the students used the concepts nozem and Provo often in the chat, in the text, and in the associations task, and that they were able to give better definitions of these concepts. This finding is in line with the literature on concept learning, which suggests that students learn concepts by using them (Van Boxtel, 2000). However, more analyses on these data are needed to investigate the relation between the results on the interaction, the text, and test.

The comparison between the two conditions showed that the type of inquiry question the students had to work on affected historical reasoning in the student interaction (chat) and in the jointly written text. First, the students who worked on the evaluative question showed more historical reasoning in the chat (M evaluation = 82, M explanation = 40.2), $t(8) = 2.15$, $p = .06$. Although the p value is not significant the .05 level, we do think this is worth mentioning, because the study was conducted with a small sample. They talked more about their point of view and about arguments to support that viewpoint, whereas students who had to explain a historical phenomenon talked more often about causes and explanations. In addition, the students in the evaluative condition more often contributed to the historical reasoning and therefore showed more coconstructed reasoning. Furthermore, the students in the evaluative condition produced text of a significantly higher quality and the texts showed a more thorough historical reasoning. Furthermore, they scored higher on the aspect point of view, which was also more often discussed in the chat. However, although the students in the explanatory condition discussed more about explanations in the chat, they did not score higher on this aspect in the text. The students in the evaluative condition, who hardly discussed explanations, did mention explanations in the text. Therefore, this finding suggests that an explanatory question elicits historical reasoning about explanations in the chat and text, whereas the evaluative question elicits historical reasoning about a point of view in the text and chat, and the giving of explanations in the text. Concerning the individual learning outcomes, we expected to find the same differences in scores on the items concerning explanation and point of view. Contrary to this expectation, we did not find that these differences had an impact on the individual learning outcomes. Although the mean scores of the items point in the direction we expected, the differences were not significant.

In interpreting the results we have to take into consideration that this study was a small-scale study in which only 10 dyads and students from one school were participating. Although the two groups were randomly assigned to one of the conditions and did not show difference in scores on the pretest, we have to handle the outcomes with care. A replication of this study in which more individuals participate would be necessary to generalize the conclusions to a broader setting. The differences between the two types of inquiry tasks found here do not indicate that an explanatory task is a less useful task. The results mainly indicate that the tasks elicit different kinds of historical reasoning. Using an explanatory inquiry question can be very useful if the goal of the teacher is to focus on the explanation of historical events, which is an important aspect of learning history.

From this study it can be concluded that a computer-supported inquiry task is a type of task that elicits historical reasoning and learning. In particular, an evaluative inquiry question seems to have the potential to elicit co-constructed historical reasoning in the chat and a higher quality of historical reasoning in the text. However, although students did reason about history, they did not always use all aspects of reasoning, nor did they use all the selected concepts so often. Also, the argumentation of students' point of view in the text were often of poor quality, as hardly any arguments were given to support this viewpoint, nor were counterarguments given or different arguments weighed. This finding is in line with the statement of Spoehr and Spoehr (1994) that the hardest part of historical thinking and reasoning is learning to anticipate counterarguments, to weigh alternate explanations for the phenomena being explained, and to be able to explain why one interpretation seems preferable to others. Therefore, students should be better supported to reason collaboratively about their point of view and discuss and weigh different arguments.

Adding extra tools to the CSCL environment might support collaborative historical reasoning. Research has shown that several tools can support the construction of knowledge, the communication between the students, and the co-construction of a group product, such as argumentative diagrams, matrices, and concept maps (Suthers, 2001; Veerman, 2000). Graphical representations such as an argumentative diagram can be especially meaningful because of their communicative and cognitive function (Erkens, Kanselaar, Jaspers, & Schijf, 2001; Suthers & Hundhausen, 2001). From a communicative perspective, it contributes to a shared understanding and a joint problem space between colearners, and enables them to focus on salient knowledge (Crook, 1998; Suthers & Hundhausen, 2001; Veerman & Treasure-Jones, 1999). From a cognitive perspective, a graphical representation can be meaningful for two reasons. First, it focuses attention on central problems, relations, and structures in the task, helping to distinguish central, main, or core issues from more peripheral ones (Suthers & Hundhausen, 2001). Second, it stimulates the process of elaboration, for it can refine and structure the content of students' knowledge and makes participants aware of gaps in their knowledge, for instance, about what specific relations are present or about the balance between arguments against and in favor of a position (Suthers & Hundhausen, 2002). In our next study we intend to compare different tools for supporting coconstructed historical reasoning. We will compare an argumentative diagram, which is a graphical representation, with an argument list (a linear representation) and a matrix (a different form of a graphical representation). In an experimental design these three tools will be compared to a control group. Each condition will consist of 30 dyads. We will use the evaluative inquiry question for this type of question because it seems to have more potential to elicit historical reasoning. We expect that the use of the graphical tools will elicit more co-constructed historical reasoning.

REFERENCES

Brown, A. L., Collins, A., & Duguid, P. (1989). Situated cognition and the culture of learning. *Educational Researcher, 18*, 32–42.

Brown, A. L., & Palincsar, A. S. (1989). Guided cooperative learning and individual knowledge acquisition. In L. B. Resnick (Ed.), *Knowing, learning and instruction: Essays in honor of Robert Glaser* (pp. 395–452). Hillsdale, NJ: Lawrence Erlbaum Associates.

Carretero, M., Jacott, L., Limón, M., López-Manjón, A. & León, A. (1994). Historical knowledge: Cognitive and instructional implications. In M. Carretero & J.F. Voss (Eds.), *Cognitive and instructional processes in history and the social sciences* (pp. 357–376). Hillsdale, NJ: Lawrence Erlbaum Associates.

Carretero, M., Jacott, L., & López-Manjón, A. (1997). Explaining historical events. *International Journal of Educational Research, 27*, 245–253.

Carretero, M., & Voss, J. F. (1994). Introduction. In M. Carretero & J. F. Voss (Eds.). *Cognitive and instructional processes in history and the social sciences* (pp. 1–14). Hillsdale, NJ: Lawrence Erlbaum Associates.

Crook, C. (1998). Children as computer users: The case of collaborative learning. *Computers Education, 30*, 237–247.

Dillenbourg, P., Baker, M., Blaye. A., & O'Malley, C. (1995). The evolution of research on collaborative learning. In E. Spada & P. Reiman (Eds.); *Learning in humans and machine: Towards an interdisciplinary learning science* (pp 189–211). Oxford, UK: Elsevier.

Duffy, T. M., & Jonassen, D. H. (1992). Constructivism: New implications for instructional technology. In T. Duffy & D. Jonassen (Eds.), *Constructivism and the technology of instruction* (pp. 1–16). Hillsdale, NJ: Lawrence Erlbaum Associates.

Erkens, G., Kanselaar, G., Jaspers, J., & Schijf, H. (2001). Computerondersteund samenwerkend leren [Computer-supported Collabarative Learning]. In W. A.Wald & J. van der Linden (Eds.), Leren in perspectief [Learning in perspective] (pp. 85-97). The Netherlands, Leuven-Apeldoorn: Garant.

Gere, A., & Stevens, R. S. (1989). The language of writing groups: How oral response shapes revision. In S. W. Feedman (Ed.), *The acquisition of written language: Response and revisions* (pp. 85–105). Norwood, NJ: Ablex.

294 VAN DRIE, VAN BOXTEL, VAN DER LINDEN

Giroud, A. (1999). Studying argumentative text processing through collaborative writing. In J. E. B. Andriessen & P. Coirier (Eds.); *Foundations of argumentative text processing* (pp. 149–179). Amsterdam: Amsterdam University Press.

Goegebeur, W., Simon, R., de Keyser, R., van Dooren, J., & van Landegem, P. (1999). Historisch besef: hoe waarden-vol?! Ontwikkeling van een analyse-instrument [Historical consiousness: how valuable?! Development of an instrument of analysis]. Belgium, Brussels: Vubpress.

Halldén. O. (1986). Learning history. *Oxford Review of Education, 12*, 53–66.

Husbands, C. (1996). *What is history teaching? Language, ideas and meaning in learning about the past.* Buckingham, UK: Open University Press.

Jacott, L., López-Manjón, A., & Carretero, M. (2000). Generating explanations in history. In J. F. Voss & M. Carretero (Eds.), *Learning and reasoning in history: International review of history education.* (Vol. 2; pp. 294–306). London: Woburn.

Jeismann, K. E. (1997). Geschichtsbewusstsein. [Historical consciousness] In K. Bergmann, K.Fröhlich, A. Kuhn, J. Rüsen, & G. Schneider (Eds.). Handbuch der Geschichtsdidaktik [Handbook of Didactics of History] (pp. 42–44). Germany, Seelze: Kalmeyersche.

King, A. (1990). Enhancing peer interaction and learning in the classroom through reciprocal questioning. *Educational Psychologist, 27,* 111–126.

Kuhn, D., Weinstock, M., & Flaton, R. (1994). Historical reasoning as theory-evidence coordination. In M. Carretero & J. F. Voss (Eds.); *Cognitive and instructional processes in history and the social sciences* (pp. 377–401). Hillsdale, NJ: Lawrence Erlbaum Associates.

Kumpulainen, K., & Mutanen, M. (1999). The situated dynamics of peer group interaction: An introduction to an analytic framework. *Learning and Instruction, 9,* 449–473.

Leinhardt, G., Stainton, C., & Virji, S. M. (1994). A sense of history. *Education Psychologist, 29,* 79–88.

Lethinen, E., Hakkarainen, K., Lipponen, L., Rahikainen, M., & Muukonen, H. (2001). *Computer supported collaborative learning: A review. CL-Net Project* [Online]. Retrieved September 4, 2001, from http://www.kas.utu.fi/clnet/clnetreport.html

Mercer, N. (1995). *The guided construction of knowledge: Talk amongst teachers and learners.* Clevedon, UK: Multilingual Matters.

O'Donnell, A. (1999). Structuring dyadic interaction through scripted cooperation. In A. M. O'Donnell & A. King (Eds.), *Cognitive perspectives on peer learning.* (pp. 179-198). Mahwah, NJ: Lawrence Erlbaum Associates.

Palincsar, A. S., & Herrenkohl, L. R. (1999). Designing collaborative contexts: Lessons from three research programs. In A. M. O'Donnell

& A. King (Eds.), *Cognitive perspectives on peer learning* (pp. 151–178). Mahwah, NJ: Lawrence Erlbaum Associates.

Perfetti, C. A., Britt, M. A. Georgi, M. C. (1995). *Text-based learning and reasoning: Studies in history.* Hillsdale, NJ: Lawrence Erlbaum Associates.

Roderigo, M. J. (1994). Discussion of the chapters 10–12: Promoting narrative literacy and historical literacy. In M. Carretero & J. F. Voss (Eds.); *Cognitive and instructional processes in history and the social sciences* (pp. 309–320). Hillsdale, NJ: Lawrence Erlbaum Associates.

Roschelle, J. (1992). Learning by collaborating: Convergent conceptual change. *Journal of the Learning Sciences, 2,* 235–276.

Rouet, J., Britt, M. A., Mason, R. A., & Perfetti, C. A. (1996). Using multiple sources of evidence to reason about history. *Journal of Educational Psychology, 88,* 478–493.

Salomon, G., & Perkins, D. N. (1998). Individual and social aspects of learning. In P. D. Pearson & A. Iran-Nejad (Eds.), *Review of research in education* (pp. 1–24). Washington, DC: American Educational Research Association.

Spoehr, K. T. & Spoehr, L. W. (1994). Learning to think historically. *Educational Psychologist, 29,* 71-77.

Stearns, P. N. (2000). Goals in history teaching. In J. F. Voss & M. Carretero (Eds.), *Learning and reasoning in history: International review of history education.* (Vol. 2, pp. 281–293). London: Woburn.

Suthers, D. D. (2001). Towards a systematic study of representational guidance for collaborative learning discourse. *Journal of Universal Computer Science, 7,* 3.

Suthers, D. D., & Hundhausen, C. D. (2001). Learning by constructing collaborative representations: An emperical comparison of three alternatives. In P. Dillenbourg, A. Eurelings, & K. Hakkarainen (Eds.), *Proceedings of European perspectives on computer-supported collaborative learning* (pp. 577–584). The Netherlands, Maastricht: Universiteit Maastricht.

Suthers, D. D., & Hundhausen, C. D. (2002). The effects of representation on students' elaborations in collaborative inquiry. In *Proceedings of CSCL 2002* (pp. 472–480).

Van Boxtel, C. (2000). *Collaborative concept learning: Collaborative learning tasks, student interaction, and the learning of physics concepts.* Enschede, Germany: Print Partners Ipskamp.

Van der Linden, J. L., Erkens, G., Schmidt, H., & Renshaw, P. (2000). Collaborative learning. In P. R. J. Simons, J. L. van der Linden, & T. Duffy (Eds.); *New learning* (pp. 37–54). Dordrecht, Netherlands: Kluwer Academic.

Van Drie, J. P. (2000). Historisch redeneren in een interactieve leeromgeving [Historical reasoning in an interactive learning environment]. The Netherlands, Utrecht: Utrecht University, Department of Educational Sciences.

Veerman, A. (2000). *Computer-supported collaborative learning through argumentation.* Enschede, Germany: Print Partners Ipskamp.

Veerman, A., & Treasure-Jones, T. (1999). Software for problem solving through collaborative argumentation. In J. Andriessen, & P. Courier (Eds.), *Foundations of argumentative text processing* (pp. 203–229). Amsterdam: University Press.

Von Borries, B. (1997). Concepts of historical thinking and historical learning in the perspective of German students and teachers. *International Journal of Educational Research, 27,* 211–220.

Voss, J. F., Carretero, M., Kennet, J., & Ney Silfies, L. (1994). The collapse of the Soviet Union: A case study in causal reasoning. In M. Carretero & J. F. Voss (Eds.); *Cognitive and instructional processes in history and the social sciences* (pp. 403–430). Hillsdale, NJ: Lawrence Erlbaum Associates.

Voss, J. F., Ciarrochi J., & Carretero, M. (2000). Causality in history: On the "intuitive" understanding of the concepts of sufficiency and necessity. In: J. F. Voss & M. Carretero (Eds.), *Learning and reasoning in history: International review of history education.* (Vol. 2; pp. 199–213). London: Woburn.

Voss, J. F., & Wiley, J. (1997). Developing understanding while writing essays in history. *International Journal of Educational Research, 27,* 255–265.

Webb, N. M. (1991). Task-related verbal interaction and mathematics learning in small groups. *Journal of Research in Mathematics Education, 22,* 366–389.

Wertsch, J. V. (1991). *Voices of the mind.* Cambridge, MA: Harvard University Press.

Wiley, J., & Voss, J. F. (1996). The effects of "playing historian" on learning in history. *Applied Cognitive Psychology, 10,* 563–572

Wineburg, S. S. (1991). Historical problem solving: A study of the cognitive processes used in the evaluation of documentary and pictorial evidence. *Journal of Educational Psychology; 83,* 73–87.

Chapter 12

Effects of Collaboration and Argumentation on Learning from Web Pages

Jennifer Wiley

Jeannine Bailey

University of Illinois at Chicago

Many recently developed learning environments incorporate collaborative learning as well as the use of technology in their design. However, at least within the social psychology literature that has investigated groups as information processors, studies have found that groups of people working together are frequently less effective than individuals working alone, or than the combined efforts of an equal number of individuals working alone (Diehl & Stroebe, 1987; Gigone & Hastie, 1997; Hastie, 1986; Hill, 1982). On the other hand, among studies of collaborative learning in educational contexts, advantages of the performance of a group over individuals have been reported (Hertz-Lazarowitz & Miller, 1995; Johnson & Johnson, 1989; Webb & Palincsar, 1996). The focus of this chapter is to begin to explore what may be responsible for the discrepancy between the findings of these two literatures, the kinds of processes that may underlie gains and losses in group contexts, and finally, the use of technology to promote successful collaborative problem solving and reasoning.

Factors Determining Process Loss

Intact groups are less productive, less creative, and often biased or unduly-influenced by one member (Diehl & Stroebe, 1987; Gigone & Hastie, 1997; Hastie, 1986; Hill, 1982). The term *process loss* was coined by Steiner (1972) to describe the loss in productivity that occurs when individuals must coordinate their efforts in a group. On the other hand, when there is a synergetic or value-added effect observed among individuals working as a group versus individuals working alone, this has been termed process gain (Steiner, 1972).

The social psychology literature has identified a number of factors that seem to contribute to process loss. For this discussion, we have grouped their observations into four aspects of group problem solving: motivation and effort, evaluation and conflict, task coordination, and use of resources. Proponents of collaborative learning who have suggested that working in groups may contribute to better learning cite these same aspects of group settings as potential reasons for learning gains (e.g., Webb & Palinscar, 1996). Thus, it seems that each factor may have opposing effects on performance in different contexts. The goal is to figure out which contexts lead to positive outcomes, (i.e., process gain), and which contexts result in negative outcomes, (i.e., process loss).

Changes in Motivation and Effort

Since the late 19th century, researchers have recognized that the mere presence of others can be motivating, whether it is turning fishing reels (Triplett, 1898), or generating word associations (Allport, 1920). When observers are present, especially when they may be in a position to evaluate performance, individuals become more productive. This has been termed *social facilitation* (Allport, 1924).

On the other hand, classic studies have also demonstrated that as soon as more than one person is responsible for a task, there is a risk that not all will participate fully (Ringelmann, 1913). When an individual is solely responsible for a task then she or he must be motivated or involved for it to be accomplished. As soon as more than one person is responsible for a task, *social loafing* may occur (Kerr & Bruun, 1983). This term refers to the fact that as more people are responsible for performing a task, each individual feels less responsibility for its actual completion, and as a result, each may contribute less than he or she would individually. Process loss has frequently been attributed to losses in motivation, a lowered sense of responsibility, and less effort by each individual (see Sheppard, 1993). Group problem solvers contribute fewer guesses in a group than alone (Mullen, Johnson, & Salas, 1991; Taylor, Berry, & Block, 1958), and group decision makers feel less investment in (and responsibility for) their decisions (Gigone & Hastie, 1997).

Potential for Evaluation and Conflict

One potential explanation for the loss of motivation or effort is anxiety or fear about being evaluated by others. The presence of others introduces an element of evaluation and conflict, not usually present when people act alone. This can have advantages, and theoretically could improve the quality of the group's contribution. For example, others may detect errors and provide immediate feedback to any individual in the group. On the other hand, the potential for being evaluated can also have an inhibiting effect, and working with others can cause evaluation apprehension, causing poorer performance and the generation of fewer or less creative ideas (Allport, 1924; Camacho & Paulus, 1995).

The potential for conflict and disagreement may exist as soon as a second person is added to the task. Further, the presence of at least three people in a group may make evaluation, conflict; and negotiation of positions even more likely, as the third person establishes majority and minority stances. Evaluation becomes especially important, as groups need to choose which information to consider and which opinion which to give more weight. A single person has only his or her own opinion. Multiple people need to consider other perspectives and determine which perspective is correct. Problem-solving studies have demonstrated that in unsuccessful groups, the minority positions are not attended to, or the opinion of the most talkative member is accepted (Maier & Solem, 1952; Thomas & Fink, 1961, 1963).

There is an additional level of social factors that can seriously impact the evaluative activity of a group. Perceptions of inequality in power, status, and knowledge about the topic all impact who contributes in a group and whose opinions are attended to in a discussion. Further, there is often a strong push toward conformity and avoidance of conflict in group settings, which can result in convergence on nonoptimal solutions, or *groupthink.*

Task Coordination

One person acting alone does not need to reflect on the task or the process for solution. A group must make these processes explicit. To the extent that the group fails to reach an understanding of the task, or a process for coordinating actions, there will be wasted effort and resources. However, the potential exists for the group to engage in more reflective and mindful problem representation than an individual (Moreland & Levine, 1992).

Studies have directly observed that some process loss occurs due to coordination difficulties by comparing intact groups (people who have worked together) with ad hoc groups (individuals put together for the first time). Ad hoc groups need some time together to get past organizational issues. When ad hoc groups are given an extended period of time, deficits go away (Anderson, 1961; Watson, 1928). On the other hand, intact groups have their own set of additional problems. Intact groups have coordination schemes in place, but may also have biases about which group members are usually the best source of information. In a classic study, Torrance (1954) nicely demonstrated that B-27 bomber teams disproportionately weighted the opinion of the pilot on problem-solving tasks completely unrelated to flying, even though that weighting was irrelevant in the new problem-solving context.

Use of Resources

One of the most obvious reasons for expecting two heads to be better than one is due to the ability of group members to pool resources. The group has the advantage of multiple frames with which to select relevant or important information to attend to, multiple long-term memory stores from which to retrieve relevant knowledge, and multiple buffers that may allow for more elaborate processing. The presence of collaborators increases the amount of information that can be brought to the table, increases the probability that any particular person will be aware of a critical piece of information, and increases the amount of information that can be considered simultaneously. Individuals can also prime others or remind them of relevant facts from long-term memory.

From an information processing approach, the presence of multiple perspectives, stores, and buffers should improve performance on complex learning tasks, which may tax the abilities of a single individual. However, this benefit from collaborators can only be the case when all people actually participate and freely share the unique perspective that they have. Unfortunately, studies from the social psychology literature suggest that this rarely happens (Hinsz, Tindale, & Vollrath, 1997; McGrath, 1984). Group members tend to offer more shared than unique information into discussion (Larson, Foster-Fishman & Keys, 1994; Stasser & Titus, 1985) and as noted briefly earlier, individuals with unique information are often ignored by the rest of the group. For the minority position to have an influence, the person needs to be confident, talkative, or able to demonstrate that his or her solution is correct, or there needs to be a leader who is responsible for making sure minority positions are heard (Hastie, 1986; Maier, 1967; Oxley, Dzindolet, & Paulus, 1996). Alternatively, expert roles can be assigned to encourage the sharing of unique information (Hollingshead, 1996; Stewart & Stasser, 1995). In these cases, role assignment can lead to some increases in group performance.

Even more discouraging are the most recent findings in this literature, which suggest that group work can actually increase the processing load on individuals. Interacting in groups increases the amount of information available immediately, but this means an increase in the amount of information that needs to be processed. Working with others adds information that needs to be attended to (individuals need to consider the task at hand, their own thoughts, and other people's thoughts and opinions). In addition, the individual has less time to state his or her own thoughts out loud, and others' contributions may interrupt the individual's own processing, knocking them off their train of thought. Further, more time may be spent on off-task topics (Dugosh, Paulus, Roland, & Yang, 2000). In the end, individuals may be more burdened and enjoy less intact cognitive processing than when working alone. Studies have directly tested this notion of interrupted cognitive processing among groups, which has been called production blocking and support an account of process loss as a function of increased disruption in group situations (Diehl & Stroebe, 1987; Stroebe & Diehl, 1994).

Thus, the social psychology literature has demonstrated that poorer group performance can result due to many possible factors. As a result of changes in motivation and effort, fear of evaluation, and coordination and communication burdens, groups are often observed to perform more poorly than individuals. However, the social group problem-solving literature has largely ignored classroom or educational contexts (e.g., Gigone & Hastie, 1997); the studies in this literature generally do not have authentic or naturalistic classroom tasks, and they tend to study short-lived interactions of ad hoc groups. Nevertheless, studies of group information processing have identified several ways in which working in groups may lead to losses in performance. As educational and cognitive researchers delve deeper into explaining successful collaborative learning, a valuable contribution may be made by addressing the factors that have been seen to cause process loss outside learning contexts, and discovering how successful learning environments may be circumventing these potential losses.

Educational Research on Collaborative Learning

Researchers in educational psychology have viewed collaborative learning from a number of perspectives. Through interaction with others, learners jointly construct or instantiate knowledge structures for themselves. Some theoretical advantages of working in groups are based in mechanisms of cognitive development, where learning is prompted by conflict with others (Perret-Clement, 1980; Piaget, 1932), internalization of social processes from working with others (Vygotsky, 1978), and modeling of or for others (Bandura, 1986; Brown & Palincsar, 1989). Other approaches hinge positive outcomes on the creation of interdependence among group members (Johnson & Johnson, 1989; Slavin, 1987). These perspectives have guided the design of collaborative learning environments that support interaction among peers.

Most collaborative learning studies that have demonstrated positive educational outcomes have investigated how better learning may result from different kinds of learning activities. Most often comparisons are between structured and unstructured collaborative learning, and advantages are found for supportive or structured collaboration. For example, Coleman (1998) investigated the development of student understanding of photosynthesis by either having students interact in scaffolded explanation groups, or in nonscaffolded groups. The scaffolding prompted students to give evidence, build on others' ideas and to try to understand others' positions. With these prompts, the scaffolded collaboration groups acquired a better understanding than the nonscaffolded groups. In another line of research, King (1990) found that instruction in reciprocal questioning strategies is more effective for learning than class discussion or reviewing material (see also Fantuzzo, Riggio, Connolly, & Dimeff, 1989).

Alternatively, researchers have looked at the interactions within small groups to determine what aspects of collaboration may actually contribute to learning gains. Studies in this vein include work by Webb, Troper, and Fall (1995), which find that student-generated explanations are related to better learning, both in the students who generate the explanations and in students who hear the explanations, as long as the hearers actually apply the explanation on their own after they hear it.

Only a few studies have directly compared learning or transfer of learned material among students learning in collaborative groups to individual learning using similarly structured tasks or environments. O'Donnell and Dansereau have been responsible for a number of studies in the literature that explore the effectiveness of interventions developed for collaborative learning settings, in both collaborative and individual learning contexts. Examples from their findings include that students who unexpectedly review a lesson in pairs perform better than individuals who reviewed alone, or dyads who expected to collaborate (O'Donnell & Dansereau, 1993). In another study, dyads learned more successfully when both students in a pair were simultaneously given a script (a learning organizer that scaffolded their activity), as opposed to individuals with or without scripts, and dyads who were not given scripts (O'Donnell, Dansereau, Hall, & Skaggs, 1990).

In a comparison of individual versus collaborative mathematical problem solving, Vye, Goldman, Voss, Hmelo, and Williams (1997) found that dyads explored more solution paths and had more coherent reasoning about the problem than did individual problem solvers. More recently, Barron (2000) found that collaborative problem solving among triads can also lead to improved mathematical problem solving. Triads outperformed individual problem solvers on an initial complex mathematical problem. More important, students who had collaborated on the initial problem then outperformed students who had worked individually on transfer problems. In general, the literature on collaborative learning tends to lack comparisons among individuals learning in a single context versus a matched collaborative context, and rarely are there tests of whether or not individual learners can transfer their learning to new material following the collaboration. The demonstrations just described are thus critical pieces of evidence that at least in some cases, collaborative learning contexts may be circumventing or capitalizing on the aspects of group interaction that might otherwise lead to losses.

Why So Little Process Loss in Studies of Collaborative Learning?

If we look for conditions that seem to maximize the potential of collaborative learning, we might expect process gain to be found in contexts that address the four areas of potential losses outlined previously: loss due to motivation, fear of evaluation, coordination, and communication burdens. Following from that logic, conditions that may make process gain most likely could be contexts that require the integrated effort of all members, contexts that provide a basis for evaluation, contexts that scaffold coordination and planning, and contexts that structure communication.

Motivation Through Interdependence

Several researchers have commented that successful collaboration directly depends on the extent to which the task can be completed without contributions of all the members (Steiner, 1972). In a similar vein, Hertz-Lazarowitz and Miller (1995) suggested that successful collaboration only occurs when the task requires the integration of the thinking of all members. Only on these interdependent tasks, where students must cooperate for the goal to be achieved, will all students be motivated to participate (Johnson & Johnson, 1989). It is these kinds of cooperative, collaborative tasks that are related to increases in student effort and drive, and that result in the findings that classrooms that employ more collaborative learning activities result in more student time on task and fewer absences (Slavin, 1987). Larson and Christensen (1993) also suggested the need for interdependence, true interaction, and complexity to see benefits. Tasks in the social psychology literature have rarely required this. The work of Johnson and Johnson (1989) suggests that studies in the social literature may be collapsing across cooperative and competitive groups. Only the former will promote better learning from groups.

Norms for Evaluation

Other research, such as the Coleman (1998) study described earlier, suggests that the potential for evaluation and conflict may only lead to higher levels of reasoning and learning when students are given norms for evaluation. When ground rules are set such that students must rely on a comparison of evidence as means to reconcile conflict, when they need to explain their position to others, and when they need to justify their opinions, only then might we find better learning in group contexts. Once these ground rules are established, then the generated questions, explanations, and proofs may provide important models for students to emulate and internalize.

Better Task Representation

Similarly, the need to discuss the task with others can also support better
task definition, goal setting, and planning activities. When students are put
in contexts with specific tasks, it may help them to plan their problem solving or learning, and they may get past coordination problems faster. Finally, contexts that structure interaction, and especially tasks that focus
learners on important information, and encourage the contribution of prior
knowledge and unique perspectives, will be important for effective group
activity.

Supporting Collaborative Learning with Argumentation Tasks

Fulfilling these conditions may be the mechanism by which successful
learning contexts can achieve performance gains from collaborative learning. This study will investigate whether positive outcomes in collaborative
learning studies may be seen in educational contexts with several key elements: when small groups are given a specific learning task that requires
full participation, provides norms for evaluation, and channels attention
toward important information and communication toward explanatory behaviors.

The learning task that we think may fulfill these demands is an argumentation task. As such, this study investigates the effects of collaboration
in the context of an argument writing task from multiple sources. In previous studies, it has been demonstrated that argumentation is a task that supports better understanding in students working alone (Wiley, 2001; Wiley &
Voss, 1996, 1999). In these studies, learners were provided with several
texts about a topic, presented in a Web site, and were asked to construct an
argument of "What produced the significant changes in Ireland's population
between 1846 and 1850?" or "What produced the eruption of Mt. St. Helens
in 1981?" When students were given an argument writing instruction, as
opposed to a narrative writing or essay writing instruction, they wrote more
causal and integrated essays, and performed better on outcome measures
such as inference and analogy recognition tests, suggesting that argument
writing led to better understanding of the subject matter. The advantage
was especially pronounced when students learned from multiple sources,
presented in a Web site, than when they learned from a single text. When
students were put in a browser environment that explicitly supported the
comparison and integration of multiple documents, and were given an argumentation task that also prompted integrative and constructive activity,
they demonstrated better conceptual understanding of the texts as compared
to more traditional textbook learning conditions (Wiley, 2001; Wiley &
Voss, 1999).

There are several reasons why argumentation itself may be a powerful learning instruction (Voss & Wiley, 2000). Implicitly, the instruction to construct an argument may require that students develop their own personal thesis or theory. Additionally, students may also perceive the argument instruction as constructing an account that includes evidence to support or justify a position (as in the sense of a legal argument). The term *argument* may imply that a position needs to be defended to others, and may cause the learner to represent an external discourse. A final reason why the argument writing task may be especially powerful is that in supporting a thesis, the learner must transform the presented information, and integrate it into a new coherent explanatory structure to fulfill the argument writing task. Especially the act of finding new connections across texts, to justify and explain in an argumentation task, may be critical for the better understanding achieved in this context (Wiley & Voss, 1999).

In many respects, the ways that argumentation tasks promote understanding appear similar to notions of how collaborative tasks are thought to facilitate learning. Further, it seems that argumentation tasks may be effective in collaborative learning contexts for reasons over and above the reasons why they may help individual learning. As a task, argumentation tasks may motivate learners by seeming to be personally relevant. Both learners may have an investment in developing an argument that they agree with. Second, argumentation may provide collaborative learners with an evaluation structure that may help them avoid many of the pitfalls of group problem solving. Giving groups a task that explicitly prompts the generation of hypotheses, and the need to support and justify those hypotheses may attenuate many issues of evaluation. Evaluation no longer runs as big of a risk of being personal or alienating as it is in the best interest of all students to espouse a position that can be supported by evidence. Further, the use of claims and evidence can make solutions demonstrable or thinking observable to other students. This not only helps modeling, but is also consistent with the notion that groups are more effective when solutions can be demonstrated as correct. Third, argumentation is a specific task that can be reflected on and planned for. Students may be more likely to engage in planning activities with a specific task than with a vague one that may be fulfilled by any product. Finally, the argumentation task can be used to structure interaction or communication by keeping students focused on explanatory activity (attending to important information in the text, and using it to construct an explanation). Thus, the use of an argumentation task may not just reinforce the strengths of collaborative learning; a task like argumentation may in fact be necessary to reap the benefits of working in groups. In line with this perspective, it seems particularly fitting that Webb and Palincsar (1996) suggested that there is heightened interest among the collaborative learning community in situations that require elaboration, interpretation, explanation, and argumentation. These processes may specifically fulfill the needs of collaborative learners as information processors, and allow them to support each other rather than impede each other's learning.

The Present Study

Pairs of learners were observed as they navigated through Web sites related to volcanic eruptions, to write a summary or an argument of "What caused the eruption of Mt. St. Helens?" Pairs were asked to jointly compose the essay. Following the reading and writing phase, all students individually completed two learning outcome measures: an inference verification task and an analogy rating task that required the recognition of similar and dissimilar geological events.

The main questions of interest are these: What do successful collaborative learners do as they complete the reading and writing tasks? Does argumentation lead to better collaborative learning? If so, what behaviors can we identify among collaborative arguers that may be responsible for supporting understanding? To assess whether collaboration is impacting motivation, we look at time on task across conditions, and number of utterances. We also look at the perceived interdependence of the group, by looking at the number of questions they ask each other. To examine the extent of evaluative activity among pairs, we look at whether conflict occurs, whether students evaluate the sources or each other, and whether they evaluate their own understanding. In terms of coordination of activity, we look at whether time is spent explicitly planning, discussing, or coordinating the execution of the reading and writing tasks. Finally, to examine communication-related effects, we examine how much information is exchanged, and what kind of information is stated in each condition.

Although the study as presented is exploratory, it is hoped that the interaction of collaborative and argumentative task environments may provide for better understanding of the subject matter, and the goal is to be in a position to describe in detail behaviors and patterns of interactions that may be contributing to success in this learning context.

METHOD

Participants

Four pairs of undergraduates participated in this study. The undergraduates were recruited from the University of Illinois at Chicago participant pool and received course credit for their participation. Pairs were not familiar with each other before engaging in this task. Two pairs were given each writing task. Of the two pairs given the summary writing task, one had two men and the other had two women. Both pairs given the argument task had one man and one woman. This is an unfortunate chance occurrence, and it should be noted that any differences in group dynamics between the two conditions could be attributed to the differences in dyad composition.

Materials

The reading material for this study was made to mimic the output of a Google search using these keywords: causes volcanic eruptions. There were two output pages, each with links to five Web sites. On the first page, the sources listed were a NASA page on volcanoes; an astrology site "Blast from the Past" on how Mt. St. Helens erupted because of the alignment of planets; a United States Geological Survey site on earthquakes, volcanoes, and plate tectonics; a *Scientific American* site where an expert explains the causes of volcanic eruptions; and a page from Vocanolive.com on how tides relate to eruptions. The second Google search page had links to five more sources: a commercial site for the Iben Browning Newsletter, written by a consultant who predicts earthquakes and volcanic eruptions; a PBS site for the series *Savage Earth*; a PBS site on plate tectonics for the series *A Science Odyssey*; a commercial site for the Cook Internal Propulsion Engine that claims that oil drilling is the cause of earthquakes and volcanic eruptions; and a site from CPB/Annenberg on volcanoes. Most sites contained many pages. The amount of information potentially available to the students was intentionally more than could be read in an hour. This was meant to necessitate decision making and negotiation among the pairs, as well as increase the chances of finding an advantage for multiple learners, because there was clearly more information than a single information processor could handle. The inclusion of a range of sources that varied in their reliability was also intentional, and was intended to prompt evaluative comments on the part of the learners.

Procedure

Participants were tested in pairs in front of a single computer. The experimenter was present in the room for the entire session. Sessions lasted 1 hour. On arrival, students were informed of the video recording and signed a consent form. They were then each given a pretest and told to complete the five short-answer questions to the best of their ability (e.g., What is a volcano? Why do volcanoes occur?). They were then told that they would be writing either an argument or a summary about the cause of the eruption of Mt. St. Helens. To help them with their task, we told them that we had done a Google search for them using the keywords of causes volcanic eruptions. The results of the search were on the screen in front of them and consisted of two pages of output with a total of 10 links that they could use to write their essay. They were also told that they were to work together on this task and that they would have around 30 minutes to both read the web pages and write their essay. They were given paper to write their essay and extra paper to take notes if they wanted. The experimenter stayed in the room and took notes as they worked. With 10 minutes left, the experimenter encouraged them to finish their essay. On completion, the video camera was turned off and they completed a posttest booklet individually and without the computer.

The posttest booklets consisted of three parts: the inference task, the analogy task, and the final survey page. The inference task consisted of 25 items. Five items were distractors that were not explicitly addressed in the reading material. Ten items were directly related to central concepts in the reading. The remaining 10 items were related to less central details in the texts.

The analogy task required students to judge the similarity of several short scenarios describing potentially analogous events. The task consisted of five items. Students were asked to rate the similarity of the cause of each event to the cause of the Mt. St. Helens eruption on a 10-point scale with 10 meaning *very similar*. The first item was a practice item on Hawaiian volcanoes. Two items concerned events that were not causally similar to the Mt. St. Helens eruption: California wildfires and the New Madrid, Missouri, earthquakes. These items are included in the dissimilar events rating measure later. Low scores on these items indicate understanding. Two items concerned causally similar events: the Kobe earthquake and the eruption of Mt. Pinatubo. These items are included in the similar events rating measure later. Higher scores on this measure indicate understanding. Finally, a discrimination index was computed by subtracting the average rating for dissimilar items from the average rating for similar items. Higher positive scores represent better discrimination of similarity.

The last page of the booklet was used to gather other information regarding the participants. Descriptive information included their age, gender, and intended major. They were also asked to define an argument and a summary, what the major difference was between them, and whether or not they liked learning with a partner and why.

Coding

Several categories were established a priori based on the literature and our predictions. We were interested in the number of utterances, number of questions (regardless of content), number of interactions, number of evaluative statements, number of planning-related statements, and kind of information shared. In reviewing our protocols, we operationalized these categories and developed the detailed coding scheme for each utterance pre-

sented in Table 12.1. Two independent raters coded all four protocols with
category agreement on 89% of utterances.

TABLE 12.1

Coding Categories

Code	Name	Definition	Example
U	Propositional utterance units	Each utterance broken into propositions	
Q	Questions	Questions double-coded with categories	The planets caused the volcano? Ready for page 2?
P	Polite expressions	Turn-taking prompts, clarifications, or acknowledgments	Are you done reading? Yeah.
O	Off-task behavior	Anything not related to reading or writing	That's real good for my self-esteem.
E	Evaluation	Value judgments	This stuff is just garbage. It's not telling us why...
M	Metacognition	Assessment of understanding	I'm not sure I get this. Do you understand this?
R	Planning of reading	Comment on reading goals or process	I don't think we have to read that.
T	Comment about writing task	Comment on task process or demands	I think this is long enough.
W	Comment about content	Suggestion of content for writing	I guess we need to lead into this subduction part.
C	Claim	A theory or summary statement of a claim	The planets caused the volcano? It's how every volcano erupts. This guy's talking about Turkey...
S	Evidence from source	Statement of a piece of information	A 5.1 earthquake opened a vent.
K	Evidence from knowledge	Statement of a piece of knowledge	I think I remember this.

RESULTS

Prior Knowledge Assessment

The prior knowledge of each participant was assessed individually in a pretest with these five questions: What is a volcano? Why do volcanoes occur? How do volcanoes erupt? Where are volcanoes located? What kinds of volcanoes are there? The conceptual model possessed by each student was categorized using the answer to these questions and a taxonomy of volcanic understanding developed by Hemmerich and Wiley (2002). Incorrect models of volcanic eruptions, such as that they are caused by the weather or gods, are coded as Level 0. Partially correct models that only include a single local cause, of either plate movement, heat flows, or pressurized magma, are coded as Level 1. Models that contain more than one correct cause are coded as Level 2. A model that integrates plate movement with heat or pressure factors represents a mature understanding of volcanic activity and is coded as Level 3. Of our four pairs, one pair in each condition had no prior understanding of volcanoes (i.e., both members started at Level 0). The other two pairs each had one member with some understanding of the role of earth movement or plate tectonics (at Level 1), and the other member with a Level 0 understanding. Thus, in some sense, our pairs were matched for prior conceptual understanding about volcanoes.

Essay-Based Pair Learning Outcomes

The essays that the students wrote together were again coded in relation to the taxonomy of volcanic understanding. In their essay, Pair 1 asserted that the alignment of the planets caused the eruption of Mt. St. Helens. This is an incorrect model, and was coded as Level 0. Pair 2 wrote in their essay that Mt. St. Helens erupted because the plates at Mt. St. Helens crunched together, that plates move because of heat flow, and that an earthquake opened a vent that caused the eruption of pent up gases and magma. Thus in their essay, they recognized the relation between plate movement and heat flow, and that these two factors and pressure relate to volcanic eruptions. Because the explanations of plate movement and heat flow are integrated, the essay is coded as demonstrating a Level 3 model of volcanic activity. This is a more complex model than either participant held before the learning activity. Pair 3 wrote in their essay that plate tectonics causes rifts and ridges in the Earth's crust. They also asserted that volcanoes are formed when hot rocks move and fill chambers in the Earth's crust. This is a model that contains both elements of movement and heat, but because the heat is not directly related to the movement of plates or to the melting of the plate, it is coded as a Level 2 model. The final pair, Pair 4, wrote an essay that included the ideas that plate movements cause the formation of magma in subduction zones, and that this magma is especially stiff, which leads to the tremendous buildup of internal gases. By mentioning both plate movement and pressure, and linking them through the formation of viscous magma, these students created an integrated model of volcanic activity, and the essay is coded as Level 3. Unfortunately, the students then went on to say that "another contribution to volcanic eruptions is the drilling of too much oil." This pet theory of the inventor of a perpetual motion engine gets assimilated into an otherwise good account of the causes of the eruption of Mt. St. Helens.

Individual Learning Outcomes

To assess the amount of learning in each partner as a result of the reading and writing tasks, we examined each student's individual performance on inference and event similarity posttests. Average performance was better on the inference and the dissimilar events rating task for pairs who had an argument task than pairs who had a summary task. As presented in Table 12.2, the outcome measures were more systematic in the argument condition than in the summary condition. Students in the argument condition tended to recognize more critical inferences ($M = 6.75$, $SD = .75$) than students in the summary condition ($M = 4.5$, $SD = 2.08$). No differences were seen in the Similar Event ratings (Argument $M = 5.13$, $SD = .85$; Summary $M = 4.75$, SD 1.19). However, the argument participants were more likely to recognize the dissimilarity of the two scenarios ($M = 3.25$, $SD = 1.5$) than were participants in the summary condition ($M = 5.75$, $SD = 1.5$). They also had better discrimination between similar and dissimilar events. These data suggest generally positive learning outcomes in the argument condition, but also for one pair in the summary condition. The question of interest is whether we can observe any discourse patterns that may be related to the development of understanding, which in turn could support better learning.

Dialogue-Based Analyses

To answer these questions, we coded the interactions of the pairs as they read and wrote their essays. The results of our protocol analysis are presented in Table 12.3. There was very little off-task behavior in the protocols, so this category is not included. No one spoke about the weather or classes or anything outside the task. Although this is quite a small sample, there are a few patterns in the data that can be identified. In general, the two pairs in the argumentation condition seemed to interact more than the summary pairs. Both argumentation pairs had a high number of total utterances, asked a good number of questions, and made many polite remarks. More important, the three dyads (Pairs 2, 3, and 4) that showed positive learning outcomes all spent more time talking specifically about essay content and negotiating the writing process than did the nonlearning pair (Pair 1).

TABLE 12.2

Learning Outcomes by Pair and Individual

Task	Summary				Argument			
Pair	1		2		3		4	
Student	1	2	3	4	5	6	7	8
Sex	F	F	M	M	M	F	F	M
Pretest score	0	0	0	1	1	0	0	0
Essay score	0	0	3	3	2	2	3	3
Inference score	4	7	2	5	8	7	6	6
Similar event rating	5	3	5.5	5.5	5.5	5	6	4
Dissimilar event rating	7	5	7	4	1	3.5	4	4.5
Discrimination score	-2	-2	-1.5	1.5	4.5	1.5	2	-.5

These preliminary results suggest that collaborative learning will be most successful when students interact well and negotiate their understanding of the bject matter. When learning partners do not engage each other, then an opportunity may be lost. This comparison suggests that argumentation tasks may support collaborative learning through providing students with a specific task and medium for interaction about the task and content. More successful groups, regardless of the writing task, engaged in more coordination of understanding about the topic. Interestingly, there were not a large number of evaluative statements in either writing condition, and those that were made did not seem to contribute much to learning (this was true considering the number of evaluations made by either member of the pair). Hence, it does not seem that the argumentation task necessarily promotes better evaluation of content.

In addition to these attempts to code and quantify the interactions among the pairs, examples of the actual dialogue better illustrate the dynamics of each dyad. For example, here is an exchange from Pair 1:

Betty reads from NASA site: Quieter volcanoes, like Iceland and Hawaii, are found mostly where plates are coming apart or in the middle of a plate.
Veronica: Go on to the next one.
(Goes to Blast From the Past astrology site).
Betty reads from site "Earthquakes and volcanoes have long been associated with planets."

This exchange is typical of the interaction between these two women. When they did speak, they were reading information from the site to each other. They did not negotiate either the writing of the essay or their understanding of the material. Here is an example of Pair 2:

Archie (clicks on *A Science Odyssey* Web site): Let's just check on these other ones really fast and see what they are.
Ralph: Yeah, so this says the movement of plates is what causes earthquakes and volcanoes and you could maybe write this down—what causes plates to move is unknown. Let me write. Okay, one theory is heat convection from the earth's inner core.
Archie: Okay.

In this pair, the second man (Ralph) takes the lead, produces almost all the claims and text on his own, and eventually takes over the actual writing. There is limited discussion, however, about the subject matter and content of the essay. In the next example, Pair 3 engages in more negotiation:

Frank: OK, Here we go (points at PBS site). Hot mantle rises up from the mantle and triggered the weak parts of the crust within the interior of the continental plate. Yeah, that's good.
Alice winces.
Frank: You don't think so?
Alice: Yeah, hold on a second, hot mantle material.
Frank: Let's go back to the first page. That was the best one.

The man in this pair takes the lead. He produces most of the claims himself, but also involves his partner with questions, and gives her an opportunity to make responses. He also makes a number of evaluative comments about the sources. Here is an example of the interaction of the final pair, Pair 4:

Rick: Alright, the first one is like because of plate tectonics.
Lucy: Want me to go back to that one? Rick: Yes, I know how to describe it so basically the continental disturbance and the ocean floor are elements that cause earthquakes and stuff like that and lava and pressure build up.
Lucy: So it causes disturbance and that makes the magma?
Rick: Yeah, that thing right there leads into this, about subduction.

This pair has the most even production of writing content and claims. They question each other, they evaluate the sources, and they strategically plan their reading to a greater extent than the other pairs.

TABLE 12.3

Number of Discourse Moves by Each Pair and Partner

Task	Summary				Argument			
Pair	1		2		3		4	
Student	1	2	3	4	5	6	7	8
Total utterances	18	18	19	64	49	26	40	67
Total questions	0	3	6	6	14	4	10	11
Total polite expressions	1	5	3	9	17	19	15	4
Evaluative remarks	3	1	0	4	6	1	5	17
Metacognitive remarks	2	2	2	3	1	0	0	1
Planning of reading	3	2	3	8	2	2	5	10
Planning of task	0	0	3	5	4	0	1	5
Negotiation of content	0	1	3	13	9	2	4	10
Claims	3	2	4	14	3	2	8	16
Evidence from text	6	4	1	5	5	0	1	2
Evidence from knowledge	0	1	0	3	0	0	1	2

Reading Time on Reliable and Unreliable Sources

Another interesting variable to examine is the time spent reading the different sources across pairs. The sources were divided into reliable (credible authorities with accounts of volcanic activity that converged on plate tectonic theory) and unreliable (commercial or personal sites) sources. Pairs in the argument condition did tend to spend more time on reliable sources (M = 1417 seconds, SD = 30) than pairs in the summary condition (M = 982 seconds, SD = 356). However, on average, pairs in both conditions spent a similar amount of time on unreliable sources (argument M = 587.5, summary M = 597). These reading time results suggest that the argument task may be prompting students to spend a larger amount of time on relevant information than they would otherwise, but it is not generally improving the ability to discriminate and disregard irrelevant accounts.

Absence of Behaviors

Finally, it is interesting to note what behaviors were not observed in our pairs. In these protocols there was an absence of criticism of others' statements, no direct conflict, no direct comparison of theories and evidence, and few attempts to develop coherent and sufficient models of volcanic activity. It is perhaps this lack of deeper evaluation of evidence and theories that relates to the overassimilation and inclusion of causes that we saw in all four essays. Even our best collaborating pair (Pair 4) considered unreliable information (the sources on astrology, the tides, and oil drilling) and no student directly questioned the reliability of these sources, or how these explanations fit with the other theories they were reading. Finally, there were few references to prior knowledge, which a student might have used as a source of evidence. Almost all of the evidence that was considered was from the text that the students had in front of them.

GENERAL DISCUSSION

This line of research has been concerned with investigating the kinds of learning contexts that may promote the best understanding when learning from technology, such as web pages. At least at first blush, the results of this study suggest that argumentation tasks may be a promising design element for collaborative learning environments. A related area that we can draw our attention to is how we may use the technology more interactively to further support collaborative learning. In the introduction, we suggested that the critical features of successful collaborative learning contexts could be that they maximize participation, interaction, and investment of all individuals; provide a grounds for evaluation that makes criticism less personal; give students the tools by which to accept or reject ideas as they attempt to supporting a thesis or interpretation; and help students to focus on relevant and reliable information. The exploratory study included here seems to support some of these notions, and specifically that argumentation tasks may in particular prompt more interaction and co-construction of understanding. Interestingly, in these dyads, an argumentation task did not seem to prompt more extensive evaluation of the reliability of sources, or more critical evaluation of claims or evidence. In turn, these may be prime candidates for direct instruction or prompting within a technology-supported collaborative learning environment. Technology can contribute perhaps by playing an interventionist role, such as by promoting recognition of conflict, or by forcing justification or explicit discrimination between theories.

These results are consistent with some findings in the social psychology literature that suggest that triads and not dyads may be the optimal size group for collaborative learning and problem solving (Steiner, 1972). Although the small size of a dyad is beneficial for maintaining motivation and participation, pairs tend to avoid conflict. For many reasons, differences in two-person groups tend to be glossed over rather than addressed head on. Triads, on the other hand, afford conflict by their number, and any difference in opinion leads to majority and minority positions, which in turn requires each member to evaluate those positions. Hence, one potentially advantageous role that a computer might play is as a third member of a triad. This may be better than a human triad, as the computer can assume the role of critic, push minority positions, and prompt evaluation and justification. At the same time, the computer partner will not monopolize the conversation, or read aloud while the partners are trying to think, or perhaps lessen the motivation of the two human participants. In preserving the inherent advantages of human and peer interaction, a human pair interacting with a computer may have advantages over models of a computer as learning partner where a single student is paired with a computer interface.

In this study, the students did not seem to take advantage of their partner as a catalyst for active evaluation of the available evidence. We do not know if there was anything about the dyad learning context that might have made either member of the pair less likely to achieve an understanding. The possibility remains that interacting in groups can make learning more difficult due to interruptions in each member's thought process. To the extent that this is true, then there are other ways in which technology may improve collaborative learning, as there are several areas in which virtual collaboration may supercede face-to-face settings. Within an educational context, Linn and Hsi (2000) showed that locating student discussions in online chat groups allows all members to contribute more. Similarly, there is a parallel electronic brainstorming literature that has demonstrated some advantages for virtual groups over face-to-face collaboration (Gallupe, Cooper, Grise, & Bastianutti, 1994; Valacich, Dennis, & Connolly, 1994). For example, Paulus and Yang (2000) found that putting brainstorming sessions online minimizes the interruptive effects of others comments, but still allows for members to prime ideas and facilitate the cognition of others. These electronic methods of supporting participation so that each student has the ability to pursue his or her line of thought, while still contributing to a discussion, seem promising. On the other hand, attempts at structuring online dialogue have yet to result in learning gains (Hron, Hesse, Cress, & Giovis, 2000). Further, the effects of virtual collaboration are also likely to be highly specific to context. In direct opposition to Paulus and Yang's (2002) results, Straus and McGrath (1994) found that virtual groups can be less productive than face-to-face groups. As a result, although the use of technology to support collaborative learning is certainly a promising area of study, there is much work to be done before we can definitively assert which contexts may lead to effective group performance, what contexts should be supported with technology, and what allows group members to learn more successfully than they would alone.

ACKNOWLEDGMENTS

This research was supported by grants to the first author from the Office of Naval Research and the National Science Foundation. We thank Ivan Ash and Cara Jolly for their assistance with this project.

REFERENCES

Allport, F. H. (1920). The influence of the group upon association and thought. *Journal of Experimental Psychology, 3,* 159–182.

Allport, F. H. (1924). *Social psychology.* Boston: Houghton.

Anderson, N. (1961). Group performance in an anagram task. *Journal of Social Psychology, 55,* 67–75.

Bandura, A. (1986). *Social foundations of thought and action: A social cognitive theory.* Upper Saddle River, NJ: Prentice Hall.

Barron, B. (2000). Achieving coordination in collaborative problem-solving groups. *Journal of the Learning Sciences, 9,* 403–436.

Brown, A. L., & Palincsar, A. S. (1989). Guided, cooperative learning and individual knowledge acquisition. In L. B. Resnick (Ed.); *Knowing, learning, and instruction: Essays in honor of Robert Glaser* (pp. 393–451). Hillsdale, NJ: Lawrence Erlbaum Associates.

Camacho, L. M., & Paulus, P. B. (1995). The role of social anxiousness in group brainstorming. *Journal of Personality & Social Psychology, 68,* 1071–1080.

Coleman, E. B. (1998). Using explanatory knowledge during collaborative problem solving in science. *Journal of the Learning Sciences, 7,* 387–427.

Diehl, M., & Stroebe, W. (1987). Productivity loss in brainstorming
    groups: Toward the solution of a riddle. *Journal of Personality &
    Social Psychology; 53*, 497–509.
Dugosh, K. L., Paulus, P. B., Roland, E. J., & Yang, H. (2000). Cognitive
    stimulation in brainstorming. *Journal of Personality & Social Psy-
    chology, 79*, 722–735.
Fantuzzo, J. W., Riggio, R. E., Connolly, S., & Dimeff, L. A. (1989). Ef-
    fects of reciprocal peer tutoring on academic achievement and
    psychological adjustment: A component analysis. *Journal of Edu-
    cational Psychology, 81*, 173–177.
Gallupe, R. B., Cooper, W. H., Grise, M., & Bastianutti, L. M. (1994).
    Blocking electronic brainstorms. *Journal of Applied Psychology,
    79*, 77–86.
Gigone, D. & Hastie, R. (1997). Proper analysis in the accuracy of group
    judgments. *Psychological Bulletin, 121*, 149–167.
Hastie, R. (1986). Review essay: Experimental evidence on group accu-
    racy. In G. Owen & B. Grofman (Eds.), *Information pooling and
    group decision making* (pp. 129–157). Westport CT: JAI.
Hemmerich, J., & Wiley, J. (2002). Do argumentation tasks promote con-
    ceptual change about volcanoes? In *Proceedings of the
    Twenty-Fourth Annual Conference of the Cognitive Science Soci-
    ety* (pp. 453-458). Mahwah, NJ: Lawrence Erlbaum Associates.
Hertz-Lazarowitz, R., & Miller, N. (1995). *Interaction in cooperative
    groups: The theoretical anatomy of group learning.* New York:
    Cambridge University Press.
Hill, G. W. (1982). Group versus individual performance: Are N+1 heads
    better than one? *Psychological Bulletin, 91*, 517-539.
Hinsz, V. B., Tindale, R. S., & Vollrath, D. A. (1997). The emerging con-
    ceptualization of groups as information processors. *Psychological
    Bulletin, 121*, 43–64.
Hollingshead, A. B. (1996). The rank-order effect in group decision mak-
    ing. *Organizational Behavior & Human Decision Processes, 68*,
    181–193.
Hron, A., Hesse, F. W., Cress, U., & Giovis, C. (2000). Implicit and explicit
    dialogue structuring in virtual learning groups. *British Journal of
    Educational Psychology, 70*, 53–64.
Johnson, D. W., & Johnson, R. T. (1989). *Cooperation and competition:
    Theory and research.* Edina, MN: Interaction Book Company.
Kerr, H., & Bruun, S. (1983). The dispensability of member effort and
    group motivation losses: Free-rider effects. *Journal of Personality
    and Social Psychology, 37*, 822–832.
King, A. (1990). Enhancing peer interaction and learning in the classroom
    through reciprocal questioning. *American Educational Research
    Journal, 24*, 664–687.

Larson, J. R., & Christensen, C. (1993). Groups as problem-solving units: Toward a new meaning of social cognition. *British Journal of Social Psychology, 32,* 5–30.

Larson, J. R., Foster-Fishman, P. G., & Keys, C. B. (1994). Discussion of shared and unshared information in decision-making groups. *Journal of Personality & Social Psychology, 67,* 446–461.

Linn, M. C., & Hsi, S. (2000). *Computers, teachers, peers: Science learning partners.* Mahwah, NJ: Lawrence Erlbaum Associates.

Maier, N. R. F. (1967). Assets and liabilities in group problem solving: The need for an integrative function. *Psychological Review, 74,* 239–249.

Maier, N. R. F. & Solem, A. R. (1952). The contribution of a discussion leader to the quality of group thinking. *Human Relations, 5,* 277–288.

McGrath, J. E. (1984). *Groups: Interaction and performance.* Englewood Cliffs, NJ: Prentice Hall.

Moreland, R. L., & Levine, J. M. (1992). Problem identification by groups. In S. Worchel Wood & J. A. Simpson (Eds.), *Group processes and productivity* (pp. 17–47). Newbury Park, CA: Sage.

Mullen, B., Johnson, C., & Salas, E. (1991). Productivity loss in brainstorming groups: A meta-analytic integration. *Basic and Applied Social Psychology, 12,* 3–23.

O'Donnell, A., & Dansereau, D. F. (1993). Learning from lectures: Effects of cooperative review. *Journal of Experimental Education, 61,* 116–125.

O'Donnell, A. M., Dansereau, D. F., Hall, R. H., & Skaggs, L. P. (1990). Learning concrete procedures: Effects of processing strategies and cooperative learning. *Journal of Educational Psychology, 82,* 171–177.

Oxley, N. L., Dzindolet, M. T., & Paulus, P. B. (1996). The effects of facilitators on the performance of brainstorming groups. *Journal of Social Behavior & Personality, 11,* 633–646.

Paulus, P. B., & Yang, H. (2000). Idea generation in groups: A basis for creativity in organizations. *Organizational Behavior & Human Decision Processes, 82,* 76–87.

Perret-Clement, A. N. (1980). *Social interaction and cognitive development in children.* New York: Academic.

Piaget, J. (1932). *The language and thought of the child.* London: Routledge & Kegan Paul.

Ringelmann, M. (1913). Recherches sur les moteurs animes: Travail de l'homme [Research on animate sources of power: The work of man] *Annales de l'institut National Agronomique, 12,* 1–40.

Sheppard, J. A. (1993). Productivity loss in performance groups: A motivation analysis. *Psychological Bulletin, 113,* 67–81.

Slavin, R. E. (1987). Developmental and motivational perspectives on co-operative learning: A reconciliation. *Child Development, 58,* 1161–1167.

Stasser, G., & Titus, W. (1985). Effects of information load and percentage of shared information on the dissemination of unshared information during group discussion. *Journal of Personality & Social Psychology, 53,* 81–93.

Steiner, I. D. (1972). *Group processes and productivity.* New York: Academic.

Stewart, D. D., & Stasser, G. (1995). Expert role assignment and information sampling during collective recall and decision making. *Journal of Personality & Social Psychology, 69,* 619–628.

Straus, S. G., & McGrath, J. E. (1994). Does the medium matter? The interaction of task type and technology on group performance and member reactions. *Journal of Applied Psychology, 79,* 87–97.

Stroebe, W., & Diehl, M. (1994). Why groups are less effective than their members: On productivity losses in idea-generating groups. *European Review of Social Psychology, 5,* 271–303.

Taylor, D. W., Berry, P. C., & Block, C. H. (1958). Does group participation when using brain storming facilitate or inhibit creative thinking? *Administrative Science Quarterly, 3,* 23–47.

Thomas, E. J., & Fink, C. F. (1961). Models of group problem solving. *Journal of Abnormal & Social Psychology, 63,* 53–63.

Thomas, E. J., & Fink, C. F. (1963). Effects of group size. *Psychological Bulletin, 60,* 371–384.

Torrance, E. P. (1954). Some consequences of power differences on decision making in permanent and temporary three man groups. *Research Studies, State College of Washington, 22,* 130–144.

Triplett, N. (1898). The dynamogenic factors in pacemaking and competition. *American Journal of Psychology, 9,* 507–533.

Valacich, J. S., Dennis, A. R., & Connolly, T. (1994). Idea generation in computer-based groups: A new ending to an old story. *Organizational Behavior and Human Decision Processes, 57,* 448–467.

Voss, J. F., & Wiley, J. (2000). A case study of understanding in history. In P. Stearns, S. Wineburg, & P. Seixas (Eds.), *Knowing, teaching and learning in history,* (pp. 375–389). New York: NYU Press.

Vye, N. J., Goldman, S. R., Voss, J. F., Hmelo, C., & Williams, S. (1997). Complex mathematical problem solving by individuals and dyads. *Cognition & Instruction, 15,* 435–484.

Vygotsky, L. S. (1978). *Mind in society: The development of higher psychological processes.* Cambridge, MA: Harvard University Press.

Watson, G. B. (1928). Do groups think more efficiently than individuals? *Journal of Abnormal and Social Psychology, 23,* 328–336.

Webb, N. M., & Palincsar, A. S. (1996). Group processes in the classroom. In D. C Berliner & R. Calfee (Eds.), *Handbook of educational psychology* (pp. 841–873). New York: Macmillan Library Reference.

Webb, N. M., Troper, J. D., & Fall, R. (1995). Constructive activity and learning in collaborative small groups. *Journal of Educational Psychology, 8*, 406–423.

Wiley, J. (2001). Supporting understanding through task and browser design. *Proceedings of the Twenty-Third Annual Conference of the Cognitive Science Society* (pp. 1136-1143). Mahwah, NJ: Lawrence Erlbaum Associates.

Wiley, J., & Voss, J. F. (1996). The effects of "playing" historian on learning in history. *Applied Cognitive Psychology, 10,* 63–72.

Wiley, J., & Voss, J. F. (1999). Constructing arguments from multiple sources: Tasks that promote understanding and not just memory for text. *Journal of Educational Psychology, 91*, 301–311.

Chapter 13

Collaborative Learning through Electronic Knowledge Construction in Academic Education

Arja Veerman
TNO-Human Factors, Soesterberg, The Netherlands

Else Veldhuis-Diermanse
Wageningen University, Wageningen The Netherlands

In this chapter, we assess collaborative learning facilitated by computer-mediated communication (CMC) systems in academic education. We examine collaborative learning as a process of knowledge construction. We present four studies that all took place as part of an academic course, in which students had to work collaboratively on complex tasks by the use of a CMC system. The four studies involved different tasks, students, tutors, and CMC systems. In each study, we analyzed how students constructed knowledge together and we related these findings to some main factors in the educational context: the role of the student, peer-student, tutor, or moderator, and characteristics of the CMC systems used. The results showed that effective use of educational technology to support collaborative learning in academic education relates to these factors, including the modes of communication in asynchronous and synchronous CMC systems. It was indicated that asynchronous media provide student groups with more options to think and reflect on information, to organize and keep track of discussions, and to engage in large-group discussions compared to synchronous media. In addition, a clear need was shown for more transparent and user-friendly CMC systems.

The use of Internet and network-based computer systems for educational purposes is "hot." Each self-respecting educational institute provides at least a Web site full of information about their educational institute, program, and activities. A move forward is the delivery of complete studies and courses through the Internet. This presumes that learning materials are digitized and structured in such a way that students can have easy access, use, and guidance. However, advantages of independence of time and place are not enough and do not lead automatically to better education. Many times, new wine is put into old bottles. Possible affordances such as the flexibility of information exchange, storage, multiple representations, increased accessibility, and various forms of electronic communication are not yet fully exploited to enhance students' academic learning (Andriessen & Veerman, 1999).

The question is how electronic environments can be effectively used to enhance education and learning. Although it is impossible to answer this question in a straightforward manner, one thing is clear: To implement thoughtlessly as much computer technology as possible can be compared with Californian day hikers who have to carry a complete outfit to survive a winter in Alaska. Although the water belt is essential and a compass is always nice to play with, the rest can only lead to a sore back, a lot of sweat, and many delays. Thus, the issue is to think about the goals first and then identify and arrange suitable equipment.

In this chapter, we work from a constructivist[1] view on learning. From this perspective, it is important to use a student-centered approach in which students' initiatives and activities are stimulated as well as collaboration processes and the exchange of information. By exchanging ideas, "old" knowledge can be revised or related to "new" knowledge. Thus, students can construct knowledge collaboratively. We assess how to use electronic environments effectively to stimulate knowledge-construction processes among academic students in collaborative learning situations.

The first issue in this contribution centers on the role of collaborative learning. What is the rationale behind this phenomenon? Next, we focus on the meaning of academic learning. In addition, we elaborate on the concept of knowledge construction. How can knowledge be constructed (collaboratively) and which contextual factors play a role? We discuss the role of the student, peer-student, tutor, task, instruction, and communication medium. Then, we describe four studies in which students work together on different tasks and assignments by the use of various CMC systems. Before we describe the CMC systems in detail, an example is provided to show how we assess collaborative learning as an explicit process of knowledge construction. The next step is to compare the process of knowledge construction across the four studies and to relate the results to the earlier defined contextual factors. Finally, a range of conclusions and practical implications are put forward considering the effective use of electronic environments in collaborative learning situations for academic education.

Collaborative Learning

Interest in collaborative learning can be enlightened by both social and theoretical issues (Van der Linden & Roelofs, 2000). Our modern society

---

[1] In the remainder of the chapter, the terms *constructivism* and *constructivist learning* are used with regards to socio-constructivist learning theory.

requests competent people who know how to communicate, to work in teams, to deal with information, and to handle computers. Based on constructivist principles for learning, research has shown that collaboration can contribute to positive learning effects and also can have social effects with respect to motivational issues, self-confidence, and relationships between students (Bossert, 1988; Johnson & Johnson, 1993). Different backgrounds and points of view can trigger students to construct knowledge and to elaborate or revise information during discussion (Baker, 1994; Dillenbourg & Schneider, 1995; Erkens, 1997; Scardamalia & Bereiter, 1994; Veerman, 2000). Recently, collaborative learning research has focused in particular on interaction processes that indicate learning or on the collaborative work structures (Dillenbourg, 1999). In collaborative situations, interaction effects caused by interrelated factors often trouble researchers to yield effects of independently designed main variables. Effects of group composition, award structures, preparation activities, or prior knowledge can heavily interact with characteristics of the student, peer-student, tutor, task, or the communication medium used. Research on collaborative learning can be divided into two kinds: effect-oriented and process-oriented research. Effect-oriented research deals with effects of collaborative learning in comparison with other teaching methods or learning situations (Van der Linden, Erkens, Schmidt, & Renshaw, 2000). In process-oriented research, analyses of the collaborative process as such are at the center. Process-oriented research offers the opportunity to assess specific interactions that contribute to learning in collaborative situations. In contrast to individual learning results, process-oriented research centralizes on constructing knowledge together through interaction, dialogue, and discussion. In this chapter, the effect-oriented trend was not relevant because collaborative learning was not compared to other learning situations; the process-oriented trend was most important.

Academic Learning

In general, universities aim at a deep level of learning (Biggs, 1999; Gokhale, 1995). Deep learning is characterized by having the intention of fully understanding the learning material, interacting critically with the learning content, relating ideas to prior knowledge and experience, using organizing principles to integrate ideas, and examining the logic of the arguments used (MacFarlane Report, 1992). Deep learning is opposed to surface learning, which is characterized by having the intention of simply reproducing parts of the content, accepting ideas and information passively, concentrating on assessment requirements, not reflecting on purpose or strategies of learning, memorizing facts and procedures routinely, and failing to recognize guiding principles or procedures (MacFarlane Report, 1992).

In university education, students have to deal with abstract, ill-defined, and not easily accessible knowledge as well as with open-ended problems, and deep learning is best achieved when learning takes place in ill-structured domains (Kirschner, 2000). It should be clear that the goals of higher education cannot be reached with (only) traditional ways of teaching. Research shows that skills that are required to achieve deep learning are more likely to be developed by students in constructivist settings than in traditional settings (Lethinen, Hakkarainen, Lipponen, Rahikainen, & Muukkonen, 2001; Paolucci, Suthers, & Weiner 1995; Reeves, 1998; Tynjäla, 1999). Learning at university is the process of discovering and generating acceptable arguments and lines of reasoning underlying scientific assumptions and bodies of knowledge (Veerman, 2000). In this context, important skills are critical thinking, creative thinking, logical thinking, creating ideas, debating and arguing subjects, using knowledge in new situations, solving problems, formulating questions, linking different insights, summarizing information concisely, sharing knowledge, and elaborating on each others' ideas and results (De Klerk, 1992; Gokhale, 1995; Jonassen, 1992; Van Ginkel, 1991).

In recent literature, skills such as the ones just described are called *competencies*. In educational contexts, there is a growing call for competency-based education (Kirschner, 2000; Kirschner, van Vilsteren, Hummel & Wigman, 1997; Mulder, 2000, 2001). Van Merriënboer (1999) characterized competencies as a mix of complex cognitive and higher order skills, highly integrated knowledge structures, interpersonal and social skills, and attitudes and values. Acquired competencies enable learners to apply these skills and attitudes in a variety of situations (transfer) and over an unlimited time span (lifelong learning; Van Merriënboer, 1999). Van der Sanden, Terwel, and Vosniadou (2000) also preferred to take a broad perspective of competence and point to the organized whole of knowledge, skill, attitudes, and learning abilities. We assume that deep learning will lead to knowledge construction. In the next section, we discuss the concept of knowledge construction.

Knowledge Construction

From a constructivist perspective, learning can be viewed as a dynamic process of knowledge construction. Knowledge can be regarded as a composition of many chunks of information that has been given meaning in complex networked relationships. A knowledge network can be viewed as a dynamic construct, ever changing due to internal and external stimuli. A continuous flow of information affects the knowledge network through perception from the outside. The meaning and relevance of information may also change under the influence of higher goals, norms, values, or expectations. Thus, each personal knowledge network is a unique construct by principle.

The construction of knowledge can be accomplished individually, hidden deep in the head of the learner, and invisible to the outside world. It can also be externalized by writing or discussing ideas and points of view. Although there is no way (yet) to trace what knowledge is really constructed in the head of the learner, written and verbal expressions can give at least some indications (Hewitt & Scardamalia, 1998). As long as we are not able to open the brain to watch and interpret the learning processes in detail, we are bound to use the thin cues of often poorly expressed information. In the CMC systems used, ideas and concepts are written down and discussed. This explicit or statable knowledge was analyzed and used to indicate what goes on considering the learning processes (Baker, 1999; Hewitt & Scardamalia, 1998).

Contextual Factors

In this chapter, we assess knowledge construction in collaborative learning situations in relation to some main factors in the educational context: the role of the student, peer-student, tutor, characteristics of the learning task, and features of the communication medium (see Fig. 13.1). We concentrate on situations in which students work together on learning tasks by the use of different CMC-systems in electronic environments.

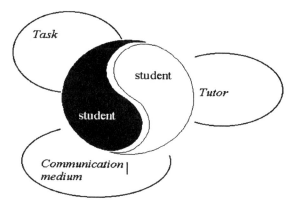

FIG.13.1. Contextual factors in collaborative learning situations.

• *The student.*
Based on constructivist principles, students have to be stimulated to engage actively in their own learning process. In collaborative learning situations, students actively search for information, engage in critical discussion, ask questions, discuss answers, make proposals, and reply to other proposals. In relation to preparation activities, prior knowledge, experience, and personal

beliefs and values, students contribute to the co-construction of knowledge (Veerman, 2000).

- *The peer-student.*

Collaboration with other students provokes activity, makes learning more realistic, and stimulates motivation. Students can ask questions to each other and discuss problems from different perspectives. They can propose various answers and solutions and evaluate them on different criteria (Petraglia, 1997). Sometimes politeness strategies inhibit students to be critical to each other. To prevent students from being too nice to each other, conversational rules can be introduced (Wegerif, Mercer, & Dawes, 1998).

- *The tutor.*

A tutor can appoint students to relevant information, misconceptions, discussion issues, conversational rules, and so on. In addition, tutors may be involved in the content of a discussion and thus participate in students' processes of collaborative knowledge construction. However, from a constructivist point of view the tutor has to be particularly reflective, guiding students from the sidewalk (Petraglia, 1997). The students have to construct knowledge, but the tutor can facilitate this process.

- *The task.*

Collaborative learning is more likely to occur in certain educational situations. Optimal learning tasks should be open-ended, thus students can share and learn from each other's differences in perspective, prior knowledge, experiences, beliefs, and values (Baker, 1994; Veerman, 2000; Veldhuis-Diermanse, 2002). To arrive at a shared conclusion or solution, information exchanges and discussion are necessary. To aim at a common end product stimulates students to share information, and to discuss and learn from each other's knowledge, experiences, beliefs, and values (Erkens, 1997). In addition to instruction aimed directly at the learning task, students can also receive instruction with respect to collaboration and communication processes. Communication rules can be provided for certain situations, procedures can be given for how to contact tutors and experts or how to handle technical help devices (e.g., Van Boxtel, 2000).

- *The communication medium.*

Internet and network-based computer programs offer new opportunities for collaboration, communication, and learning. Collaboration can take place at a distance, by the use of asynchronous and synchronous CMC systems. Examples are the use of a chat-box through the Internet for synchronous communication or e-mail and newsgroups for asynchronous communication. Communication by the use of such systems usually takes place by just typing text. Text-based communication can enhance reflection, because messages can be reread and changed whenever needed. In addition, texts can be saved easily and read or rewritten at a later moment. Text-based discussions are much slower than verbal conversations, in particular when asynchronous CMC systems are used. This provides the users with an easy way to follow the line of discussion and to discover various points of view, different interpretations, or knowledge conflicts. A structured interface can also affect the form of communication. By the use of buttons or menus, messages can be put into the communication window and, for example, be labeled with message types: a question, thought, argument, and so on. Sometimes graphical tools can be used to present information, which can support the construction of knowledge in addition to a chat window (Veerman & Treasure-Jones, 1999). In short, features of the communication medium can affect collaboration processes, communication and knowledge construction heavily through the user interface. However, they have to be viewed in relationship to the other contextual features, such as previously mentioned.

To summarize, in this chapter we assess how to use electronic environments effectively in educational settings designed to enhance knowledge construction in collaborative learning situations. The following factors will be taken into account: the role of the student, peer-student, tutor, task, and communication medium.

FOUR STUDIES

In this section, we describe four studies that each involved different groups of undergraduate students at Utrecht University and Wageningen University. All studies took place as part of a real course, in which students had to work collaboratively on complex tasks by the use of a CMC system. The studies involved different tasks, students, tutors, and CMC systems. Guidance or moderation was sometimes provided in various constructions. Before we describe the studies in more detail, we explain our system of analyses that was used to assess the amount and types of knowledge construction in all four studies.

Data Analyses

In all four studies students, peer-students and tutors had to communicate by sending each other text-based messages through a synchronous or asynchronous CMC system. All messages were automatically logged as text files on the computer. Messages could contain explicit expressions of task-related knowledge construction, such as new ideas, explanations, or evaluations. In addition, messages could contain information about planning the task, technical problems considering the CMC system, conversational rules and references to other facts, issues, summaries, or remarks elsewhere in the discussion. Moreover, some messages only referred to non-task-related issues such as the weather, jokes, and so on. In this research, we are specifically interested in messages that contain explicit expressions of knowledge construction. We regard such expressions as signals of collaborative learning in process (Scardamalia & Bereiter, 1994). In Table 13.1, we present our categories for analysis with some examples.

TABLE 13.1

Categorizing Messages

Message	Example	Knowledge Construction
Not task-related		
Planning	"Shall we first discuss the concept of 'interaction'?"	—
Technical	"Do you know how to change the diagram window?"	—
Social	"Smart thinking!"	—
Nonsense	"What about a swim this afternoon?"	—
Task-related		
New idea	"Interaction means: responding to each other."	X
Explanation	"I mean that you integrate information of someone else in your own reply."	X
Evaluation	"I don't think that's a suitable description because interaction means also interaction with computers or materials, see Laurillard's definition!"	X

We particularly focus on task-related messages that we categorize as new idea, explanation, and evaluation. A new idea can be described as a task-related message, focused on relevant content that is not mentioned before. An explanation is a message in which information is refined or elaborated that was already stated before, but elsewhere in the discussion. An evaluation is a message in which an earlier contribution is critically discussed on strength and relevance in the light of the task. An evaluation is more than a "Yes, what a good idea," and often involves reasoning processes, justifications, and relations to the content of earlier messages, task parts, or task goals. In principle, an explanation or evaluation can be constructed by the same person who posted an earlier message that is referred to, but mostly will be done by someone else.

After describing the four studies in the next sections, we present the results in terms of frequencies of messages per category and per study. We related these findings to some main factors in the educational context: the role of the student, peer-student, tutor, or moderator, and characteristics of the CMC systems used.

Study 1: NetMeeting

NetMeeting is a synchronous CMC system that facilitates synchronous communication and the sharing of applications among several users. The communication mode is not structured and there are no restrictions considering turn taking. In this study, NetMeeting was used as a chat box and combined with shared Notepads that students used as simple text editors. In Figure 13.2, it is shown that students communicate by use of the chat box, they edit in their own Notepads, and they write their final conclusions down in a shared Notepad. Students cannot view each other's messages before the Send button is pushed and the message becomes part of the shared chat history.

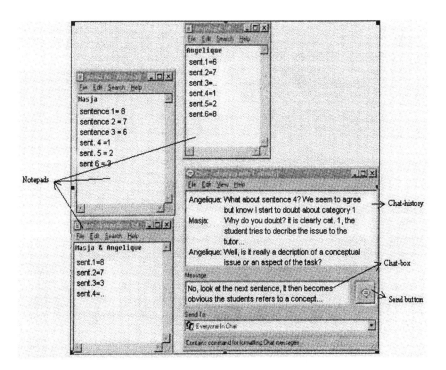

FIG.13.2. Chat box in NetMeeting and three Notepads.

In 1997 and 1999, the NetMeeting study was integrated as an actual undergraduate course on educational technology at the Department of Educational Science at Utrecht University (Veerman, 2000; Veerman, Andriessen, & Kanselaar, 1999). In 1997, the whole course took 8 weeks, and in 1999 it was extended to 12 weeks. The course structure of the first 4 weeks was the same, the period in which the NetMeeting study was conducted. One of the main learning goals was to reach insight and understanding in the conversational framework (Laurillard, 1993), a discussible model that one can use for analyzing teacher–student interaction. An electronic discussion task was designed for discussing this framework in the third week of the course, after the students were asked to study the framework at home.

In sum, 20 pairs of students engaged in a 45-minute discussion task by use of the NetMeeting system. The students' task was to analyze sentences in a protocol of a tutor–student dialogue considering various categories of the conversational framework. First, the students categorized these sentences individually. Then, the students compared electronically their answers in pairs. The collaborative task goal was to finally come to a shared answer through comparison, questioning, and discussion of the categorized sentences (see Fig. 13.2). Student pairs were randomly assigned to a guided and nonguided condition. In the guided condition, an additional peer-student was instructed to focus on triggering critical discussion by asking justification questions and triggering (counter) argumentation. It was expected that this form of guidance would enhance students to engage in processes of knowledge construction.

Study 2: Belvédère

The Belvédère environment is a synchronous networked software system developed by Suthers and others at the Learning Research and Development Center at the University of Pittsburgh (Suthers, Toth, & Weiner, 1997). In Belvédère, students can use a synchronous chat box and an argumentative diagram construction tool at the same time. As in the NetMeeting system, the communication mode in the chat box is not structured and there are no restrictions considering turn taking. In the diagram window, students can add data into the argumentative diagram window by using a predefined set of text boxes *(hypothesis, data, unspecified)* and links *(against, for, and)*. Although these boxes and links are predefined, students can organize, link, and fill them in their own way and in any possible combination with the chat (see Fig. 13.3). Because Belvédère provides students with the opportunity to construct an argumentative diagram as a graphical overview or form of reflection of an ongoing chat discussion, it was expected that this would support and enhance discussions and knowledge construction.

In 1998, the Belvédère study was integrated as part of a regular 8-week undergraduate course on computer-based learning at the Department of Educational Science at Utrecht University (Veerman, 2000; Veerman et al., 1999). In this course students had to design an educational computer program by group work. In sum, 20 undergraduate students took part in the course and formed eight small groups of their own choosing to work with during the course (four dyads and four triples).

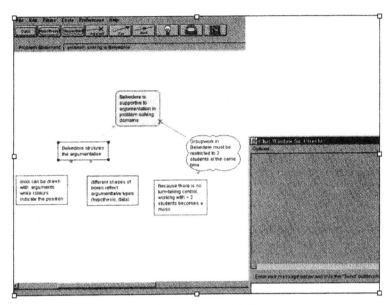

FIG.13.3. Screen dump of the Belvédère system (v2.0).

In the first week of the course all student groups got the assignment to make a plan for a design of an educational computer program of their own choice. They were asked to define the target group, the learning goals, and how they thought their program would have to be constructed to reach these goals. This plan was subject to a verbal tutoring session with one of the tutors in the second week of the course. After this session, in the third week the student groups had to elaborate their plans and justify pedagogical choices considering learning goals and target group, specifically what learning strategy to use and how to sequence the learning activities. With respect to these issues, the students were instructed to use the Belvédère system. This part of the course was specifically designed as a scientific study, but also functioned as part of the course for the students.

In the third week, all students were instructed to log on the Belvédère system, to start a chat discussion, and to build an argumentative diagram with their group members about two main pedagogical choices in their design: (a) what pedagogical strategies to use to reach the learning goals, and (b) how to sequence learning activities. The students were first instructed to produce conflicting claims for each of these pedagogical aspects. These claims served as the starting points for one or two discussion sessions, in

334   VEERMAN AND VELDHUIS-DIERMANSE

which the students all logged in at private computer stations. The sessions took about 60 to 90 minutes each. The instruction was to hand in the diagrams afterward, for usage in some additional tutoring sessions during Week 4. In sum, the student groups produced 13 chat discussions and 13 diagrams.

Study 3: Allaire Forums

Allaire Forums is an asynchronous CMC system, in which messages can be organized by threading and branching them around themes. The system is comparable to common newsgroups on the Internet. Students can read and send messages and reply to each other's contributions. Administrators can organize new discussion threads and branches and organize discussions on themes and dates. In Figure 13.4 a threaded discussion is shown, including some branched replies.

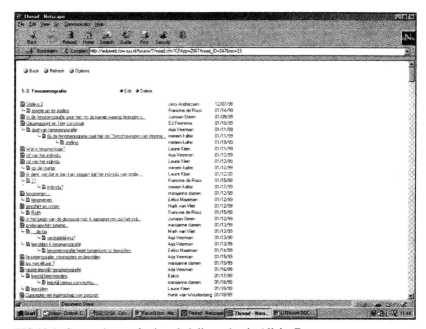

FIG.13.4. Screen dump of a threaded discussion in Allaire Forums.

In 1999, the study on Allaire Forums was organized as part of a 3-month course on educational technology at the Department of Educational Science at Utrecht University (Veerman, 2000; Veerman et al., 1999). Every 2 weeks, four to six discussions were organized. Some were aimed at theoretical issues, and others at practical issues in the field of education and technology. About 30 undergraduate students were randomly appointed to participate in one of the theoretical discussions and one of the practical discussions every 2 weeks. As a consequence, in each discussion group 8 to 12 students were involved. All students had access to an Internet-connected computer at home. They were instructed to make at least two contributions a week and to keep them short for readability and ease of interpretation (maximum of 15 lines per message). After 2 weeks, the course lecturer closed the discussions and provided the students with general feedback and comments on a separate web page. At the same time, new discussions were started.

Two course assistants reflectively moderated more than half of the discussions, and the others were self-regulated. In self-regulated discussions, the claim was given but no further support was offered. Reflective moderators were instructed to check information on meaning, strength, and relevance and to question connections between claims and arguments. In addition, they were asked to summarize information particularly when focus had been lost, and to nurture students' motivation especially when discussion volumes went down. The moderators were instructed not to interfere in the discussions without reason and not to state their own positions. Experts (including the course lecturer) could be contacted by e-mail. It was expected that moderation would support students to construct knowledge together.

Study 4: Web Knowledge Forum

Web Knowledge Forum (WebKF, 2000) is an asynchronous CMC system developed by the Ontario Institute for Studies in Education (OISE). The construction of the program is based on knowledge construction theory, which states that it is important for students to share ideas and reflect on these ideas to build knowledge together (Scardamalia & Bereiter, 1996). The program has been used in different educational settings for almost 15 years, at elementary schools as well as at universities. The OISE team is still working on new versions of the program, considering renewed theoretical insights and practical experiences. In addition, the team developed the Analytic Tool Kit, which can be used for running different basic analyses in WebKF.

In WebKF, students can log into a shared database through the Internet. On the introduction page, tutors and students can select a view in which to work. A view can be defined as a thematic discussion list and is comparable to a thread in Allaire Forums (see Fig. 13.5). In a view, students can read and write messages (notes). Additionally, they can label notes with a thinking type. Using a thinking type can force students to think about the type of note (question, answer, comment, idea, solution, argument, information) and help them to keep the discussion well-organized. Students can read messages and react by means of a build-on note (similar to a reply in Allaire Forums). Furthermore, it is possible to link a number of notes (within a view or from different views) and to select them based on theme, author, or date. Tutors have the additional option to create views.

The WebKF study took place in the context of an academic course at Wageningen University in the academic year 1998–99. This 6-week course was called "Quasi Land Evaluation and Variability for Explorative Land Use Studies" (Veldhuis-Diermanse, Mulder, & Biemans, 1999).

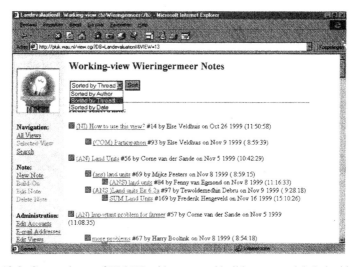

FIG.13.5. Screen dump of WebKF with notes and build-on notes, labeled with thinking types.

At the start, students were informed about the course, the various tasks, the digital learning environment, the concept of collaborative learning, and the practical use of WebKF. Furthermore, they had to make some exercises in the first couple of weeks and received lectures on land evaluation tools and models. Subsequently, students worked collaboratively at two cases. In addition, they carried out some other activities such as a NetMeeting discussion, a test, and the tryout of several tools.

The two cases students had to work on were designed as open-ended problems. In one of the cases, students worked in a multidisciplinary team in which each of them took a particular perspective (regional planner, local politician, tourism, citrus farmer). The task for the students was to reformulate the problem. Then they had to solve the problem by using specific models studied in the first couple of weeks of the course. This is an example of a formulated problem:

> The prime goal in land use planning is economic sustainability of agriculture. The agriculture in Alora depends mainly on subsidy and not on a market. Without subsidy, agriculture in Alora

would not be profitable. What is the most optimal land use to let
agriculture survive in this area?

The problem-solving process was subsequently supported by subtasks,
exercises, and a planning schedule. First, students had to make the subtasks
and exercises individually, then they had to respond to each other's contributions. Finally, they had to evaluate different problem solutions and make
a shared decision about the best solution.

In sum, 14 students were organized in two groups (7 students each).
These groups worked independently on two problem cases, in two different
databases within WebKF. The first group received technical help and a
view to keep the discussion organized. The second group received additional support from a tutor, who tried to stimulate the collaborative learning
process. This tutor was trained in intervening discussions by formulating
positions, asking critical questions, providing explanations, or drawing attention to messages of peer-students. No instruction was given considering
the frequency and timing of interventions. It was expected that students in
the guided discussions constructed more knowledge than students in the
nonguided condition.

Pedagogical Affordances of the CMC Systems Used

NetMeeting

NetMeeting is a network-based software system that facilitates synchronous
communication and the sharing of computer applications between several
users. The communication mode is not structured and there are no restrictions considering turn taking. NetMeeting does not include specific pedagogical affordances, except for the fact that students cannot view each
other's messages before the Send button is pushed and the message becomes part of the shared chat history. This characteristic provides students
with support for coordinating their interaction, which can be viewed as an
important factor for fruitful collaborative learning (Erkens, 1997).

Belvédère

Literature on graphical representation and comprehension generally shows
that representations foster comprehension when they support a focus by
transparency on salient and important features of a task (Ghyselink & Tardieu, 1999; Reimann, 1999). In its most basic form, a discussion can be
seen as a set of arguments with related claims and evidence, oriented for
and against the claims. This structure is essentially not linear (Adam, 1992;
Coirier, Andriessen, & Chanquoy, 1999; McCutchen, 1987). Hence, linear
interfaces may not be optimal for supporting and representing such a struc-

ture. A nonlinear diagram as a representation of discussion may be easier to understand and serve as a better source for further debate than linear text. The diagram could be particularly supportive if it is used in a manner closely linked to the chat and serves to trigger discussion about arguments that are still unclear, or not yet stated, discussed, or justified (Veerman & Treasure-Jones, 1999). The diagram construction tool, therefore, may help students to organize their discussion and keep track of the main issues.

Input into the Belvédère diagram construction tool is constrained by a labeled set of argument boxes and links. Students, nevertheless, are free to fill in boxes with any information they like. A general expectation is that students will be cued by the labeled argument boxes and links, which correspond to the input of arguments that can be oriented and organized for and against a claim (Kozma, 1991). In other words, they will use the tool to represent the discussion and not procedural matters.

The Belvédère environment may enhance the process of collaborative learning through diagram-mediated discussion. The diagram construction tool may support students in organizing their arguments and keeping track of the discussion by representing (discussed) information. This may trigger new discussion in the chat about issues raised by the organized representation, maybe in the form of elaboration of discussed content or as arguments that have not yet been discussed or justified. In addition, use of a diagram may affect task approaches, in the sense that the argumentative orientation of the discussion may be fostered, displayed by a focus on meaning negotiation.

Allaire Forums

Allaire Forums is an asynchronous CMC system, in which messages can be organized by threading and branching them around themes. Thus, questions and answers, arguments and elaborations, statements, and counters all can be linked together hierarchically. This serves students by offering them an organized overview of the discussion(s) in which they are engaged.

In contrast to synchronous discussion systems, in an asynchronous discussion system such as Allaire Forums, students are not pushed for immediate responses. This may facilitate rereading, reflection, and keeping track of the discussion over time (Moore, 1993). However, students may experience asynchronous discussions more as printed text than as an ongoing dialogue, leading to less 'argumentative' forms of discussion (Mason, 1992). Since asynchronous discussions are generally slower than synchronous discussions, due to the extended time-delays, discussions can be more focused on content (conceptually oriented) and include a higher density of constructive activities.

Web Knowledge Forum

WebKF is assumed to support the advancement of knowledge in different ways. Students can use various forms of hypertext commands to respond to others' notes. Messages can be referenced and linked together simply by mentioning a note number. Images, charts, and graphics, created as a web page or downloaded from the Internet, can also be incorporated into one's message. WebKF is a system that allows users to take advantage of current Web-based technology to develop a shared database of knowledge and teach others what they have come to know. This shared database makes use of an educational technique called scaffolding—a changing level of support that matches learners' competency levels (Vygotsky, 1978). As more teacher–student or student–student interactions take place, more ideas are shared, explored, and discussed, leading to additional opportunities for higher levels of learning. The sophistication of presentation can also be negotiated dependent on the user's needs. WebKF thus promotes progressive interaction because it is a many-to-many communication platform that evolves with the users rather than being just a holding tank of information. It also promotes scaffolding in other ways.

Both social and technical networks can be used in WebKF for online encouragement, qualitative and quantitative data analyses, and monitoring collective progress and goal attainment. The potential to move beyond one's normal boundaries of exploration is there. Due to the ability to access and interact within the class database, participants can learn about the assumptions and practices of many disciplines. Thus, opportunities for interdisciplinary dialogue and collaboration can take place. This type of learning, however, is not a given. WebKF exemplars try to promote a philosophy of developing what is called a knowledge-building community (KBC); (Hewitt, 1996). A KBC can be thought of as a group of people who assemble because they believe and are willing to continuously work toward advancing what is known about objective and subjective worlds, including themselves. It is a community that works towards fulfilling a shared, almost lofty vision of continuous improvement, recognizing that many disciplines (human and technical) are required to get there. Through the efforts of the participants and the technical advancements of WebKF, academic messages or "publications" to advance knowledge are possible. Reviewing and reflecting on one's own and others' published ideas can prompt new general ideas or theories. Ultimately, this is what WebKF exemplars hope to support—a community of scientists who through collaborative efforts enhances what has been shared before. WebKF then is more than a sophisticated software program. It provides supports for rethinking about and practicing learning (Bereiter & Scardamalia, 1996).

RESULTS

First, we present an overview of the mean number and type of messages for each study in Table 13.2. Then, we compare the four studies on the number of messages, task-related versus non-task-related messages, constructive versus nonconstructive messages, and the various types of constructive messages across the four studies. In each study, background information is given concerning differences within studies and between conditions. In addition, we report some remarkable facts.

Notice that our aim was not to compare the different systems to assess the usefulness of each system. Four different educational courses are described and analyzed to get insight into students' learning processes in computer-supported collaborative learning related to the following contextual factors: role of the (peer)-student, role of the tutor, task characteristics, and synchronous versus asynchronous CMC systems. Comparing the results is possible because of analyzing the data in each study identically.

Table 13.2 can be read in the following way. For example, in the WebKF study four discussions were analyzed. The mean number of messages per discussion was 98. These messages were so long that they could be divided into 272 separate contributions. The mean number of words per contribution was 205. The total number of all messages analyzed across the four discussions was 1,088. It was only necessary to divide messages into contributions in the WebKF study. In the other three studies, each message equaled one contribution. Thus, in WebKF 272 messages were analyzed per discussion. A mean number of 40 messages was coded as non-task-related. These messages concerned issues such as planning the task or were more socially oriented. The remainder of the 232 messages were coded as task-related. All task-related messages were subsequently coded as constructive or nonconstructive. On average, 157 of the 232 messages were coded as constructive; the other 75 messages were coded as task-related but not constructive. Finally, all constructive messages were categorized as a new idea, elaboration, or evaluation. In WebKF, 157 constructive messages were divided into 67 new ideas, 67 elaborations, and 23 evaluations.

Number of Messages

NetMeeting and Belvédère were used to execute short, synchronous discussion tasks in pairs or triples. In Belvédère, students were instructed to conduct the task in 90 minutes. In NetMeeting, students got about 45 minutes. The mean number of messages was comparable, as well as the mean number of words. In Belvédère, students had to construct an argumentative diagram during discussion, which left them less time to send messages.

TABLE 13.2

Number and Type of Messages and Percentages in the Four Studies

	Net-Meeting	Belvédère	Allaire Forums	WebKF
Total # of analyzed discussions	20	13	28	4
Mean # of messages per discussion	102	99	34	98
Mean # of contributions per discussion	102	99	34	272
Mean # of words per message	10	11	120	205
Total # of analyzed messages	2,040	1,287	952	1,088
Mean per discussion (100%):				
Non-task-related messages	40 (39%)	57 (58%)	4 (12%)	41 (15%)
Task-related messages	62 (61%)	42 (42%)	30 (88%)	232 (85%)
Mean per discussion of the task-related messages (100%)				
Non-constructive messages	42 (67%)	22 (52%)	8 (27%)	75 (32%)
Constructive messages	20 (33%)	20 (48%)	22 (73%)	157 (68%)
Mean per discussion of constructive activities (100%)				
New idea	8 (40%)	9 (45%)	7 (32%)	67 (43%)
Explanations	3 (15%)	3 (15%)	11 (50%)	67 (43%)
Evaluation	9 (45%)	8 (40%)	4 (18%)	23 (14%)

In NetMeeting, a student who was instructed to provoke critical argumentation by asking questions and (counter) argumentation guided 12 of the 20 small student groups. In the guided discussions one and a half as many messages were sent compared to the nonguided discussions (on average).

In Allaire Forums, students had 2-week discussions to discuss asynchronous claims. The mean number of words per message was 120. It seems that students acted in accordance with the instruction to keep messages brief. In Allaire Forums, a reflective moderator guided half of the discussions. Students started to copy the moderator's behavior in the first rounds of discussions. Because all students were randomly distributed across moderated and nonguided discussions over time, they cross- influenced each other. Consequently, differences in the total number and types of messages between the two conditions were minimal.

In WebKF, students also engaged in asynchronous discussions. Students worked in groups of seven, for about 2.5 weeks. Students were instructed to use WebKF for all types of communication and collaboration. In an evaluative questionnaire, students were asked to estimate how much communication was done by WebKF and how much they communicated face to face. On average, 88% of the students mentioned that all communication was done online, by using the CMC system. Students discussed all information electronically, put literature on the forum, contributed pieces of text written within the framework of the problem task, and combined all such issues in one message. Therefore, the mean number of words per message was very high and messages had to be split into multiple contributions. In WebKF, the two student groups received two different types of task assignments. The results showed that discussions triggered by various perspectives provoked students to write one and a half as many messages compared to the regular condition.

Task-Related Versus Non-Task-Related Messages

Figure 13.6 shows an overview of task-related versus non-task-related messages sent across the four studies. Remarkable are the high percentages of non-task-related messages in the NetMeeting and Belvédère synchronous systems. Percentages of non-task-related messages in the Allaire Forums and WebKF systems are much lower. In these systems students communicated asynchronously during a much longer period.

In the NetMeeting study, students experienced many technical troubles. Despite some training and instruction, they had difficulty using the tool. Besides, sometimes the network connection broke down, which interfered with their discussions. In the Belvédère study there was another reason that could explain the high number of non-task-related messages. Students had to construct an argumentative diagram during their discussion. This required much planning and conferencing. For example, students talked a lot about who had to make which part of the diagram, how to do that technically, and how the diagram should finally look. This left the students with less time to send messages.

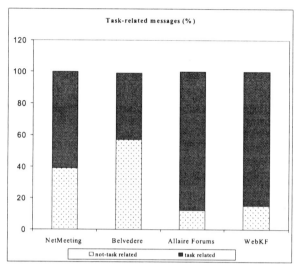

FIG.13.6.   Percentages of non-task-related messages per study.

With respect to the asynchronous CMC systems, the results show that not many non-task-related messages were sent. Students from Wageningen judged WebKF to be user-friendly and there were only a few technical problems. In Allaire Forums, hardly any time was lost to discover the possibilities of the tool. Therefore, non-task-related messages mainly concerned the task approach and the planning of all kinds of other activities. Sometimes some social or irrelevant comments were made, but this happened only a few times.

With respect to the different forms of guidance in the various studies, hardly any differences could be found. In NetMeeting, the guided student groups (triples) experienced some more trouble keeping track of the line of discussion compared to the nonguided discussion groups (pairs). As already mentioned, the multidisciplinary teams in WebKF triggered students to produce more messages. In the problem case in which students viewed the problem from a particular perspective, one and a half times as many messages were sent to the discussion compared to the problem case without the use of roles. Focusing on the content of the messages, we see the same pattern: The multidisciplinary teams contributed one and a half times as many task-related messages compared to the groups without roles.

Constructive Versus Nonconstructive Messages

Again, the synchronous media NetMeeting and Belvédère can be distinguished from the asynchronous media Allaire Forums and WebKF. In NetMeeting and Belvédère, less than half of the messages were coded as types of knowledge construction. In Allaire Forums and WebKF more than 60% of all task-related messages were coded as knowledge construction types. In the NetMeeting and Belvédère study, many contributions contained questions that were directed at the content but were formulated without containing any new information. Examples are, "Are you sure?" or "What do you mean?" Other questions and remarks repeated information that was stated earlier in the discussion but neither added new information nor insights.

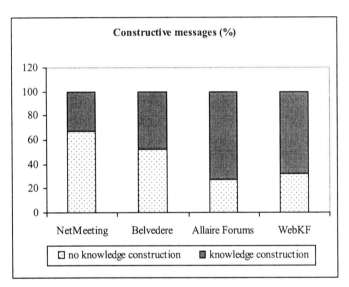

Figure 13.7 presents the percentages of constructive versus nonconstructive messages of the total number of task-related messages per study.

In Allaire Forums, question messages often contained more information. These messages were longer, ideas were more elaborated and arguments were given to a question. The additional information was sometimes repeated information, but often it was new and constructive in the discussion. In WebKF, students could use an information module with specific information about land evaluation. Students often used this module and, consequently, more than half of all nonconstructive messages were coded as using external information. These messages were not coded as constructive because they concerned literally repeated information from other sources.

In contrast to what we expected, the different types of guidance did not have many effects on the knowledge construction found in the discussions. In NetMeeting, guidance was directed at stimulating critical argumentation. Little effect was found on the number of questions asked and the extent of interactivity in the discussions; information was exchanged at a high rate by creating short messages that were sent to each other. These messages were not constructive and empty questions did not support knowledge construction by definition (for more detail see Veerman, 2000). As mentioned before, in Allaire Forums students started to copy the moderator's behavior already in the first rounds of discussions, thus, no overall effects were found. Also in WebKF, guidance did not effect knowledge construction heavily. The total number of constructive messages in the guided as well as in the nonguided discussion did not differ very much. However, considering the first problem case, an interesting observation was made. The teacher in the guided case characterized his function as follows: "My function was being a catalyst; I helped the students getting started." It was shown that this discussion started faster than the nonguided case. In the second problem case, this difference could not be found.

Types of Knowledge Construction

Table 13.3 shows the various types of constructive messages across the four studies. The difference between evaluations and explanations is remarkable. In the synchronous studies of NetMeeting and Belvédère almost half of all constructive messages were coded as evaluation, which is in contrast to the low percentage of evaluations in the asynchronous studies with Allaire Forums and WebKF.

TABLE 13.3

Percentages of Knowledge Construction of all Task-related Messages per study

	Software Type			
Message Content	NetMeeting	Belvédère	Allaire Forums	WebKF
New Idea	40%	45%	32%	43%
Explanation	15%	15%	50%	43%
Evaluation	45%	40%	18%	14%

Considering the percentage of explanations, it is just the other way around. The four studies differ the least in the type of knowledge construction we called new idea. We did not analyze different types of constructive activities related to different conditions of guidance. By dividing the constructive messages into three categories of knowledge construction it was not useful to divide the small numbers of messages again.

DISCUSSION AND CONCLUSIONS

In this section the results of the various studies are evaluated. We draw conclusions are drawn and put forward points for discussion. Effects of the main factors in the educational context on forms and amounts of knowledge construction are systematically put forward and discussed in the following paragraphs: the (peer-) student, tutor or moderator, learning task, and communication medium. At the end of the section, we provide a list of practical tips for the effective use of educational technology in collaborative learning situations.

Role of the (Peer-) Student

All students in the four studies were undergraduates. They were used to working in groups in various educational settings and were experienced with assignments in which they had to develop their own ideas and insights. Therefore, we expected them to participate in electronic discussions in an active, critical, and constructive way. This should be reflected in the production of various types of constructive activities: new ideas, explanations and evaluations. Especially messages coded as evaluations should reflect a critical attitude of the students, because they refer to the discussion of information and ideas on strength and relevance in the light of the task (goals).

The results show that students using the asynchronous CMC systems Allaire Forums and WebKF sent more constructive messages to each other than students using the synchronous CMC systems NetMeeting and Belvédère. Viewed from the perspective of the role of the student and peer-student, we searched for an explanation considering individual (group) differences such as task preparation and differences in group size. In Net-Meeting and Belvédère, students had difficulties carrying out the task. Technical troubles bothered them in NetMeeting, and in Belvédère students had to coordinate a chat discussion and the production of an argumentative diagram at the same time. If students had been more used to the synchronous CMC tools, they probably would have sent each other more constructive messages without being disturbed by technical or coordination problems. Allaire Forums and WebKF were much more user-friendly and transparent. Student groups did not show technical or coordination troubles.

Concerning group size, in the synchronous NetMeeting system, triples had more troubles keeping track of the discussion than dyads. In Belvédère, triples had no more problems than dyads in following lines of arguments. The diagram supported students in keeping focused. In the asynchronous CMC systems, groups of 7 to 12 students engaged in discussions without losing track. Because different perspectives and multiple ideas can trigger and support discussion, we prefer large and heterogeneous groups over small homogeneous groups. However, we do not think it is fruitful to discuss ideal group size in relation to knowledge construction. Among other factors, this depends on how group communication is organized, how the task is designed, and what tools are available. For example, in asynchronous discussions it can be important to keep a clear view of many messages sent but it can also be the case that students have to be provoked to generate enough messages to keep the discussion going. Highly intensive discussions can be organized with small sets of students; in slow discussions large groups can be more effective.

Role of the Tutor

In various studies, we used peer-students, assistants, moderators, and tutors to guide and support the electronic student discussions. We expected student groups to construct more knowledge in guided discussions compared to nonguided discussions. However, we did not find this effect in any of the four studies.

In the NetMeeting study, students sent more messages in the guided discussions than in the nonguided discussions. The number of participants could explain this: dyads in nonguided discussion groups and triples in the guided groups. In this particular case, more students meant a more intensive flow of discussion, and thus, more messages sent. Relatively, the number of constructive messages did not increase. In NetMeeting, guidance was aimed at stimulating critical argumentation. As an effect, students engaged in discussions that were more critical. However, they did not construct more knowledge. This result was also found in the Belvédère study. Creating an argumentative diagram in relation to a chat discussion stimulated student groups to engage in critical discussion, but no effect was found on the amount of knowledge constructed. However, critical discussion appeared to influence the type of knowledge constructed. In NetMeeting and Belvédère, more constructive messages were coded as evaluation, whereas in Allaire Forums and WebKF more messages were coded as explanation.

In Allaire Forums and WebKF, the total amount of messages was more or less equal in guided and nonguided discussions. In Allaire Forums, students copied the moderator's activities rapidly. They checked each other's information critically on strength and relevance and constructed knowledge together. They discussed issues in an indirect or mild manner, did not attack each other but explained a lot, and completed each other's ideas. In

WebKF, the tutor showed a lack of time to contribute many notes to the discussion. Reading students' (long) messages alone took about 1 day a week, which was not well-thought-out beforehand. Most likely, due to the low amount of the tutor's contributions, no effects of tutorial interventions were found.

Task Characteristics

Four different tasks were organized across the studies: an analyzing task, a design task, a discussion task, and a problem-solving task. In each task it was important to communicate, to share information, and to collaborate to interpret difficult information and to solve complex problems. Although the context of the four studies differed, the learning objectives in the Net-Meeting and the Allaire Forums study were comparable. In both courses, the object of the courses was formulated as "reaching insight in." In the Belvédère and the WebKF study, learning objectives were comparable; in both courses students had to think about a solution for a specific problem. Based on the results there is no reason to assume that these learning objectives as a characteristic of the task affected the amount and type of students' knowledge construction.

The tasks were structured in different ways. In NetMeeting and Belvédère, students worked at a complex but not heavily structured task. In NetMeeting, students analyzed a protocol with respect to a theoretical model. Students could carry out this task in different ways; for example, they could discuss the total model or fragments of it. In Belvédère, students had to discuss the design of an educational computer program. They could approach the task in different ways: discuss the design by using mainly the chat, the diagram construction tool, or both at the same time. In Allaire Forums and WebKF, tasks were more clearly structured. In Allaire Forums, the moderator put predefined claims for discussion on the forum, whereas in WebKF the tutor divided the task into subtasks beforehand.

Earlier research suggests that students construct more knowledge when a task is more structured. A task that requires structure because of complexity demands regulation activities. Students have a need to make plans, make appointments, distribute subtasks among group members, monitor planning, and so on. Thus, they need much time to regulate issues that do not directly relate to the content of the task, which leaves them with less time for knowledge construction. Results of our studies confirm these findings. More knowledge was constructed in the studies that were defined or pre-structured, such as in Allaire Forums and WebKF, compared to the less structured tasks in NetMeeting and Belvédère. In the NetMeeting and Belvédère studies, students used much more time to make plans and to organize a proper approach to execute the task.

Another aspect referring to the relation between task characteristics and the building of shared knowledge is the use of different roles. In half of the

WebKF discussions, specific roles were assigned to the students to stimulate collaboration from different perspectives. Students working in these so-called multidisciplinary teams produced one and a half times as many messages compared to students who did not discuss issues from different positions. In the evaluative questionnaires, students stated that in their experience debating was more useful within a multidisciplinary team. Some quotes support this idea: "It was much more discussion, because everyone had a different point of view" or "The discussion was more sparkling, because people were defending their own interest," and "The discussion was more based on opinions and arguments." In addition, working from different perspectives provoked more discussion and led to more knowledge construction.

Synchronous Versus Asynchronous CMC Systems

In the four studies, we used four different CMC systems; two synchronous CMC systems (NetMeeting and Belvédère) and two asynchronous systems (Allaire Forums and WebKF). With respect to the amount of time that students worked in these systems (synchronous systems at maximum some hours, asynchronous systems a couple of weeks), students sent a high frequency of short messages in the NetMeeting and Belvédère studies compared to the studies on Allaire Forums and WebKF. However, in Allaire Forums and WebKF, frequencies were lower, but messages were much longer. These differences characterize the different types of collaboration and communication across synchronous and asynchronous CMC systems. Synchronous collaboration has to be fast, due to a high psychological pressure to respond as soon as possible (Moore, 1993). Consequently, students have less time to search for information, produce extended explanations, evaluate information thoroughly, ask elaborated questions, and so on. In general, asynchronous collaboration is much slower. In relation to the educational design and task characteristics, students have more time to think, search for information, elaborate ideas, explain ideas, and reflect on each other's contributions. Students can take time to reach shared understanding, create their own ideas, and formulate points of view as clear as possible.

Another factor that seems to be important is that students in Allaire Forums and in WebKF worked within separated discussion themes or threads. This made it easier for them to follow the development of the discussion compared to the NetMeeting and Belvédère discussions. Content-related messages were separated from organizational and technical issues. Moreover, in contrast to the synchronous systems, messages in the asynchronous CMC systems got a clear title; in WebKF they even got an additional thinking type. A better overview and explicit subject titles support the students in focusing on the task, keeping track of the discussion, and using most of the time for the construction of knowledge.

It has to be emphasized that features for organizing discussions and supporting focus maintenance can be implemented in both asynchronous and synchronous CMC systems.

We conclude with a list of practical tips for the effective use of educational technology in collaborative learning situations, with an emphasis on the construction of knowledge:

- Use an open-ended task in which information can be discussed from multiple perspectives and problems can be solved in many different ways.
- Use task structures that regulate organizational and planning issues, particularly when such issues are not related to task and learning goals.
- Arrange heterogeneous group compositions and, if possible, provide students with different discussion roles.
- Check students' assumptions and expectations. Provide guidelines about participation, collaboration, and communication.
- Choose transparent and user-friendly CMC systems. Provide students, tutors, and moderators with sufficient time and exercises to get used to the system.
- Organize clear discussion threads. Separate discussion themes, technical issues, planning aspects, and social issues. Support the use of clear titles when sending contributions.
- Give preference to asynchronous CMC systems, especially considering larger groups of students.
- Use synchronous CMC systems only for small groups (dyads, triples), especially when interaction is not structured.

ACKNOWLEDGMENTS

Jerry Andriessen, Gellof Kanselaar, and Jos Jaspers from the Department of Educational Science at Utrecht University have to be thanked for their extensive support on the work on computer-supported collaborative learning between 1996 and 2000. Dan Jones and Dan Suthers deserve a word of appreciation for their ongoing help with the Belvédère computer system throughout the years.

REFERENCES

Adam, J. M. (1992). *Les textes: Types et prototypes—Recit, description, argumentation et dialogue* [The texts: Types and prototypes—Story, description, argumentation, and dialogue]. Paris: Nathan.

Andriessen, J. E. B., & Veerman, A. L. (1999). Collaborative distance learning in higher education. *Pedagogische Studiën, 6*(76), 157–178.

Baker, M. (1994). A model for negotiation in teaching–learning dialogues. *Journal of Artificial Intelligence in Education, 5,* 199–254.

Baker, M. (1999). *Argumentation and constructive interaction. In P. Coirier & J. E. B. Andriessen (Eds.),* Foundations of argumentative text processing *(pp. 179–202). Amsterdam: Amsterdam University Press.*

Bereiter, C., & Scardamalia, M. (1996). Rethinking learning. In D. R. Olson & N. Torrance (Eds.), *The handbook of education and human development: New models of learning, teaching and schooling* (pp. 485–513). Oxford, UK: Blackwell.

Biggs, J. B. (1999). *Teaching for quality learning at university: What the student does.* St. Edmundsbury, UK: Society for Research into Higher Education & Open University Press.

Bossert, S. T. (1988). Cooperative activities in the classroom. *Review of Research in Education, 15,* 225–253.

Coirier, P., Andriessen, J. E. B., & Chanquoy, L. (1999). *From planning to translating: The specificity of argumentative text processing.* Amsterdam: Amsterdam University Press.

De Klerk, V. (1992) A cognitive model of language: The network approach." *South African Journal of Linguistics.* (Special edition), 186–190.

Dillenbourg, P., & Schneider, D. (1995). Mediating the mechanisms which make collaborative learning sometimes effective. *International Journal of Educational Telecommunications, 1*(2–3), 131–146.

Dillenbourg, P. (1999). *Collaborative learning: Cognitive and computational approaches.* Amsterdam: Pergamon.

Erkens, G. (1997). *Cooperative problem solving with computers in education: Modeling of cooperative dialogues for the design of intelligent educational systems.* Utrecht, Netherlands: Brouwer Uithof.

Ghyselink, V., & Tardieu, H. (1999). The role of illustrations in text comprehension: What, when, for whom and why? In H. van Oostendorp & S. Goldman (Eds.), *The construction of mental representations during reading* (pp. 195–218). Mahwah, NJ: Lawrence Erlbaum Associates.

Gokhale, A. A. (1995). Collaborative learning enhances critical thinking. *Journal of Technology Education.* Retrieved April, 27, 1998, from http://scholar.lib.vt.edu/ejournals/JTE/jte-v7n1/gokhale.jte-v7n1.html

Hewitt, J. G. (1996). *Progress toward a knowledge-building community.* Toronto: University of Toronto.

Hewitt, J., & Scardamalia, M. (1998). Design principles for the support of distributed processes. *Educational Psychology Review, 10, 75-96.*

Johnson, D. W., & Johnson, R. T. (1993). Creative and critical thinking through academic controversy. *American Behavioral Scientist, 37,* 40–53.

Jonassen, D. H. (1992). Evaluating constructivist learning. In T. M. Duffy & D. H. Jonassen (Eds.), *Constructivism and the technology of instruction: A conversation* (pp. 137–148). Hillsdale: Laurence Erlbaum Associates.

Kirschner, P. A. (2000). *The inevitable duality of education: Cooperative higher education.* (Inaugural address). Maastricht, Netherlands: Maastricht University.

Kirschner, P., van Vilsteren, P., Hummel, H., & Wigman, M. (1997). The design of a study environment for acquiring academic and professional competence. *Studies in Higher Education, 22,* 151–171.

Kozma, R. B. (1991). The impact of computer-based tools and embedded prompts on writing processes and products of novice and advanced college writers. *Cognition and Instruction, 8,* 1–27.

Laurillard, D. (1993). *Rethinking university teaching: A framework for the effective use of educational technology.* London: Routledge.

Lehtinen, E., Hakkarainen, K., Lipponen, L., Rahikainen, M., & Muukkonen, H. (2001). *Computer supported collaborative learning: A review.* (CL-Net Project). Retrieved January 26, 2001, from http://www.kas.utu.fi/clnet/clnetreport.html

MacFarlane Report. (1992). Retrieved September 1, 2000, from http://www.northern-college.ac.uk/internal/courses/BEd/deep_learning.html

Mason, R. (1992). The textuality of computer networking. In R. Mason (Ed.), *Computer conferencing: The last word* (pp. 22–38). Victoria, BC, Canada: Beach Holme.

McCutchen, D. (1987). Children's discourse skill: Form, and modality requirements of schooled writing. *Discourse Processes, 10,* 267–286.

Moore, M. G. (1993). Theory of transactional distance. In D. Keegan (Ed.), *Theoretical principles of distance education* (pp. 22–38). London: Routledge.

Mulder, M. (2000). *Development of competence in business and education,* (Inaugural address). Wageningen, The Netherlands: Wageningen University.

Mulder, M. (2001). *Development of competences in organizations: Perspectives and practices.* Gravenhage, The Netherlands: Elsevier Bedrijfs Informatie.

Paolucci, M., Suthers, D., & Weiner, A. (1995). *Belvedere: Stimulating students' critical discussion* [Online]. Retrieved May 26, 1998, from http://www.pitt.edu/~suthers/belvedere/chi95.html

Petraglia, J. (1997). *The rhetoric and technology of authenticity in education.* Mahwah, NJ: Lawrence Erlbaum Associates.

Reeves, T. C. (1998, June). *Answering critics of media and technology in education.* Paper presented at Ed-media & Ed-telecom, Freiburg, Germany.

Reimann, P. (1999). Commentary: The role of external representations in distributed problem-solving. Learning & Instruction, 9, 419–424.

Scardamalia, M., & Bereiter, C. (1994). Computer support for knowledge-building communities. *Journal of the Learning Sciences, 3,* 265–283.

Scardamalia, M., & Bereiter, C. (1996). Student communities for the advancement of knowledge. *Communications of the ACM, 39,* 36–37.

Suthers, D., Toth, E., & Weiner, A. (1997). An integrated approach to implementing collaborative inquiry in the classroom. In *Proceedings of the conference on Computer Supported Collaborative Learning: CSCL'97* (pp. 272–279).

Tynjälä, P. (1999). Towards expert knowledge? A comparison between a constructivist and a traditional learning environment in university. *International Journal of Educational Research, 31,* 357–442.

Van Boxtel, C. A. M. (2000). *Collaborative concept learning. Student interaction, collaborative learning tasks and physic concepts.* Enschede, The Netherlands: Print Partners Ipskamp.

Van der Linden, J. L., & Roelofs, E. (2000). *Leren in dialoog* [Learning in dialogue]. Groningen, Netherlands: Wolters-Noordhoff.

Van der Linden, J. L., Erkens, G., Schmidt, H., & Renshaw, P. (2000). Collaborative learning. In P. R. J. Simons, J. van der Linden, & T. M. Duffy (Eds.), *New learning* (pp. 37–54). Dordrecht, Netherlands: Kluwer Academic.

Van der Sanden, J., Terwel, J., & Vosniadou, S. (2000). New learning in science and technology. In P. R. J. Simons, J. van der Linden, & T. M. Duffy (Eds.), *New learning* (pp. 21–36). Dordrecht, Netherlands: Kluwer Academic.

Van Ginkel, J. A. (1991). Education and inquiry. In G. Coebergh & W. Kramer (Eds.), Academic education: The problem of quality of scientific education viewed from another perspective (pp. 19–30). Culemborg, The Netherlands: Phaedon.

Van Merriënboer, J. J. G. (1999). *Cognition and multimedia design for complex learning,* (Inaugural address). Heerlen, The Netherlands: Open University.

Veerman, A. L. (2000). *Computer-supported collaborative learning through argumentation.* Enschede, The Netherlands: Print Partners Ipskamp.

Veerman, A. L., Andriessen, J. E. B., & Kanselaar, G. (1999). Collaborative learning through computer-mediated argumentation. In C. Hoadly & J. Roschelle (Eds.), *Proceedings of the third conference on Computer Supported Collaborative Learning* (pp. 640–650). Palo Alto, CA: Stanford University.

Veerman, A. L. & Treasure-Jones T. (1999). Software for problem solving through collaborative argumentation. In P. Coirier & J. E. B. Andriessen (Eds.), *Foundations of argumentative text processing* (pp. 203–230). Amsterdam: Amsterdam University Press.

Veldhuis-Diermanse, A. E. (2002). *CSCLearning? Participation, learning activities and knowledge construction in computer-supported collaborative learning in higher education.* Wageningen, Netherlands: Wageningen University.

Veldhuis-Diermanse, A. E., Mulder, M., & Biemans, H. J. A. (1999). Computer-supported collaborative learning: Useful to use in higher education? *Tijdschrift voor Hoger Onderwijs, 20,* 223-245.

Vygotsky, L. S. (1978). *Mind in society: The development of higher psychological process.* Cambridge, MA: Harvard University Press.

WebKF. (2000). Information and demo. Retrieved December 7, 2004, from http://www.learn.motion.com/lim/Webkf/WebKF1.html

Wegerif, R., Mercer, N., & Dawes, L. (1998). Software design to support discussion in the primary classroom. *Journal of Computer Assisted Learning, 14,* 199–211.

Chapter 14

Learning to Argue

Clark A. Chinn

Rutgers, The State University of New Jersey

A commonsense definition of *argumentation* is that it is discourse in which learners take positions, give reasons and evidence for their positions, and present counterarguments to each other's ideas when they have different views. By this definition, the authors of nearly all of the chapters in this volume explicitly or implicitly advocate argumentation as an instructional strategy. The authors of four chapters (Andriessen et al., chap. 9; Erkens, Prangsma, & Jaspers, chap. 10; van Drie, van Boxtel, & van der Linden, chap. 11; Wiley & Bailey, chap. 12) explicitly employ argumentation in their instructional systems. The authors of four other chapters (Bielaczyc & Collins, chap. 3; Chen, Zhang, & Wu, chap. 6; Hmelo-Silver, chap. 7; Veerman & Veldhuis-Diermanse, chap. 13) develop or employ instructional systems in which students have ample opportunities to engage in argumentative discussion of opposing views and reasons. Bielaczyc and Collins also note that exceptional knowledge-creating communities such as Silicon Valley are marked by "stimulating discussion of alternative views." Collectively, these chapters reflect a rapidly growing interest in argumentation as an instructional tool (e.g., Anderson, Chinn, Chang, Waggoner, & Yi, 1997; Voss & Means, 1991; Yackel & Cobb, 1996).

The growing use of argumentation in classrooms raises important issues for research. The first set of questions is about whether argumentation is in fact worth doing in the classroom. Does argumentation offer instructional benefits? If so, what are these benefits? Then, assuming that argumentation does enhance learning in some way, the next set of questions addresses instructional goals. Argumentation can vary in quality, and it is not easy to try to define what it means to argue well. Exactly what should students learn when they engage in argumentation? Finally, once instructional goals are identified, one can turn to instructional issues. What kinds of instructional methods can help students learn to argue well? My purpose in this chapter is to address these three sets of issues.

Instructional Benefits of Argumentation

There are at least four possible benefits to having students engage in arg-
mentation in the classroom. Argumentation in the classroom might improve
understanding of course content, enhance student interest, improve performance on problem-solving tasks, or foster the development of students'
argumentation ability. Each of these potential benefits is supported by research, including some classroom research. Next I examine research that
investigates the effects of individual argumentation as well as the effects of
argumentation in groups.

Understanding Course Content

Argumentation involves elaborative processing of information; students
connect ideas they are learning to reasons and evidence that support or re-
fute these ideas. Theoretically, one might expect deep, elaborative processing to promote learning of the ideas (Pressley & Woloshyn, 1995). Against
this idea, however, some might worry that argumentation might focus students' attention on part of the content to be learned at the expense of other,
equally important content that is less relevant to the topic of debate. Thus,
there is also a possibility that argumentation could distract students from
learning some key ideas.

In several studies, curricula featuring argumentation have helped students learn key concepts and principles, such as the physics of forces
(White & Frederiksen, 1998), arithmetic (Wood & Sellers, 1996), and the
nature of good scientific conclusions (Chinn, O'Donnell, & Jinks, 2000).
Van Drie et al. (chap. 11, this volume) add to this literature in showing that
high school students' collaborative work on an argumentative essay improved their understanding of causes of Dutch social changes in the 1950s
and 1960s. However, although these studies are suggestive, the comparison
groups in these studies were not groups in which students learned without
argumentation, so it is impossible to tease out the specific role of argumentation.

Zohar and Nemet (2002) conducted a study that manipulated whether
students engaged in argumentation. The students were ninth graders learning genetics. About half of the students learned through instruction in effective argumentation followed by participation in group argumentation
around genetics dilemmas. The other half learned through materials covering the same content but without the argumentation. The students who participated in argumentation exhibited gains in biological knowledge that
were not found in the control group. Smith, Johnson, and Johnson (1981)
found that sixth graders working in groups of four with frequent teacher
guidance learned more when they treated their problem-solving task as an
argumentative task than when they treated it as a consensus-building task
on which argumentation was to be avoided. In a study with individual un-

dergraduates, Wiley and Voss (1999) found that students asked to write arguments about the causes of population changes in Ireland from 1846 and 1850 exhibited greater mastery of central causal principles than students asked to write narratives, summaries, or explanations. Together, these studies support the conclusion that argumentation can enhance learning of important course content.

Interest and Motivation

Argumentation has the potential to increase students' intrinsic motivation because controversy might be inherently interesting (Johnson & Johnson, 1979). Students' interest may be piqued when they discover that their peers have different ideas about issues, and students might find it engaging to try to resolve conflicting perspectives. In addition, in argumentation students typically have greater freedom to express their own ideas than they have in traditional recitations (Chinn, Anderson, & Waggoner, 2001). This greater freedom may also enhance motivation. However, there are also reasons to worry that argumentation could decrease motivation. Argumentation might foster aggressive verbal interaction, even *ad hominem* attacks, that intimidate less assertive students. In particular, some scholars have suggested that argumentation can promote a confrontational style of discourse that some girls may be uncomfortable with (Anders & Commeyras, 1998).

Although the research on this issue is still sparse, there is some initial, limited support for positive effects of argumentation on interest and motivation. In their comparison of consensus versus controversy formats for group work, Smith et al. (1981) found that sixth graders who engaged in debate were more interested in the topic, as indicated by ratings scales, greater willingness to give up recess time to watch a film on a related topic, and more relevant materials voluntarily checked out from the library. Chinn et al. (2001) used several measures of participation in discourse, including the rate of talk, to examine the level of engagement in argumentative discussions about issues raised by stories. They concluded that argumentation was marked by higher levels of engagement than was the discourse of traditional recitations. They also found no differences between boys and girls on several measures of preference for assertive talk. It should be noted that both of these studies included instruction to teach children norms for polite, respectful discussion. This instruction may have fostered a climate that discouraged some of the potential negative outcomes of argumentative discourse.

Problem Solving Performance

A large body of research supports the conclusion that argumentation during a variety of problem-solving tasks—ranging from writing essays to relatively simple decision-making tasks—enhances the quality of problem solutions. Both self-directed argumentation by individuals and argumentation in groups appear to be beneficial.

In a review of a broad range of studies covering many different problem-solving tasks, Arkes (1991) found that problem solving often improves when reasoners are directed or cued to articulate alternate arguments or reasons, which is equivalent to asking the reasoners to engage in a simple form of internal mental argumentation. The general procedure of considering alternatives also improves performance on hypothesis testing tasks (Wharton, Cheng, & Wickens, 1993). Argumentation can also improve writing. When teachers provide some training in argumentation skills, students do better at writing persuasive essays (Page-Voth & Graham, 1999). However, the formulation of arguments appears to improve other aspects of writing as well, such as increasing the causal connections in texts (Wiley & Voss, 1996, 1999).

Argumentation within groups can also improve group problem solving. Poor policy decisions by groups of government officials have often been attributed to groupthink, in which leaders discourage contrary arguments from being voiced or considered (Janis, 1982). Argumentation by groups of students working together can promote better, more creative problem solutions (Johnson & Johnson, 1979). Two chapters in this volume extend these ideas to pair writing tasks. The study presented by Wiley and Bailey (chap. 12) suggests the possibility that argumentation might promote better reasoning about scientific evidence. The study by Erkens et al. (chap. 10) suggests that argumentation during pair writing improves the quality of the resulting essays.

A plausible explanation for the benefits of argumentation on problem-solving performance is that argumentation helps people overcome their natural tendency to satisfice (Simon, 1955; see also Perkins, Allen, & Hafner, 1983). Ordinarily, people appear to be content to think about an issue just long enough to come up with a solution that seems, at first glance, to be acceptable. However, such quickly generated solutions are likely to be suboptimal; in particular, they are likely to be biased by initial beliefs that may be incorrect. Both intraindividual and group argumentation provide a source for contrary ideas that can both provide better solutions and more extensive comparison of alternatives. However, it should be noted that these processes alone do not guarantee that groups will reach good solutions to problems. In an analysis of John F. Kennedy's misguided decision to invade the Bay of Pigs and Lyndon Johnson's decisions to escalate fighting in Vietnam, Kramer (1998) argued on the basis of recently released documents that, contrary to claims that these presidents discouraged dissent, both actively encouraged dissent. Poor decisions were reached because of faulty weighting of arguments and inappropriate goals.

Argumentation Ability

It seems plausible that practice at argumentation, like practice at other skills, would improve students' ability to argue. In the study in this volume by van Drie et al. (chap. 11), students who engaged in argumentation showed improvement on two measures of reasoning skill: selecting information from a source and evaluating the trustworthiness of sources. However, practice without instruction may have only small benefits. Adults who repeatedly engage in argumentation about capital punishment show only modest change in their ability to generate arguments on this topic (Kuhn, Shaw, & Felton, 1997).

Recent studies that include teacher instruction or guidance in argumentation have shown some promise in improving argumentation skills. In Zohar and Nemet's (2002) study, high school students who engaged in argumentation exhibited greater ability to argue on new topics than students who did not engage in argumentation. Reznitskaya et al. (2001) found that elementary school students who participated in teacher-led argumentative discussions about issues raised by stories were better able to provide persuasive arguments and counterarguments when writing essays, even though the training did not involve any practice or instruction in writing arguments.

Summary

Argumentation has the potential to improve multiple aspects of student learning. Particularly important is the robust finding that argumentation benefits performance on a broad range of problem-solving tasks. This means that if students learn to argue well in schools, they will be able to apply this ability to improve their future problem-solving performance on a wide array of problems. Learning to argue well will prepare students to be good thinkers and problem solvers. Therefore, learning to argue well should be a central goal of education.

Instructional Goals for Argumentation

If argumentation should be a central goal of education, then educators will need to work hard to be clearer about what it means to argue well. More than a decade ago, I worked with a fourth-grade teacher on facilitating argumentative discussions about stories with small reading groups. Within several lessons, the children demonstrated proficiency in most of the argumentation skills that were the focus of our study: taking positions, giving reasons, backing up reasons with textual evidence, and challenging other students' ideas. Very shortly, we were faced with the question, "What next?" Once students demonstrate mastery of the basics, what else do they need to learn? What does it mean to argue really well? Answering this question is far from trivial. In this section I suggest several kinds of knowledge that students are likely to need to be able to argue well.

When people argue well in groups, they do three things. First, they construct good individual arguments (e.g., "I don't agree that this study shows that pellagra is caused by a virus because those neighborhoods without sewers were also likely to be poorer neighborhoods, and people in poorer neighborhoods might also have poorer diets; so there is a confound here"). Second, they collectively weave their individual arguments together into a coherent, productive group discourse in which many different perspectives are presented and pondered. Third, they weigh all the evidence together and draw reasonable conclusions from the entire tapestry of arguments pro and con. Different students will undoubtedly reach different conclusions, but they should all endeavor to do their best to take all the relevant evidence into account.

This analysis suggests that to understand how to teach students to argue well, one needs answers to three questions: (a) What knowledge do students need to construct good individual arguments? (b) What knowledge do students need to weave together individual arguments effectively in an overall group discourse? (c) What knowledge is needed to draw good conclusions from the complex network of arguments, pro and con? In this section, I discuss some elements of the knowledge that students need to argue well. These elements of knowledge readily translate to instructional goals for curricula designed to promote argumentation.

Constructing Individual Arguments

Philosophers have proposed different conceptualizations of what the basic form of an argument is (see Voss & Van Dyke, 2001). Common to most is the idea that a reason is used to support a claim, as in Figure 14.1, which presents an argument made by many Mars enthusiasts in the late 1800s. There is a usually unspoken warrant or rule that links the reason to the claim (Toulmin, 1958). In the well-known system developed by Toulmin (1958), the argument may be qualified (e.g., "probably" or "possibly"), and the warrant may be supported with further backing.

Learning to argue well can be viewed as learning a repertoire of specific argument forms. The argument in Figure 14.1 is an example of an argument form relating to sample size. Argument forms vary in how specific they are to a particular domain (cf. Brewer & Chinn, 1995). *Domain-specific* argument forms are highly specific to a particular field of study. For instance, a psychologist might argue that a study is invalid because a particular IQ test used has only a moderate level of reliability; the knowledge that this particular IQ test is only moderately reliable is highly specific to this field of research. *Cross-domain* forms of argument are more general and can be used across different but somewhat related domains, such as across both biology and physics, across both sociology and psychology, or across both medicine and psychology. The argument that a study is more believable if the measures are reliable is common to many fields from biology to sociology; however this argument is not used in other fields, such as literary criticism or music history. *Global cross-domain* argument forms can be used in virtually all domains. Offering counterexamples is an argument form that is probably common to almost all domains of human reasoning.

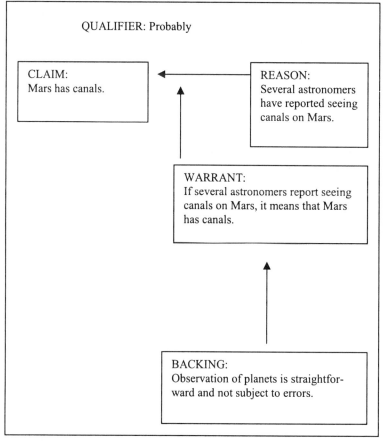

FIG.14.1. An argument.

K–12 education, and even much undergraduate education, will probably focus mainly on global cross-domain and cross-domain argument forms. These are forms that have the most general power to promote good reasoning and problem solving.

Global Cross-Domain Argument Forms

Much of the research on global cross-domain argumentation has focused on several very basic argument forms: stating positions, giving reasons, and stating objections to one's own position (e.g., Kuhn, 1992; Perkins, 1985). The general picture that emerges from this research is that although young children—even preschoolers—can and do make these argument moves in everyday conversations (Stein & Albro, 2001), performance is poor in more formal settings (Kuhn, 1992; Perkins et al., 1983). Even undergraduates are often able to generate surprisingly few arguments for their own positions on issues, and they generate even fewer arguments for opposing positions. These general argumentative strategies can be an initial focus of instruction so that students will learn to apply these strategies more extensively, but it is likely that students will soon master them and be ready to move on to other strategies.

Comparative research is needed to identify other forms of argument that are common to diverse domains, from literary criticism and editorial writing to psychology and physics. Candidates include the following: giving examples, giving counterexamples, mistrusting sources that have a bias, giving preference to credible sources, rejecting *ad hominem* attacks, considering alternative causes and consequences, questioning reports of biased individuals, and giving concrete evidence to support reasons. Several strategies of this sort are considered in this volume by van Drie et al. (chap. 11) and Wiley and Bailey (chap. 12). Ennis (1987) presented a broad range of candidate argument forms. Some global cross-domain argument forms may be arguments that students, at least by high school, are capable of using but do not necessarily use spontaneously. Others, such as giving concrete evidence to support reasons, may be difficult because students have difficulty clearly distinguishing evidence from the claims that the evidence supports (Kuhn, 1992). Developmental research is needed to gain a better understanding of when, if ever, students develop the ability to use these various strategies without special instruction and which of these strategies, if any, become part of people's regular repertoire of strategies.

Cross Domain Argument Forms

Many of the most useful cross-domain argument forms link claims to evidence or address the quality of evidence. For example, in many areas of the social and physical sciences, reasoners argue on the basis of a particular pattern of data that there is an interaction between two variables. Arguments about sample size or the presence of appropriate comparison groups are used to argue for or against particular conclusions. Different cross-domain argument forms might be prevalent in fields such as history and jurisprudence. For instance, arguments about memory processes can be used to credit or discredit the testimony of an eyewitness in both fields.

Arguments about how people adapt their words to cater to different audiences could be used to try to work out what a person really believes.

Many of these useful cross-domain argument forms can be treated as the backing that supports the warrant linking a reason with a claim. For example (see Fig. 14.2), suppose that a reasoner is considering the cause of the disease pellagra. The reasoner argues that the disease is caused by poor diet because of a study (Study #1 in Fig. 14.2) in which children in an orphanage who were given a better diet were cured, whereas children in orphanages that did not improve the children's diet continued to suffer from pellagra. The reasoner believes that the study supports this claim because the study used careful controls and had a large enough sample. Thus, both careful controls and sample size are used to bolster the validity of the link between the study and the conclusion that pellagra is caused by poor diet.

An important task of research is to identify cross-domain strategies that can be fruitfully taught to students at different ages. One part of this research task is to identify those strategies that are actually used among experts across several domains. Another part is to identify appropriate ages and grade levels at which it is best to introduce the various argument forms.

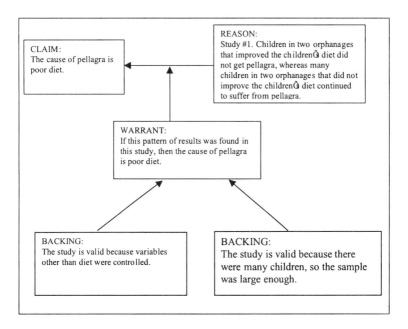

FIG.14.2. An argument based on controlled variables and sample size.

The Structure of Argument Schemas

When students learn an argument form, I propose that they learn an argument schema that enables them to deploy the argument form appropriately. Different proposals exist for the structure of argument schemas. One possibility is that an argument schema such as an argument based on sample size is like what is shown in Figure 14.2. For example, the argument schema for sample size would consist of a claim, qualifier, reason, warrant, and backing stating the rule for sample size. In this view, the key step in learning a particular argument form would be learning the appropriate rule to use as the backing in an argument about the validity of a study. Similarly, some researchers have treated arguments or reasoning strategies as rules that can be captured by a sentence or phrase such as "Results are more reliable when the sample size is larger" (e.g., Fong, Krantz, & Nisbett, 1986; Germann, Aram, & Burke, 1996). In a more linguistic approach to argument schemas, Anderson et al. (2001) treated arguments in children's discussions as stratagems with particular linguistic structures, such as "Yeah, but" with an objection added, or "If you were <name of story character>, wouldn't you feel" with a particular way of feeling added to complete the sentence.

All of these viewpoints treat argument schemas as fairly simple forms of knowledge. I have taken this approach in my own previous work. However, as I have continued to work on projects directed at helping students learn to learn argument forms, I have come to conclude that there is much more to knowing an argument form than knowing a simple rule or simple structure. Mastery of even a seemingly simple argument form requires very large funds of knowledge. Consider some of what an expert knows about the role of a control group in evaluating the quality of studies. The expert certainly knows the basic principle: Studies are more or less believable depending on whether it includes a control group. However, the expert also knows much more. The expert knows that a study without a control group may not support any conclusion whatsoever. The expert also has an underlying model that justifies the application of this argument (e.g., a model of situations being represented as causes and effects, with something like John Stuart Mill's method of differences used to infer causation). The expert knows when control groups need not be explicitly incorporated in a study. For instance, when a disease is known historically to be 100% fatal, a study showing that 20 patients did not die when given a drug is convincing, even in the absence of a second group of patients not receiving the drug. The expert knows when control groups are especially crucial, as when people would likely improve even without any treatment. The expert knows that some variables can be regarded as causally irrelevant and need not be carefully controlled (e.g., whether people take the drug while standing in the kitchen or the dining room). The expert also knows that random assignment to treatment provides a way to assume that variables are controlled on average without explicitly controlling them. The expert knows pitfalls that can arise when attempting to control variables (e.g., matching on one variable can lead to unmatching other variables that are not perfectly correlated). The expert knows possible counterarguments to the application of this argument form (e.g., it does not matter that a variable was not controlled because it is completely irrelevant). This list is far from exhaustive.

This analysis suggests that expert knowledge of an argument form embraces a very deep pool of knowledge. In Table 14.1, I present a schema showing some of the components of knowledge of sample size. The table presents the knowledge of a moderately knowledgeable student who has taken statistics (schemas, of course, may differ from one individual to another). Each row in the schema specifies a slot that would be present in the schema for any commonly used argument form. I propose that learning an argument form well means learning the various components of such a schema. Instruction should develop ways to help students learn all of these components of knowledge.

Constructing Group Argumentation

As the authors of several of the chapters in this volume emphasize, argumentation is not just a matter of deploying individual arguments. Argumentation in classrooms means that students must construct interlocking networks of arguments in an overall coherent discourse. But what are the characteristics of such discourse? What instructional goals should teachers have for the shape of group argumentation? I discuss five issues that seem to be central.

Argumentation About Content

A striking finding common to four of the chapters in this volume (Andriessen et al., (chap. 9); Erkens et al., (chap 10); van Drie et al, (chap.11); and Wiley & Bailey, (chap. 12) is that most of the talk in the online and real discussions was not, in fact, argumentation. Although the tasks were intended to afford argumentation, argumentation was infrequent. In particular, students seemed very reluctant to express disagreement with their peers. In chapter 10, Erkens et al., additionally found that even when students did engage in actual argumentation while writing an essay, little of the argumentation (less than 10%) was about the content of the essay. Rather, any argumentation that occurred was focused on plans for writing the papers, as distinct from the content of what was to be written. In work with fifth graders (Chinn et al., 2000), my colleagues and I have found that about a third of elementary schoolchildren in groups of four engaged in little argumentation at all when given a task that encouraged argumentative discourse.

Although argumentation often seems to entail disagreement, argumentation can in fact occur without disagreement. Two students could construct a variety of arguments for and against a position while agreeing on every point they raised; these students might be engaged in constructing excellent arguments without ever disagreeing with each other. However, given that individuals rarely think of substantial numbers of counterarguments to their own position (Perkins, 1985; Perkins et al., 1983), argumentation seems much more likely to promote learning if students do express disagreement; otherwise, argumentation is likely to include too little consideration of alternative perspectives.

These considerations suggest that an obvious, but far from trivial, goal of argumentation in classrooms is that students actually do argue. They should articulate claims, reasons, and evidence. Ideally, they will sometimes express disagreement and attempt to resolve this disagreement. The expressions of disagreement should be marked by politeness and fundamental respect for others' viewpoints, as is suggested by Wiley and Bailey (chap. 12, this volume). Students' knowledge of group argumentation should include an understanding of the importance of all of these goals.

TABLE 14.1

Components of a Knowledgeable Individual's Argument Schema for Sample Size

Schema Component	Example of Contents of Slot for Reasoning About Sample Size
Goal of using the argument form	To help determine whether a study provides support for a conclusion.
Positive form of argument	Study A supports Conclusion X in part because the study has a sufficiently large sample size.
Negative form of argument	Study A does not support Conclusion X in part because the study has a sample size that is too small.
Common situations of use, with typical numerical parameters	Examples of situations in which the schema is invoked: (a) psychological laboratory studies, with appropriate sample size of 25+ people per cell; (b) classroom studies, with appropriate sample size of 5 when sample size per cell is 5+ classrooms per cell; (c) medical studies with genetically identical mice, with appropriate sample size of 5 mice per cell; (d) and so on. Note: Many other specific situations and typical rule-of-thumb sample guidelines may be associated with the schema.

TABLE 14.1(cont'd)

Explanation underlying the schema	Each unit of analysis (person, classroom, mouse) in each treatment condition can be treated as one of a sample drawn from a population of interest. Differences between conditions must be greater than would be expected by the random drawing of units into each condition. The larger the sample, the less likely it is that medium-sized or large differences would occur just by chance, so any real differences are likely to result from real differences between the treatments.
Inferences that can be made on the basis of this schema	When sample size is small: (a) Reduce confidence in claims of a difference between treatment, when p values are not provided; (b) reduce estimate of real size of difference between treatments; and (c) reduce confidence in estimate of any population values.
Inferences that should *not* be made using this schema	The probability value of a statistical test already takes sample size into account, so that one does not revise one's estimate of p values when the sample size is too small.
Schema component	Example of contents of slot for reasoning about sample size.
When the schema implies that a study is worthless	When the sample size is 1 or 2, no credence whatsoever can be given to the study.
Other numerical relationships	The greater the variability, the larger the sample size that is needed to permit conclusions. A change in sample size matters more when sample size is small than when sample size is large.
When the schema is not applicable	When differences between treatments are astonishingly large (e.g., in a classroom study with one classroom in an experimental method, students at an underperforming school make a four-grade-level improvement in mathematics).
Counterarguments to using the schema	Every individual is so different that conclusions cannot be drawn from an aggregate of individuals.

TABLE 14.1(cont'd)

Correctives	Inferences about treatment differences when sample size is small size can be mitigated by a more uniform sample.
Cost–benefit issues	The reasoner knows that there are costs associated with increasing sample size, so that one cannot demand extremely large samples, because the cost would be prohibitive.
Collocated schemas (i.e., other schemas that are often invoked at the same time as the sample size schema)	One typically evaluates sample size at the same time as one evaluates the representativeness of the sample, whether the sample is random, and whether there are any biases in the sample.

Depth and Breadth of Argumentation

Andriessen et al. (chap. 9, this volume) raise the important issue of the depth and breadth of argumentation. Group argumentation may often consist of simple lists of reasons for and against a position, with little or no elaboration of any of these reasons. For instance, students debating whether the American colonists in the 1770s should have opted for peaceful resistance rather than armed revolt might simply give a list of reasons pro and con, such as, "The government of England would not have listened" or "Colonialism is wrong" on the pro side, without any further elaboration or exploration. Deeper argumentation would explore each reason further, considering whether each reason was in fact defensible, whether there was adequate backing for the warrants linking the reasons to the claims, and whether there were any rebuttals that could undermine each reason.

Chinn et al. (2000) found evidence in fourth-grade argumentation in groups that deeper development of reasons was associated with greater learning; in contrast, students who tended to advance a simple reason without any further development of that reason learned less. Teachers and students should thus make deep elaboration of arguments a central goal of argumentation. Participation in deep argumentation could help students learn some of the complex knowledge in argument schemas such as the one in Table 14.1. For example, if one student argued that a study with mice failed to support a conclusion because of a small sample size, another student might counterargue that because there was little variance in the sample, a large sample size was not necessary. Through further discussion of these ideas, students could construct some of the more complex knowledge that is a part of a mature argument schema.

A Focus on Evidence

Participants in group argumentation often advance little real evidence to support their claims (see Chinn & Anderson, 1998; Kuhn, 1992). Chinn and Anderson (1998) found that fourth graders arguing about what a character in a story should do next discussed possible consequences of different actions but seldom provided evidence about the likelihood of various actions (e.g., they did not consider textual evidence from the story that would bear on whether a story character would be happier moving away from home or not). In an analysis of U.S. senators' debate about the war to expel Iraq from Kuwait in 1991, Voss, Wiley, Kennet, Schooler, and Silfies (1998) reported that there were many arguments in which the senators noted possible positive or negative consequences of an attack on Iraq (e.g., war would lead to a prolonged quagmire as in Vietnam, or war would promote Middle East stability). However, it appears that few senators adduced concrete evidence to support the relative likelihood of the various consequences they envisioned. These results suggest that students and teachers should understand that an important goal of group argumentation should be to infuse greater consideration of evidence in the discussions.

Making the Discourse Structure Salient

It is well established that readers learn more from written texts when the text structure of those texts is clearly signaled and when referential connections are clearly marked (Spyridakis & Standal, 1987). Little is known about how students learn from oral discourse, but it seems plausible to draw an analogy from written text and assume that students might learn more from argumentative discourse in which the structure of the discourse is clearly signaled and referential connections are made clear. For examples, participants could clearly signal claims, reasons, and evidence. They could periodically summarize the main arguments pro and con. They could clearly specify when they are initiating a new line of argument, when they are adding to or rebutting a current argument, and when they are returning to consider an older argument. Students can also explicitly note whose argument they are addressing (e.g., "I would like to add to Emily's argument" or "I don't agree with what Jevon said a few minutes ago"). Andriesson et al. (chap. 9, this volume) emphasize the value of making referential connections by explicitly noting whose work is being referred to. Andriessen et al. found that without interventions, such references were uncommon in online posts. Students' appreciation of these signaling techniques would likely improve the quality of group discussion.

Co-construction of Arguments

Van Drie et al. (chap. 11, this volume) highlight an important distinction between arguments that are constructed by individual students and arguments that are coconstructed in a collaborative fashion by two or more participants. They found that as high school students wrote an essay together, 39% of arguments were coconstructed and 53% were constructed individually. This raises the question of whether one kind of argument—coconstructed or individual—is preferable to the other. Before considering possible answers to this question, I would note that individually constructed arguments can be simple unelaborated reasons or complex elaborated arguments. Simple reasons are unlikely to promote the elaborated knowledge structures that would promote learning. However, it might be valuable for individuals to construct more complex arguments individually, because they would be learning to generate many components of a complex argument on their own, without assistance. Co-construction of arguments could also be valuable. As two students elaborate on an argument, whether in supportive ways or through rebuttals, both students might learn something about how to construct complex arguments by adding further information or considering counterarguments. In accordance with these hypotheses, Chinn et al. (2000) found with fourth graders that both co-construction of arguments and individual construction of complex arguments facilitated learning, whereas individual construction of simple, unelaborated arguments was negatively associated with learning. If this finding proves to hold for other situations, then teachers and students should be aware that both modes of complex argument construction are valuable.

Drawing Conclusions

An interesting conclusion from Andriessen et al. (chap. 9, Experiment 2) is that few undergraduates actually drew conclusions from their online discussions. This finding is echoed in Wiley and Bailey's (chap. 12, this volume) study, in which the four undergraduate dyads did not compare different theories of volcanic action with each other. Apparently, integrating multiple arguments based on multiple sources of information is difficult even for undergraduates. The psychological processes involved in drawing conclusions from a complex network of arguments and counterarguments are poorly understood. In general, it is likely that some sort of explanatory coherence process occurs, so that reasoners end up taking the position that is best supported by the known evidence and arguments (see Thagard, 1992). However, there are many different ways in which evidence and arguments might be weighted as the explanatory coherence processes occur, and there is little research that illuminates these processes. In the physical and social sciences, reasoners may reach conclusions on the basis of formal techniques such as meta-analysis or, more simply, counting studies for and against a claim. In history, the process of accounting for evidence appears to involve a process of developing a complex narrative that can account for the multi-faceted evidence available from a broad range of source documents (Gottschalk, 1950). At this point, little is known about how experts draw conclusions when clear quantitative methods such as meta-analysis are not possible.

INSTRUCTION THAT PROMOTES THE DEVELOPMENT OF ARGUMENTATION

Identifying the knowledge students need to argue well, as I have attempted to do in the previous section, is the first step to developing effective instruction in argumentation. The second step is developing instructional methods to achieve these goals. Instructional researchers, including the authors of many of the chapters in this volume, have developed tasks that promote argumentation and have provided scaffolding for students as they engage in argumentation. Less commonly, instructional researchers have developed explicit instruction to help students learn to argue; some, but not all, of these efforts have been successful (Sedlmeier, 1999; Zohar and Nemet, 2002).

Instruction designed to promote argumentation should help students learn the three types of knowledge needed for effective argumentation: learning individual argument schemas, learning to contribute to effective group argumentation, and learning to draw conclusions. I explore each of these areas in this final section of the chapter.

Learning Argument Schemas

Educational researchers have explored several ways of promoting the development of argument schemas. One is simply to give students extensive practice in argumentation. Although this technique does promote improvement, the improvement from practice alone appears to be modest (Kuhn et al., 1997). Three other commonly used techniques have had greater success. One is to prompt students to use particular argument types. For instance, a teacher could explicitly prompt students to make counterarguments during a discussion to promote the development of a general schema for counterarguments, or a computer program could provide prompts to students to explain their reasoning. As Hmelo-Silver (chap. 7, this volume) discusses, complex tasks can be broken down in computer simulations so that students are prompted to carry out one step at a time. Prompting students to use particular reasoning strategies such as explaining experimental designs or to vary one thing at a time has positive effects on performance

(Lin & Lehman, 1999; Vollmeyer, Burns, & Holyoak, 1996); in some studies, strategy use transfers to new tasks (Lin & Lehman, 1999).

Closely related to prompts is the technique of having students evaluate
their own performance at using particular argument forms. For instance,
students can be asked to evaluate how well they generated hypotheses and
explanations during their discussion, or they could be asked whether they
considered sample size when evaluating a study. Criteria for evaluation can
be provided to students, or students can help generate their own criteria.
Evaluation is typically combined with prompting (e.g., White & Frederiksen, 1998), and it can also be combined with having students set goals for
their performance before they begin the argumentation activity (Nguyen-
Jahiel, Anderson, Waggoner, & Rowell, in press). One large classroom
study that investigated this technique found strong positive effects, both on
learning science concepts and learning to reason scientifically (White &
Frederiksen, 1998). The effectiveness of evaluation may arise in part because when students are comparing their own performance to an ideal, they
are made aware of ideal argument forms and are helped to see where their
own performance can be improved.

A third technique designed to improve argumentation is to explicitly
provide students with model schemas and then have students construct
similar schemas in which they fill in the slots themselves. For example,
several projects have developed computer-based systems in which students
construct diagrammatic arguments akin to the ones presented in Figures
14.1 and 14.2. Students construct arguments by filling in the various parts
of the argument, which presumably helps them improve their understanding
of the relationship between claims and evidence. In several studies, these
spatial representations of arguments have improved students' reasoning
ability (Bell, 2001; Erkens et al., chap. 10, this volume; Cavalli-Sforza,
Weiner, & Lesgold, 1994). A more complex version of the model schema
approach has been developed by Reiser et al., (2001), who provided students with model evolutionary explanations with slots to fill in to help students learn to construct these explanations.

As I reflect on the instructional methods that have been used to promote argumentation skill, including methods I have worked on, it seems to
me that current research has taken too little account of the difficulty of the
argument schemas to be learned. Because argument schemas are highly
complex, with many interrelated conceptions to be learned, learning a
schema can involve the need to make major changes in conceptions. Just as
learning scientific theories often involves conceptual change, learning argument schemas may also involve major conceptual changes, and there is a
need for a theory that takes more account of this. In general, I propose that
new argument schemas have different levels of difficulty. Levels of difficulty can be defined according to the relationship between the new argument schema and learners' current ideas. Different instructional techniques
will be needed for schemas at different levels of difficulty. Next I discuss

five different levels of difficulty and consider implications for instructional techniques.

In considering the level of difficulty of new argument schemas, two issues arise (see Chinn & Samarapungavan, 2001). One is whether students understand the components of the new schema. Many students undoubtedly do not understand key ideas of probability that underlie argument forms such as arguments based on sample size. The second is whether students believe the new ideas. Students may understand why the teacher thinks that explicit measurement of length is important, but nonetheless believe that they can get good enough results just by eyeballing an object.

Level 1: Known Schemas

In this situation, students are already familiar with a schema. They may occasionally use it on their own, but the frequency of use is low. An example is the strategy of offering counterexamples. Elementary schoolchildren occasionally produce counterexamples in argumentation (see Anderson et al., 1997), but the frequency of use is not high (Chinn & Anderson, 1998).

For known schemas, instructional techniques such as modeling, prompting, and self-evaluation should be very effective. It may also be effective for teachers simply to label strategies as they are used (e.g., "That was a good counterexample"), to help students recognize argument forms and gain metacognitive control over them. Simple practice without any specific instruction at all may provide a context in which students begin to use known schemas more frequently. Simple practice is most likely to promote improvement when one or more students in a group begin spontaneously to use a known strategy; once one student begins to use a known argument form, the use rapidly spreads throughout the group (Anderson et al., 2001). However, without any prompting or labeling, many relevant known argument forms may never be articulated by any student and so have no chance to spread among students.

Level 2: Consistent Schemas

Students do not already know *consistent schemas*, but when they first encounter these schemas, they instantly understand them and see their usefulness because the schemas are generally consistent with the students' existing ideas. An example would be the argument of rejecting the results of a study because the study was not run long enough (e.g., a clinical drug trial is more believable if measures of improvement are made after the drug has had an appropriate amount of time to take effect). In a recent study with middle school students (Chinn, unpublished data), I found that almost no students generate this argument on their own, but once they hear it, many understand it and use it regularly. The idea of waiting for things to take effect before measuring results is likely to be consistent with students' everyday views of how the world works.

A number of instructional methods seem likely to promote the development of consistent argument schemas. These techniques probably include all the techniques that appear to be effective for known schemas: labeling, prompting, self-evaluation, and modeling. Teacher questions and statements that direct students' attention to the new argument forms may be highly effective. Examples include, "Has anyone thought about whether they checked the results too soon?" or "Erin made a good point about the length of the study—maybe we need to think about when they checked the results." Prompts and self-evaluation built into computer simulations may be also very effective at helping students learn consistent schemas (e.g., White & Frederiksen, 1998). With consistent schemas, one key to learning is probably to help students construct an abstract representation that goes beyond the immediate situation (cf. Fong et al., 1986; Reeves & Weisberg, 1994). Practice alone is unlikely to promote development of this schema, unless one or two participants do already know the argument and regularly use it so that use can spread to other students.

Level 3: Disbelieved Schemas

By *disbelieved schemas*, I mean argument schemas that students do not find worth using, even after they learn about them. Disbelieved schemas are sufficiently congruent with students' prior ideas that the students can readily understand them, but students do not believe that these schemas are valid or appropriate, or they do not believe that are very broadly applicable. For some students, even undergraduates, the sample size schema may fall into this category. Undergraduates readily employ the sample size schema in situations that obviously involve probability, but in more subjective situations they may not view sample size as relevant (Fong et al., 1986). Instead, students may believe that an argument supported by a large sample should carry less weight than an argument based on a vivid case (see Nisbett & Ross, 1980). Even when students come to understand the idea that large samples are more reliable, they may persist in treating a single vivid case as extremely important to decision making.

Another example of a disbelieved schema might be the use of counterarguments in school discourse. Although people are familiar with counterarguments and use them readily in selected contexts (e.g., a couple debating which of several cars to buy), they may not believe them to be useful in academic settings. The results presented in three chapters in this volume (Andriessen et al., chap 9; Erkens et al., chap. 10; Wiley & Bailey, chap. 12) suggest that undergraduates are reluctant to challenge others directly when working on an academic task together. Students may not appreciate the usefulness in argumentation in helping them construct new ideas, or they may not think that counterarguments are sufficiently valuable to risk negative interpersonal affect.

I am not aware of any research that specifically addresses how to promote belief in disbelieved schemas. Current instructional techniques such as prompting and self-evaluation are unlikely to be effective with disbelieved schemas. These techniques may enforce use of the argument forms within the classroom, but they do little to convince students that the schemas are valuable. As a result, students will present in not believing that the schemas are valid or useful, and they are likely to stop using the schemas as soon as they walk out of the classroom. In cases when students do not want to use argument forms such as counterarguments because they want to avoid interpersonal conflict, instruction should aim at reducing interpersonal barriers to using the strategy. For example, teachers could work to foster social norms in which counterarguments are seen as knowledge-building strategies rather than personal attacks. Research is needed to develop and investigate instructional techniques that can be effective at promoting belief in argument forms that students find implausible.

Level 4: Inconsistent Schemas

Inconsistent schemas are argument schemas that are conceptually inconsistent with students' current schemas. Students typically do not know the reasoning schema at all, and when they encounter it, they understand it only partly at best. They may also be unwilling to believe that the new schema is a valid argument form. An example of an inconsistent schema comes from middle school students learning about masked observation procedures in experiments. In a recent experiment I conducted with middle school science students, some students find it very difficult to understand the argument that observers who are unaware of experimental condition are less likely to make errors in observation than observers who are aware of experimental conditions. They think that aware observers will be more careful and fair because they know what to look for, which is, of course, approximately the opposite of the scientific viewpoint. It appears difficult for these students to understand the rationale for the argument that masked observations enhance the believability of the study.

In this situation, effective instruction is difficult, because students must both develop an understanding of a qualitatively new reasoning schema and become convinced of its validity. Once again, the current methods of instruction (prompts, self-evaluation, etc.) are unlikely to be broadly effective with inconsistent schemas. If students are regularly prompted to give preference to studies with blind observation procedures, without more elaborated instruction, they are unlikely to come to understand much about this schema beyond rote application of the basic rule. They are also unlikely to believe it sufficiently to apply to situations outside of school.

Level 5: Incommensurable Schemas

Incommensurable schemas are fundamentally at odds with the concepts that underlie students' current ideas about good argumentation. Incommensurable schemas are not merely inconsistent with the students' prior conceptions; they are fundamentally incompatible in the sense that students even lack the concepts needed to make sense of the new schemas. Students must undergo fundamental conceptual change to learn these schemas. Examples of incommensurable schemas include schemas that are based on treating everyday events as events drawn randomly from a sample of events. For example, arguing that the result of a study is an artifact of regression to the mean requires people to treat events as sampled randomly from a population of events. It is difficult for many people to view events in this way; it seems more natural to regard events as determined by specifiable causes than to treat them as outputs of stochastic processes.

It seems likely that extensive instruction akin to methods used to promote conceptual change in science (Guzzetti, Snyder, Glass, & Gamas, 1993) will be needed to help students learn and believe incommensurable argument schemas. There is no research at present that provides information on how to adapt principles of instruction for conceptual change to the goal of helping students learn incommensurable argument schemas.

Summary

When one takes seriously that schemas vary in difficulty, it indicates the need for a more differentiated theory of instruction that takes these various levels into account. In addition, it is important to note that different components of different argument schemas are likely to vary in difficulty. Students may adopt the sample size schema fairly readily yet fail to understand the probabilistic underpinnings. Indeed, students may advocate a sample size schema for a rationale wholly different from the rationale of scientists (e.g., medical researchers should use a large sample because more people will be helped if the medicine works). A theory of instruction of argument forms must take into account both the many aspects of knowledge within argument schemas and the different levels of difficulty of each aspect of knowledge.

Learning to Construct Group Argumentation

In comparison with research on learning individual argument schemas, there is less research on techniques for improving the quality of group argumentation, and much of what does exist remains fairly speculative. Several general techniques used to improve the quality of group argumentation include the assigned task, establishing norms, goal setting and evaluation, teacher scaffolding during discussions, and spatial representations of arguments. There are few studies that isolate the effects of any of these variables on particular processes, so this section is speculative.

One aspect of the *assigned task* that can affect the quality of group argumentation is the question under discussion. Obviously the question needs to be one that students find interesting, and one on which they need enough information to be able to marshal arguments. It is also desirable for opinion on the question to divide, as argumentation is more likely if students disagree with each other (Waggoner, Chinn, Anderson, & Yi, 1995). The formulation of the question matters, as well. In a study by Chinn et al. (2000), fifth graders discussing which of three conclusions was best and which was worst had more elaborated group argumentation than fifth graders discussing whether each of the same three conclusions was satisfactory. The instructions to identify the best and worst evidently triggered more disagreement among the students.

Respectful argumentation might be facilitated by *establishing norms* for the argumentation beforehand. Smith et al. (1981) provided small groups with norms for interaction prior to having the groups engage in argumentation. These norms included "I am critical of ideas, not people," "I listen to everyone's ideas, even if I do not agree with them," and "I first bring out all the ideas, then I put them together." In research by Anderson and his colleagues with students in teacher-led groups (e.g., Anderson et al., 1997; Chinn et al., 2001), students have been introduced to similar norms, and by and large these discussions are free from personal attacks. Establishing such norms may make students more willing to disagree with each other because criticism is less likely to be viewed as a personal attack. Students may also come to understand that disagreement can play an important role in the knowledge-building process.

Goal setting and student evaluation of group performance can be used to promote a variety of discourse features. Teachers can direct students to engage in particular argument moves (e.g., challenging each other, adding to others' arguments, asking for clarification, referring explicitly to each other's ideas, not interrupting, giving textual evidence, or giving evidence from experiments that groups have conducted), or they can ask students to generate their own goals (Nguyen-Jahiel et al., in press). Through appropriate goals, students can be made aware of any feature of good discussions, and they can be encouraged to embody these features in their own discussions. Postdiscussion evaluations of performance can further improve performance (Nguyen-Jahiel et al., in press; White & Frederiksen, 1998). Andriessen et al., (chap. 9, this volume) demonstrate that referential connections among messages can be increased by requesting that students make these connections when they contribute to online argumentation.

Although many projects—including most of those described in this volume—have been designed for group work without extensive teacher guidance during the group work, other argumentation projects have relied on *teacher scaffolding* during discussions to help students collaboratively construct high-quality argumentation in teacher-led groups or classes. Collaborative reasoning is a discussion format in which children discuss issues raised by stories. Collaborative reasoning envisions a central role for the teacher, who fosters high-quality discussions by prompting students to develop arguments in various ways (e.g., by encouraging students to give textual evidence or to follow up on what other students are saying), modeling good argumentation by thinking aloud, challenging students, and summarizing (Waggoner et al., 1995). These techniques can potentially be used to ensure that discussions have any of the desirable features of group argumentation (e.g., deeper argument development, clearly signaling relations among arguments, summarizing, etc.). To help students gain better meta-awareness of the structure of discussions, teachers can combine these scaffolding techniques with other techniques such as goal setting and self-evaluation to promote greater learning.

Spatial representations have been used to help students learn to formulate complete arguments and keep track of the arguments on each side of the question. The projects using spatial representations have usually been computer based; different systems have different representational formats and differ in the elements of arguments that are represented. Erkens et al., (chap.10, this volume) provide an example. In a typical system, students type claims in one box and reasons in another box, and they link reasons to supported claims with arrows (Cavalli-Sforza et al., 1994). Spatial representations can benefit students by focusing their attention on the content of arguments as well as on the overall pattern of evidence presented for and against various claims.

The available research indicates that spatial representations are beneficial to students (Toth, Suthers, & Lesgold, 2002). However, some of the findings presented by Erkens et al. (chap. 10, this volume) suggest a cautionary note. Erkens et al. note that most of the argumentation by students writing a paper together was about the process of writing papers rather than about the content of the paper. When students spend a great deal of time filling in boxes in a chart, it could lead to considerable talk about the mechanics of entering information that could detract from the content of what is being entered. An additional worry is that the time needed to draw the figures and type in the key ideas is probably substantial, and this time takes away from time that could be used to discuss a wider range of ideas.

Drawing Conclusions

Spatial representations are one main instructional approach that has been used to improve students' conclusions from argumentation. When students clearly lay out each argument pro and con, it highlights the number of arguments supporting each position. In addition, when students see arguments arrayed together in front of them, they might be able to weigh the relative strength of rival arguments more easily. A particularly interesting exemplar of this method is a system developed by Ranney and his colleagues. Basing his system on Thagard's (1992) computational theory of how scientists combine evidence to make theory choices, Ranney's system directs students to arrange the evidence in support of alternative theories and then run Thagard's computations to generate what the preferred theory should be. At this point, students can debate whether they think the computations yielded the best solution (Ranney & Schank, 1995).

A second approach to improving conclusions is to encourage students to be open-minded and willing to change their minds in response to evidence. In collaborative reasoning discussions (Waggoner et al., 1995), teachers encourage students to change their minds in response to the best arguments, if they think the best arguments are on the other side. Teachers also welcome initial positions of "I'm not sure" and assure students that it is entirely appropriate to wait to hear arguments before making up their mind. Finally, teachers often wrap discussions up by asking students who have changed their minds to explain their reasoning.

I am not aware of any research that specifically tests what students learn about drawing conclusions from either of these two instructional approaches. This is a fruitful area for future research.

SUMMARY AND CONCLUSION

In this chapter, I have discussed several key issues surrounding the use of argumentation in classrooms. An encouraging finding for proponents of argumentation is that argumentation appears to offer a number of benefits, from increasing students' interest to improving learning and problem solving. However, to help students learn to argue well, teachers need a better conceptualization of what the instructional goals of argumentation should be. An idea that is central to this chapter is that expert knowledge of argument forms does not consist of simple rules; rather, knowledge of argument forms is organized in complex schemas. Knowledge of how to argue well also includes knowledge of desirable features of good group argumentation. Researchers—including many of the researchers represented in this volume—have made strong progress in identifying these features—such as deep development of arguments, a focus on evidence, and co-construction of arguments. Instructionally, it will be important to help students learn both the many components of argument schemas and the features of good group argumentation. Instructional methods should also pay more heed to the relationship between the argument forms that students are learning and the argument forms that students currently use and believe. As research on argumentation advances, teachers will have a knowledge base to move beyond a simple emphasis of giving reasons and counterarguments, and they will be able to develop a sociocognitively grounded curriculum to help students learn to argue well.

ACKNOWLEDGMENTS

This material is based upon work supported by the National Science Foundation under Grant No. 9875485. Any opinions, findings, and conclusions or recommendations expressed in this material are those of the author and do not necessarily reflect the views of the National Science Foundation.

REFERENCES

Anders, P., & Commeyras, M. (1998). A feminist commentary on four science education vignettes. In B. Guzzetti & C. Hynd (Eds.), *Perspectives on conceptual change: Multiple ways to understanding knowing and learning in a complex world* (pp. 133–144). Mahwah, NJ: Lawrence Erlbaum Associates.

Anderson, R. C., Chinn, C., Chang, J., Waggoner, M., & Yi, H. (1997). On the logical integrity of children's arguments. *Cognition and Instruction, 15,* 135–167.

Anderson, R. C., Nguyen-Jahiel, K., McNurlen, B., Archodidou, A., Kim, S. Y., Reznitskaya, A. (2001). The snowball phenomenon: Spread of ways of talking and ways of thinking across groups of children. *Cognition and Instruction, 19,* 1–46.

Arkes, H. R. (1991). Costs and benefits of judgment errors: Implications for debiasing. *Psychological Bulletin, 110,* 486–498.

Bell, P. (2001). Using argument map representations to make thinking visible for individuals and groups. In T. Koschmann, R. Hall, & N. Miyake (Eds.), *CSCL 2: Carrying forward the conversation (Computers, cognition, and work)* (pp. 449–485). Mahwah, NJ: Lawrence Erlbaum Associates.

Brewer, W. F., & Chinn, C. A. (1995, September). *Cross-domain and within-domain reasoning and beliefs about the world in children and scientists.* Paper presented at Conference on the Psychology of Science, Memphis, TN.

Cavalli-Sforza, V., Weiner, A. W., & Lesgold, A. M. (1994). Software support for students engaging in scientific activity and scientific controversy. *Science Education, 78,* 577–599.

Chinn, C. A., & Anderson, R. C. (1998). The structure of discussions that promote reasoning. *Teachers College Record, 100,* 315–368.

Chinn, C. A., Anderson, R. C., & Waggoner, M. A. (2001). Patterns of discourse in two kinds of literature discussion. *Reading Research Quarterly, 36,* 378–411.

Chinn, C. A., O'Donnell, A. M., & Jinks, T. S. (2000). The structure of discourse in collaborative learning. *Journal of Experimental Education, 69,* 77–97.

Chinn, C. A., & Samarapungavan, A. (2001). Distinguishing between understanding and belief. *Theory Into Practice, 40,* 235–241.

Fong, G. T., Krantz, D. H., & Nisbett, R. E. (1986). The effects of statistical training on thinking about everyday problems. *Cognitive Psychology, 18,* 253–292.

Ennis, R. H. (1987). A taxonomy of critical thinking dispositions and attitudes. In J. B. Baron & R. J. Sternberg (Eds.), *Teaching thinking skills: Theory and practice* (pp. 9-26). New York: Freeman.

Germann, P. J., Aram, R., & Burke, G. (1996). Identifying patterns and relationships among the responses of seventh-grade students to the science process skill of designing experiments. *Journal of Research in Science Teaching, 33,* 79–99.

Gottschalk, L. (1950). *Understanding history: A primer of historical method.* New York: Knopf.

Guzzetti, B. J., Snyder, T. E., Glass, G. V., & Gamas, W. S. (1993). Promoting conceptual change in science: A comparative meta-analysis of instructional interventions from reading education and science education. *Reading Research Quarterly, 28,* 116–155.

Janis, I. L. (1982). *Groupthink: Psychological studies of policy decisions and fiascos.* Boston: Houghton-Mifflin.

Johnson, D. W., & Johnson, R. T. (1979). Conflict in the classroom: Controversy and learning. *Review of Educational Research, 49,* 51–70.

Kramer, R. M. (1998). Revisiting the Bay of Pigs and Vietnam decisions 25 years later: How well has the groupthink hypothesis stood the test of time? *Organizational Behavior and Human Decision Processes, 73,* 236–271.

Kuhn, D. (1992). Thinking as argument. *Harvard Educational Review, 62,* 155–178.

Kuhn, D., Shaw, V., & Felton, M. (1997). Effects of dyadic interaction on argumentative reasoning. *Cognition and Instruction, 15,* 287–315.

Lin, X., & Lehman, J. D. (1999). Supporting learning of variable control in a computer-based biology environment: Effects of prompting college students to reflect on their own thinking. *Journal of Research in Science Teaching, 36,* 837–858.

Nguyen-Jahiel, K., Anderson, R., Waggoner, M., & Rowell, B. (in press). Using literature discussions to reason through real life dilemmas: A journey taken by one teacher and her fourth-grade stdents. In Horowitz, R. (Ed.), *Talking texts: Knowing the world through the evolution of instructional discourse.* Hillsdale, NJ: Erlbaum Associates.

Nisbett, R., & Ross, L. (1980). *Human inference: Strategies and shortcomings of social judgment.* Englewood Cliffs, NJ: Prentice Hall.

Page-Voth, V., & Graham, S. (1999). Effects of goal setting and strategy use on the writing performance and self-efficacy of students with writing and learning problems. *Journal of Educational Psychology, 91,* 230–240.

Perkins, D. N. (1985). Postprimary education has little impact on informal reasoning. *Journal of Educational Psychology, 77,* 562–571.

Perkins, D. N., Allen, R., & Hafner, J. (1983). Difficulties in everyday reasoning. In W. Maxwell (Ed.), *Thinking: The frontier expands* (pp. 177–189). Hillsdale, NJ: Lawrence Erlbaum Associates.

Pressley, M., & Woloshyn, V. (1995). *Cognitive strategy instruction that really improves children's academic performance* (2nd ed.). Cambridge, MA: Brookline Books.

Ranney, M., & Schank, P. (1995). Protocol modeling, textual analysis, the bifurcation/bootstrapping method, and Convince Me: Computer-based techniques for studying beliefs and their revision. *Behavior Research Methods, Instruments, & Computers, 27,* 239–243.

Reeves, L. M., & Weisberg, R. W. (1994). The role of content and abstract information in analogical transfer. *Psychological Bulletin, 115,* 381–400.

Reiser, B. J., Tabak, I., Sandoval, W. A., Smith, B. K., Steinmuller, F., & Leone, A. J. (2001). BGuILE: Strategic and conceptual scaffolds for scientific inquiry in biology. In S. M. Carver & D. Klahr (Eds.), *Cognition and instruction: Twenty-five years of progress* (pp. 263–305). Mahwah, NJ: Lawrence Erlbaum Associates.

Reznitskaya, A., Anderson, R. C., McNurlen, B., Nguyen-Jahiel, K., Archodidou, A., & Kim, S. Y. (2001). Influence of oral discussion on written argument. *Discourse Processes, 32,* 155–175.

Sedlmeier, P. (1999). *Improving statistical reasoning: Theoretical models and practical implications.* Mahwah, NJ: Lawrence Erlbaum Associates.

Simon, H. A. (1955). A behavioral model of rational choice. *Quarterly Journal of Economics, 69,* 99–118.

Smith, K., Johnson, D. W., & Johnson, R. T. (1981). Can conflict be constructive? Controversy versus concurrence seeking in learning groups. *Journal of Educational Psychology, 73,* 651–663.

Spyridakis, J. H., & Standal, T. C. (1987). Signals in expository prose: Effects on reading comprehension. *Reading Research Quarterly, 22,* 285–298.

Stein, N. L., & Albro, E. R. (2001). The origins and nature of arguments: Studies in conflict understanding, emotion, and negotiation. *Discourse Processes, 32,* 113–133.

Thagard, P. (1992). *Conceptual revolutions.* Princeton, NJ: Princeton University Press.

Toth, E. E., Suthers, D. D., & Lesgold, A. M. (2002). "Mapping to know": The effects of representational guidance and reflective assessment on scientific inquiry. *Science Education, 86,* 264–286.

Toulmin, S. E. (1958). *The uses of argument.* Cambridge, UK: Cambridge University Press.

Vollmeyer, R., Burns, B. D., & Holyoak, K. J. (1996). The impact of goal specificity on strategy use and the acquisition of problem structure. *Cognitive Science, 20,* 75–100.

Voss, J. F., & Means, M. L. (1991). Learning to reason via instruction in argumentation. *Learning and Instruction, 1,* 337–350.

Voss, J. F., & Van Dyke, J. A. (2001). Argumentation in psychology: Background comments. *Discourse Processes, 32,* 89–111.

Voss, J. F., Wiley, J., Kennet, J., Schooler, T. E., & Silfies, L. N. (1998). Representations of the Gulf Crisis as derived from the U.S. Senate debate. In D. A. Sylvan & J. F. Voss (Eds.), *Problem representation in foreign policy decision-making* (pp. 279-302). Cambridge, England: Cambridge University Press.

Waggoner, M. A., Chinn, C. A., Anderson, R. C., & Yi, H. (1995). Collaborative reasoning about stories. *Language Arts, 72,* 582–589.

Wharton, C. M., Cheng, P. W., & Wickens, T. D. (1993). Hypothesis-testing strategies: Why two goals are better than one. *Quarterly Journal of Experimental Psychology, 46A,* 743–758.

White, B. Y., & Frederiksen, J. R. (1998). Inquiry, modeling, and metacognition: Making science accessible to all students. *Cognition and Instruction, 16,* 3–118.

Wiley, J., & Voss, J. F. (1996). The effects of playing historian on learning in history. *Applied Cognitive Psychology, 10,* S63–S72.

Wiley, J., & Voss, J. F. (1999). Constructing arguments from multiple sources: Tasks that promote understanding and not just memory for text. *Journal of Educational Psychology, 91,* 301–311.

Wood, T., & Sellers, P. (1996). Assessment of a problem-centered mathematics program: Third grade. *Journal for Research in Mathematics Education, 27,* 337–353.

Yackel, E., & Cobb, P. (1996). Sociomathematical norms, argumentation, and autonomy in mathematics. *Journal for Research in Mathematics Education, 27,* 458–477.

Zohar, A., & Nemet, F. (2002). Fostering students' knowledge and argumentation skills through dilemmas in human genetics. *Journal of Research in Science Teaching, 39,* 35–62.

Index

A

Activity field hypothesis, 10, 172, 173, 174, 177, 194
Adam, J. M., 337
Adventures of Jasper Woodbury, 62, 101, 102, 106, 107, 108, 109, 111, 112, 117, 119, 120
Agnew, C., 3
Agogino, A. M., 66
Ainsworth, S., 76
Albro, E. R., 362
Alessi, S., 128
Allaire forums, 334, 335, 338, 341, 342, 344, 346, 348, 349
Allen, R., 358, 362, 366
Allport, F. H., 298, 299
American Association for the Advancement of Science, 147
American Psychological Association, 4
Anchored collaborative inquiry, 106, 107, 118, 121, 122
Anchored instruction, 62, 100, 101, 100–104,107, 149
Anders, P., 357
Anderson, J. R., 222
Anderson, N., 299
Anderson, R. C., 355, 357, 359, 364, 369, 372, 377, 378, 379
Andre, T., 128
Andriessen, J. E. B., 200, 208, 219, 221, 224, 235, 239, 240, 324, 332, 334, 337
Angelillo, C., 32
Anseli, E., 99, 104, 105
Antaki, C., 237
Aram, R., 364
Archodidou, A., 359, 364, 373
Argument
   domain-specific, 356
   quality, 5, 9, 85, 233, 239, 244, 248, 251, 257, 259, 279, 355, 376
   structure, 260
   norms, 357
Argumentation
   ability, 356
   diagrams, 72, 292, 332–34, 337, 342, 347, 372, 378

group, 368
individual, 360
norms, 68, 304, 375, 377
tasks, 201, 233, 241, 266, 304, 305, 312, 315, 358, 359, 365
Arkes, H. R., 358
Aronson, E., 51, 65, 66
Assessment, 18, 20. 64, 72, 78–80, 83, 91, 103, 109, 112–13, 115, 119, 163, 164, 186, 189, 310, 325
Atwood, M. E., 149
Authentic
   activities, 32, 224, 234, 301
   activity, 172, 179
   context, 147, 175, 194, 223
   problems, 142, 149, 165
   resources, 75

B

Baker, L. M., 155
Baker, M., 196, 199, 200, 206, 214, 224, 237, 240, 266, 325, 327, 328
Ball, D. L., 104, 105, 107, 121
Ball, G., 222
Bandura, A., 301
Bangert-Drowns, R., 128
Bannon, L. J., 241
Bargh, J. A., 66
Barron, B. J. S., 101, 149, 302
Barron, L., 102
Barrows, H., 149, 177, 178, 185
Bartlett, F. C., 184
Bass, K. M., 149, 150
Bassok, M., 63
Bastianutti, L. M., 316
Baumgartner, E., 72
Becker, H. J., 82, 87
Beherend, J., 99, 104, 105
Bell, P., 68, 73, 75, 76, 77, 78, 79, 80, 153, 372
Belvedere, 208, 337, 344
Bereiter, C., 7, 44, 45, 62, 67, 68, 103, 142, 148, 149, 152, 200, 208, 220, 223, 225, 234, 239, 240, 241, 325, 330, 335, 339
Berenfeld, B., 3
Bernas, R. S., 238

T